No. 1876
$25.95

GETTING GREAT GRAPHICS

CARY N. PRAGUE & JAMES E. HAMMITT

This book is dedicated to Northeast Utilities where I spent the first seven years of my corporate life. It is especially dedicated to Dave Mathews, who taught me how to get the job done. To Allen Wright, who taught me the meaning of walking the line, and most of all to Rose Hanley who helped me make the transition from technician to manager. To these people I will always be grateful.

- CNP

To my wife Lee, for all her patience.

- JEH

Special Dedication

This book is also dedicated to my newborn son, David Harold Prague, who came into this world just in time to make this book.

FIRST EDITION

FIRST PRINTING

Printed in the United States of America

Library of Congress Cataloging in Publication Data

Prague, Cary N.
Getting great graphics.

Includes index.
1. Computer graphics.
I. James. E. Hammitt II. Title.
T385.P73 1985 001.64'43 85-7970
ISBN 0-8306-0876-1
ISBN 0-8306-1876-7 (pbk.)

Contents

Acknowledgments

We wish to thank the vendors featured in this book for lending us hardware and software to make this book possible. We would like to especially thank five corporations who really helped us out above and beyond the call of duty.

To the Polaroid Corporation for providing us with the Polaroid Palette, which enabled us to produce the many screen images you see in this book.

To Hewlett-Packard Corporation for the use of a HP-7475A plotter and HP-150 Touch Screen.

To Microsoft for letting us beta-test Microsoft CHART, which was used to produce almost all the graphs in Chapters 1 through 6.

To Computer Graphics Group for breathing new life into us with their PC Illustrator package, which was used to draw many of the pictorial representations in this book.

To Ashton-Tate for the copy of Framework that was used to do the word processing in this and many of our other books.

Finally, to all the other vendors who sent beta-test copies of their software, spent countless hours with us on the phone, and went out of their way to make this book a success. We thank you!

Introduction

Anyone can prepare a simple bar graph or line chart, but preparing them effectively is an art by itself. To make a graph effective, you must be concerned with two disciplines: the scientific aspects that make the graph correct, and the humanistic aspects that make the graph easy to understand.

Preparing effective graphics is not complicated when you are using today's microcomputer graphics packages. They do much of the work for you. Unfortunately most of what they do are the scientific functions of calculating and plotting points. The humanistic aspects of an effective graph can be overlooked. *Getting Great Graphics* examines all the different types of graphs, the elements of graphs, and the proper techniques for creating graphics; finally it presents an analysis of today's best selling graphics software packages and hardware devices.

This book is divided into two major sections and contains 15 chapters. The first three chapters are a general introduction to graphics. They cover the basics of graphics and provide a look at the terms used when dealing with graphics. They also provide an overview of the different type of graphs. These first few chapters discuss the different components of a graph, from the raw data to the finishing touches of color, patterns, labels, axis scaling, and letter selection.

The next five chapters provide an in-depth look at the many different types of graphs. Each chapter is filled with illustrations. These chapters explain when to use each type of graph, how to properly create each type of graph, and how to present them effectively.

The second section of the book includes pictorial exhibitions of the best selling graphics packages and descriptions of what they are specifically designed to do best. This final section is subdivided into chapters concerning stand-alone graphics packages, integrated packages, text/slide packages, picture processors/graphic enhancers, highly specialized packages, and little known packages that do wonderful things and should be known. You will see the programs in action, the input required, and the most effective way to use the programs to produce graphs for presentations. A final chapter is devoted to graphics hardware.

All who use a personal computer for their business or personal applications will find excellent advice and guidance in these pages.

Section 1

The Design and Presentation of Business Graphics

Presentations, reports, studies, demonstrations, classes, textbooks, manuals, memos—these are the instruments of persuasion used throughout corporate America. Fortunes are won and lost, contracts are signed or cancelled, political campaigns succeed or fail, all based on the ability of an individual or group to get The Message across.

Most of us have not had professional training in creating and presenting arguments effectively. There is, however, a simple rule that any grade-school teacher can tell you: *What I hear, I know; what I read, I understand; what I see, I remember.* Fully 85 percent of all information that a human being assimilates comes through the channel of the eyes.

The graphic presentation of ideas and opinions is a valuable tool in the hands of even the least able persuader. Pictures affect the audience directly, through the major information channel available to them. Peoples' emotions are tied directly to what they see; subliminal pictures, flashed faster than the human optic center can record, can produce emotional and even *physical* reactions in an unsuspecting audience.

The ability to design and present business graphics effectively is probably the most important ability that today's manager can have. The manager must convince superiors and subordinates alike of the viability of any particular course of action. The corporate structure has a lot of inertia and will move to a new course only with difficulty and sufficient persuasion.

This first section of *Getting Great Graphics* will show you how to choose, use, and execute a graph for an effective presentation. The basic parts of a graph are discussed, and the most effective ways to use the various charting formats are explained.

This section will help to guide you through the sometimes confusing world of graphs and charts. Remember that your goal is to create an effective presentation through the effective use of graphics.

Chapter 1

Can You Picture That!

Painting, n. The art of protecting flat surfaces from the weather and exposing them to the critic.

Ambrose Bierce

The information age has caused all of us, in almost every aspect of life, to be bombarded with numbers. Prices, discounts, percentages, unemployment figures, and statistics of all kinds are shouted at us by the news media. All lines of work involve numbers or statistics of some sort.

Most of us cannot begin to assimilate the amount of information that is being pumped at us without end. Numbers do not, as a rule, mean anything at the gut level. The statistics on pollution and the environment that we see almost every day do not stir us to action; the most fanatic environmentalists are those who have seen the devastation with their own eyes, not those who have read the numbers.

Employees of large firms have found themselves in the "number quandary." When employees at a lower level of the hierarchy see something going wrong, they usually can determine the best way to fix the problem and save the company. In order to do this, however, they must first convince foremen, supervisors, managers, directors, veeps, and/or CEOs that the problem exists. So they compile statistics on the problem, present them to one or more of the above-mentioned groups, are praised (maybe) for their thoughtfulness, and sent back to work with, at best, an order to watch and wait. The painstakingly compiled statistics mean something to those immediately involved, but nothing to those who are not.

The medium best able to affect people at an emotional level is art. This is part of the human makeup—it has nothing to do with intelligent or ability. When numbers and statistics are presented to us, the emotional half of our brain receives the information only after it has been filtered by the unemotional intellect. The right brain-left brain concept means that people are affected at an emotional level by that which reaches the emotional half of the brain directly. Paintings, photographs, and colors reach the emotional side directly and reach the intellect through the emotional filter.

Figures take on new meaning when presented in a pictorial fashion. Graphs show the relationships between different amounts, percentages, and other forms of numbers so that they are grasped instantly by the viewer. Charts present a map of a process so that each action in the process can be seen in its relationship to all other actions. The purpose of this book is to show, by using graphic representations of numbers, how any report or presentation can be enhanced.

EFFECTIVE REPORTS

Many employees are put in the position of making reports to superiors about various aspects of their jobs. They are judged not only by their conduct, but also by the effectiveness of their report. If an employee cannot evoke belief and sympathy in the reader of the report, they are called poor communicators. As shown in Fig. 1-1, one sure way of evoking boredom in the reader is to load the report with reams of meaningless numbers, which are likely to be skipped over by most, if not all, readers. Communicating numbers with pictures makes reports more interesting. The point of the report is more easily grasped, and important numerical relationships are noticed instead of ignored. Color and shading can define different amounts or different periods of time, and require no calculation by the reader.

The use of graphs in reports can clarify and simplify the subject matter. Effective use of graphs and charts shortens the report substantially by summarizing large tables of numbers in a small amount of space. When graphics are used effectively, they reinforce the point of the text and make the text itself more coherent.

EFFECTIVE PRESENTATIONS

Everyone has had the misfortune to be present at a meeting where someone has stood for what seemed like forever spouting numbers about production or finance. During times like these, most people read the agenda, look out the window, talk to the person sitting next to them, and in general do everything but listen. The one thing that is more boring than reading groups of meaningless numbers is listening to someone read groups of meaningless numbers. No other single act can lose an audience faster. Presentations of all types—meetings, classes, lectures, and public speeches—can be made more interesting through the use of graphics and charts. The graphics can be designed with the audience in mind; the level of interest and the size of the audience need to be taken into account when decisions concerning graphics are made.

One good rule for the presentation of graphics

Iccam Furniture Company
Gross Sales in 1984

	Bedding	Living room	Dining room
January	$12,132.11	$14,598.00	$9,945.80
February	$9,080.00	$19,783.28	$10,675.90
March	$11,678.43	$11,876.34	$11,282.42
April	$13,630.71	$11,807.60	$10,954.00
May	$14,523.88	$12,045.34	$12,011.40
June	$20,654.39	$11,955.92	$10,956.70
July	$19,998.04	$9,756.50	$9,676.85
August	$16,856.87	$12,023.67	$10,656.70
September	$14,787.87	$11,745.02	$19,843.88
October	$11,456.32	$10,994.55	$18,876.62
November	$10,698.19	$11,456.70	$10,871.10
December	$15,206.42	$12,530.00	$22,954.00
	$170,703.23	$150,572.92	$158,705.37

Fig. 1-1. Table of sales by month, Iccam Furniture Company.

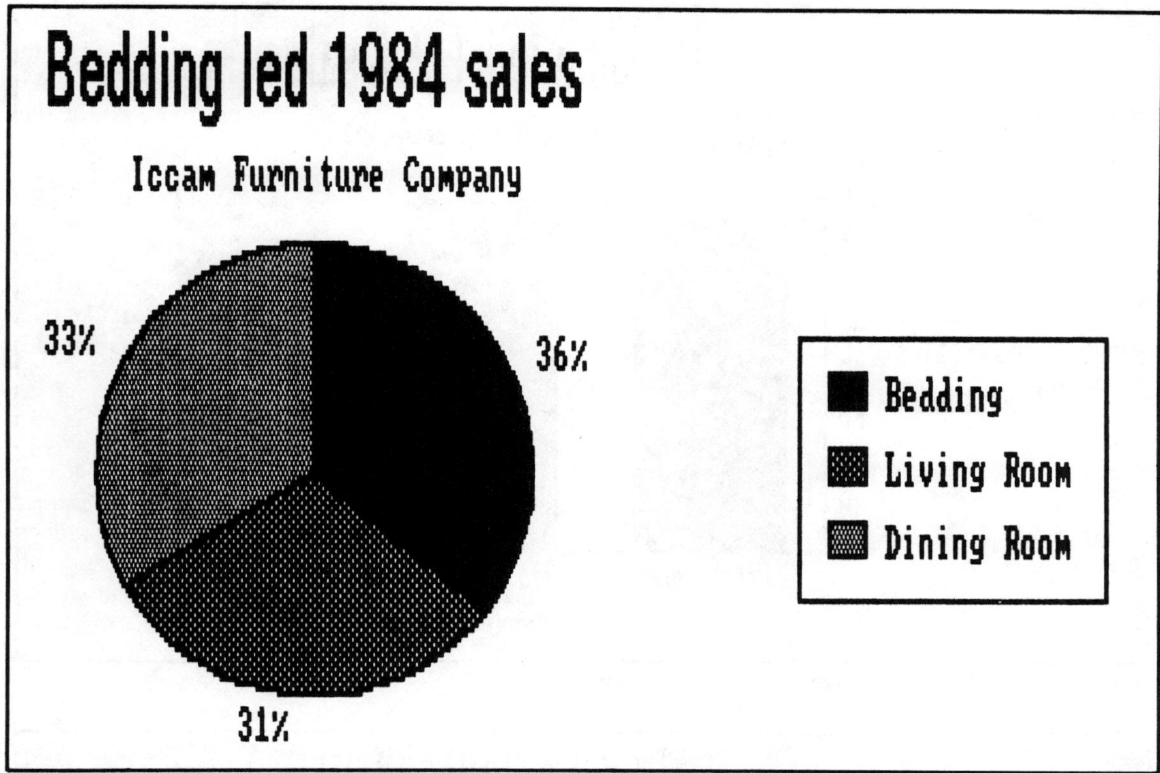

Fig. 1-2. Proportion of gross sales by department.

is that the more colorful the graphics are, the better. People tend to look at colorful pictures with more interest than at black and white drawings. Another rule is the KISS rule (Keep It Simple, Stupid!); one graph should not attempt to show too much information. A busy graph can be incomprehensible and therefore ineffective.

Figure 1-2 shows the information listed in Fig. 1-1. The pie chart, however, graphically describes the information instantly and does not require the viewer to calculate the totals mentally. Figure 1-3 shows the same information in a column chart.

DOLLARS, TIME, AND TRENDS

In many corporate settings graphs and charts are used to indicate the amount of money earned versus the year in which it was made. The graphs seem to show a "trend" in the growth of the company. It is important to remember, however, that a competent artist, whether drawing a painting or preparing a graph for a company meeting, can make us see things that are not there. Graphics of this kind are meant to impress a specific audience, probably the stockholders. Everyone perceives pictures through the emotional side of the brain, so that the first impression of a specific picture can fool the nonintellectual area of the brain and cause a feeling of joy or whatever feeling the artist was trying to evoke. By the time that the intellectual side of the brain can analyze what was seen, any good showman will have moved on to a newer and more colorful picture.

One effective way to fool an audience with graphics is to play with the scale of the graph. For instance, the rate of increase of dollars versus time appears to be greater if the time scale is shortened even slightly or the dollar scale lengthened. What

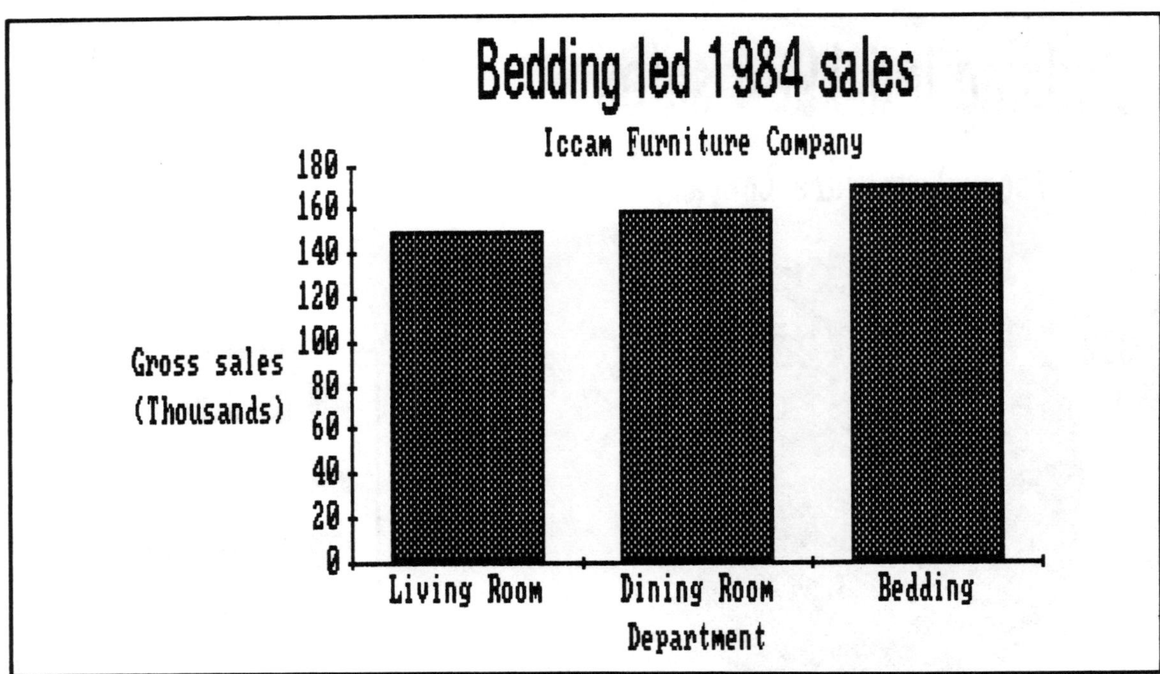

Fig. 1-3. Gross sales by department, Iccam Furniture Company.

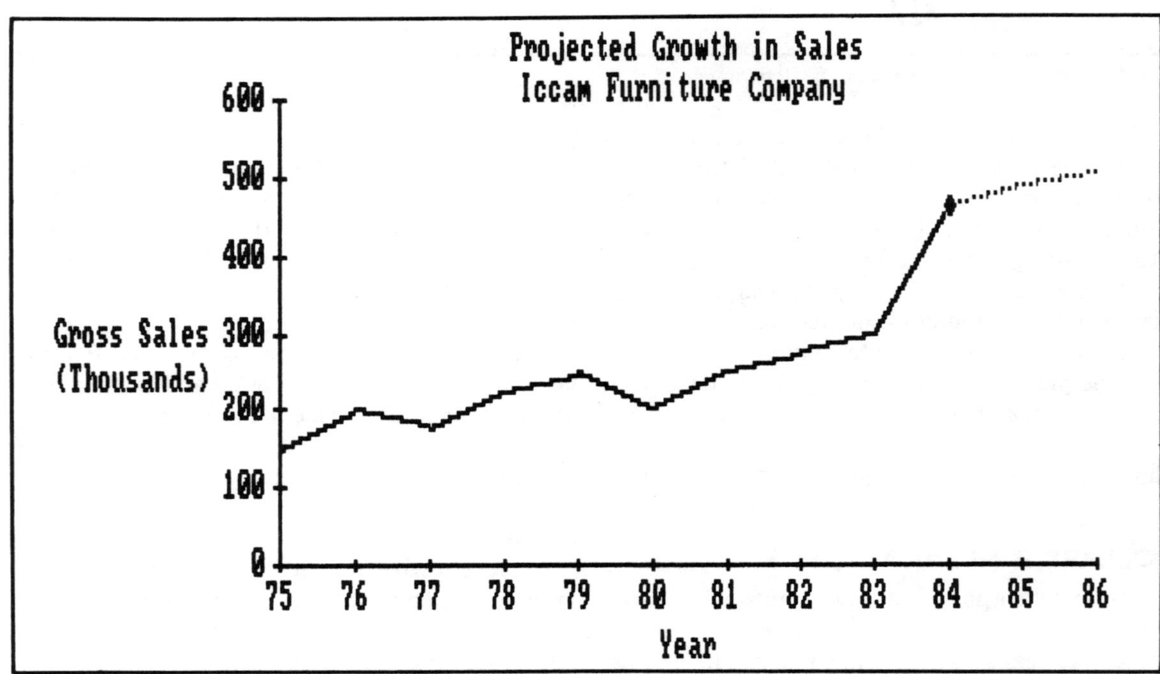

Fig. 1-4. Chart showing projected growth of sales.

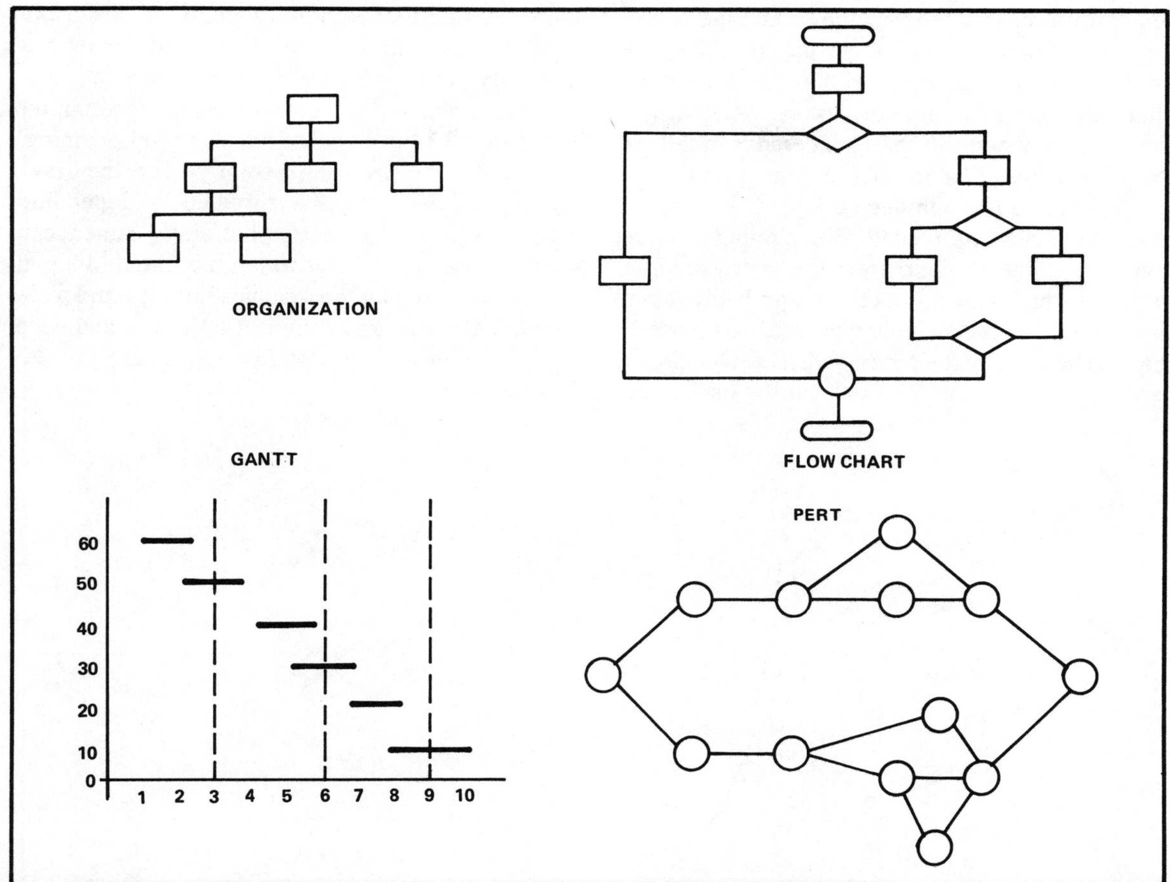

Fig. 1-5. Management charts.

may actually be a long period of constant but slow gain can be made to appear like a fast spurt of growth.

Please be advised that the authors of this book do not advocate the use of graphics to lie to anyone, even stockholders. We do feel, however, that you, as an observer of graphics need to be aware of the possibility that someone may be lying to you. Looks can deceive, both in judging people and in judging their graphs.

PROCESSES

Charts can be designed to show the flow of a process, the hierarchy of an organization, or the relationships between sets of processes. In industry, Gantt charts are used to show the time allotted for different tasks along a timeline that describes the deadlines for getting the task done. PERT charts show the relationships between tasks and the order in which the tasks can be accomplished. Flowcharts are used by programmers and engineers to map out a process into logical, linear steps.

Many software packages available today allow even nonartistic managers to produce their own graphs and charts in very little time. By entering some data and giving the software a few instructions, the manager can produce pie charts for reports, Gantt charts for managing projects, and the tables of organization for the company. Any secretary who has had to type and retype the table of organization can tell you the advantage of having a more fluid method of storing, recalling, and changing it. Any manager who has had to draw a chart for a big meeting, only to discover that new figures have made the chart outdated, can tell you the advantages of having the chart in a fluid form.

Just type a few numbers, press a few keys, and presto—the chart is updated. Wait a minute . . . just how do you get the chart from the microcomputer to the meeting? The best method is probably to take the computer to the meeting with you, with a screen that can be seen by the entire audience. One big advantage to this is that changes can be made right up to the minute before the meeting. A disadvantage is that a large screen is needed for even a modestly sized audience.

The point is that even using microcomputer graphics, there is no substitute for good planning. If a graph is drawn using a color plotter, the drawing time can be as much as three hours, depending on the complexity of the graph. Using a camera can mean waiting a few days to get the film developed into slides. Planning the graphics carefully and planning for the size and composition of the audience can pay off in an effective and productive presentation.

Chapter 2

You Ought 'a' Be in Pictures

In painting, the most brilliant colors, spread at random and without design, will give far less pleasure than the simplest outline of a figure.

Aristotle

In the first chapter of this book, graphic presentations were discussed in terms of the perception of the viewer. This chapter will talk about some of the methods that you can use to project your message to your audience.

The most important step in presenting your message is to determine just what that message is to be. This could be called "defining the problem." There are some easy steps to take when you are deciding what message you want to convey:

1. Determine the basic type of the message. Of course, in a single presentation, a number of graphics could be used to illustrate various points. Each graphic must be designed as an individual message, presenting one of the major points of the presentation. The general types of message that can be conveyed effectively with a graph are:

a. Time Series—a record of amounts, volumes, or other measurements over a period of time.
b. Portions of a Whole—a record of percentages, proportions, or ratios.
c. Comparisons—a record that compares amounts, volumes, and other data where the difference is also an important datum. For example, income can be compared to expenditures. In this case the difference (profit/loss) is a vital amount.

2. Use one graphic to present one major point. A basic mistake to make is to try to arouse your audience by presenting a large number of graphs, charts, and flashy pictures. This usually has the opposite effect—the audience first becomes overawed and then overcome by the assault on their senses—and then they will become over-bored. The graphics that you will design will constitute the high points of your presentation. Don't use your "big guns" on unworthy targets.

3. Define your message in a single sentence. This will be the topic sentence of the graph. The graph, when viewed alone with no other text or special presentation, should state your message clearly enough to be understood immediately by whoever views it.

Once you have decided on the concept you want to present, you must decide how to best convey that message to your audience. The best-designed graphic can actually detract from a presentation if the execution is faulty. The methods of presenting graphics vary with intention of the presentation.

When doing a printed presentation, a memo, or a status report, the graphs can be placed alongside the text to illustrate the point made in the text. It is important to place the graph with the text that it clarifies. The point is lost even one page later. Color graphics in a report should be limited to the major or most noteworthy points. In most cases, even with microcomputer graphics, text and color graphics are difficult to place on the same page; most likely, a separate page will be needed for color graphs and charts. This will mean that the graphs must stand alone, and the reader must divide his/her attention between the text and the graph. The message must be simple and instantly understood so that it will not be lost.

In a standup presentation, the size of the audience can make a difference in the choice of the medium for graphics. In a small meeting of five to ten people, the color monitor of the microcomputer can itself be used for the display. Audiences from ten to twenty-five people can be reached very easily with an overhead or opaque projector. Larger audiences will require a slide projector and screen to display the graphics most effectively.

Once you have determined what conceptual bridge you will build and the final form it will take, you can choose the computer software that will produce the kind of graph you desire and then get the necessary data into computer-usable form. With most graphics software packages, it is possible to switch from one chart type to another very quickly, so it will be possible to get many different views of your data.

A major advantage of the use of microcomputers is the number of hardware devices that can be used to produce graphs. Apart from the monitor screen of the computer, most computer printers will print graphics in black-and-white patterns of dots. There are also color plotters, which use colored pens to draw graphs on plain paper. Finally, there is a device known as the *palette*, which conveys the image on the computer screen to a device that will display the image for a 35mm camera. This is an excellent way to create slides of your computer graphic; without a palette you would have to stand for hours in a darkened room trying to snap pictures of the monitor screen. This can be done with patience. The camera angle must be exact, or the edges of the screen will be distorted.

The steps to designing an effective graphic for a presentation are:

1. Define the message to be conveyed.
2. Determine the best method of conveying the message.
3. Determine what medium of display will be used.
4. Find the computer software/hardware that will produce the result you need.
5. Put the data into the form necessary for your computer system.
6. Produce the graphic.

When the graphic has been produced, preview it with one or more people who are also involved with the data you are using. They should be able to divine the meaning very quickly and be able to explain what they are seeing. This sort of previewing can eliminate embarassing mistakes before the official presentation and will also give you an idea of how the graphic will affect your audience.

SELECTING THE FORMAT

There are many graphic formats that you can use to illustrate a given point in a presentation. Choosing the correct format is possibly the most confusing part of designing presentation graphics. The multitude of different graph and chart formats can be overwhelming. Different styles of graph, however, are most often associated with particular types of messages.

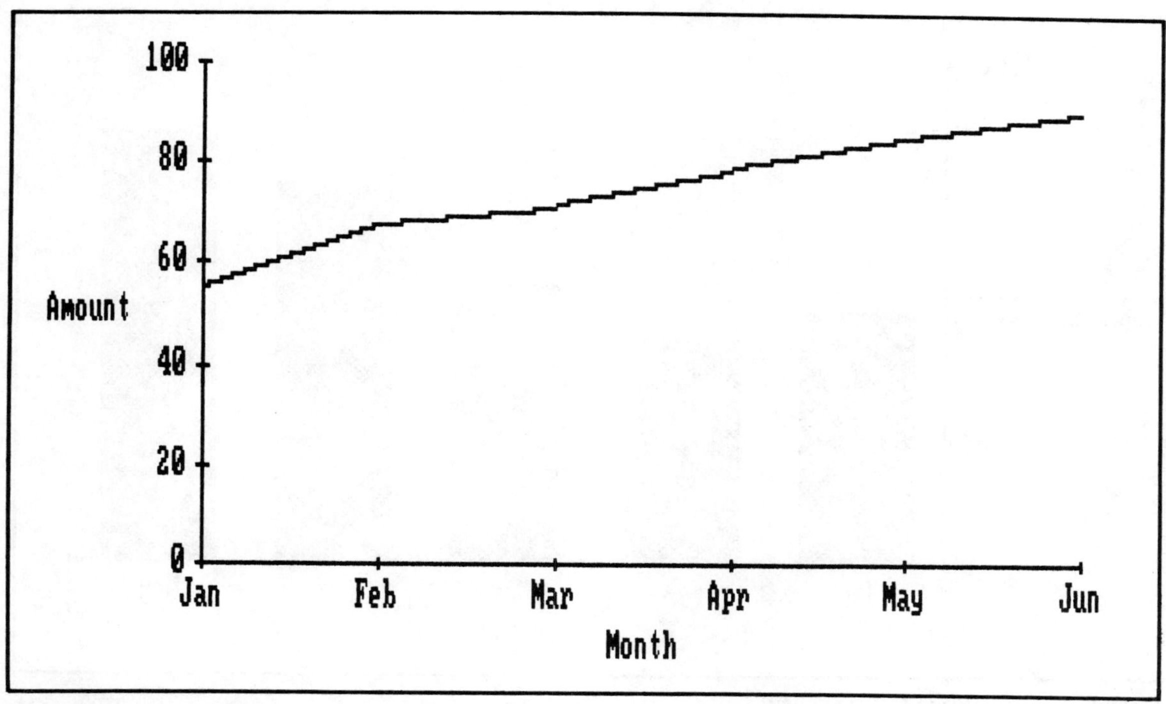

Fig. 2-1. The line chart.

Trends over a period of time are usually represented by a line chart as shown in Fig. 2-1. Line charts can also be used to plot a stream of data over a large number of time periods. Very gradual increases and decreases can be seen in the rising and falling of the line. This type of chart is effective in projecting from the already existing data into the short-term future. Line charts are often used to detail the rise or fall of a company's income, expenses, or production quotas. Usually, the plot is in terms of dollar amounts, although amounts of any kind could be used.

Time series can also be shown using the vertical bar chart (Fig. 2-2). This is most effective when the differences between the time periods are large; it can also be more effective where few time periods are involved.

Volumes of substances or items can be shown with a variation of the line chart known as the surface chart. This is a line chart that has the area below the plot line shaded or colored, as if it were a solid surface (Fig. 2-3).

Portions of a whole can best be depicted with a pie chart (Fig. 2-4). A circle, or pie, representing one hundred percent of whatever this graph is about is drawn. The pie is divided to show the proportional relationships between the various parts that make up the whole. Pie charts are very popular for showing the apportionment of funds among several groups, because by a very small manipulation of artistic perspective, the pie can become a coin.

Pie charts become ineffective when a large number of slices are needed to show the full story. When some slices must be combined, it is possible to modify the pie chart by adding a *100% bar*, which is usually seen projecting from one slice of the pie chart. A 100-percent bar is like a linear pie chart—each band of color or shading represents a portion of a whole, which is the single slice. Unfortunately, the bar calls attention to the slice thus pictured and reduces the effect of the rest of the chart. This variation should only be used when the focus of the graph is on that particular slice (Fig. 2-5).

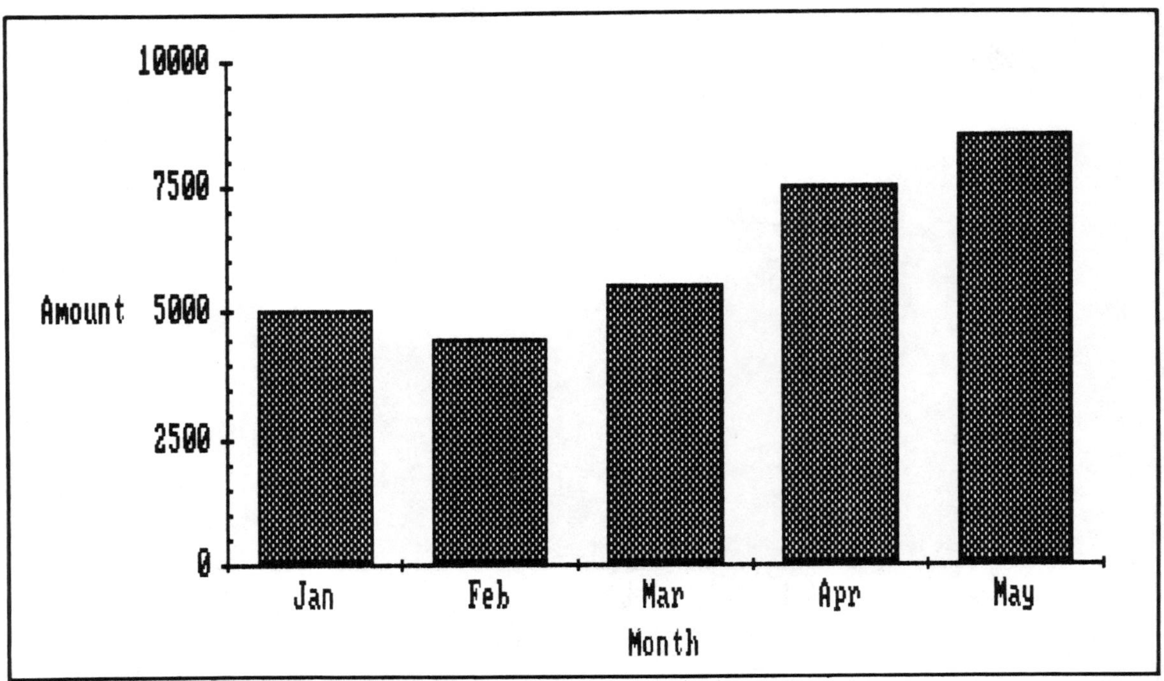

Fig. 2-2. The vertical bar (column) chart.

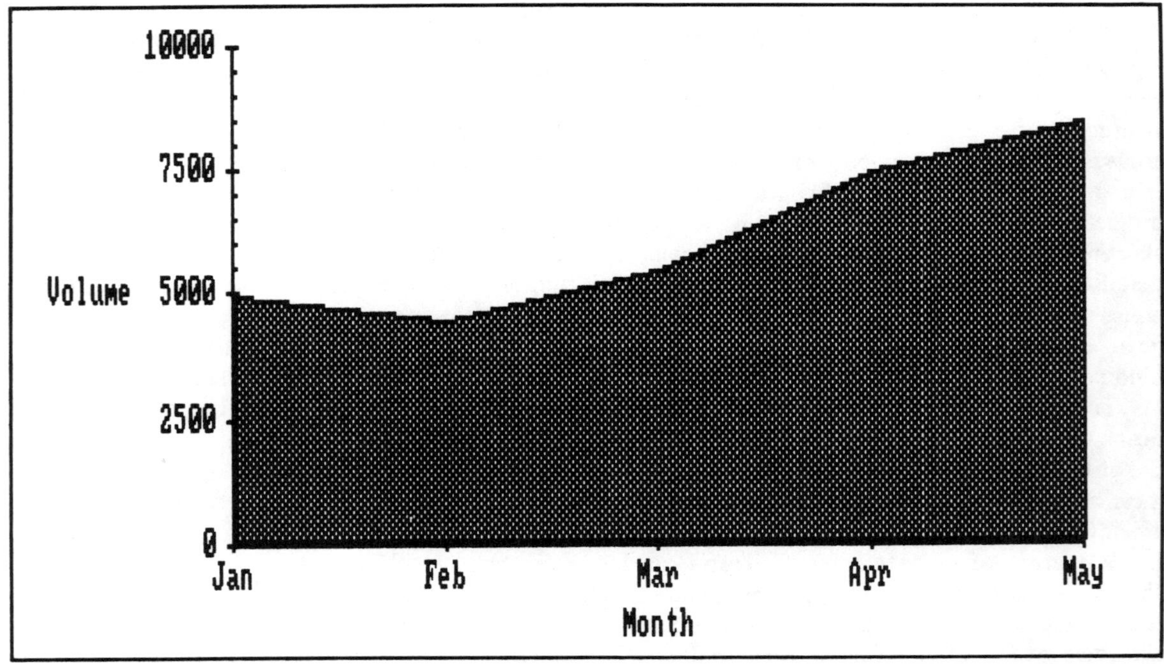

Fig. 2-3. The surface/area chart.

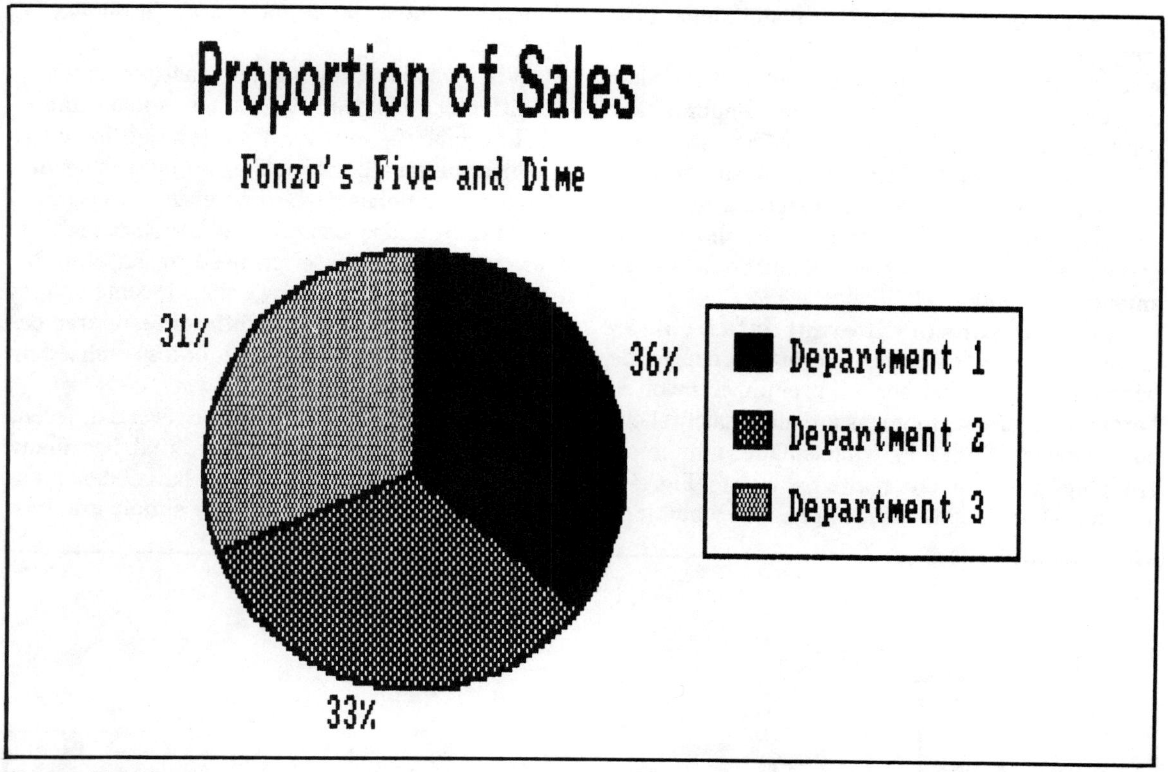

Proportion of Sales
Fonzo's Five and Dime
31%
36%
33%
Department 1
Department 2
Department 3

Fig. 2-4. The pie chart.

INSTEAD OF THIS !
DO THIS !
COMBINE INTO
ONE
SLICE
1
2
3
4
5
6
6
5
4
3
2
1

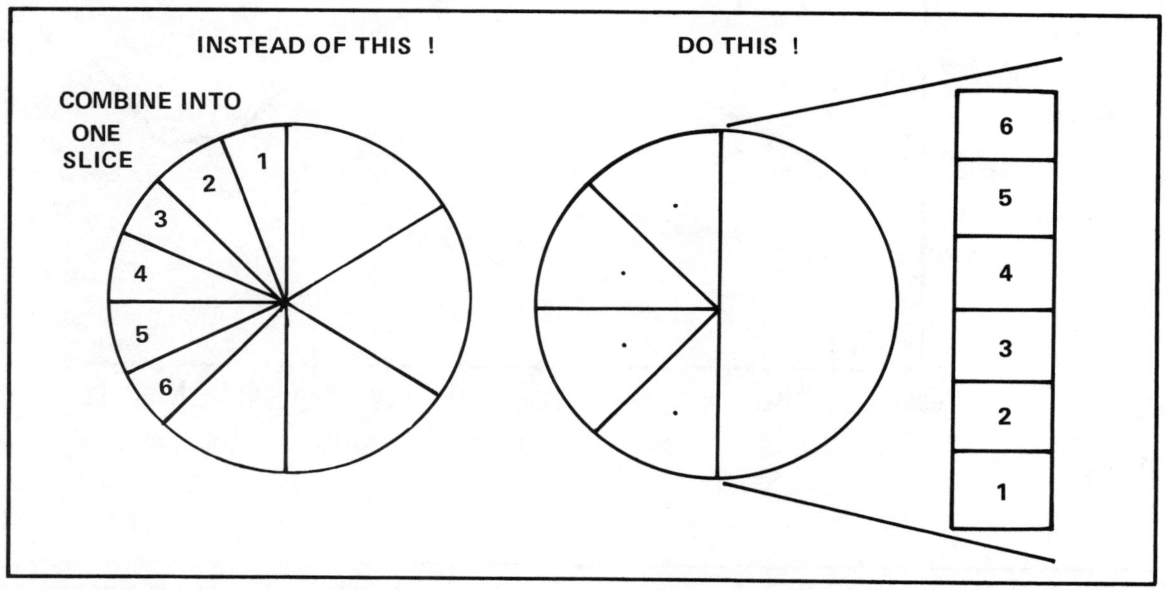

Fig. 2-5. A pie chart with a 100% bar.

100-percent bar charts that stand alone, however, are not very popular at all. Each horizontal or vertical bar represents 100 percent of a whole. Since bar charts are used mostly for amounts and volumes, a 100-percent bar chart can be easily mistaken for a regular bar chart, and the message of the chart will be distorted. In fact, a 100-percent bar chart can itself distort the data by showing only the rise or fall of a proportion, and not the actual amount or volume.

Comparisons of different data items are usually shown with either line or bar charts, depending on the number of groupings involved. Larger numbers of groupings are more easily shown on a line chart (Fig. 2-6), while smaller numbers of groupings are shown best with bar charts (Fig. 2-7). The bar chart is also most impressive when large differences must be shown from grouping to grouping.

When you are showing a comparison in which the difference between two values is itself important information, you can use a type of line chart in which the area between the two plots is shaded or colored to emphasize the difference. This is called an *area* chart and is a variation of the surface chart. This type of graph is often used to map the difference between a company's sales income and its expenditures (Fig. 2-8). The difference, or area between the two plots, is the profit or loss realized by the company.

As you have realized, there are several different kinds of charts, and each major kind has many variations, only a few of which have been mentioned so far. For the most part, a simple graph or

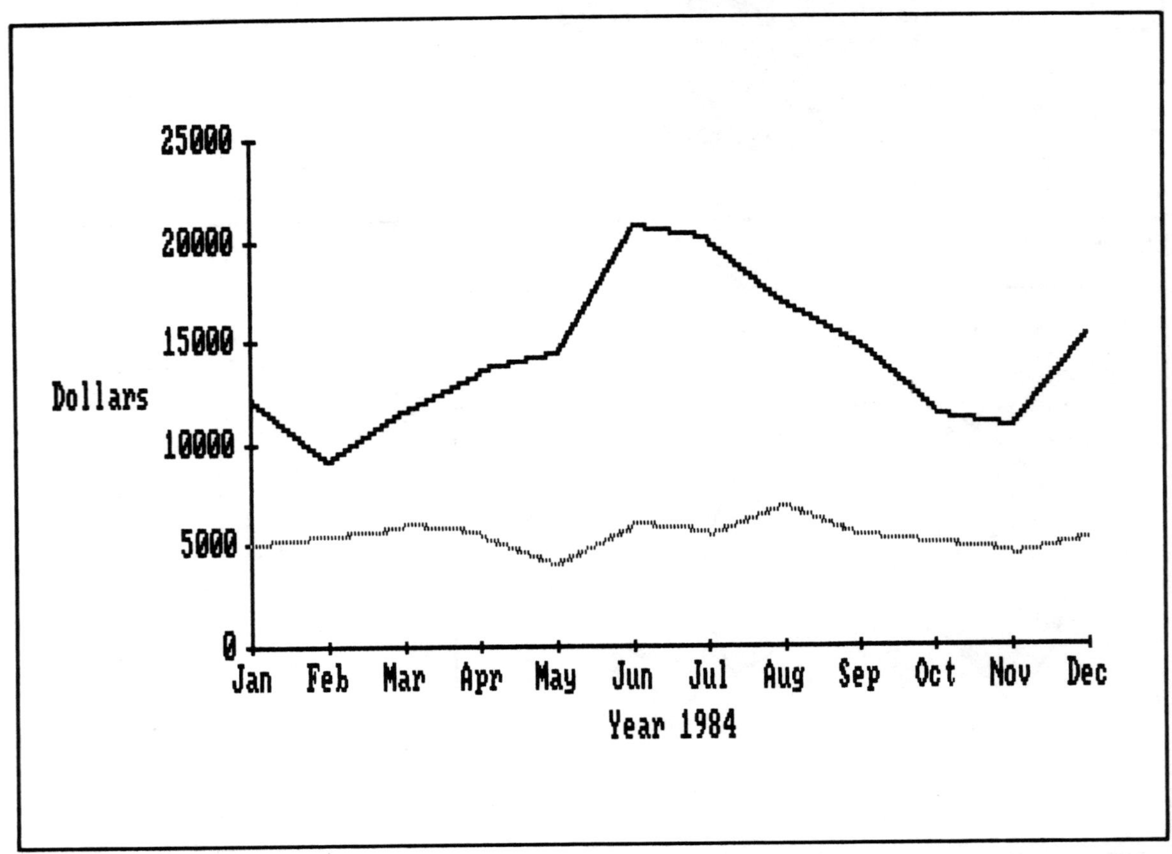

Fig. 2-6. The multiple line chart.

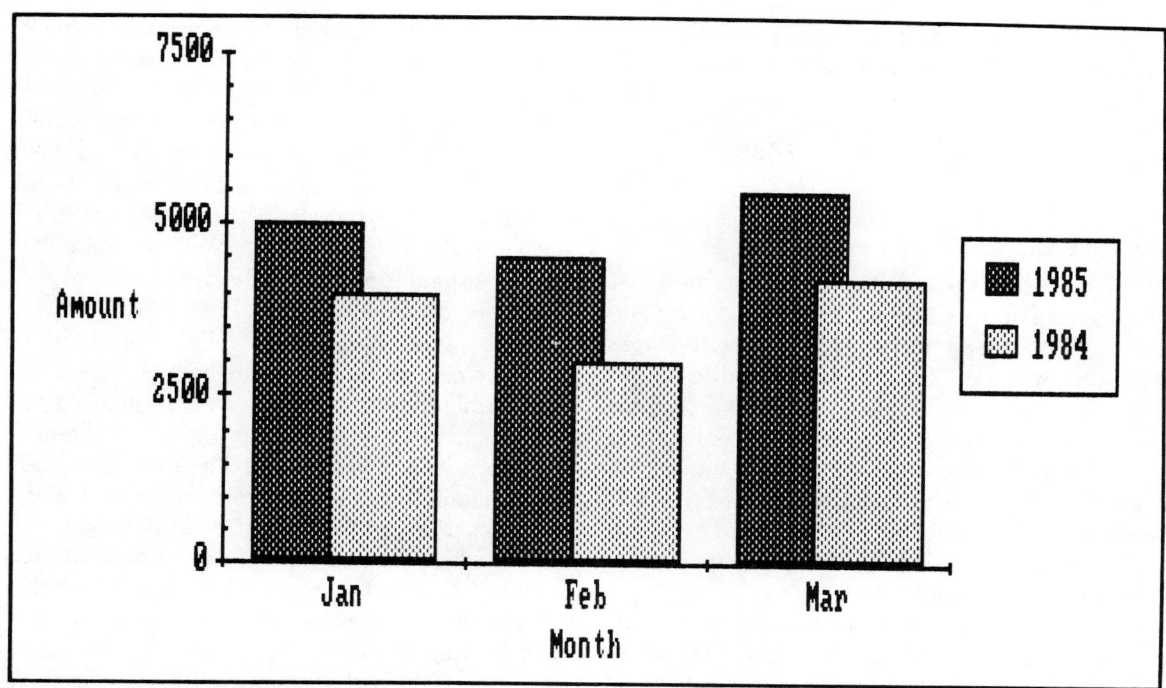

Fig. 2-7. The grouped column chart.

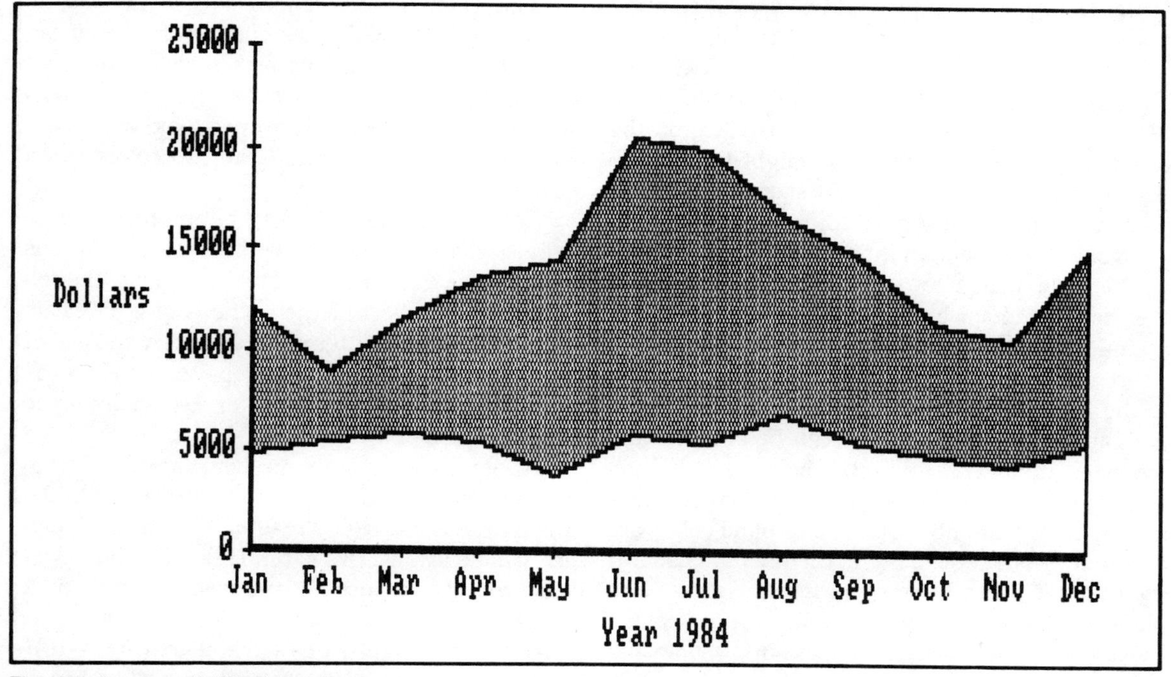

Fig. 2-8. An area-of-difference chart.

chart will suffice to make the particular point you wish to convey. The choice of which type of graph to use depends on the type of message you want to send to the audience and where you want the emphasis to lie.

CATCHY COLORATION

A great many people who have seen computer graphics software packages have come away impressed with the number of colors these packages enable them to use. Their imaginations abound with visions of charts and graphs so colorful that the viewer will need sunglasses to cut the glare. This is another of the misconceptions concerning graphics. Colors are best used to emphasize, not to overwhelm. The computer graphics in the color section following page 184 show some examples of the effective use of color.

The viewer's eye should be drawn to the part of the chart that contains the major part of the message. In a pie chart, one of the pie slices should be colored to emphasize it, and the others, while differing from each other, would be in a background color. The emphasis in a column chart would be one or more of the columns.

Colors, particularly bright colors, should be used to call attention to a particular place on the chart. For example, a company might have a vertical bar chart in their prospectus showing the dollar amounts of assets of several competing companies alongside their own. In a case like this, the competitors would be shown in yellow or gray, while their own column is bright red. This coloration calls attention to their column before the viewer is even aware of the other columns, which seem to fade into the background.

One or two bright colors can be aesthetically pleasing without being too overwhelming. Other colors, if present, should be background colors. It is important to remember that background colors are different colors depending on the medium used. If the graph is going to be reproduced using a color plotter, red, blue, and green are foreground colors. Lighter colors and pastels, such as pink, yellow, and gray, are background colors.

When you are taking photographs of a color graph on a computer monitor or palette device, yellow is a bright color, although it can still be used as background. Blue is an excellent background color in this context; red remains an emphasis color. The best test of the coloration is to see which parts of the graph draw your eye when you look at it. A good general rule for selecting colors to emphasize a part of a graphic is to use a dark color on a paper and a light color on a screen.

Grids, axis lines, and labels should be in a neutral color with respect to the background. The best combination of neutral colors is black and white—black-on-white for printing and white-on-black for slides or projectors. The axis lines and labels contain pertinent information for analyzing the graph. Through the use of neutral colors, the viewer's eye is drawn first to the focal point of the graph and then to the actual data. Neutral colors, in any medium, are more readable than any other color; it is important that the viewer can easily read the information, because it is vital to the viewer's understanding of the entire message.

The catch of coloration is that the eye is physiologically limited in the number of colors it can perceive at one time. This fact causes colors that are in close contact to *wash out* at their mutual border. This can cause the viewer to look away from that area or even to confuse the two colors when questioned later.

Color is not the only way to emphasize or to make a chart visually more interesting. Various shading patterns can be used to differentiate the columns of a bar chart or the sections of a pie chart (Fig. 2-9). Darker patterns tend to draw the eye of the viewer better than lighter patterns when the graph is reproduced on a printer, especially if the printer is black-on-white.

Slanted shading patterns should always slant to the right, because the eyes of the audience will be drawn from left to right "reading" the chart. A pattern slanted against this natural reading motion will cause the eye to become confused and get stuck before reaching the area of emphasis, which is usually on the right side of the chart (Fig. 2-10).

Many graphics software packages allow a vari-

Fig. 2-9. Shading patterns.

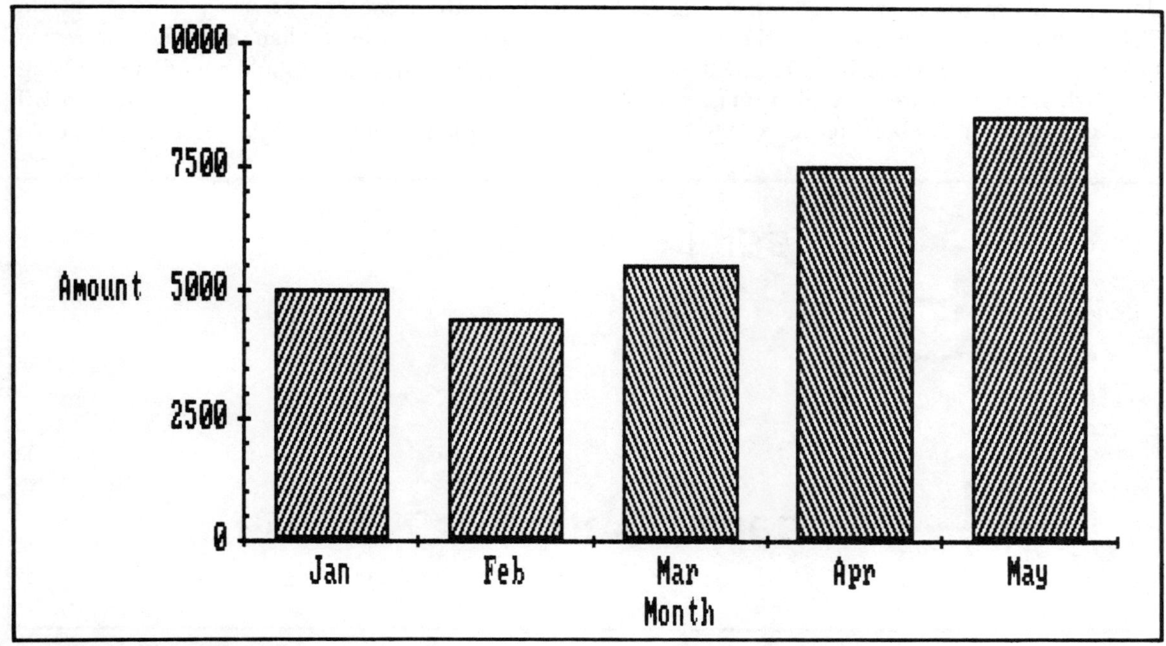

Fig. 2-10. Slanting patterns.

ety of different fonts and printing styles for labels. Using unusual printing styles, however, can detract from the emphasis of the graph. As a rule, simple, sans-serif letters and numbers can be used very effectively (Fig. 2-11). Mixing different type styles will definitely cause confusion and possibly eye strain.

THE ART OF MISDIRECTION

While most people use graphs for emphasis, it is very easy to move from over emphasizing to downright cheating. There are several common ways of misrepresenting data with graphs, which you should be aware of to avoid these traps yourself.

The main impact of a graph or chart comes from the first impression that the viewer receives. A rising trend line always looks impressive, and a good showman will talk around the graph in such a way as to keep the viewer from really examining the data. The rising trend line, however, can be distorted to look as if the trend is steeper or shallower than it actually is, and in some cases, it can be made to look as if it were dropping.

Disproportionate scaling of the axis lines can flatten or sharpen a curve as shown in Fig. 2-12. This kind of scaling occurs when the spacing between units of equal value is different. It can also occur when the units are unfamiliar; in most cases, units of five or ten are best for describing the plotted data. When the axis is labeled in increments of, for example, three-tenths (.3, or in a sequence of 1.2, 1.5, 1.8, and so on), the disproportionate spacing is more difficult to see.

Logarithmic scaling should only be used when the audience is expecting it in advance. If the audience is expecting a normally scaled line chart, the first impressions of this type of scale can be extremely misleading, as shown in Fig. 2-13. Logarithmic scaling is where the point halfway on the graph is the square root of the value of the end point. For example, the scale starts at zero, the point halfway between the endpoints is 10 units, and the end point is 100 units. This can show an extremely distorted plot of the data, and if the viewer does not have time to examine the chart at length, it can create a very inaccurate impression.

Logarithmic scaling will cause steeply rising trend lines to appear as if they were leveling off, like a ball coming to the peak of a bounce. This effect is very pronounced and becomes worse the higher the line goes toward the endpoint.

All amount axes should be based at zero. If you see a graph that is wavy across the bottom, notched at the bottom corners, or has a number at the bottom (not zero) larger than the other numbers on that axis line, an alarm should sound in your head. Graphs that have an axis not based on zero will sharpen the rise and fall of the plotted curve, caus-

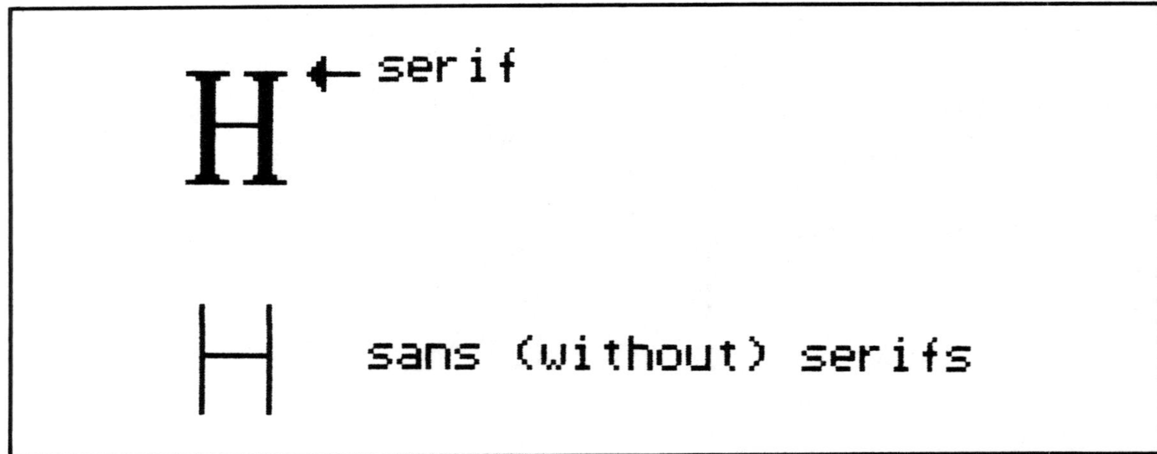

Fig. 2-11. Serif and sans-serif type faces.

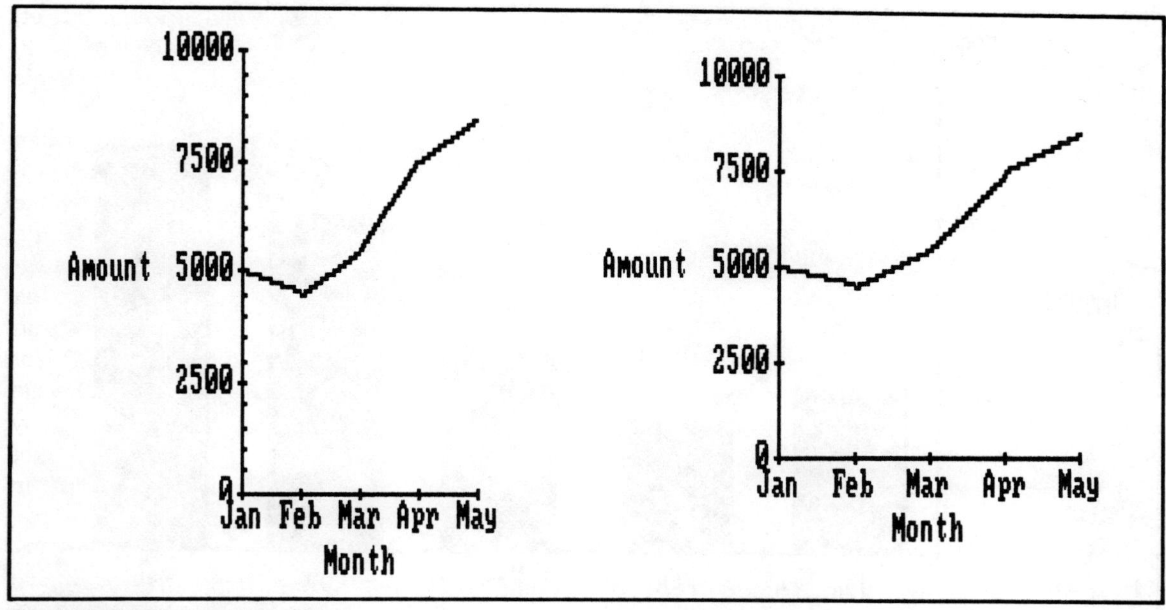

Fig. 2-12. Shortening the x-axis.

ing gradual trends to appear steeper than they actually are. The data are correct, but the first impression will be distorted. Figures 2-14 and 2-15 show the same plotted data, but the charts appear different because the chart in Fig. 2-15 is based at zero, where the one in Fig. 2-14 is not. There is no

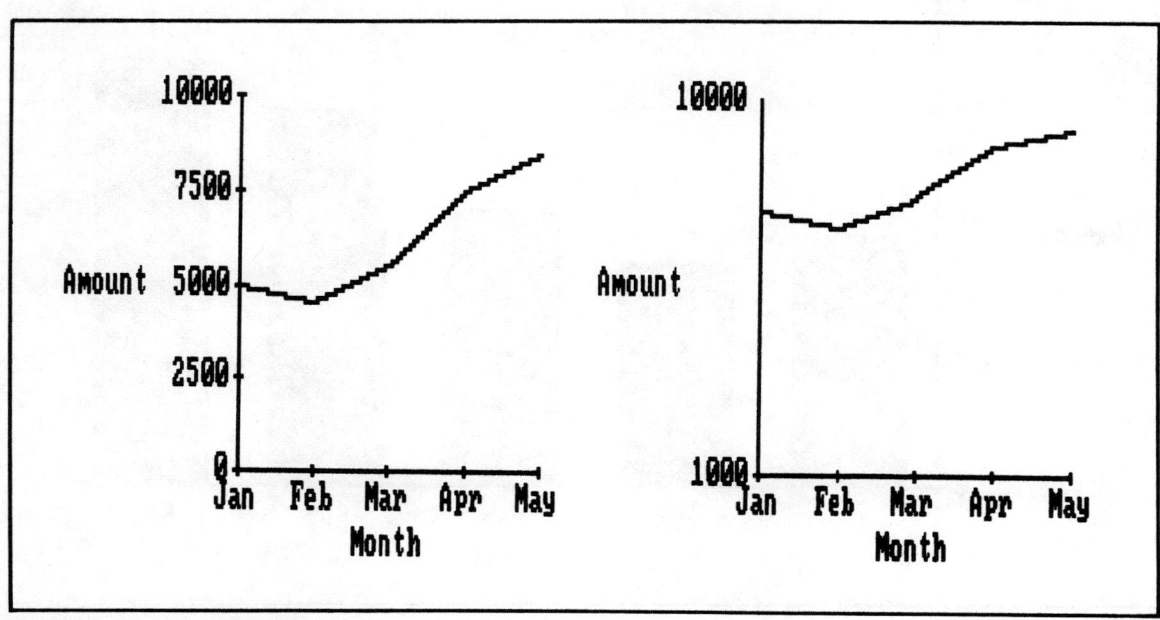

Fig. 2-13. A logarithmic scale.

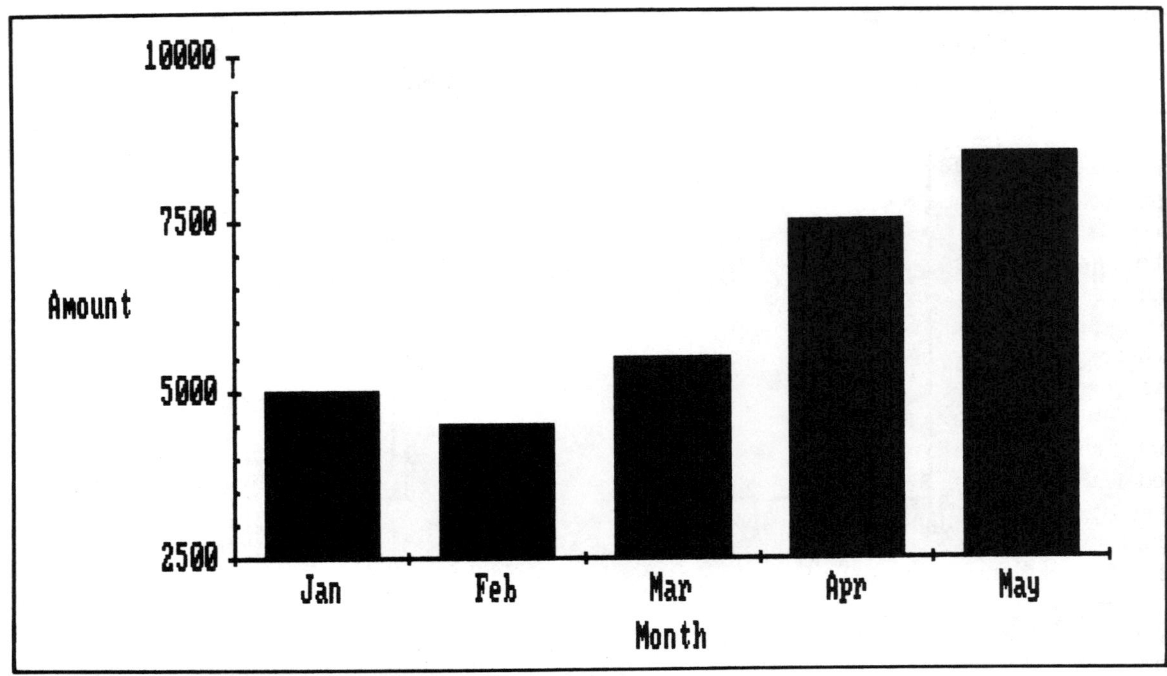

Fig. 2-14. An amount scale not based at zero.

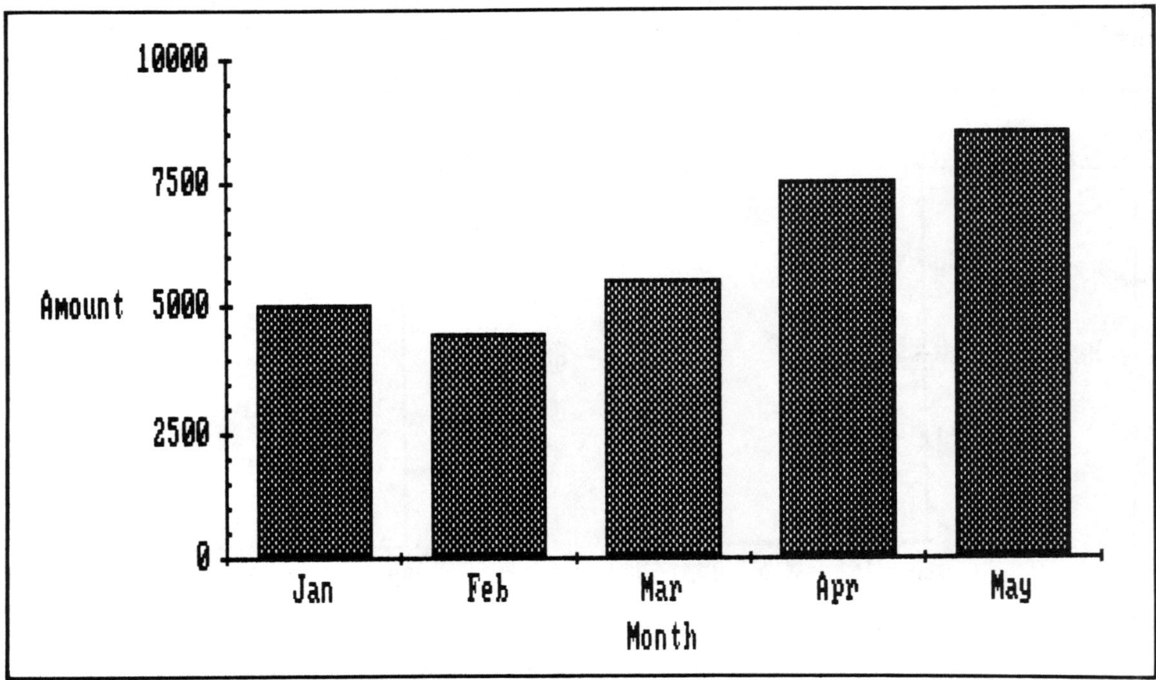

Fig. 2-15. An amount scale based at zero.

analytical difference between the figures, but the emotional impact is very different.

Certain techniques used in perspective drawing can cause a three-dimensional graph to be misleading. A three-dimensional graph creates the impression that there is a wall from which the graphic symbols (charts, pie wedges, or whatever) seem to be projecting. This projection is caused by the use of artistic perspective techniques, where the part of the object against the wall will be smaller, or higher, or lower, than the front of the object, which appears closer because of the size difference. As shown in Fig. 2-16, the grid and axis lines of a three-dimensional graph are usually at the back wall of the chart, which means that the true data is plotted at the back wall, not in the foreground where your attention will be focused. In a column chart, the column will appear larger because it is larger than the true reading at the back wall.

As if there were not enough ways of purposefully cheating, it is possible to accidentally cause graphic confusion. Almost everyone has seen the common optical illusions that are depicted on restaurant placemats and in young people's magazines, where the viewer is asked "which line is longer?" only to find that the lines are indeed the same length. This and other optical tricks of perception are caused not by the lines that you are asked to compare, but by the other lines in the drawing. This kind of optical illusion occurs most frequently in line or surface charts. You can usually avoid this by making the grid lines much lighter than the other lines on the chart. The grid lines will help overcome the illusion by projecting the axis units to the data plot.

GRAPHIC SOFTWARE

There are some important points to remember when you are shopping for graphic software. Any choice in software applies to your own situation, which the authors have no way of knowing. There are, however, certain rules that apply in almost every case.

First, it is important to know precisely what your situation is. Determine what kinds of graphs you will be using most often and the method that they will be reproduced by. If your use will be for large presentations, you must be able to produce your graphs on transparencies or slides. In a report or memo, graphs must be produced to fit in with the format of the rest of the text. They must also be positioned in the text at the points where they will be most effective.

Have a good knowledge of what kinds of graphs you will be using most. You will most likely be searching for software that can fill all of your current requirements, and you should be able to find

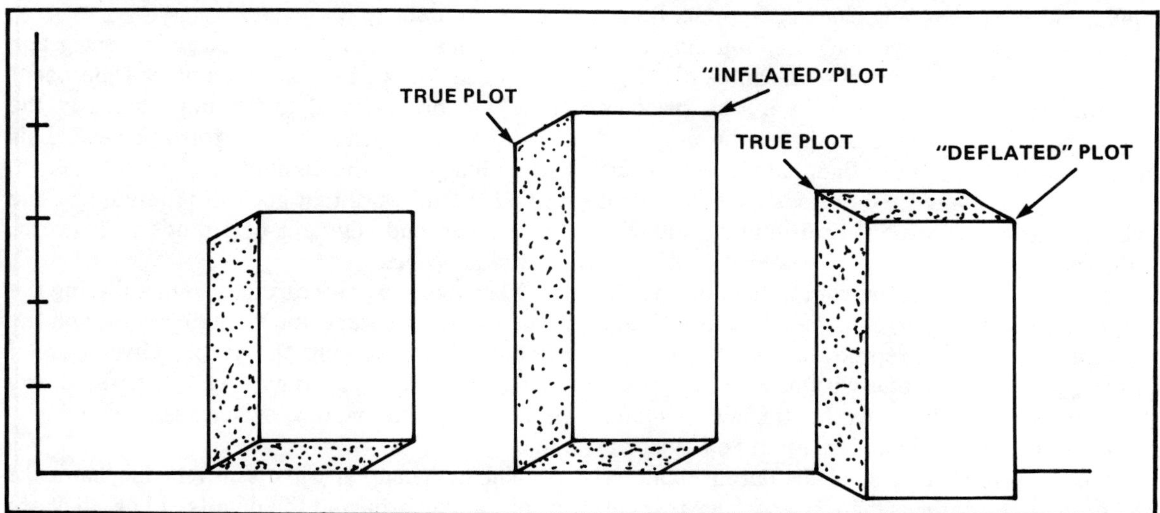

Fig. 2-16. Three-dimensional misdirection.

a software package that meets all of them. You do not have to accept second best. No matter how many extras are lumped into a package, if the program cannot produce your graphics the way you want them, you will not be pleased with it.

The amount of time that you can afford to use in learning the software may also affect your choice. In almost every case, there will be a period of learning that you will go through when attempting to use a new package. If you need a week of study to learn the package well enough to use it for your simplest requirements, perhaps you can find one that is much easier to learn.

Another important feature of a good graphics package is the ease and speed of entering your particular set of data. Many packages will accept data only in certain formats. Some packages require you to type the information into a special file used only by the package itself. One way to avoid time-consuming data entry chores is to buy a package that accepts data from the files that you already use. If all of your raw data is in dBASE III files, for example, you might want to purchase a package that will draw its data directly from the database and graph the totals of various fields or the counts of certain record types.

The ability to manipulate the graphs produced by the package, in terms of changing axis lines and labels, and even swapping chart styles quickly and easily, may also affect your choice. You may want to produce a column chart of totals and a pie chart of grand totals of the same data. The package should be able to expand or shrink the produced graphs as necessary. If you find that a column chart is covering too many time periods, you may want to be able to switch to a line chart quickly and with little work.

Once you have entered your data and seen the graph on the monitor screen, the graphics package must also be able to reproduce your graph on a printer, plotter, or palette with as little help from you as possible. This means that the output should be easy to acquire and manipulate. If you must run three other programs to send the output to a plotter, for example, perhaps there is a package that outputs directly to the plotter with no intervening steps.

The transportability of the graphics produced and the input data may be a deciding factor in companies where many different brands of microcomputers are used. The graphs developed on one machine might need to be moved to another for reproduction.

Also, the final form of the graphs produced by the package should be as close to the final form that you will use as possible. Some packages will insert graphs directly into text files, although this is uncommon. The most common form of output is letter-size (8.5 by 11 inches). If this does not meet your needs, there are packages that will produce smaller or larger graphs, and put multiple graphs on the same page.

As is the case with the purchase of all computer tools, the purchase of hardware and software to produce graphics is based on your individual situation. First, you must decide what is to be produced, then buy the software that will do it, and then buy the hardware that will best produce the most usable form of the graphics.

SUMMARY

The time spent in designing and choosing the right form of the graph will be returned in the response that can be evoked. Confusing or unclear graphs can be a liability just as much as good graphs can be an asset.

It seems like a lot of work can go into one graph in a presentation, but the amount of time spent should be proportional to the importance of the point that the graph is helping to emphasize. This can be likened to the amount of planning, design, and plain hard work that goes into filming just one 15 or 20-second segment of a motion picture or television scene.

Plan your graphics carefully, remembering the audience, the message you want to convey, and the method of reproducing the graph. Give yourself enough lead time to prepare two or three drafts prior to presentation, to allow for mistakes and new data.

The next chapter will discuss the mechanics of graphs and charts, and the details of how they are constructed.

Chapter 3

Building a Graph . . . One Step at a Time

"Begin at the beginning," the Kind said, gravely, "and go till you come to the end; then stop."

Lewis Carroll

THE AXIS LINES

Horizontal and vertical bar (column) charts and line charts are built on a *Cartesian plane*—a plane of two numbered lines that cross each other at their zero points (Fig. 3-1). The two number lines are called *axis lines,* or *axes* in the plural. Each line is numbered in units that are not necessarily the same as those on the other axis. The point where the axes cross is called the *origin.*

Data can be plotted in any or all of the quadrants formed by the axis lines. The quadrants are numbered I, II, III, and IV starting from the upper-right quadrant and proceeding counterclockwise (Fig. 3-2). Data is plotted by finding the value for one variable on the vertical axis (or y-axis), finding its value for the horizontal (or x-) axis, and plotting a point where lines drawn from the values cross at a right angle. The location of the plot point is named by its coordinates, the x-axis value followed by the y-axis value. Thus the values on the axis lines determine the placement of the plot marker for the piece of data you are plotting. Someone viewing the graph should be able to find the values of a given point from both axes.

Quadrant I is formed from the positive sections of the axis lines. This is the most frequently used quadrant for plotting data because all values/coordinates are positive on both axes (Fig 3-3). Sometimes this quadrant is turned on its side, as is the case with most horizontal bar charts.

Quadrants I and II can be combined to form a deviation chart by drawing the y-axis line in the center of the chart and plotting data on each side of the axis (Fig. 3-4). This format is used to show deviation from some value. For example, if a sales team is rated on the percentage of a quota met, the y-axis would indicate the full quota position. Columns extending to the right indicate over-quota percentage, and columns extending to the left indicate quota shortfalls.

The same type of format can be drawn vertically using quadrants I and IV. In this case, positive data are plotted above the line, and negative data below the line (Fig. 3-5). The center line of the chart

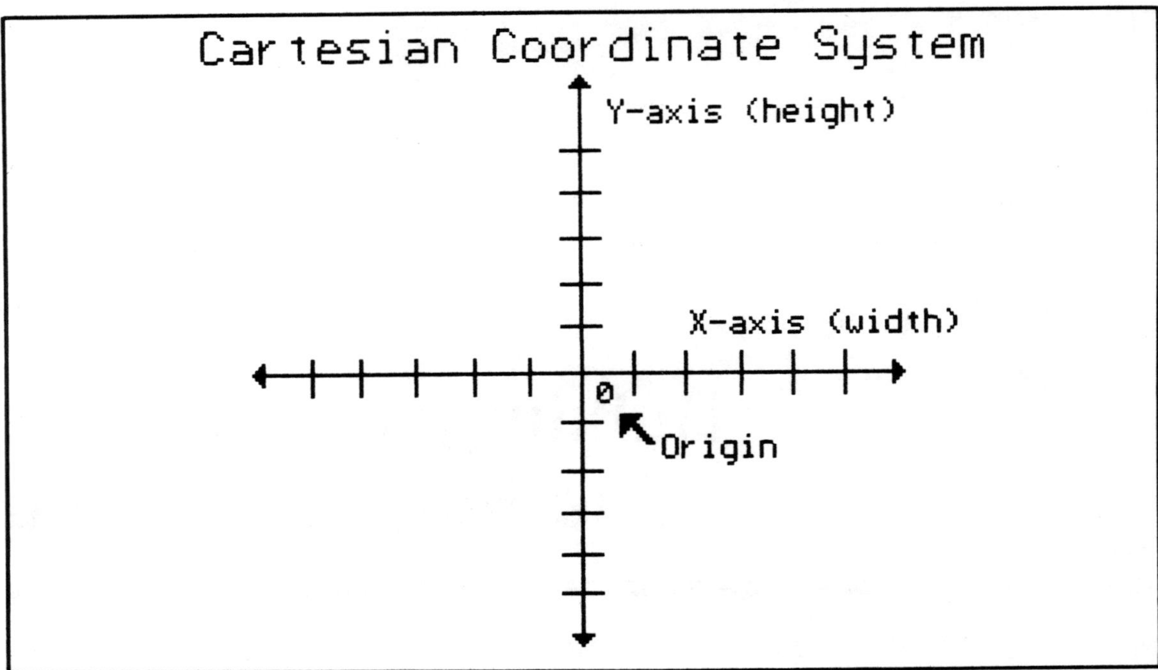

Fig. 3-1. The axis lines.

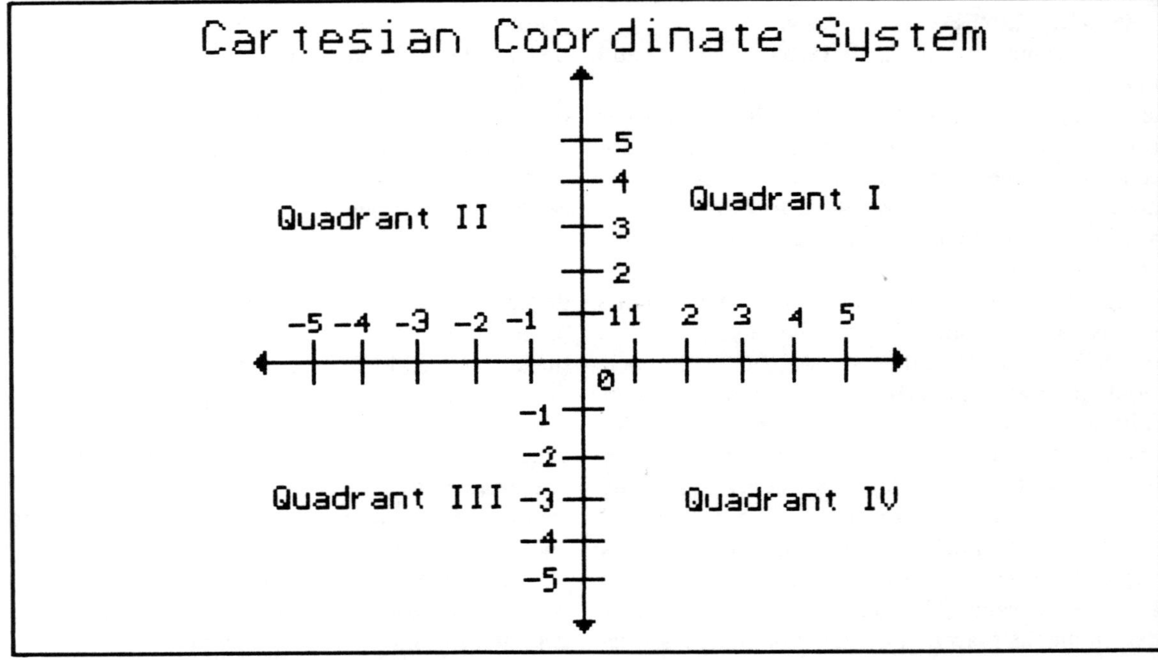

Fig. 3-2. The cartesian coordinate system.

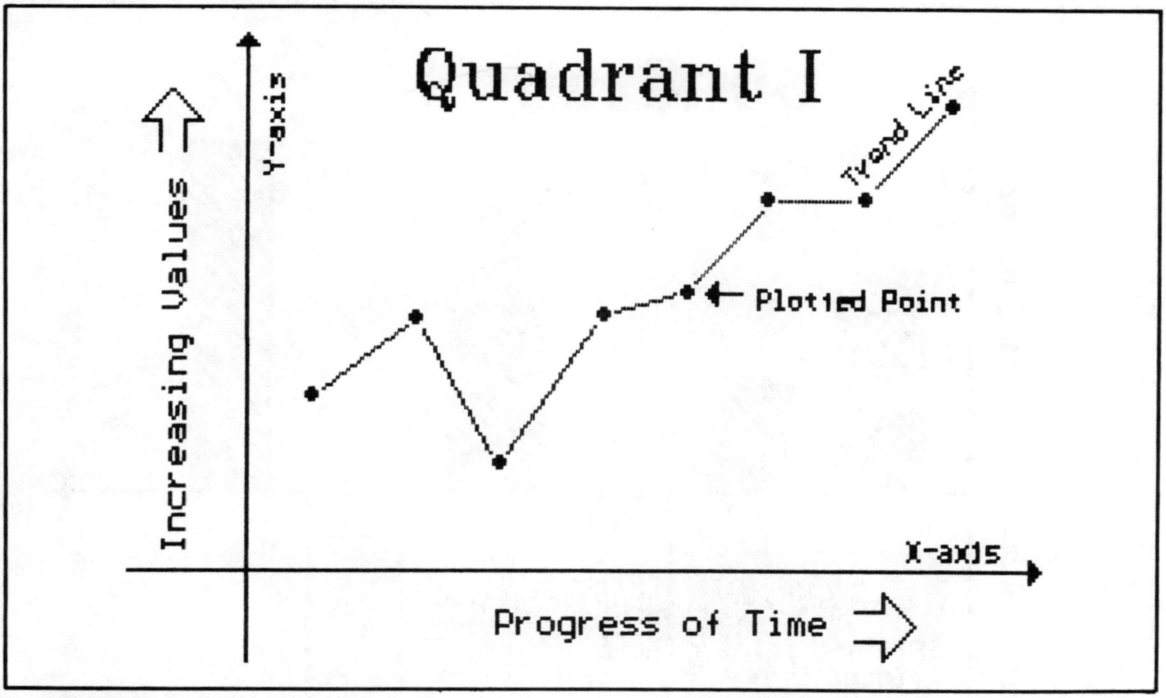

Quadrant I
Increasing Values
Y-axis
Trend Line
Plotted Point
X-axis
Progress of Time

Fig. 3-3. Quadrant I.

Quadrant II
Quadrant I
Plotted Point (positive)
Plotted point (negative)
Decreasing Values
Increasing Values

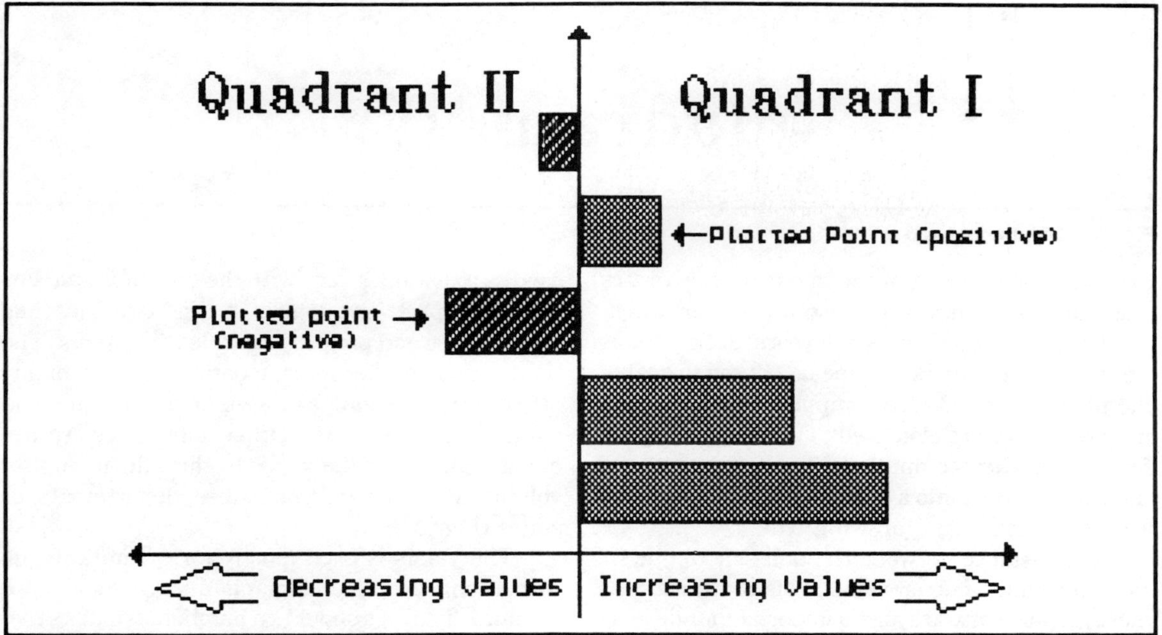

Fig. 3-4. Quadrants I and II.

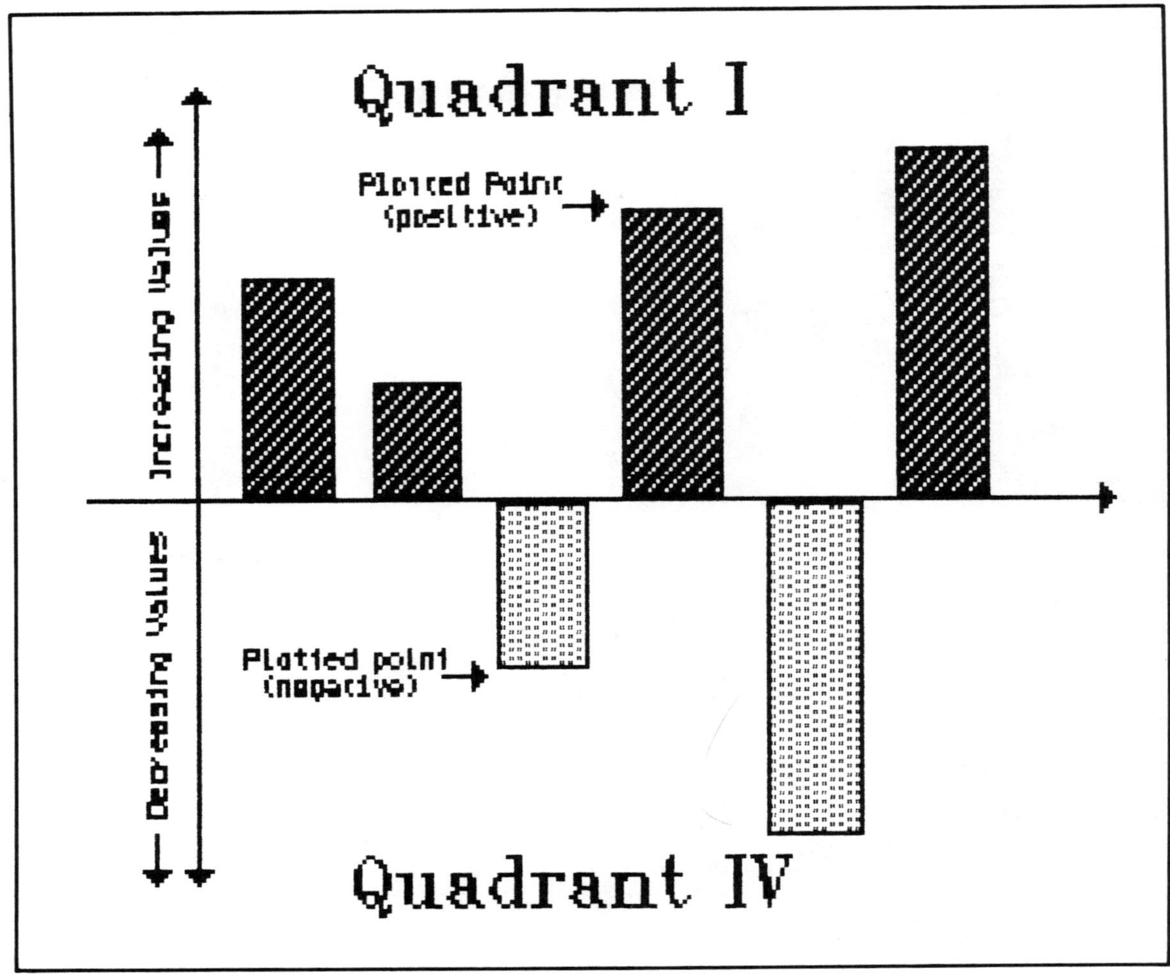

Fig. 3-5. Quadrants I and IV.

extends to the left from the center of the vertical axis, and the columns are also drawn vertically.

Units on the axis lines are years, dollars, index values, or other "marker" type units used to analyze the plotted data. Before computer graphics, these marker units were also used to plot the data in the first place. Microcomputer software packages will translate the data into a chart much faster and more accurately than hand drawing will.

The distance between the units should be the same for units of equal value. This is a function of most graphic software and is important for developing a reliable graph. The types of units that can be used as axis values vary with the type of graph. For the most part, the x-axis is graduated in time periods for trend projections, called *time series*. The time periods can be years, months, quarters, or any other period, as long as the periods are equal and equidistant on the axis. Other data series are frequently placed on the x-axis to show an amount or volume across several companies, departments, or states (Fig. 3-6).

The y-axis is used mostly for quantitative information, such as dollars, quantities of goods, or volumes. The axis should be numbered in units that are easily understood by the viewers. Numbering in multiples of five, ten, fifty, one hundred, and so on will be more recognizable than any other increments.

Another type of unit that can be used on the y-axis is the *index.* This type of unit shows the value of an item in relation to its value at a specified point on the x-axis. For example, the government's wholesale price index is based on the year 1967 = 100, which means that no matter what the value actually was in 1967, it is considered to be 100. The actual value of any other year is divided by the 1967 value and multiplied by 100. This creates a base year for comparing wholesale prices over a period of time where the actual monitary value of the items was changing due to other outside forces, such as inflation (Fig. 3-7).

Axis lines are the foundation for the chart. They should not be colored or patterned; they should be legible, but they should not detract from the plotted trend lines. Axis lines are shown best in a neutral color.

Lines may be extended from the axes to mark unit values. Small, perpendicular lines that mark the positions of values along the axes are called *tick marks,* or just *ticks.* Ticks help the viewer identify the plotted amount by marking the charted units directly on the axis (Fig. 3-8).

Data points to be plotted on the chart are expressed in the form of *coordinates.* The coordinates are in the form (x,y), where the value to be plotted on the horizontal axis is listed first, followed by the value to be plotted from the vertical axis. The point

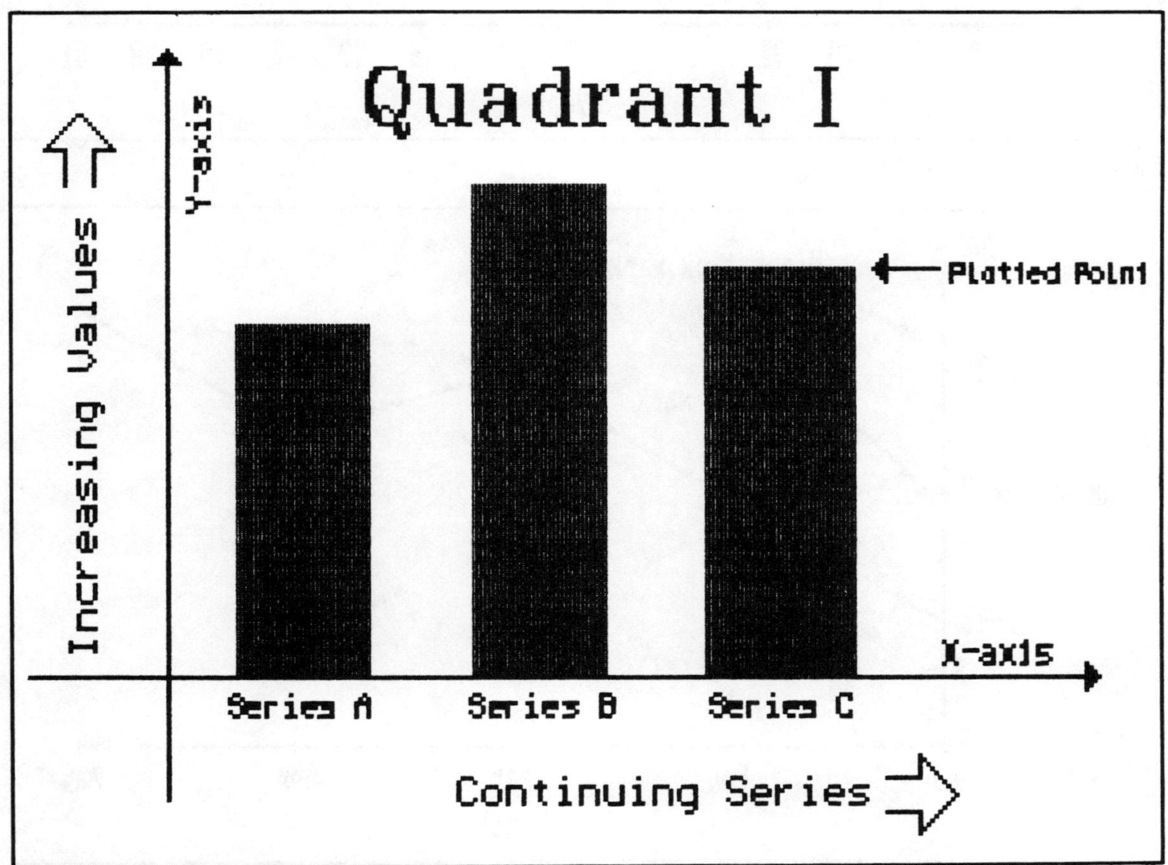

Fig. 3-6. Comparing x-axis series.

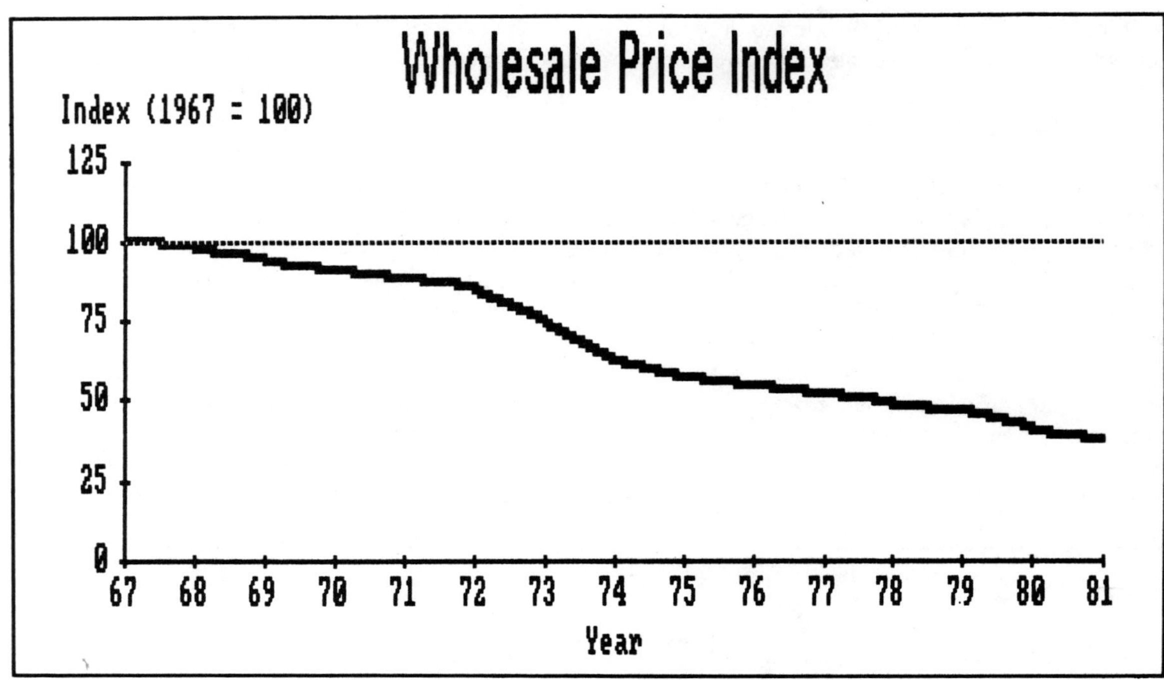

Fig. 3-7. An indexed line chart.

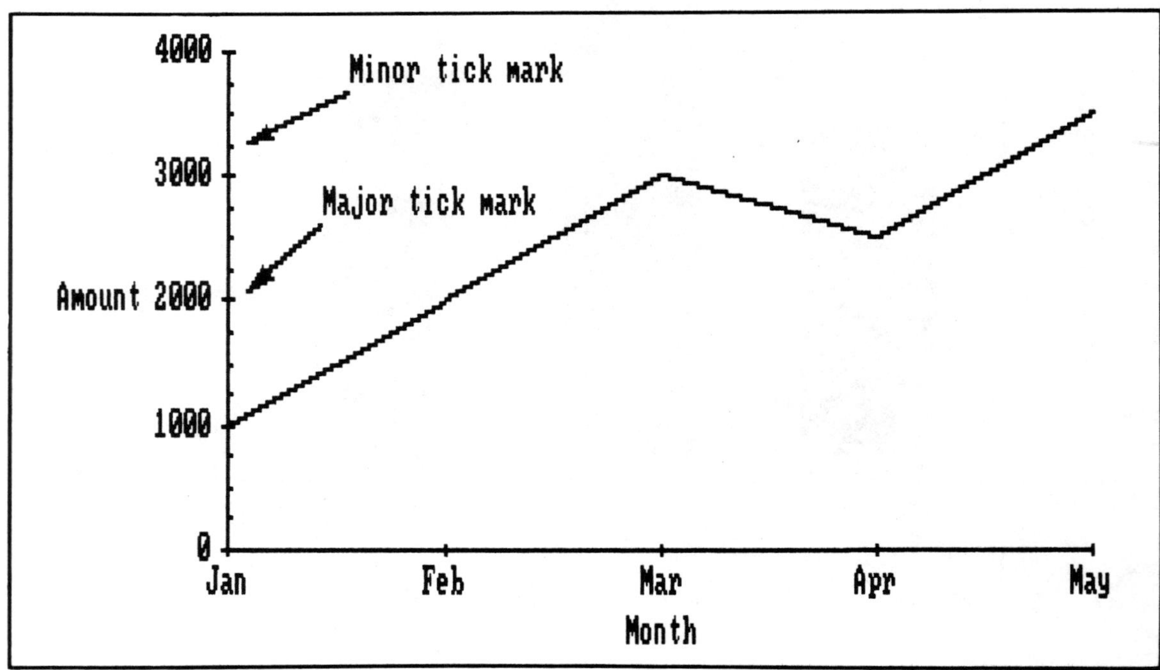

Fig. 3-8. Tick marks.

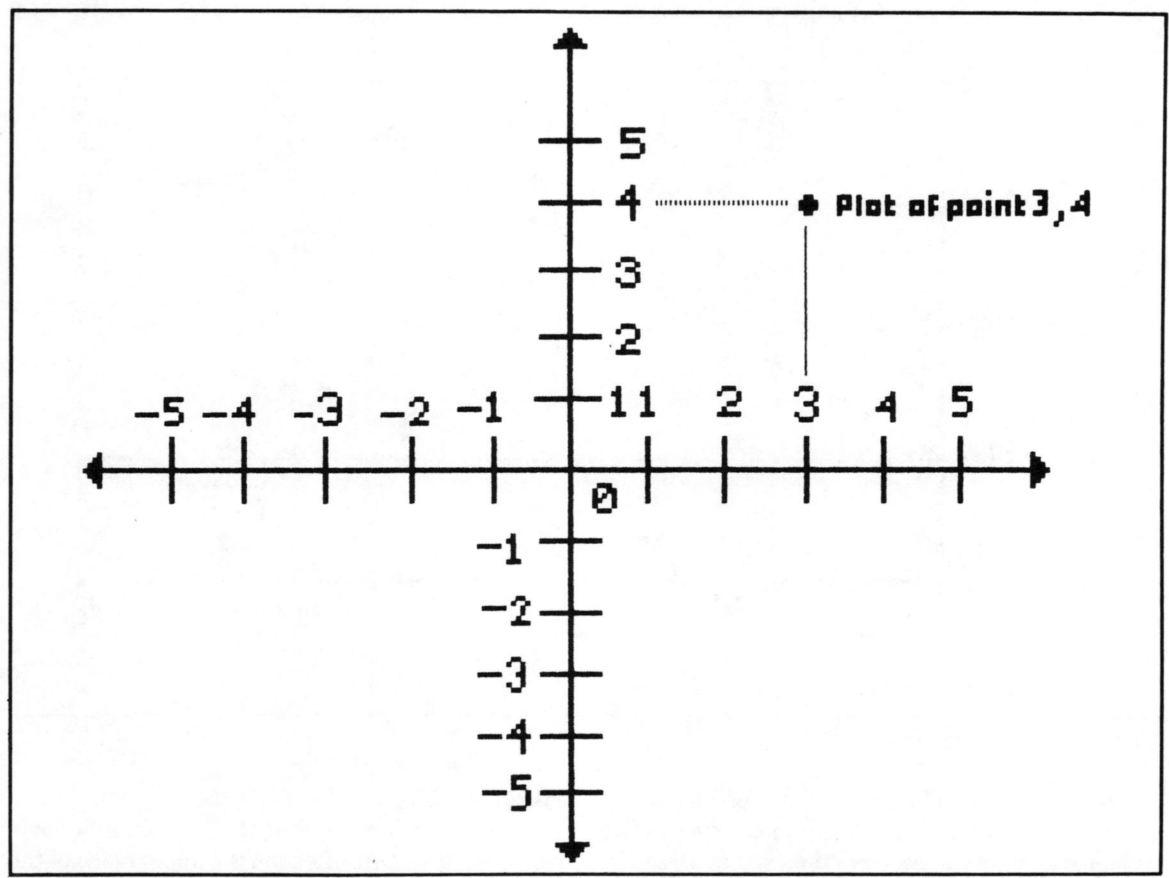

Fig. 3-9. The plotted coordinates.

where perpendicular lines drawn from the axes at the value points intersect is the plot point (Fig. 3-9).

Dependent variables are plotted on the y-axis. The values of the dependent variables are usually the focus of the graph and are generally amounts or volumes. The value of the dependent variable can be influenced by external factors, such as increasing staff or changing company policy.

Independent variables are usually plotted on the x-axis. These values are outside any control. Time periods, series groupings, and in the case of histograms, statistical groupings are independent values. The value of the dependent variable is reported for each unit of the independent variable. For example when income during a time period is charted, the time period is fixed, invarying, and uncontrollable, while the income can be changed by marketing new goods or providing new services.

The axis lines can be graduated in any multiple of the units used, but as mentioned before, the values five, ten, and their multiples are probably best, because they are familiar to everyone. Major graduations are labeled with the appropriate value, and other denominations can be marked by a grid line or just a small tick mark on the axis line.

GRIDS AND REFERENCE LINES

Extending the lines across the chart forms a grid that aids the viewer in determining the actual values of a plotted point. As illustrated in Fig. 3-10, this helps the viewer determine the values at most

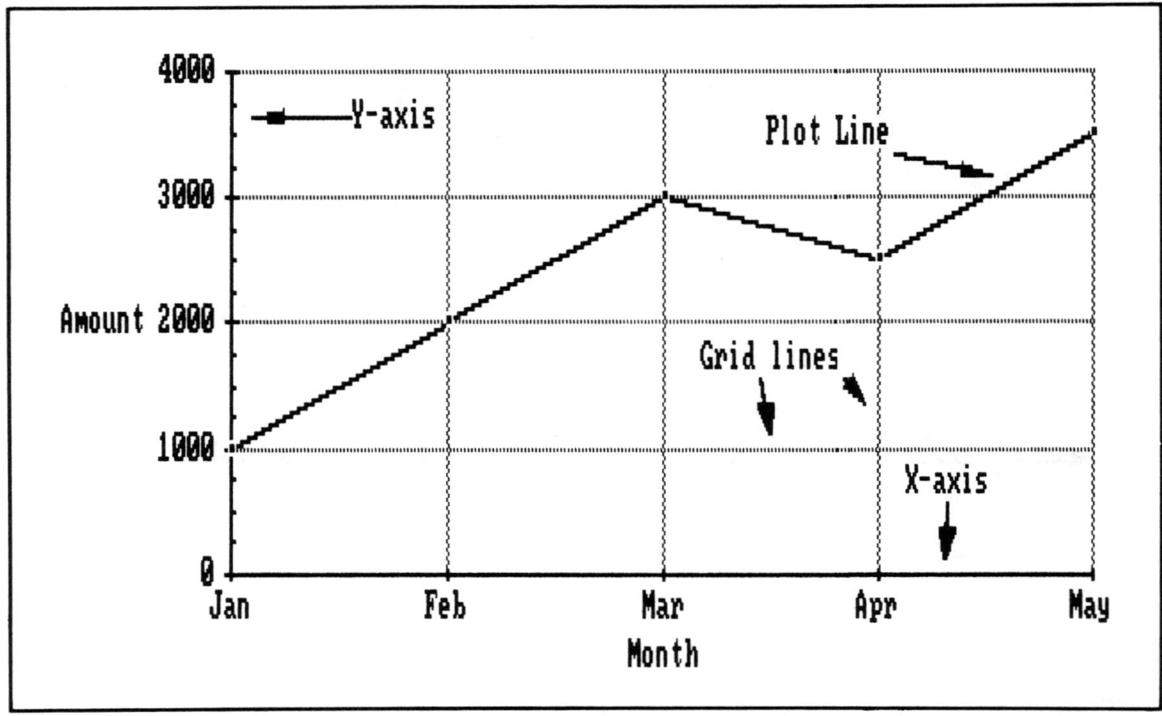

Fig. 3-10. A chart with grid lines.

points on the line. The presence of grid lines will give your graph more credibility in the eyes of the audience or readers, because they can analyze the graph more easily.

Grid lines should be just a bit lighter than the axis lines. They should not detract from your chart and should be much lighter than the plot lines. Too many grid lines will make the chart confusing and cluttered; too few grid lines can look silly. A good formula is to have grid lines for major divisions and tick-marks at minor or fractional divisions.

Reference lines are used to mark a particular unit value as important (Fig. 3-11). In index charts, a reference line would be drawn to indicate the base value 100. Other types of time-series charts might have reference lines at particular points to mark high and/or low points, or the median value.

A reference line should be the same weight as the axis lines. When used with grid lines, the reference lines should be slightly heavier than the grid, but still lighter than the plot line.

SCALING CONSIDERATIONS

Shrinking or expanding the scale of either axis can have a dramatic effect on the appearance of the plotted trend, as shown in Fig. 3-12. A gentle upward slope becomes a steep rise when the horizontal axis is shrunk without a corresponding shrinkage of the vertical axis. Conversely, shrinking the y-axis can make a steep rise look slower and shallower. The misdirection can be accidental; for example, it can be the result of trying to fit a graph or chart into a fixed-size space in a publication or report.

To avoid misdirection, the relative scales of the axes should be carefully calculated when you are drawing a graph. When you are using a computer software package, scaling is usually taken care of by the program. A good package, however, will allow you to do literally anything you want to customize the chart for your use. The ability to expand or contract either axis without affecting the other is a feature of some graphics software packages.

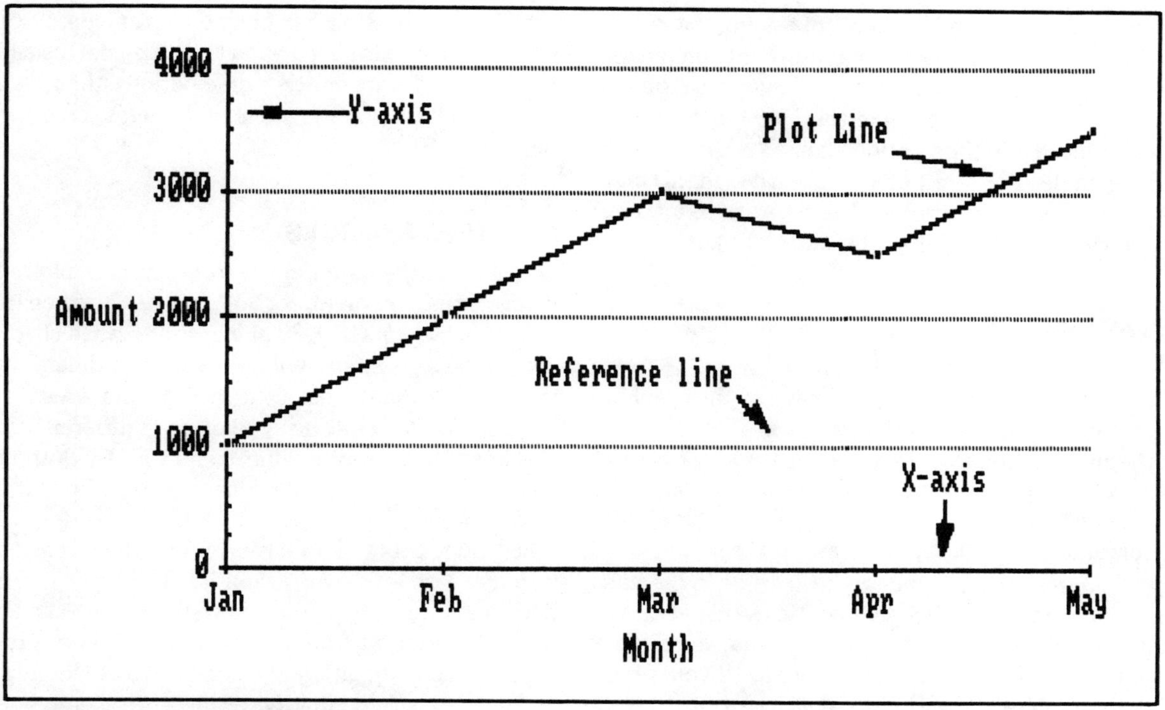

Fig. 3-11. A chart with reference lines.

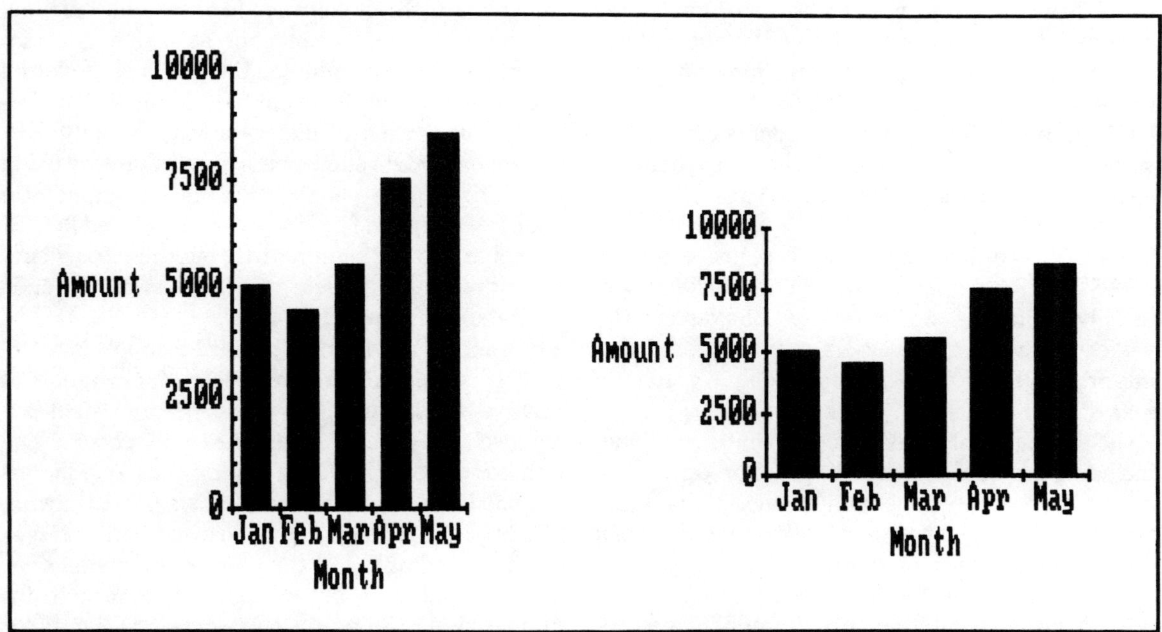

Fig. 3-12. The effect of different size axes.

The easiest and best way of scaling the axes to each other is to make one major division on the vertical axis the same length as one major division on the x-axis. This will make the plot for increasing one unit in one time period slant at a forty-five degree angle. The effect of a graph scaled in this manner will be more dramatic as the rate of increase grows and is faithful to the original data.

THE DATA

The information to be plotted must be made available in a form that can be used by the graphing program. This means that the data files that hold the information to be graphed either already exist in a computer file/database, or the totals to be graphed must be entered into the computer system somehow, so that the program can use it.

A great deal of time can be invested in the function of data entry. The only way to avoid data entry is to use a package that can use the data you already have. To reduce the data entry load, all you can do is to purchase a package that allows fast entry of only the information needed to set up the graph.

When you are graphing a series of totals over a period of time, either a series of data records can be input and totals computed by the program, or the individual period totals, calculated by some other method, can be directly entered. Your choice of software may depend on the ease of changing your data to the format required for the package.

Some graphics packages allow you to total data in certain types of database files, for example, dBASE III™ database files. The package will usually ask for the field or fields to be graphed, the values for the axes, the labels, and other pertinent information that will be used to produce a graph format of your choosing.

The content of the data can be almost anything, including the quantities of a product produced, the amount of revenues generated by sales of that product, the average person-hours it takes to produce one unit of the product, or the dollar amounts of expenses incurred in the production.

Trends are not the only form of statistical analysis that can be enhanced by charts. Histograms can be plotted using bar or line charts, simply by using the statistical population on the x-axis. Instead of a series of years or other time periods, the x-axis labels would be age groups, sex groups, or other population segments.

PLOTTING SYMBOLS

Most of the data depicted on charts is plotted using lines, or bars, or other standard chart reference markers (Fig. 3-13). These are called charting symbols. The symbol marks the coordinates of the data on the quadrant formed by the axes.

One use for plotting symbols is to differentiate the lines in a multiple-line trend chart. Plotting points are marked with a square for one line, and a triangle, a circle, an arrowhead, or a dot for another (Fig. 3-14). This type of line demarkation becomes less effective with more than three trend lines and can be confusing, even with only three lines. A better way of labeling the lines is to produce solid lines of different colors, and include a legend on the chart to identify the lines. Most software packages produce legends, but fewer packages will allow you a choice between legends and labeling.

Symbols can enhance presentation graphics when you use a symbol for the item being plotted rather than using the usual bars or lines. This format is often used in history and geography textbooks: bar charts show population figures by using little stick-figure people, and the oil output of a country is depicted by small barrels labeled "OIL." The chart can look impressive, but the plot will not be very accurate unless grid lines and good axis labels are supplied (Fig. 3-15).

Another use for nonstandard symbols is to depict the volume of an item by showing symbols of relative sizes. Charts of this type are called *pictographs.* They are also often used in text books. The number of hogs produced in a farming region during one time period is depicted by a small drawing of a hog, and a comparatively scaled (either larger or smaller) drawing of the hog represents another period. This can be an impressive format for dramatizing differences between two or three periods of production. One difficulty, though, is that

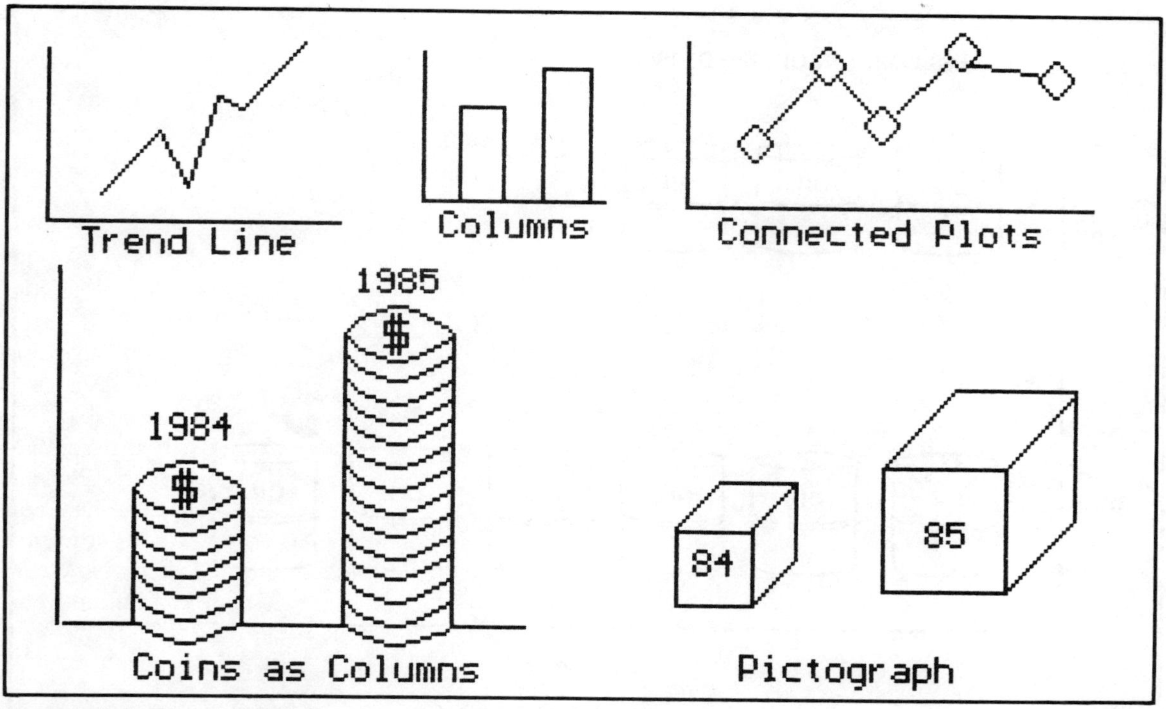

Fig. 3-13. Different types of plots.

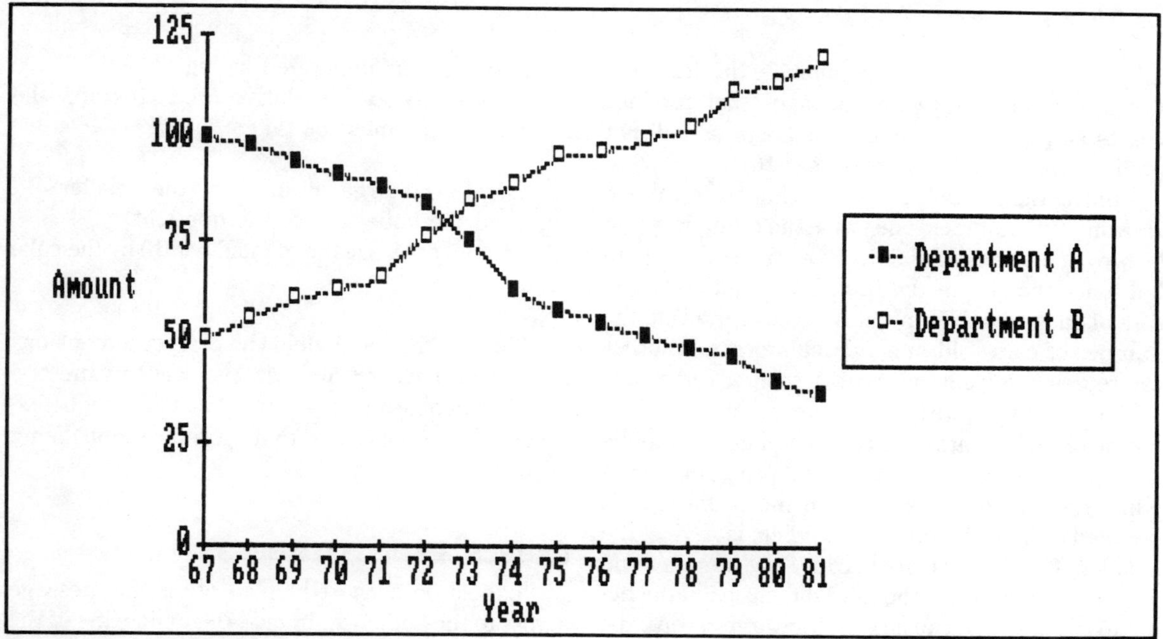

Fig. 3-14. Plotting a chart with symbols.

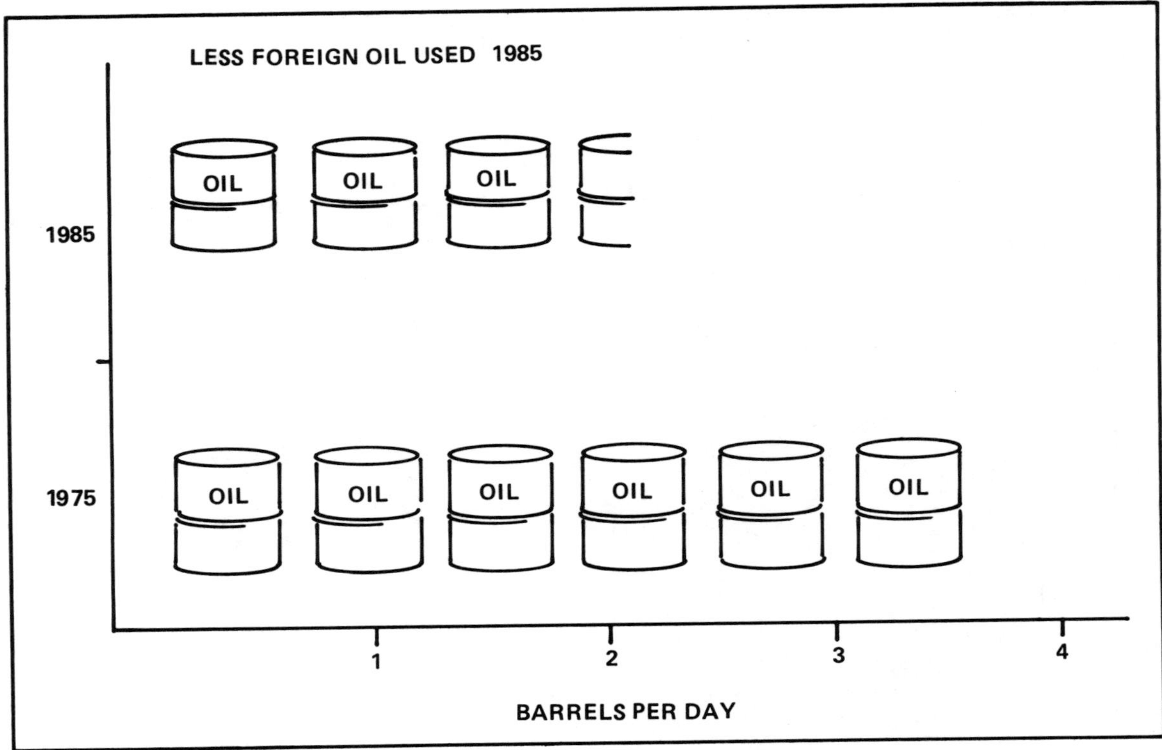

Fig. 3-15. A pictograph.

this type of chart is not popular in the business world and most software packages that produce charts and graphics suitable for business will not produce this kind of chart (Fig. 3-16).

Sizing the symbols properly is important. When showing two volumes, one twice the other, it would be wrong and misleading to show the second symbol twice the size of the first. For example, a picture of an automobile might be used to indicate the number of cars sold in a particular year. Another car, representing another year, is then placed beside it. The relative increase or decrease in the size of the pictures indicates the rise or fall of automobile sales between those years. The problem occurs when the size of the symbol in the pictograph is doubled when the larger number is twice the smaller. This is incorrect because the human mind will automatically add the third dimension of the figure to the drawing, causing the viewer to receive the impression that the volume has quadrupled rather than doubled, as illustrated in Fig. 3-17.

To properly scale a relative-size pictograph, the following steps must be taken:

1. Divide the larger number by the smaller.
2. Find the cube root of the quotient.
3. Multiply the size (height and width) by the cube root.

This method will yield the correct dimensions of the larger figure. You can also use this method on other people's pictographs that you may be exposed to—to be sure that you are not being misdirected.

LABELS, LABELS, LABELS

Labels on a chart help to bring the message across to the audience. In fact, the major title of the chart should be the single-sentence definition that

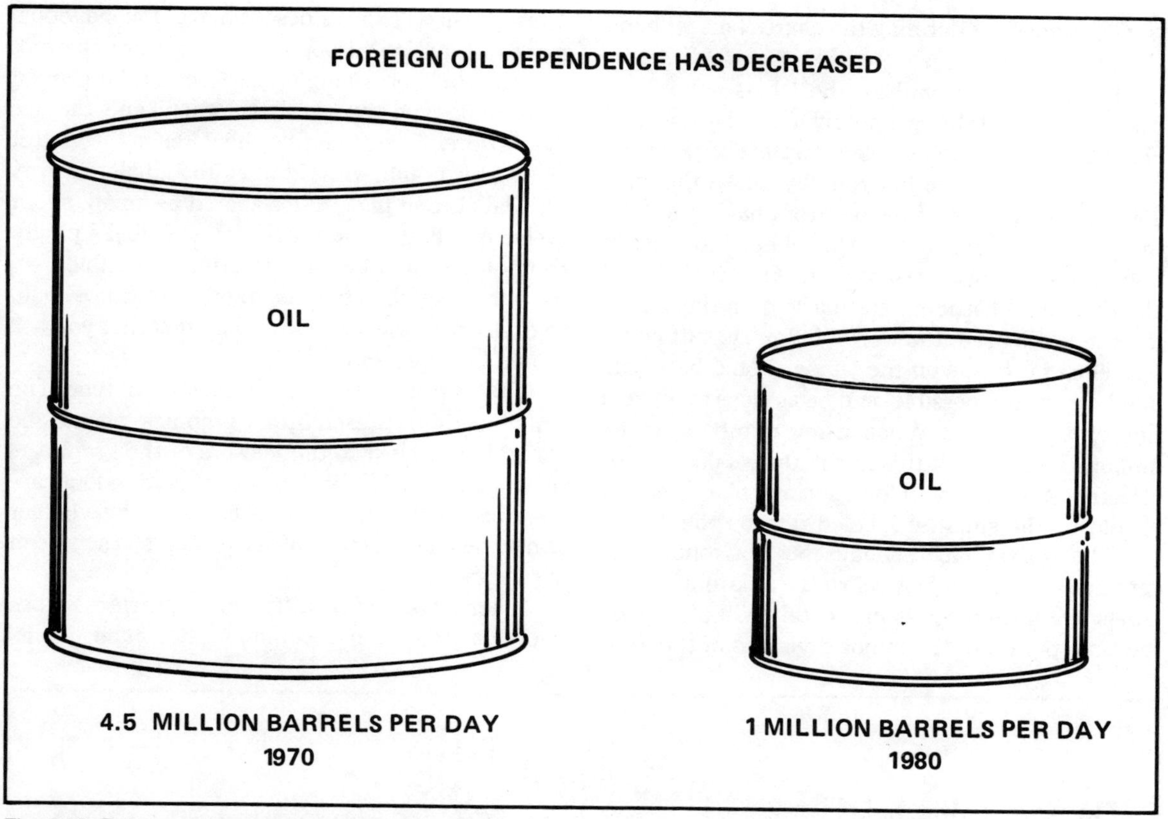

FOREIGN OIL DEPENDENCE HAS DECREASED
OIL
OIL
4.5 MILLION BARRELS PER DAY
1970
1 MILLION BARRELS PER DAY
1980

Fig. 3-16. Relative volume shown by a pictograph.

THIS IS 4 TIMES LARGER
NOT 2 TIMES !
PROPER SIZE
2 INCH
2 INCH
4 INCH
4 INCH
2.5 INCH
2.5 INCH

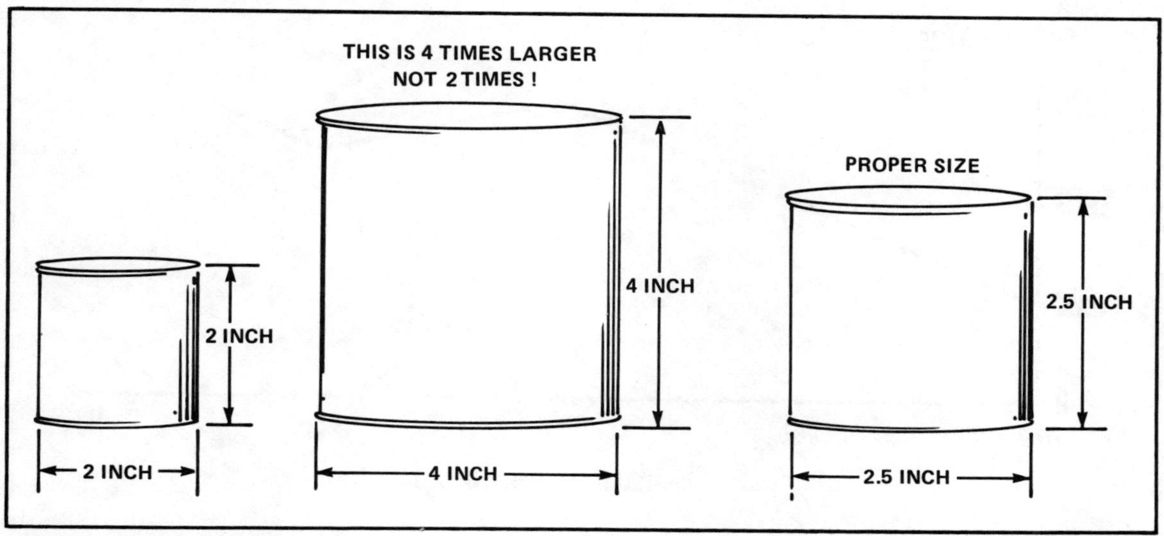

Fig. 3-17. Sizing pictographs.

you developed for defining the chart. This will emphesize your message.

Figure 3-18 shows how the labels should appear. Figure 3-19 shows a poorly labeled graph, and Fig. 3-20 shows a well labeled graph. The y-axis label should be written horizontally above the axis. This will save a lot of people from having to turn the paper sideways to read the label or to twist in their seats during a presentation. The label should clearly state what units are marked on the y-axis. If an index is used, the word "index" is sufficient.

The unit labels on the y-axis should be whole numbers (where possible) and be as close to the real figures as possible. When using numbers in the millions and billions, this is not always possible or effective. Numbers with one decimal place (tenths) should be the smallest labeled unit on the y-axis.

The x-axis label should be horizontal and centered on the line just below the axis and its unit labels. On a time series chart, this will always be the time period of the major divisions of the axis. A histogram will have a description of the individual groups or statistical populations that are charted.

All labels on a single chart should be printed in the same type style as all the others; only the size should differ. The main title should be in the largest type on the graph, with subtitles about half that size. Axis labels and unit values should be small, about twelve or fifteen letters per inch (12- or 15-pitch). Footnotes should be smaller still, if possible.

Whatever the style used, the lettering should be easily readable and clear. The *font* that you use should be selected carefully.

Font is printer's jargon for the style of type. The fonts used in presentation graphics should be readable and clear to the viewers of the graph. As shown in Fig. 3-21, differences in printing fonts are described by the shape of the characters, by whether or not the characters have serifs, and by the size of the characters.

There are many different character shapes available. The most common are plain, italic,

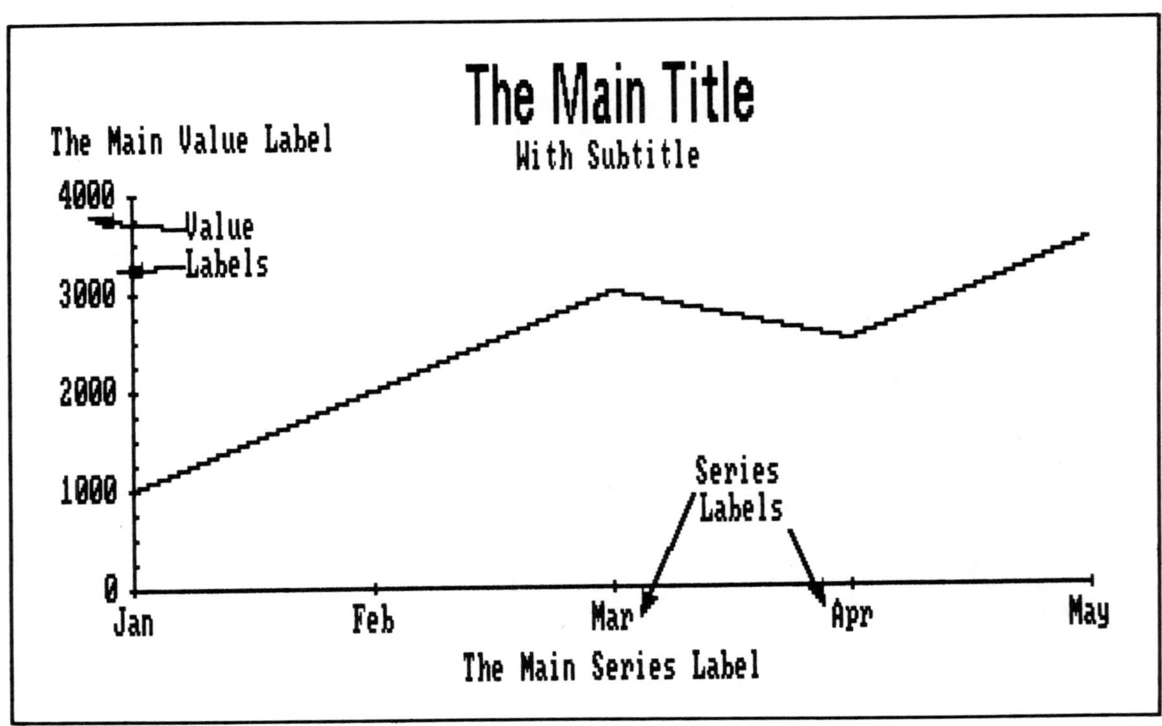

Fig. 3-18. Chart labels.

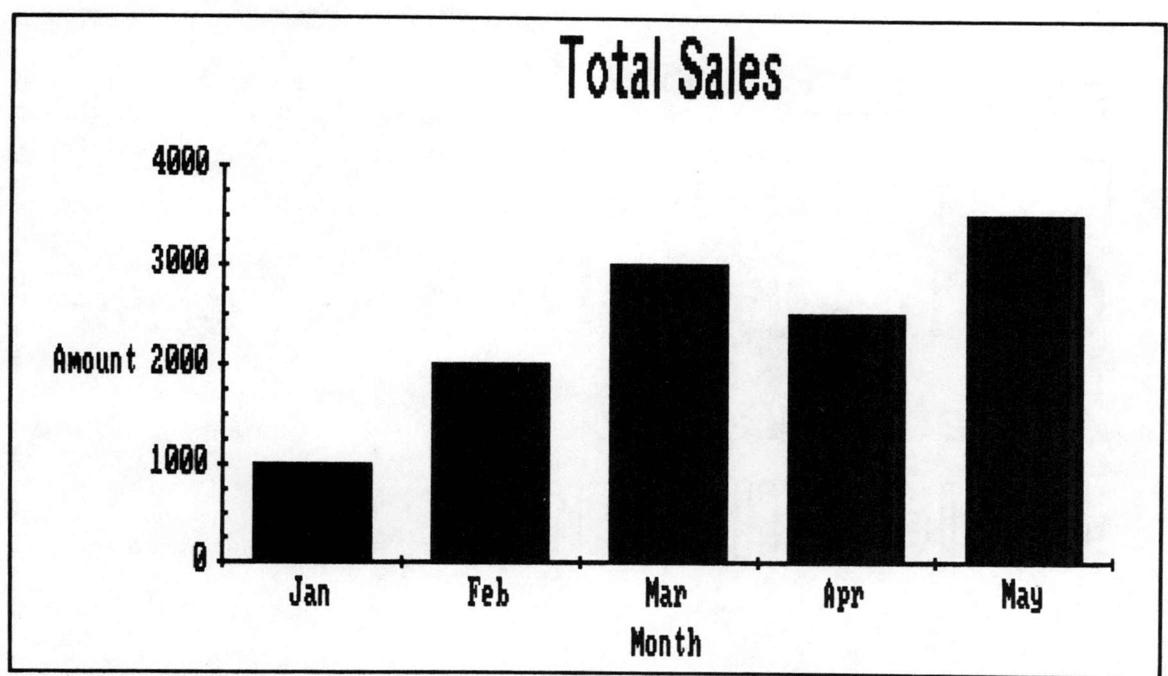

Fig. 3-19. A poorly labeled chart.

Fig. 3-20. A well-labeled chart.

Roman serif

Roman sans-serif

Olde English aka Gothic

Simplex Script

Hollow Helvita

Pica

Elite

Fig. 3-21. The printing fonts.

boldface, hollow, and shadowed. Italic fonts seem to lean to the right; boldface means that the letters are heavier (or thicker) than they normally are; hollow type styles have letters that are just outlines; shadowed characters seem to be three-dimensional because they have a shadow on one side of the letter. These character shapes have advantages and disadvantages. The advantage of using italics is that italicized words seem to be accented, as if a speaker had emphasized that *particular* word as the focus of his sentence. Italics, however, are sometimes fuzzy when produced on some computer printers. Italics and hollow letters do not reproduce well on copying machines, due to the relative lightness of the letters. Italics that are printed in boldface are much easier to read.

Serifs are little projections that are present at the ends of most letters in a character set. The term *sans-serif* means without serifs. Sans-serif fonts look more modern than the serif styles, because the serif styles were popular on manual typewriters.

The size of the type is referred to as its *pitch* (Fig. 3-22). 15-pitch means that 15 characters will fit in one inch of space. The most common ranges of types are 10-pitch (pica 10), 12-pitch (pica 12), and 15-pitch (elite). Most graphics software packages allow much larger type in titles and subtitles.

Old English and Script styles are available in most software packages. Old English printing can give an atmosphere of tradition and age to a chart, if it is easily readable and if it can be reproduced easily. Each style of Old English is different; less "flowery" styles are more easily read and reproduced than the more complicated styles. Script is the standard Script print font, the kind used on pharmacists' labels before the dot-matrix printer came along.

There are two types of script fonts, simplex and complex. *Simplex script* resembles the normal writ-

This is normal 12-pitch pica type.

This is 12-pitch Elite type.

This is 4.5-pitch.

This sentence is in 17-pitch type.

This sentence is in 10-pitch Elite type.

Fig. 3-22. The printing sizes.

ten script that everyone is familiar with. The letters in *complex script* do not necessarily connect, and the letters may be shaped differently than normal written script.

Fancy printing fonts are difficult to reproduce. The dot-matrix printers commonly used with microcomputers reproduce diagonal and curved lines awkwardly, unless the line is over-struck several times. As newer and better printers are introduced to the market, this sort of problem is slowly disappearing.

The best style of type to use on graphs, unless a specific artistic effect is to be produced, is plain, dark, sans-serif print. The effect is business-like and

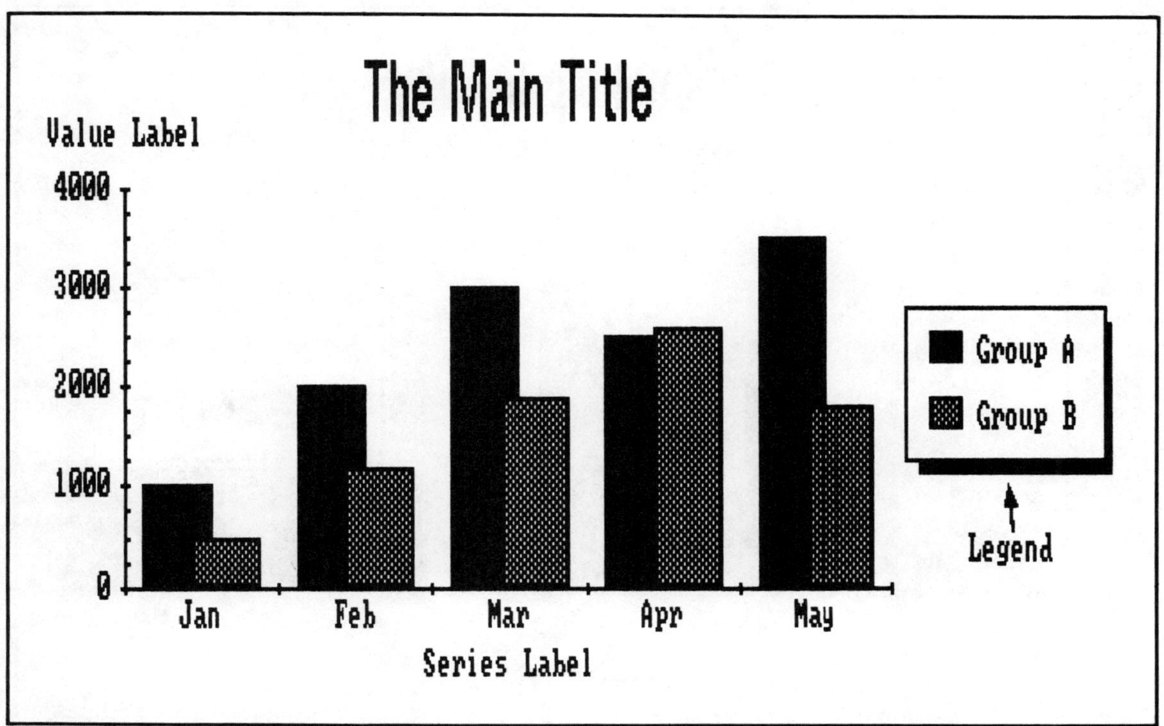

Fig. 3-23. The legend.

truthful, and the print is easily read by everyone. The intelligent use of type styles will aid in conveying your message as clearly as possible.

LEGENDS

A legend is a description of the symbols used on a chart or map. Legends are included on charts to aid viewers in understanding the chart (Fig. 3-23). A good legend will identify all of the plots on a chart by their color or pattern. For example, it should identify the color or shading of different slices of a pie chart or the different line patterns on a multiple-line chart.

Legends should be placed outside of the chart area when possible. (Fig. 3-24). The most obvious part of the page should be the chart itself (of course!), but the legend should be easily identifiable and readable. A legend can be placed within the chart area if it does not distract the viewer from the main emphasis of the chart. Some line charts and surface charts, for example, have large areas above the plot lines that are just dead space. A legend placed in one of these locations can add an air of credibility to the chart, even if the reason for placing it there is lack of space.

TITLES AND FOOTNOTES

As you remember, the main title of the graph should be a simple sentence that describes the purpose of the graph. The problem-definition sentence that you used to design your graph will usually be the best main title. Figure 3-25 shows a poor title, and Fig. 3-26 shows a good title. The message you are trying to convey will be emphasized by repetition; the main title should be the second thing the audience looks at on your graph—the first thing the viewer sees should be the area where your point is dramatized.

Subtitles can be used to specify the time period covered in the chart or the statistical population

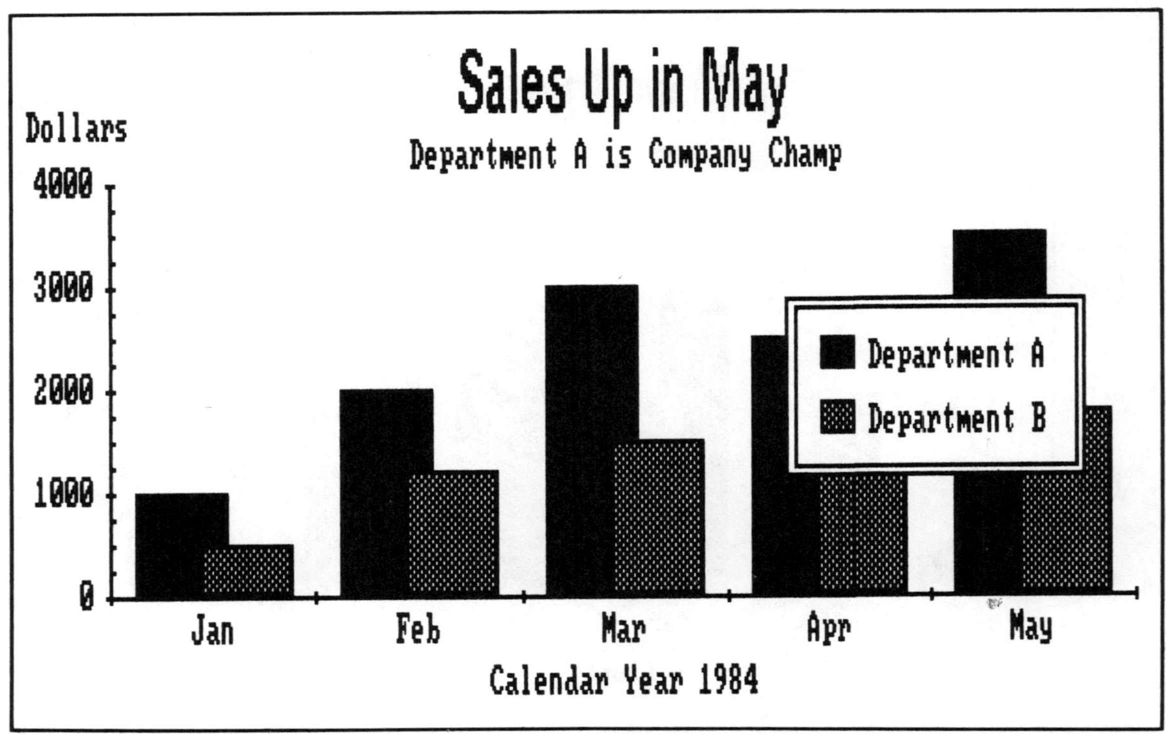

Fig. 3-24. A distracting legend in the chart area.

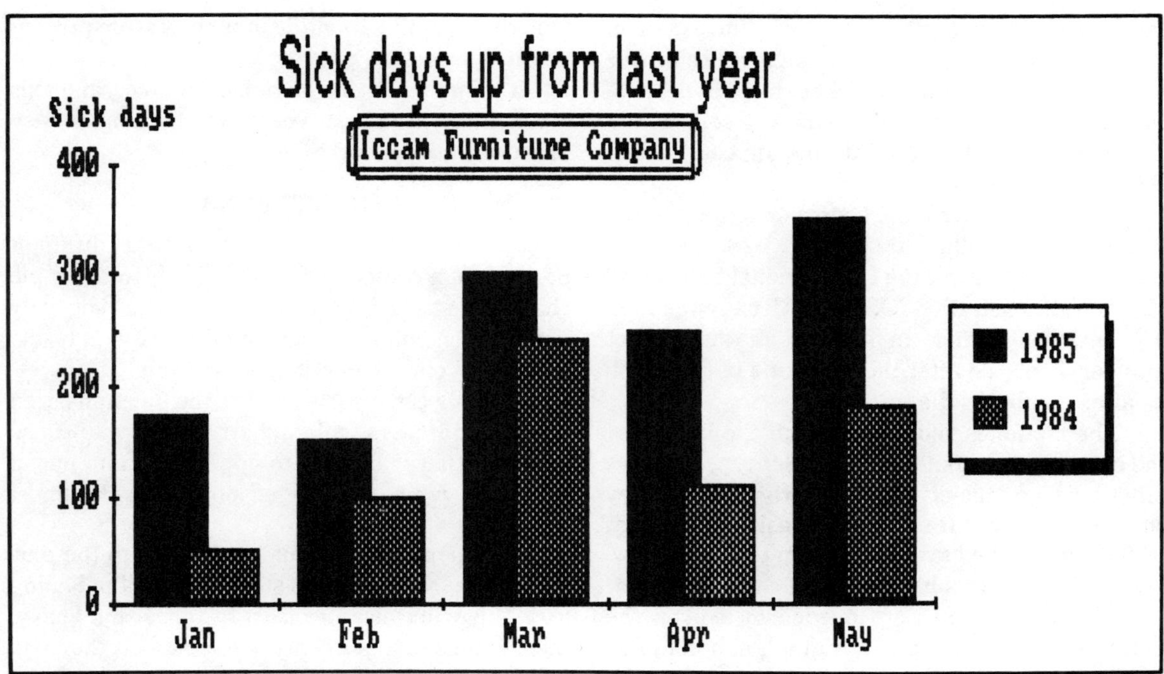

Fig. 3-25. A title with an ambiguous message.

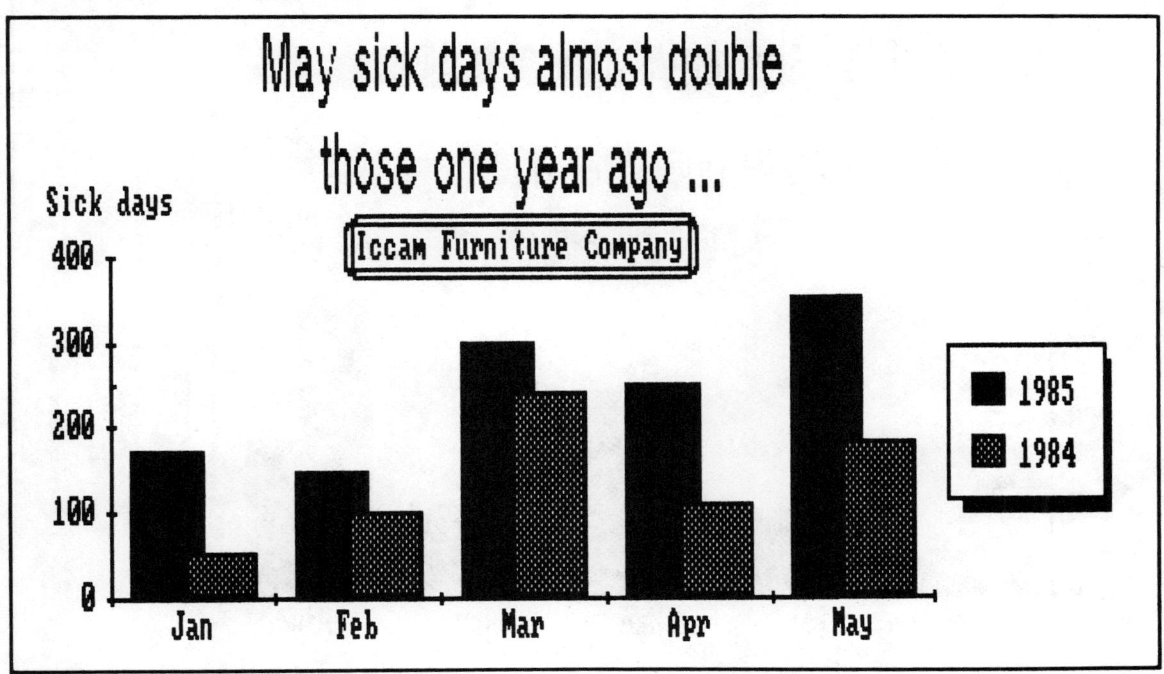

Fig. 3-26. A good title.

represented, as shown in Fig. 3-27. For example, if your chart only includes data on females or certain age groupings, this should be stated in the subtitle. Also, the area that the data was collected in might be included, if that information could affect the interpretation of the data.

Footnotes indicate the source or sources of the data graphed, as illustrated in Fig. 3-28. An example could be "Source: the Occupational Safety and Health Administration (OSHA)." Usually the footnote marker (either an asterisk or superscript number) is placed after the main title of the graph or after a subtitle if appropriate.

The footnotes should appear at the bottom of the chart. They should be in smaller type than the other labels on the chart, but clearly legible. They should not detract from the emphasis of the chart, so they should be as far away from the main viewing area of the graph as possible.

If many footnotes are needed to explain the graph, it is time to make the graph simpler. The graph should not need extensive explanations, although you will explain it in your text or presentation.

It is important that all titles, footnotes, and axis labels be in the same type style, one that is easy to read.

FILLING IN WITH PATTERNS

Shading patterns are used to contrast different portions of a component chart, that is to say, a pie chart or a stacked-bar chart. Shading is especially useful when you are producing the graph in black-on-white from a computer printer (Fig. 3-29).

Shading can also be used as the unemphasized background on a color chart. This will cause anything that is colored to appear to jump out of the chart, while the shaded portions will almost disappear.

Darker patterns should be closest to the axis line, while lighter shades should be on top. Failing to do this will cause the chart to appear top-heavy; the columns in a bar chart will look as if they will fall over. To avoid this illusion, patterns should be

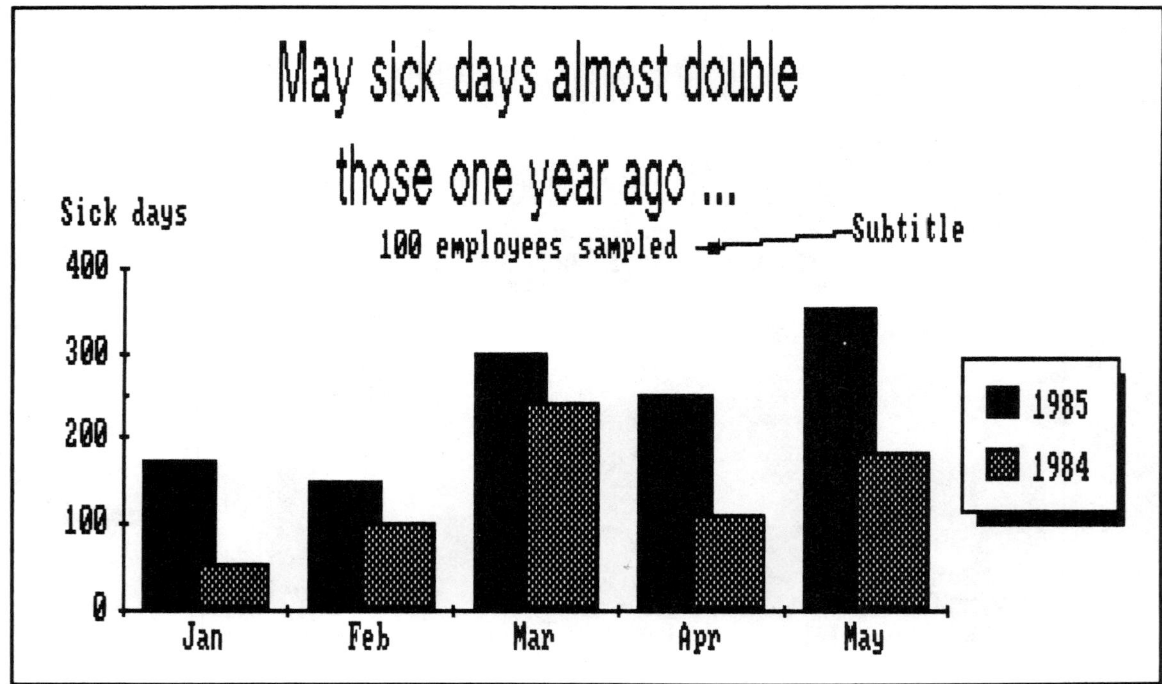

Fig. 3-27. The subtitle.

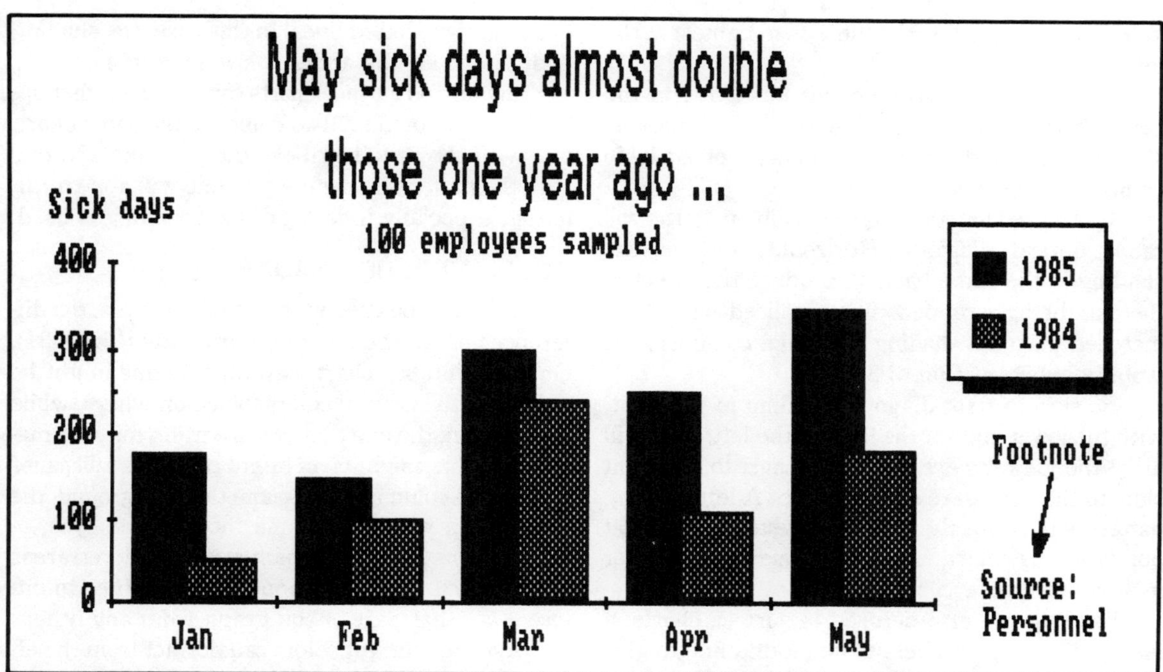

Fig. 3-28. The footnotes.

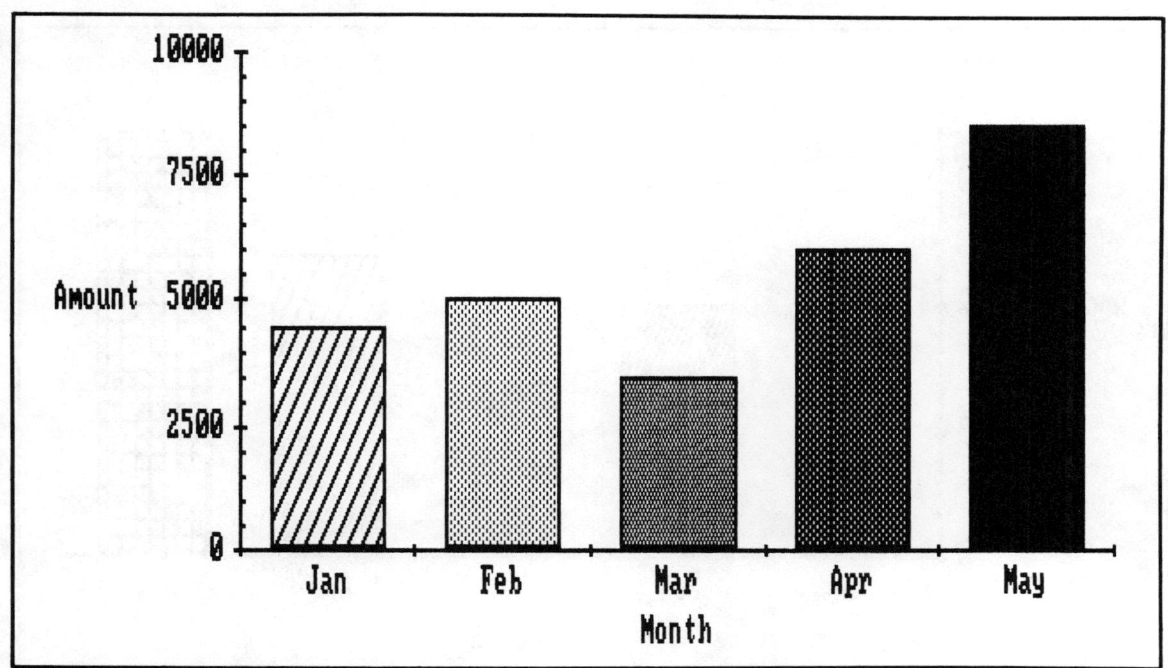

Fig. 3-29. Shading the chart.

graduated from darkest at the axis to lightest at the top.

Never leave any component unshaded in the neutral background color. This will give the impression that data on that particular item is not available or not accounted for.

When used together, some shading patterns will cause optical illusions. Horizontal and vertical shading in the same bar will produce the effect of the bar being wrapped, like a spliced wire. Mismatched diagonal shading can make columns look wobbly and bent (Fig. 3-30).

Be sure to slant diagonal shading to the right, with the lower ends of the lines to the left. This will draw the viewer's eye along the chart to the right side, in the normal reading fashion. A left-slanting pattern will cause the viewer's eye to stick at that point on the chart, and can cause confusion or misreading of the chart.

Shading can also be used in surface charts; a line graph is shaded below the plotted line to give the appearance of a rolling hill or wave. This type of shading can be used to point out the difference between two plotted lines. In this case, the shading is different for the areas below each line.

Shading on surface charts can cause another optical illusion to occur. Two copies of the same chart, one with the shading above the plot line and one with the pattern below the plot line will appear different, especially if dark or black shading is used.

COLOR VERSUS SHADING

Color can be used with shading to make the differences on your chart more dramatic (Fig. 3-31). On a column/bar chart, several columns might be shaded in the neutral colors (black-on-white), while one column, the one that you are using for your major emphasis, might be in bright red. This will cause the shaded columns to fade into the background; the red column will really catch the viewers' eyes.

Patterns are not normally used in colored areas of the chart. The color alone should suffice to differentiate that part of the graph from any other.

Too many bright colors can detract from the effectiveness of the chart. When the point to be emphasized is embodied in one or two of several plotted

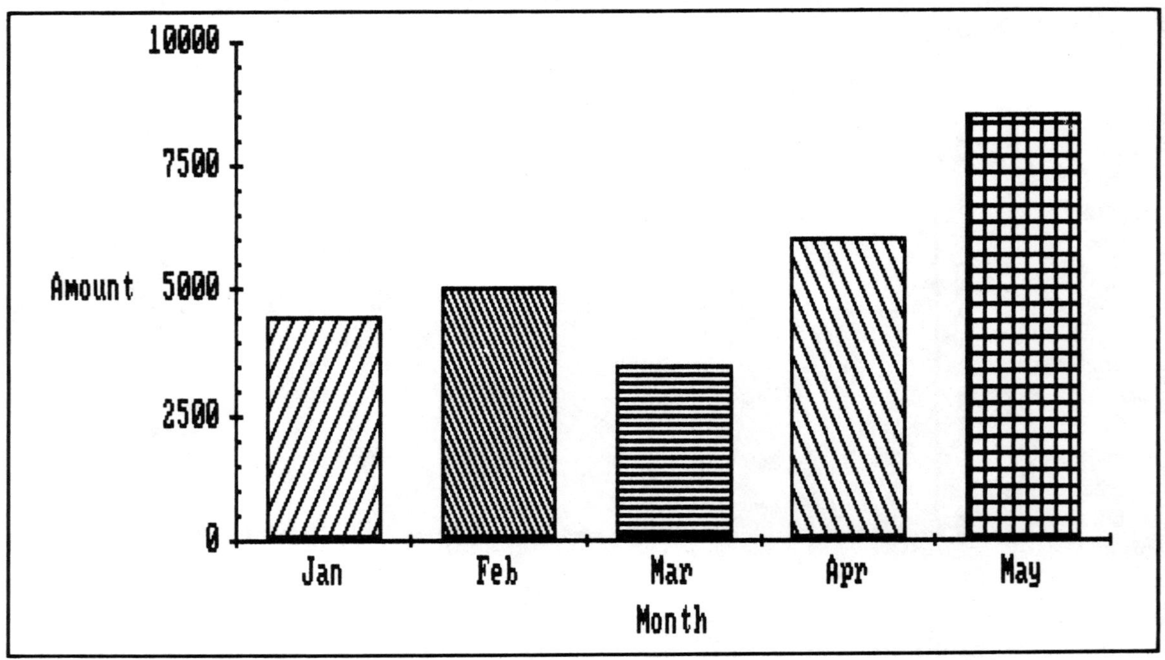

Fig. 3-30. Mismatched shading.

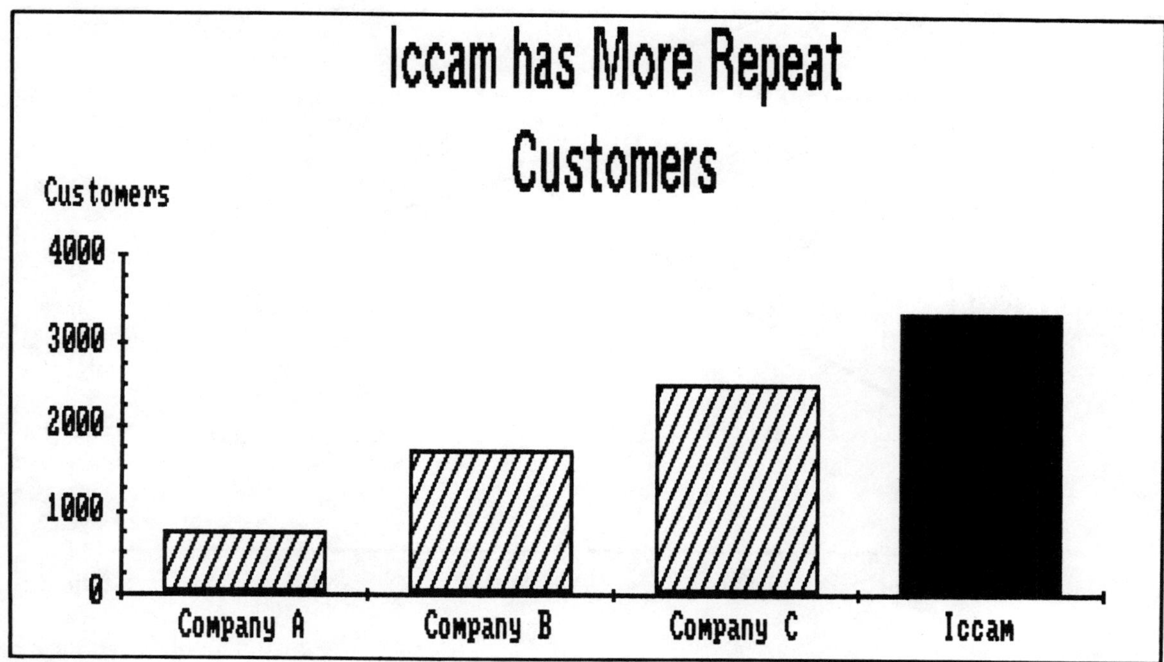

Fig. 3-31. Shading for emphasis.

areas, these areas should be colored, while the rest of the graph is shaded with lighter patterns.

Colors will look different on paper than they do on a computer monitor screen. This is because the neutral colors of the screen are the opposite of the neutral colors used on the printer or plotter. Another reason for this is that the ink might not be exactly the same hue as the one shown by the monitor. It may be necessary for you to experiment with your software and hardware to find the right combinations for your application.

Reproducing color graphics for reports is becoming easier as the copier industry becomes more technologically advanced. Some color copiers have problems with colors that have to be mixed (yellow plus blue is green, for example). Others cannot properly copy bright colors that are joined, and the border between the colors bleeds both ways. This can be very frustrating when it takes four hours to produce the graph on a plotter. You must either produce many originals, or have enough time to fiddle with the copier to get the contrast (not necessarily the colors) that you need.

CONNECTING THE DOTS AND BUILDING THE COLUMNS

The line used to connect the plotted points on a curve chart is called the *plot line.* The plot line should be thicker ("heavier" in the printer's jargon) than the axis and grid lines of the chart (Fig. 3-32). If a color chart is used, the line should be in a darker color, like blue or green. Red has a different meaning when used on a line graph instead of on a bar or pie chart. A red plot line would spell trouble to managers and corporate executives.

In a column/bar chart, the top of the column indicates the plotted data. The border of the column should be in the background color. The border does not have to be heavier than the grid lines; a heavier border will, however, make a particular column seem to jump out of the page.

Columns should be separated if there are a small number of time periods covered. The space between them should be one-half the width of the bar. This will allow the eye to see the columns as different from each other.

Step charts are column charts in which the col-

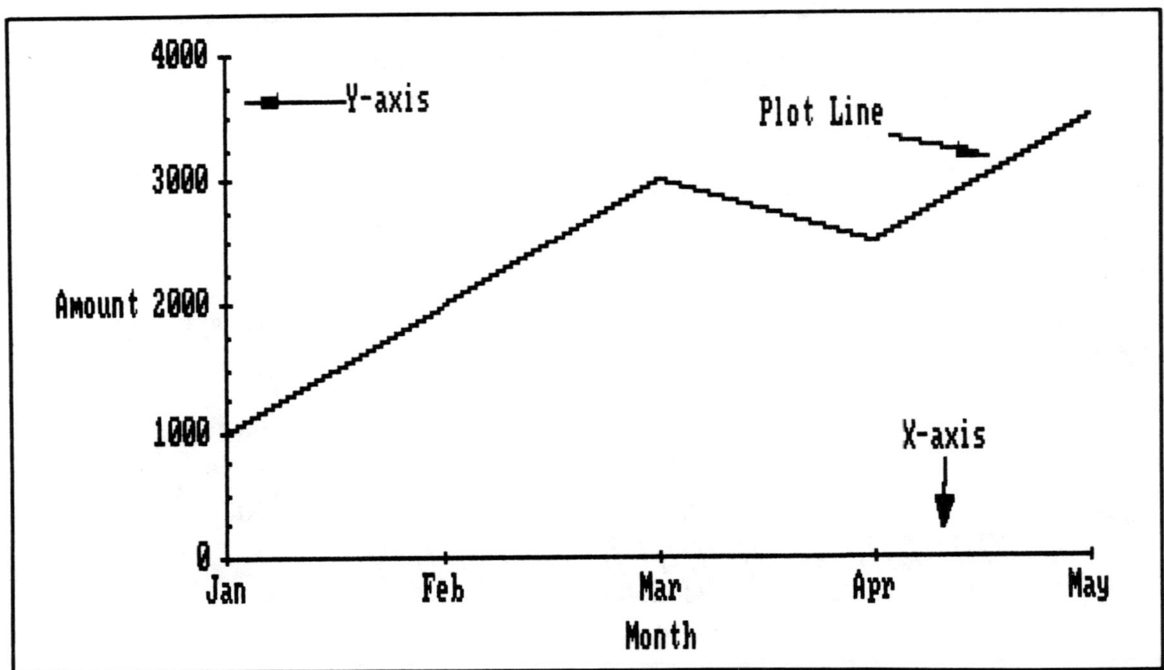

Fig. 3-32. The plot line.

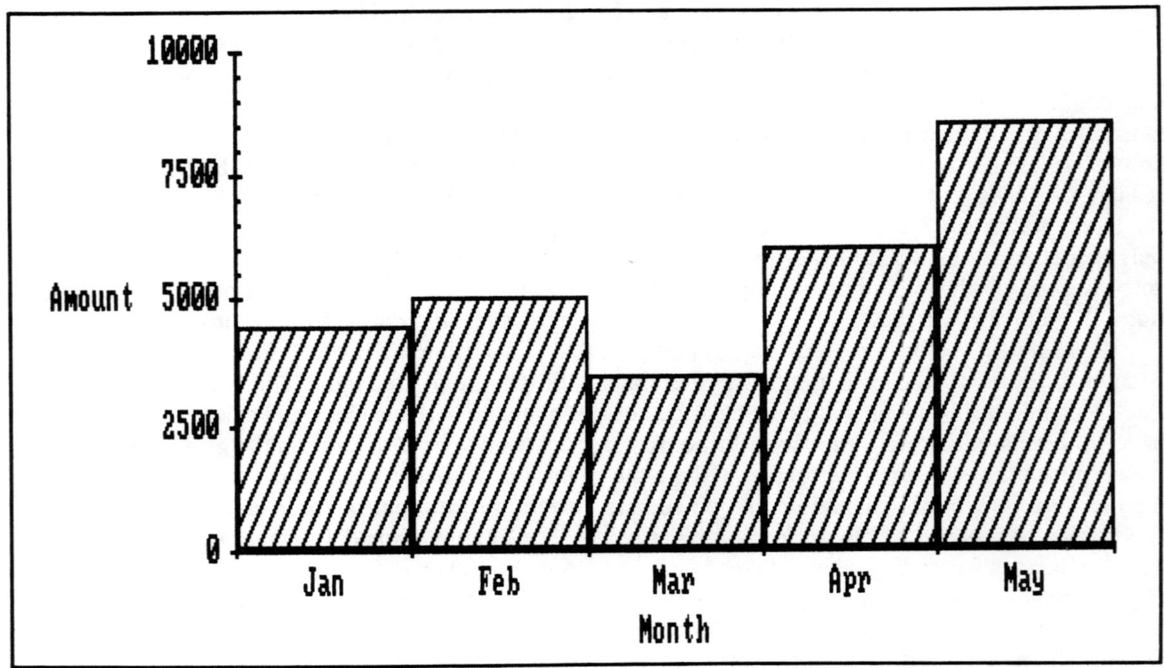

Fig. 3-33. A shaded step chart.

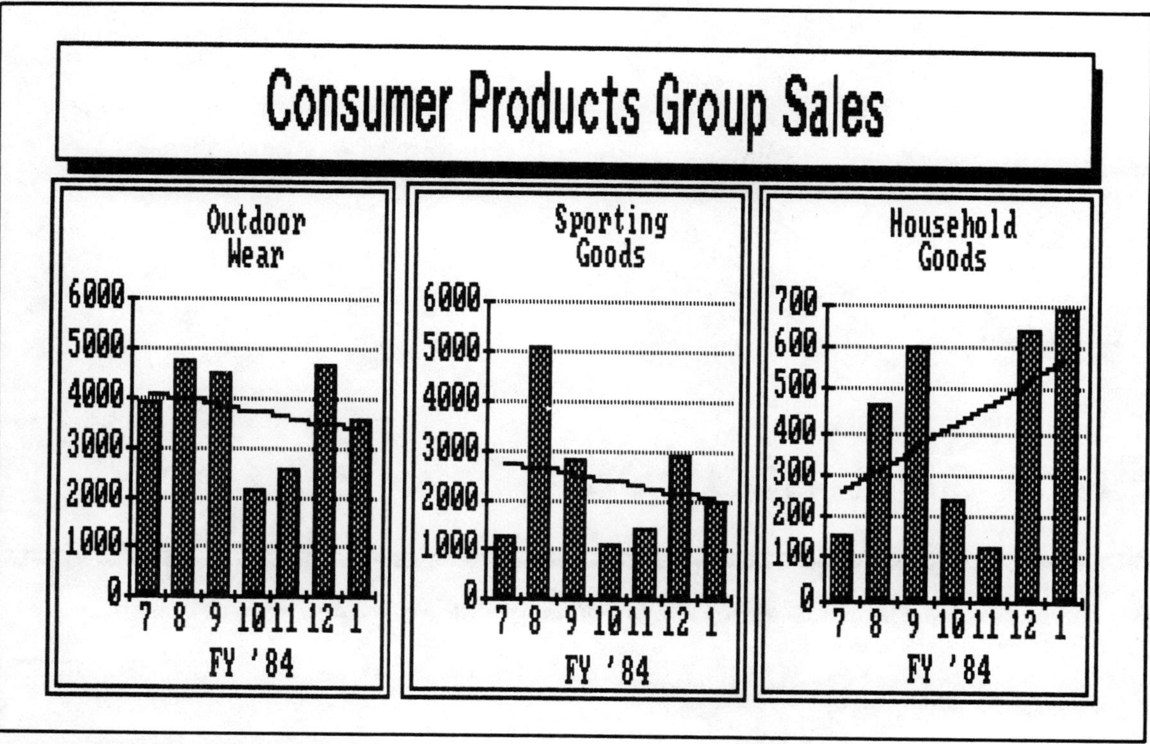

Fig. 3-34. Multiple graphs on one page.

umns are touching each other. This type of chart is used to show a larger number of time periods. As shown in Fig. 3-33 the chart is drawn with the columns sharing mutual borders. Shading or color should be consistant across the entire graph.

MULTIPLE GRAPHS ON A PAGE

Microcomputer software and reproduction techniques make it possible to place more than one chart on a single page. The graphs can be designed on the computer screen full-sized and then reduced by the software to fit on a page with other charts, as shown in Fig. 3-34.

Most plotters or printers can produce up to four readable graphs on the same page; more than four graphs means that the graphs are smaller and less easy to read. Because printers and plotters can take enormous amounts of time to produce single graphs, it is tempting to put as many on a page as will fit, but you should not yield to this temptation without careful planning. Charts placed on a single page should be related to each other. Placing unrelated charts all on the same page will cause the viewer to try to find a relationship where none exists.

Chapter 4

Bars and Stripes

It is said that one machine can do the work of fifty ordinary men. No machine, however, can do the work of one extraordinary man.

Tehyi Hsieh

The bar or column chart is probably the most common chart format used in reports and presentations. Technically, bar charts are horizontal (the rectangles are "resting" on the long side as shown in Fig. 4-1) and column charts are vertical (the bars are standing on end as shown in Fig. 4-2). Generically, all formats of this type of chart are called bar charts.

Bar charts can be used to show quantitative differences between groups of data. The groups can be divided by any variable, although the most common format is to chart the same type of data over a period of time (time series). When the bar represents quantitative data by a statistical population, the chart is called a *histogram*. A histogram depicts statistical distribution, rather than a rise or fall over time.

There are several varieties of bar chart. The bars can be stacked to show subdivisions of the whole total represented. For example, a bar chart would show the national sales total for a company, with the bars divided to show the relative contribution of each major region. This is most effective when a few subdivisions are shown; too many subdivisions will cause a stacked bar chart to look cluttered.

Grouped bars are formatted by breaking the stacked bar into individual bars for each subdivision. This is used for showing subdivision totals in relationship to each other. Each time unit or x-axis unit has several connected columns to represent subdivision totals; each group is, however, separated from the other groups to reduce confusion.

Bars on a bar chart may be touching each other, turning the bar chart into a step or Manhattan chart (because of its resemblance to the Manhattan skyline). Step chart are more effective on charts where there are many bars.

Artistic perspective can be added to a step chart or column chart to produce a three-dimensional effect. This makes the columns resemble the Manhattan skyscrapers that give the step chart its nickname. This chart format can be very impressive, although it is prone to the usual pitfalls of misdirection like any pseudo-three-dimensional drawing.

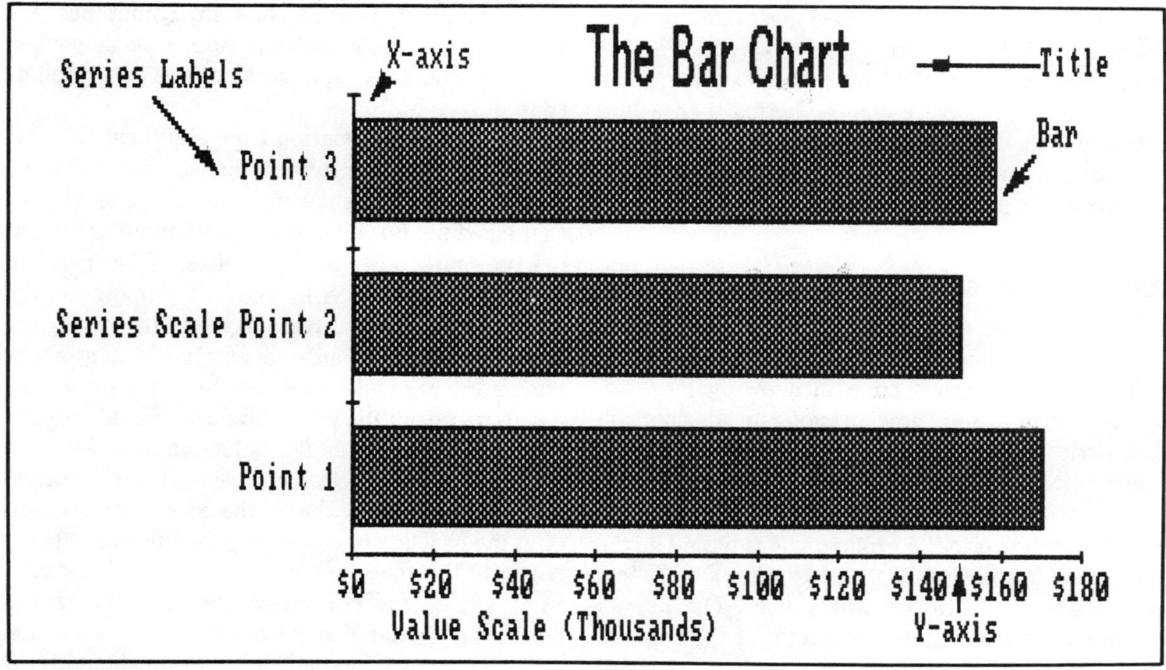

Fig. 4-1. The bar chart.

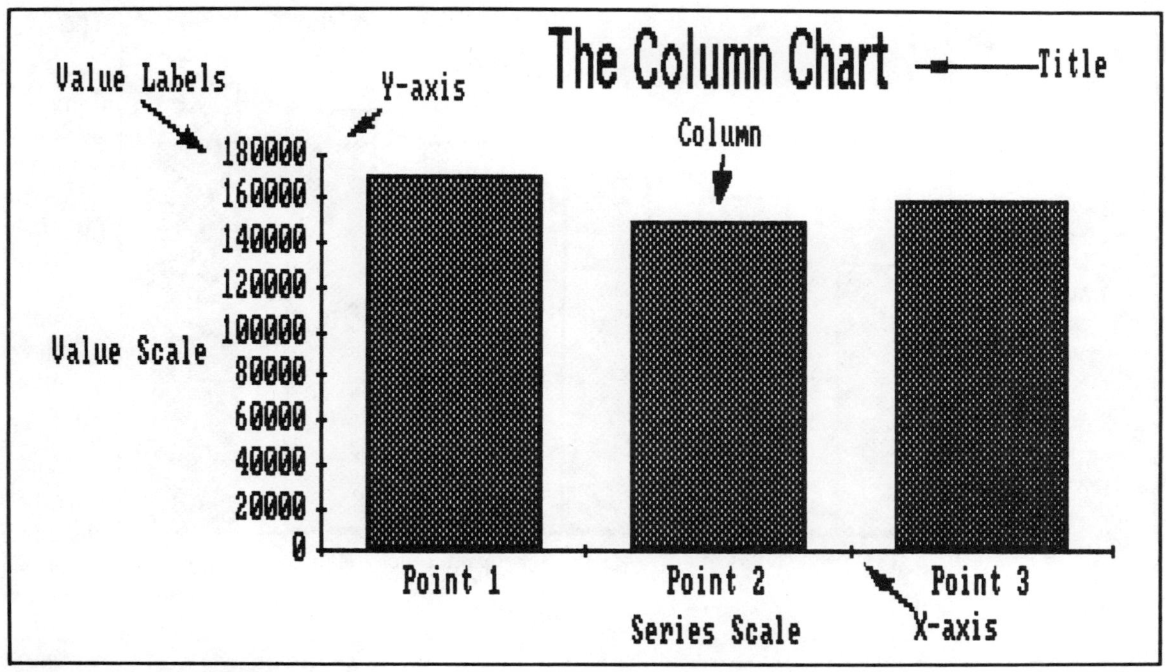

Fig. 4-2. The column chart.

Bar/column charts are used most effectively to show large differences from group to group. The difference in the size of the bars is dramatic, and a bar chart can emphasize a change better than a line chart, which would show a large increase as a steep rise, can. A bar chart gives the impression that the change occurred instantly.

VERTICAL BARS

Vertical bar charts (or column charts) are the most common chart format used in business presentations. They are effective in showing large increases from one time period to another, in comparing volumes or dollar amounts across several departments or companies, and in showing differences between statistical groupings.

The time period or group name is placed on the horizontal (x-) axis, while the plotted amount for that group is scaled on the vertical (y-) axis. The amount to be shown determines the height of the column.

The y-axis is usually at the left side of the chart, while the x-axis is at the bottom. Sometimes, the y-axis is repeated on the right side, especially when the chart contains many time periods or groupings (Fig. 4-3).

To show the deviation from a defined baseline with the vertical bar format, the y-axis is continued below the x-axis to show amounts above and below that baseline. For example, a sales manager might use the chart shown in Fig. 4-4 to show the percentage of quota reached by the salespersons on the staff. Bars starting at the x-axis and projecting upward would indicate an amount or percentage above quota for a particular salesperson. A bar projecting downward from the horizontal axis would indicate an amount or percentage below quota.

The x-axis labels for a vertical bar-deviation chart can be placed either at the bottom of the chart, or at the baseline by separating the upper and lower halves of the chart and drawing the baseline twice. In this case, the portion of the y-axis below the horizontal should also start at the base line value. The y-axis label for the lower portion should be at

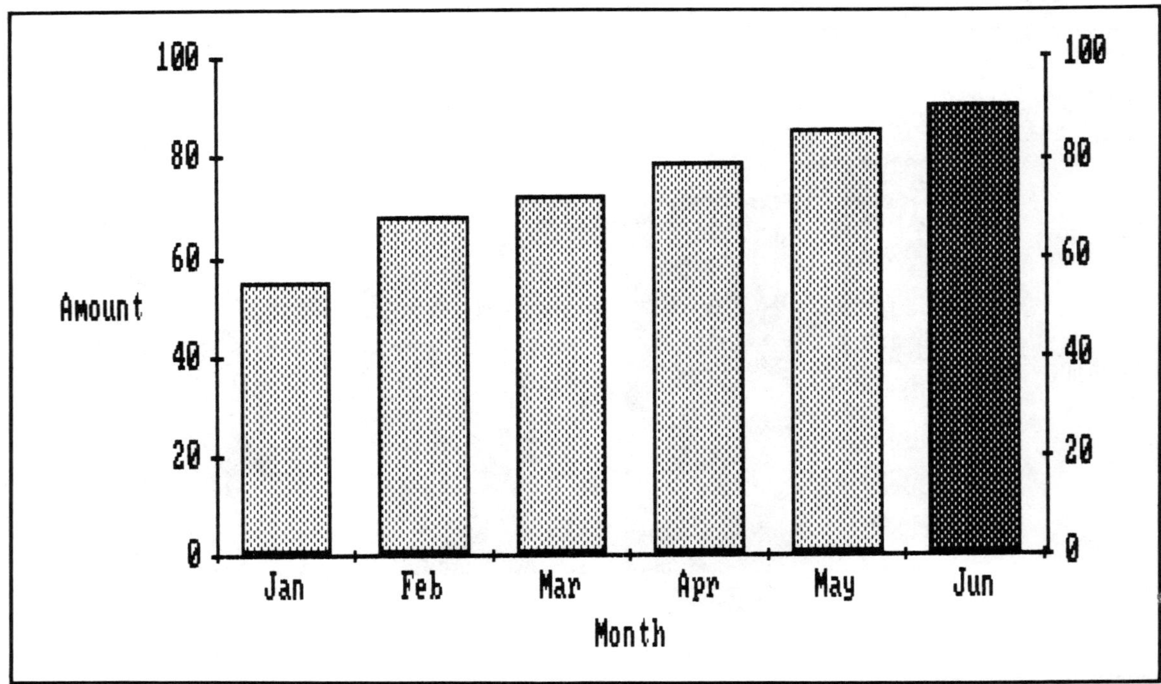

Fig. 4-3. The column chart with a repeated y-axis.

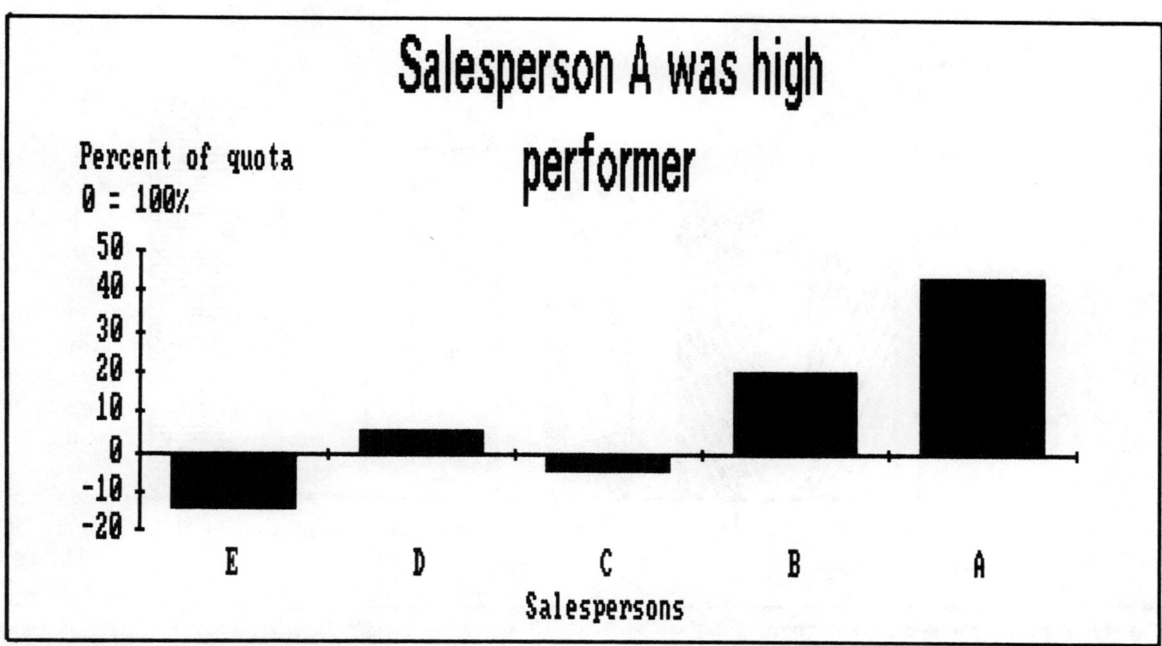

Fig. 4-4. The column deviation chart.

the end of the axis farthest from the baseline as shown in Fig. 4-5.

Vertical bar charts are most effective when few time periods or groupings are included on the chart. The ideal chart would have fewer than five groupings/time periods; too many groupings will reduce the emphasis. The emphasis of the chart should be the right-most bar on the chart, since the viewer's

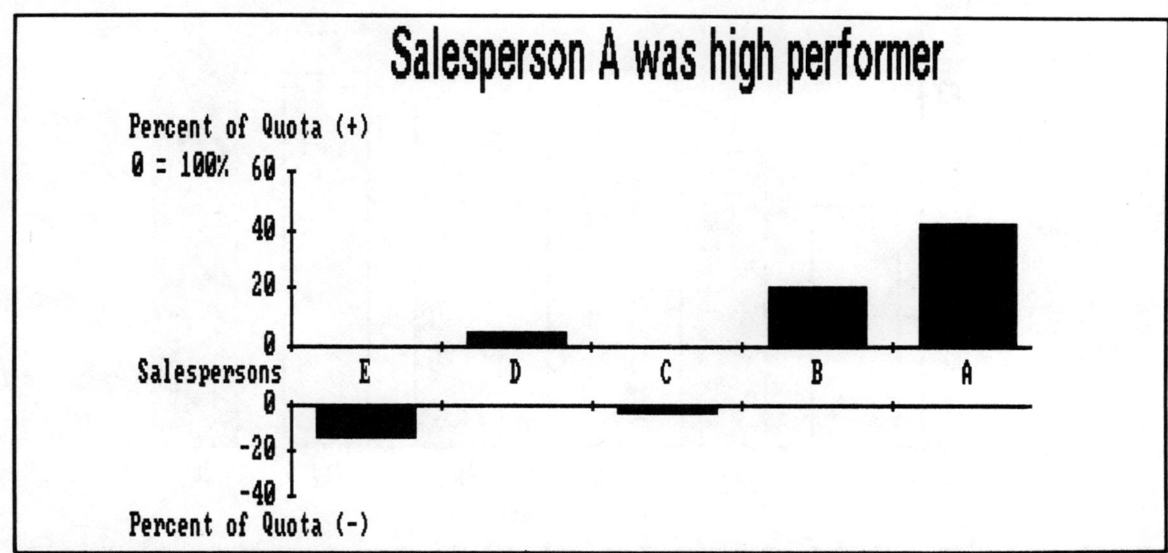

Fig. 4-5. A deviation chart with split x-axis.

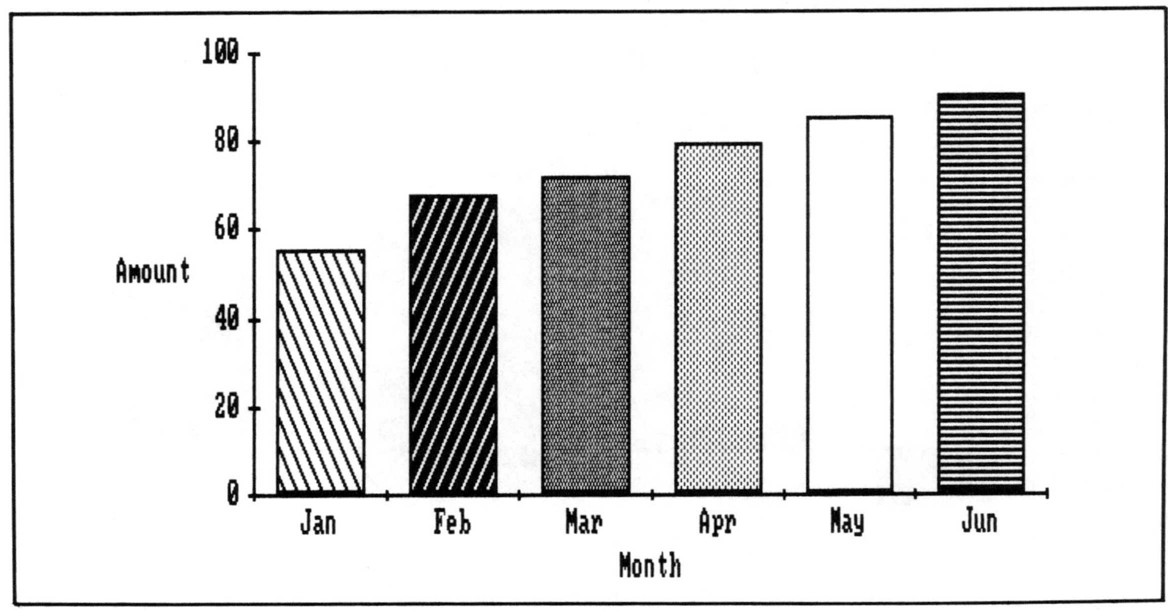

Fig. 4-6. A poorly planned column chart.

eye will be drawn from left to right on the page or screen. The eyes of the audience should sweep the chart and rest on the point where the major emphasis resides. Figure 4-6 shows a poorly planned chart and Fig. 4-7 shows a well planned chart.

As the number of groupings on the x-axis grows, the size of the bars becomes smaller. This can be counteracted by reducing the amount of

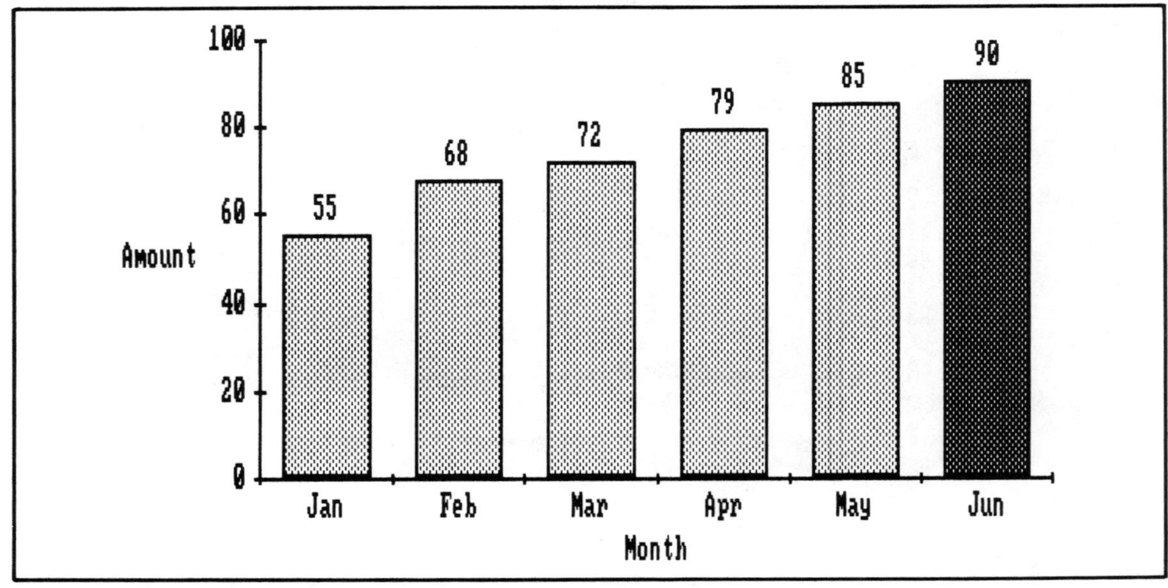

Fig. 4-7. A proper column cart with emphasis at the right side.

separation between the bars or by removing it entirely. The result is a step chart, which looks more like the plotted line chart than a bar chart. This kind of chart is used most commonly with time series when many time periods are covered, and the difference in amounts from period to period is large (Fig. 4-8).

The vertical bars can be labeled in several ways. The label can be on the x-axis, as with time periods. For groupings, the label is immediately under the bar that represents that statistical group. Different shadings can be used for different groups when the labels are too large to fit below the column; where shading is used to differentiate the groups, be sure to include a legend for the viewers' convenience.

The actual values may be difficult to determine on a vertical bar chart, unless the y-axis is graduated in very small units. One way of lending credibility to your graph is to place the actual total figure, in terms of the units on the y-axis, inside or above the bar that pictures that amount. The amount label is placed in the center of the bar at the top. If shading is used, the area immediately surrounding the amount should be neutral so that the amount can be read easily (Fig. 4-9).

Another way of making a vertical bar chart easier to read is to include grid lines for the major unit-divisions of the vertical axis. This will enable the audience to analyze the chart more easily (Fig. 4-10).

Color on a vertical bar chart should be limited to the area of emphasis. Red bars are the most noticeable, as are navy blue bars. Green and yellow bars should be used carefully, depending on the quality of reproduction that you can achieve with these colors. Bars that are to be deemphasized should be medium-shaded in the neutral colors.

Deviation bar charts can use different shadings or colors to denote positive and negative values (Fig. 4-11). Usually, dark blue is used for positive amounts, while red is used for the negative amounts.

As with all types of time series charts, a

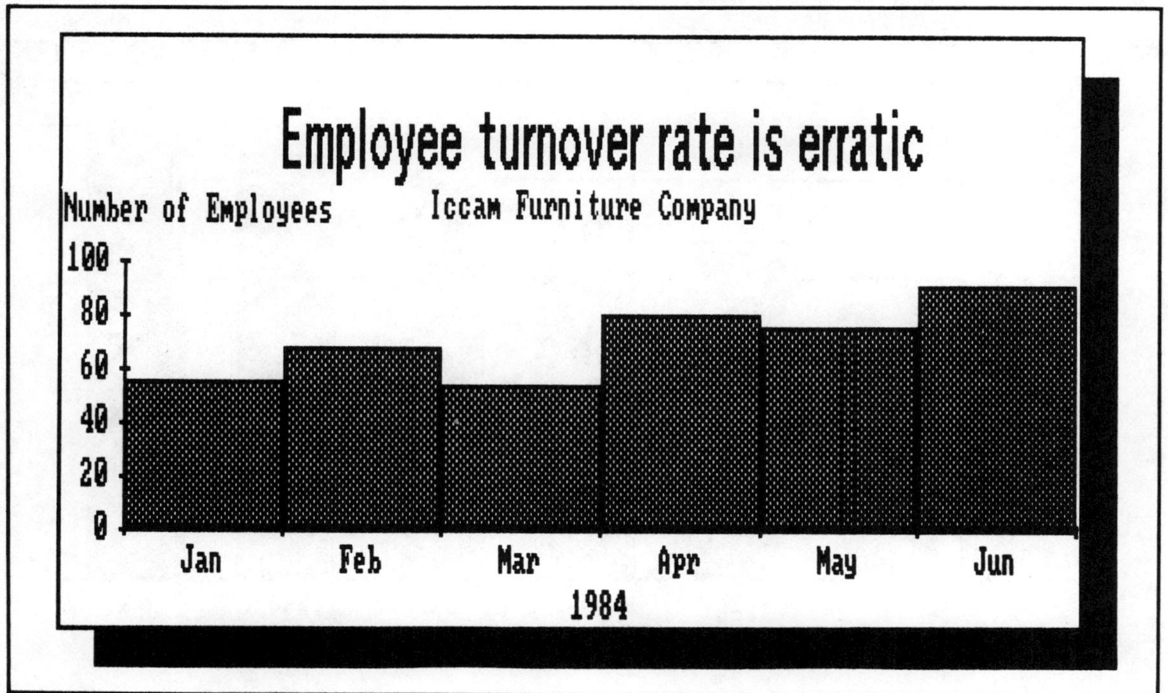

Fig. 4-8. The step (Manhattan) chart.

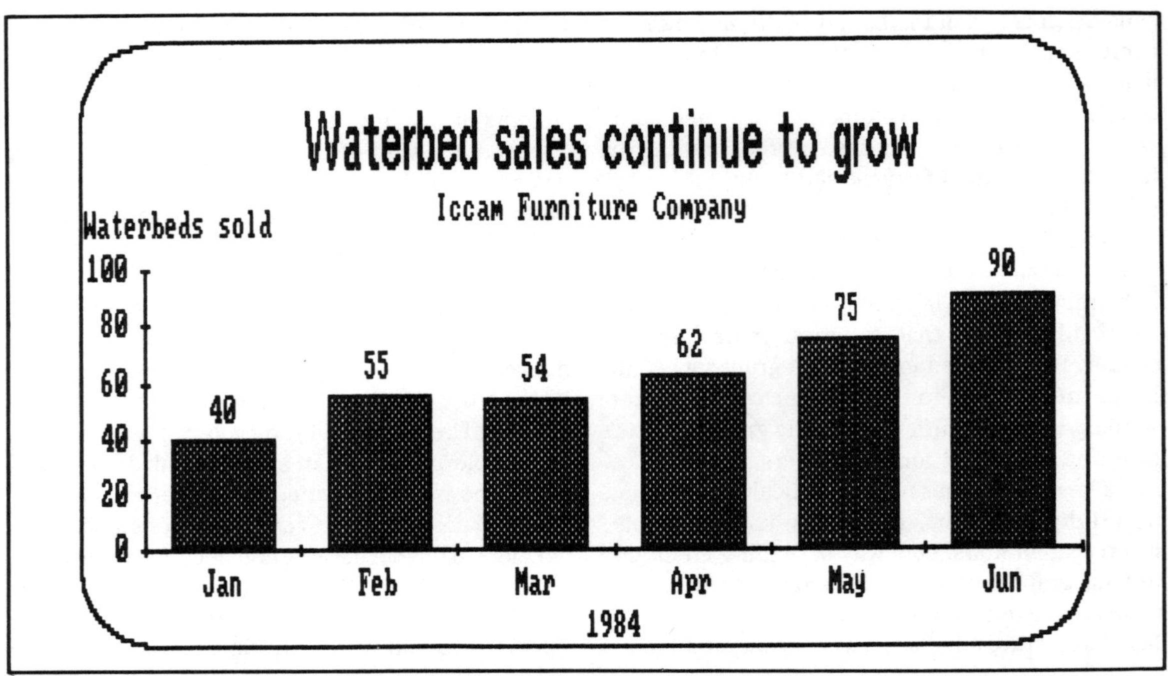

Fig. 4-9. A vertical bar chart with amount labels.

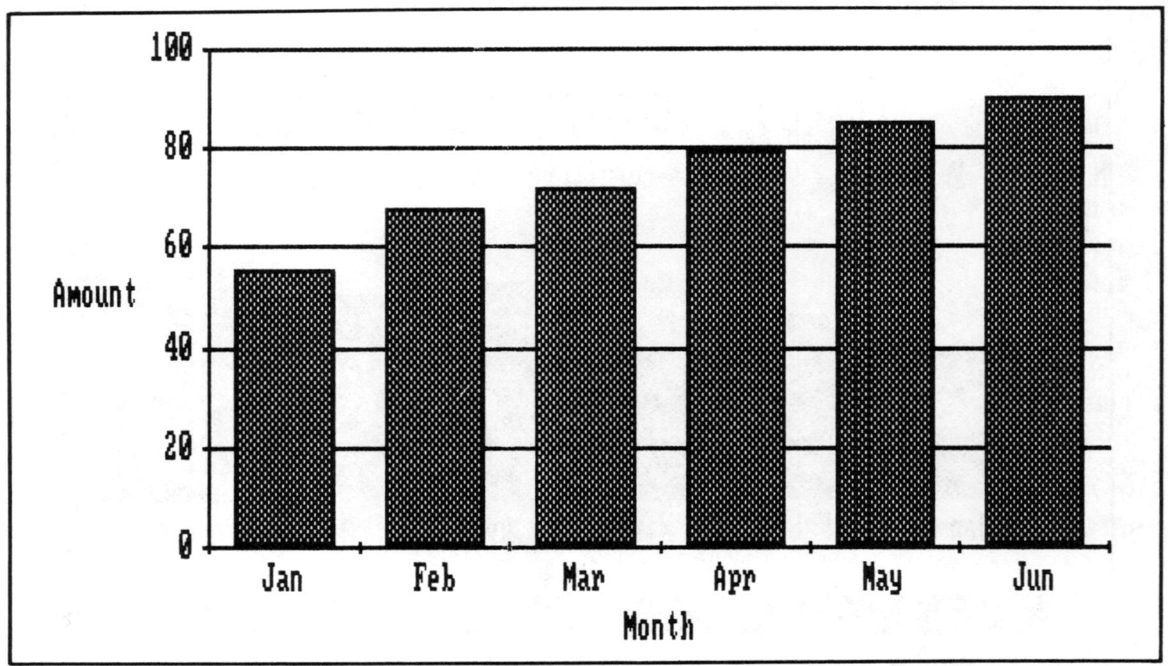

Fig. 4-10. A column chart with grid lines.

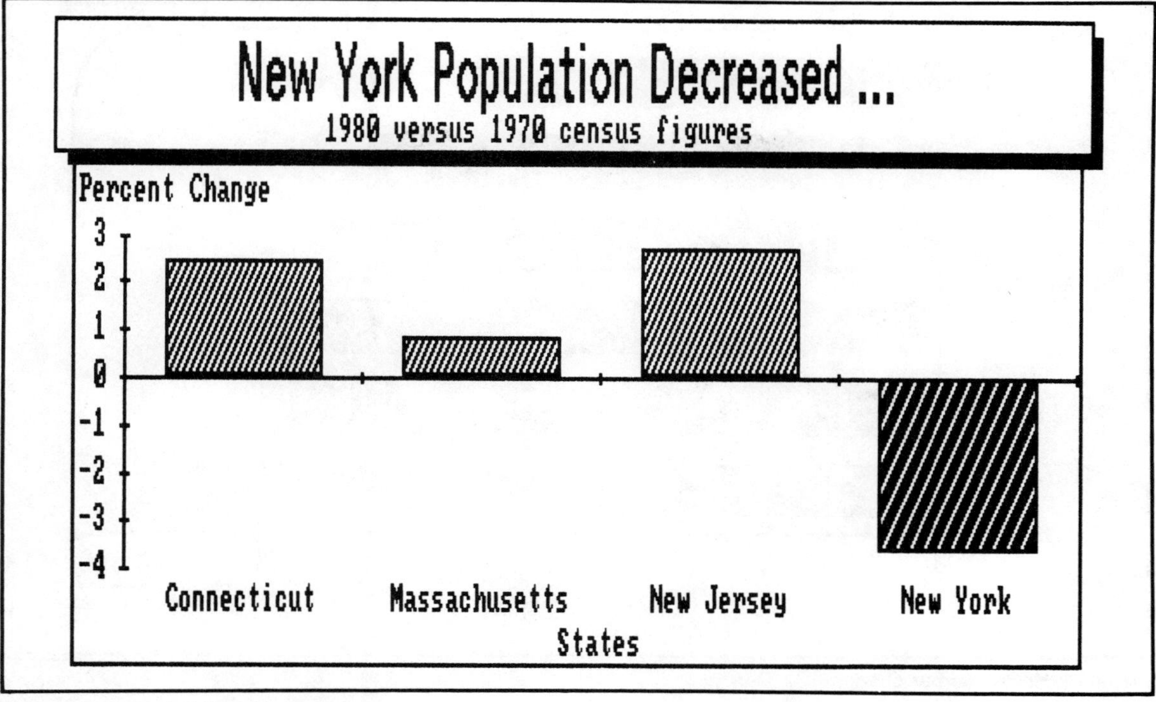

Fig. 4-11. A shaded deviation chart.

reference line may be added to mark a base year or median value to aid in making your point; this can also help the viewers in their analysis of your chart.

HORIZONTAL BARS

Horizontal bar charts are used to show two to five groupings of a statistical nature, although a specific time period ("years", for example) could be used. The group labels are at the left side on the now-vertical x-axis, while the amount scale (y-axis) is horizontal at the top or bottom.

Bars are drawn horizontally from the left to the right. The effect is that of having taken a vertical bar chart and rotated it clockwise ninety degrees. Most business graphics place the rotated y-axis at the bottom of the chart, even though this may be slightly confusing (Fig. 4-12).

The horizontal bar chart is effective in showing small numbers of groups with dramatic differences in the amount or volume plotted. The group to be emphasized should be at the top, with the less important bars below it. Bars usually range in size from largest at the top to smallest at the bottom, but any order can be used depending on the message to be conveyed.

Horizontal deviation bar charts can be used in the manner discussed for vertical deviation bar charts. The axis becomes central vertically, dividing the chart into negative amounts or percentages on the left and positive amounts or percentages on the right. The axis may be separated for labels if space allows (Fig. 4-13).

As with vertical bar charts, the horizontal bar may include the precise amount plotted in an unshaded area at the end of the bar. If one group's total is far beyond that of other groups, it may be necessary to split the bar so that the chart will fit on a page. This is done by making a ragged split to the right of the rightmost point reached by the other bars, and placing the exact figure in the bar to the right of the split (Fig. 4-14).

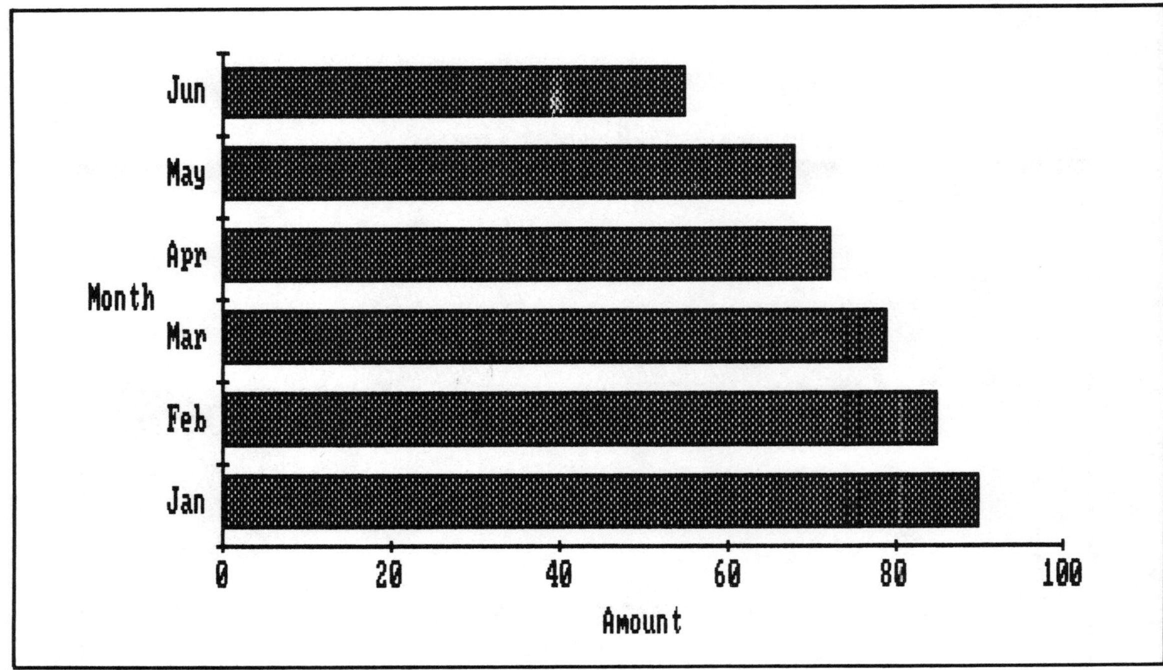

Fig. 4-12. Horizontal bar charts.

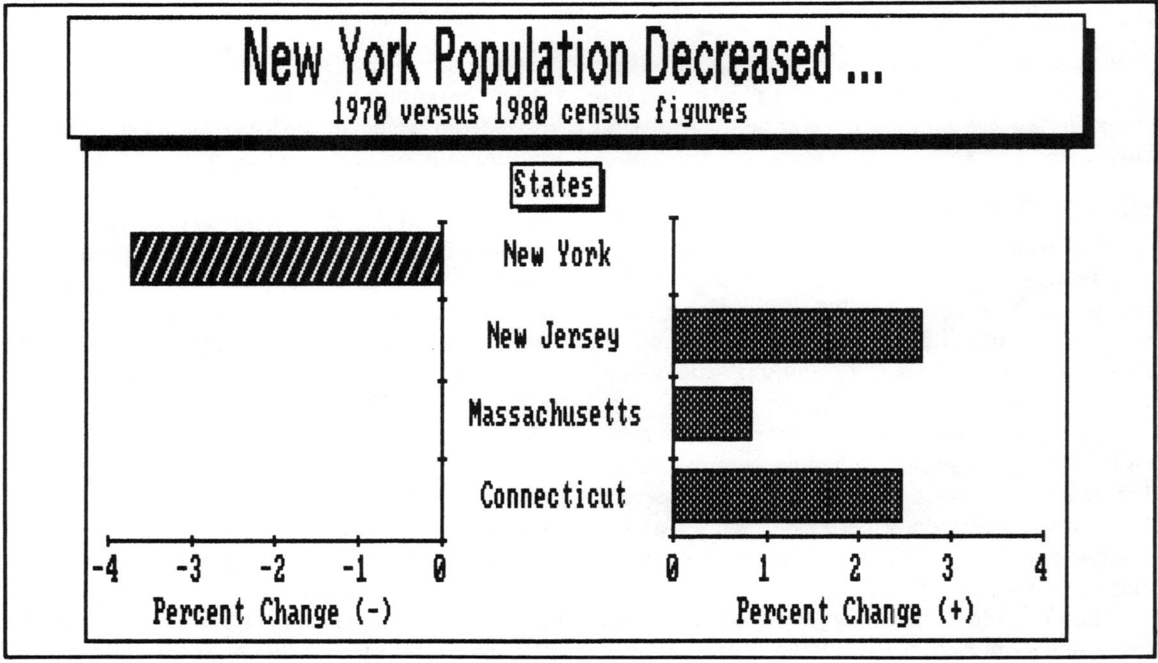

Fig. 4-13. A horizontal deviation chart.

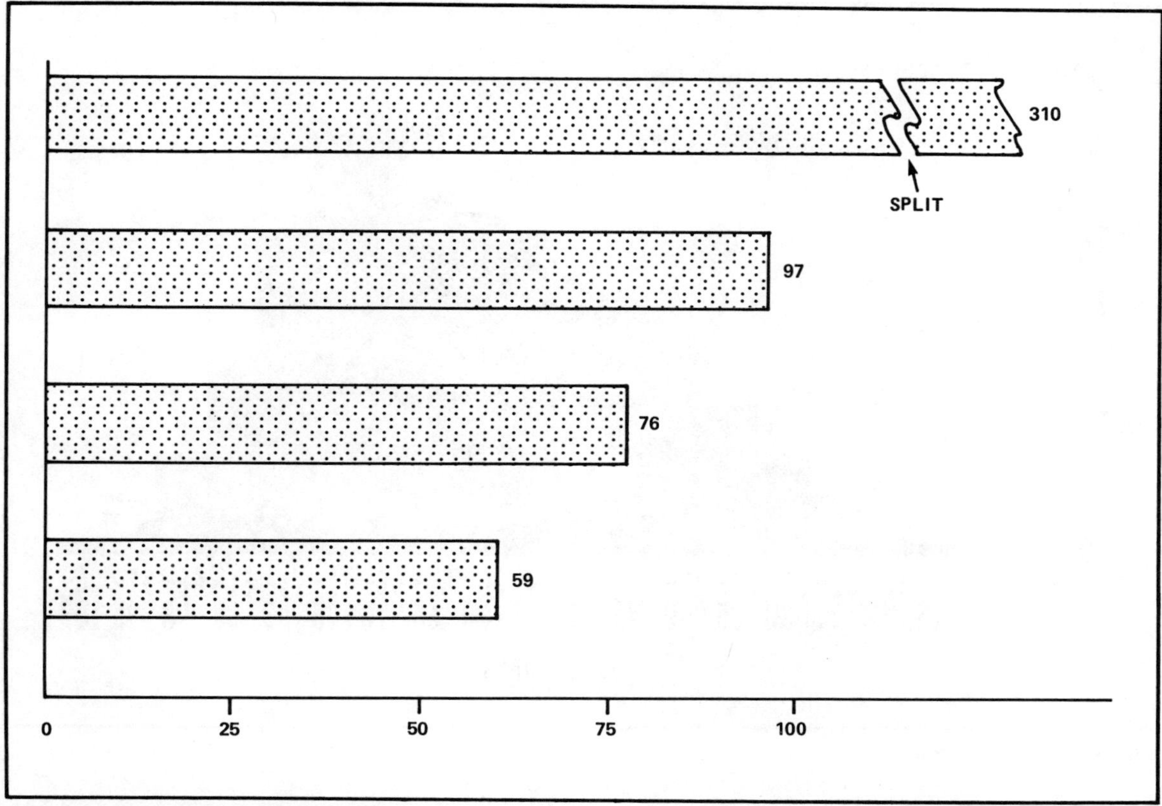

Fig. 4-14. A split horizontal bar chart.

Dark shading and bright colors should be reserved for the area of emphasis—the bar closest to the y-axis (in this case the horizontal axis) on the chart. Most textbooks and business graphics tend to place the y-axis at the bottom of the chart, making the "bar of emphasis" the lowest bar.

Grid lines are almost never used on a horizontal bar chart. Reference lines, however, may be used to mark an average value or median.

HISTOGRAMS

Histograms are a cross between a curve/line chart and a vertical bar chart. In fact, the histogram resembles a surface chart, because the bars are always shaded or colored. Histograms are used to show statistical frequency distributions over a large number of time periods or groups. Narrow bars are used to produce the plot, which will represent the distribution curve of the data tracked. Only one data item can be tracked effectively with a histogram, although a second item may be plotted if the plot of the second item is below the plot of the first item and the same units are used to measure both (Fig. 4-15).

The difference between a histogram and a regular bar chart is found in the way the groups are arranged on the x-axis. The regular bar chart uses discrete units such as sex, department, or company, for the major groupings. As histogram uses ranges of scores, ages, or years to plot the number of people or items that fall into those categories. These groups are called *interval data* in statistical terms.

Histograms are always plotted using narrow bars that are touching each other. It can be much more effective to plot this type of frequency distribu-

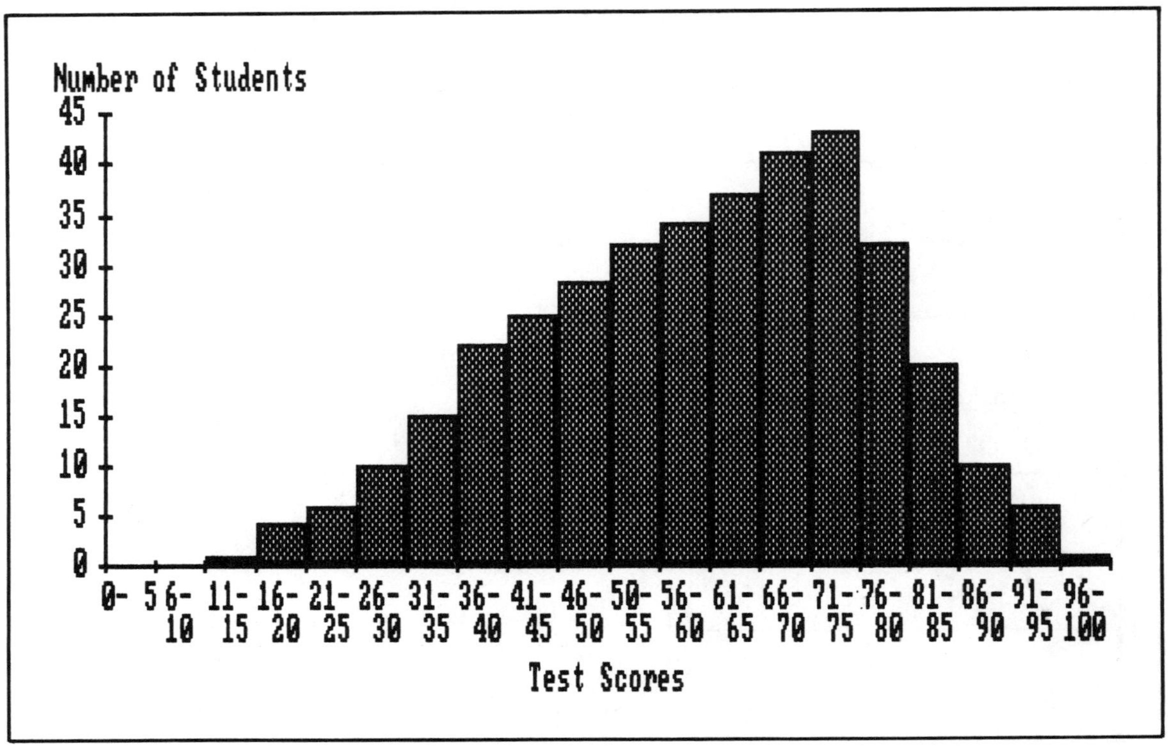

Fig. 4-15. The histogram.

tion with a vertical-bar histogram when the differences between groupings are large. If the differences are small, a line or surface chart would be more effective.

STACKING THE BARS

A vertical or horizontal bar may be divided to show subdivisions of the overall total represented by the bar. For example, a bar chart showing the total income of a company could be subdivided to show each department's contribution to that total.

This type of chart is called a *stacked* bar chart, because it looks as if several bars are set on top of each other to form the overall bar. In a grouped bar chart, these bar sections would be set beside each other (Fig. 4-16).

Each section in the stacked bar is shaded or colored differently from the others in the same bar. It is important to keep the darker shadings or colors at the bottom of the stack, graduating to lighter shades/colors at the top (Fig. 4-17). Darker shades on top of the stack will cause the stack to have a top-heavy, unstable appearance (Fig. 4-18).

The largest subdivision should appear next to the horizontal axis. Large divisions on top of the stack can also give the appearance of top-heaviness.

When using different shadings to individualize the bar sections, be sure to use patterns that are similar in slant. Patterns slanted to the right and diagonal crossing shades go well together. Using alternate vertical and horizontal shading patterns, however, can cause the bars to appear as if they are bound like wheat at harvest time. The bars will seem to become narrower at the vertical shading and then spread out at the sections of horizontal shading.

A legend should be included in a stacked bar chart to show the meaning of the divisions. Each subdivision should be true to the amount attributable to that division (Fig. 4-19).

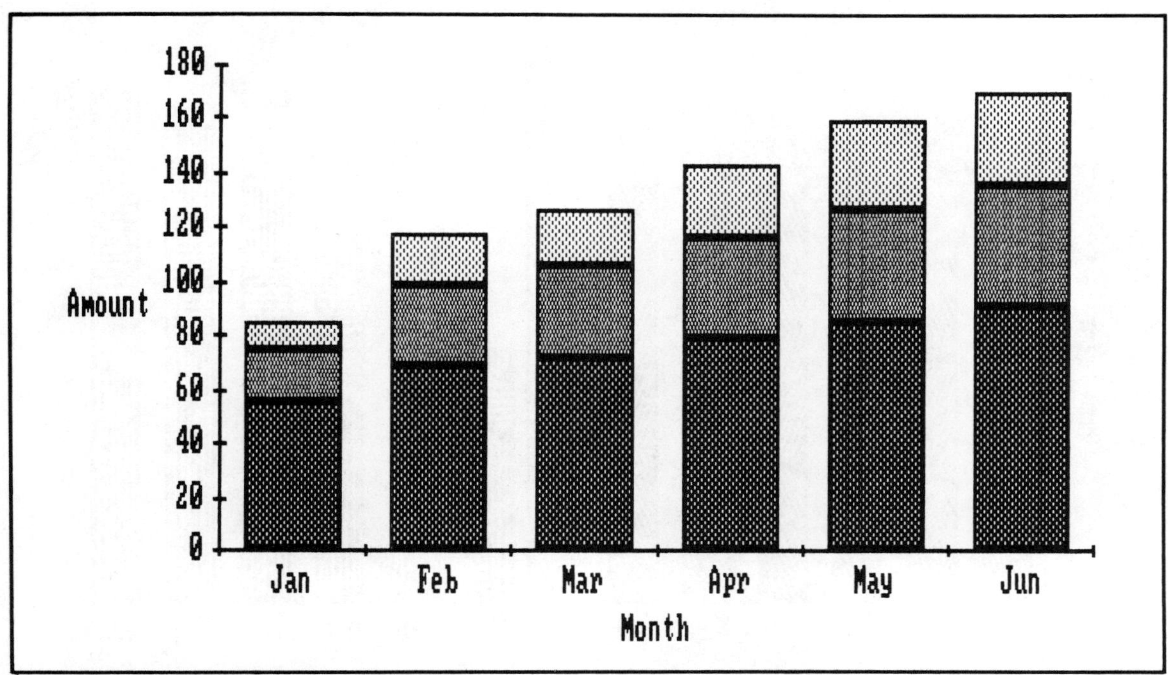

Fig. 4-16. The stacked bar chart.

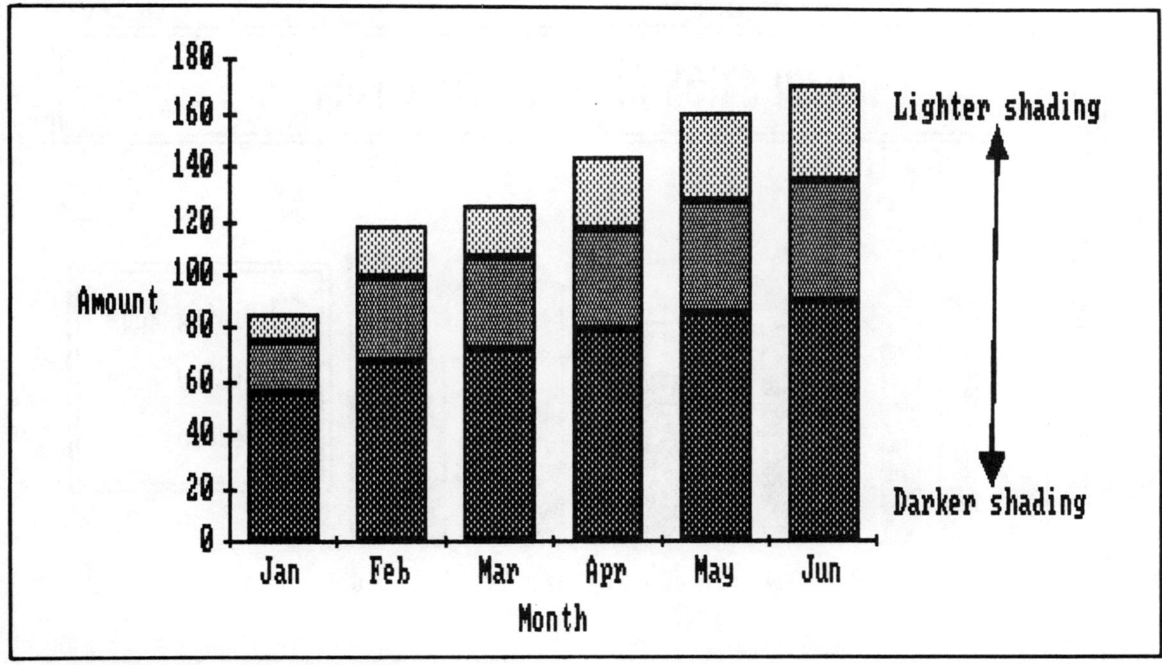

Fig. 4-17. The proper shading for stacked bars.

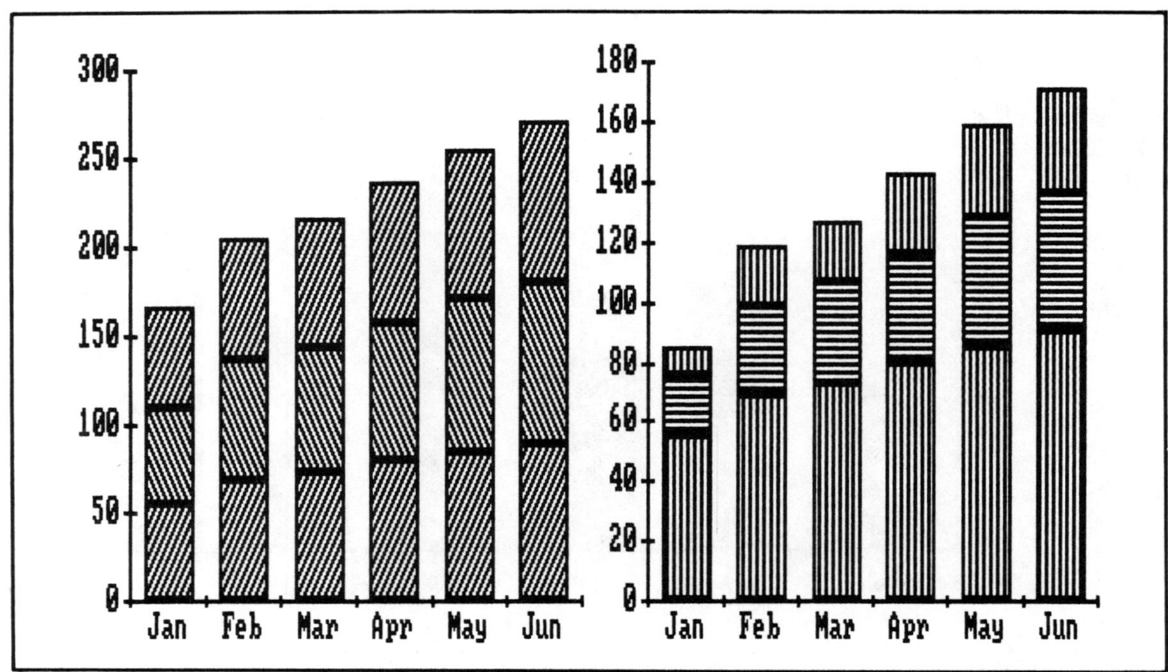

Fig. 4-18. Poor and mismatched shading.

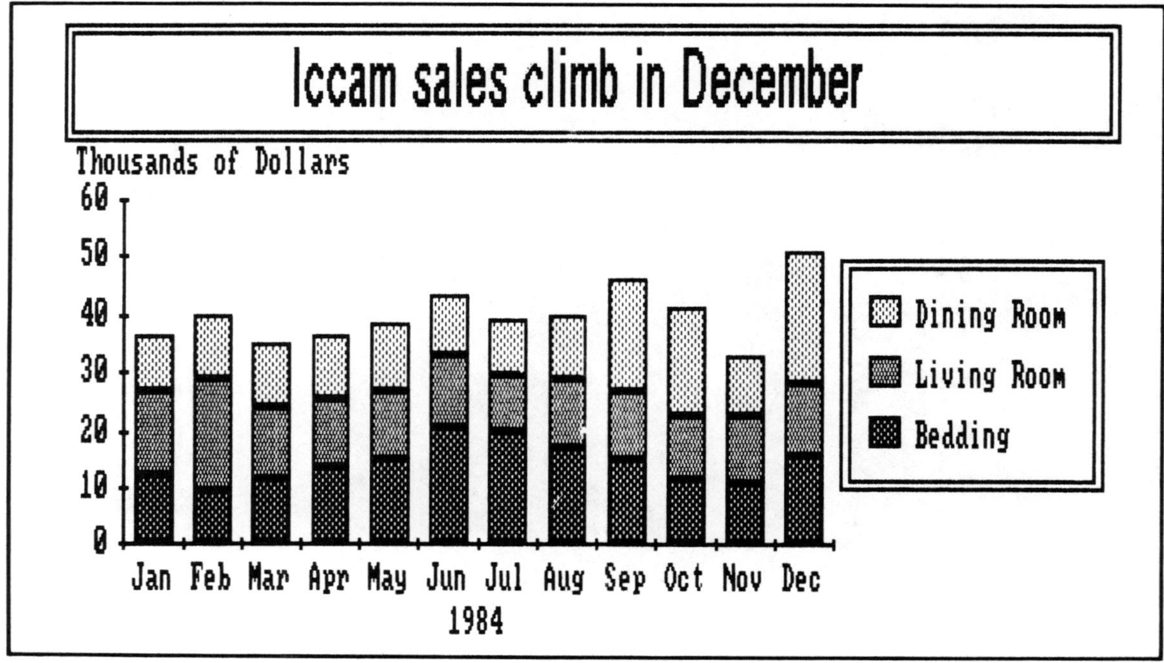

Fig. 4-19. A stacked bar with a legend.

MANHATTAN BARS AND BLOCKS

Adding perspective to the vertical bar chart gives the column the appearance of being three-dimensional. A properly drawn 3-D bar chart will look like a series of tall buildings, thus the nickname *Manhattan chart*. Manhattan charts can appear several ways. The bars can be separated or joined; "Manhattan" is also used to refer to step charts. Figure 4-20 shows a two-dimensional step chart, and Fig. 4-21 shows a three-dimensional step chart.

The addition of perspective can cause misdirection. The number of units represented by the bar should be clear to the viewer. The axis units should appear in the foreground of the perspective, indicating the plotted amount on the foreground of the bars, not on the perspective shading.

Perspective shading is produced in the background color, for example, it can be black on a printed chart. The bars can be shaded or colored in any effective manner.

Another form of Manhattan chart is the block chart. This is usually a three-dimensional representation of a flat surface with the columns rising from the surface, each in their own little block. This type of chart is good for visual effect, but not very accurate in terms of true measurements (Fig. 4-22).

Block charts can also be two dimensional grids, each with its own little chart within. The most common forms use either a single column or a group of columns to show the block-to-block variations in totals, amounts, or volumes. Pies, stacked columns, and 100% columns can also be used in block charts. Each little chart must conform to all the others on the chart. Shading/coloration, position of series on the chart, and the scaling factors cannot change between blocks.

Each block on a block chart can represent a subdivision of some whole. They are most frequently used to show time values, such as quarters of a year. The standard wall calendar can be used as a block chart for day-to-day variations. Block charts can also be used to show variations across departments within a company when the same information is being tracked.

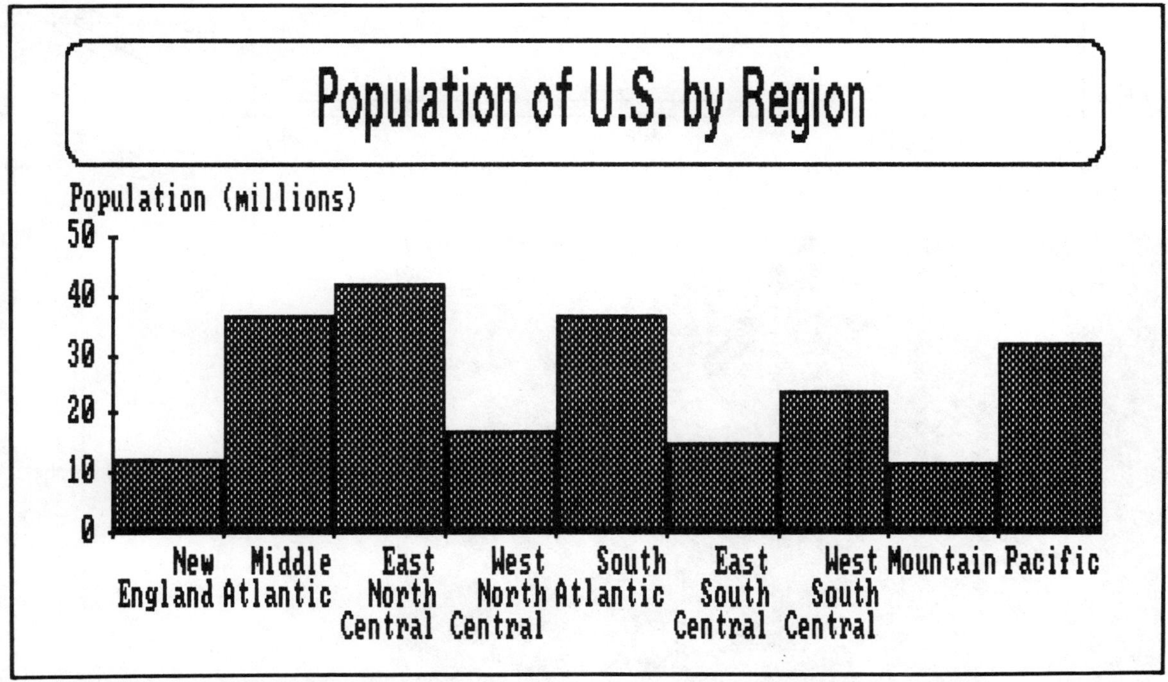

Fig. 4-20. The two-dimensional step chart.

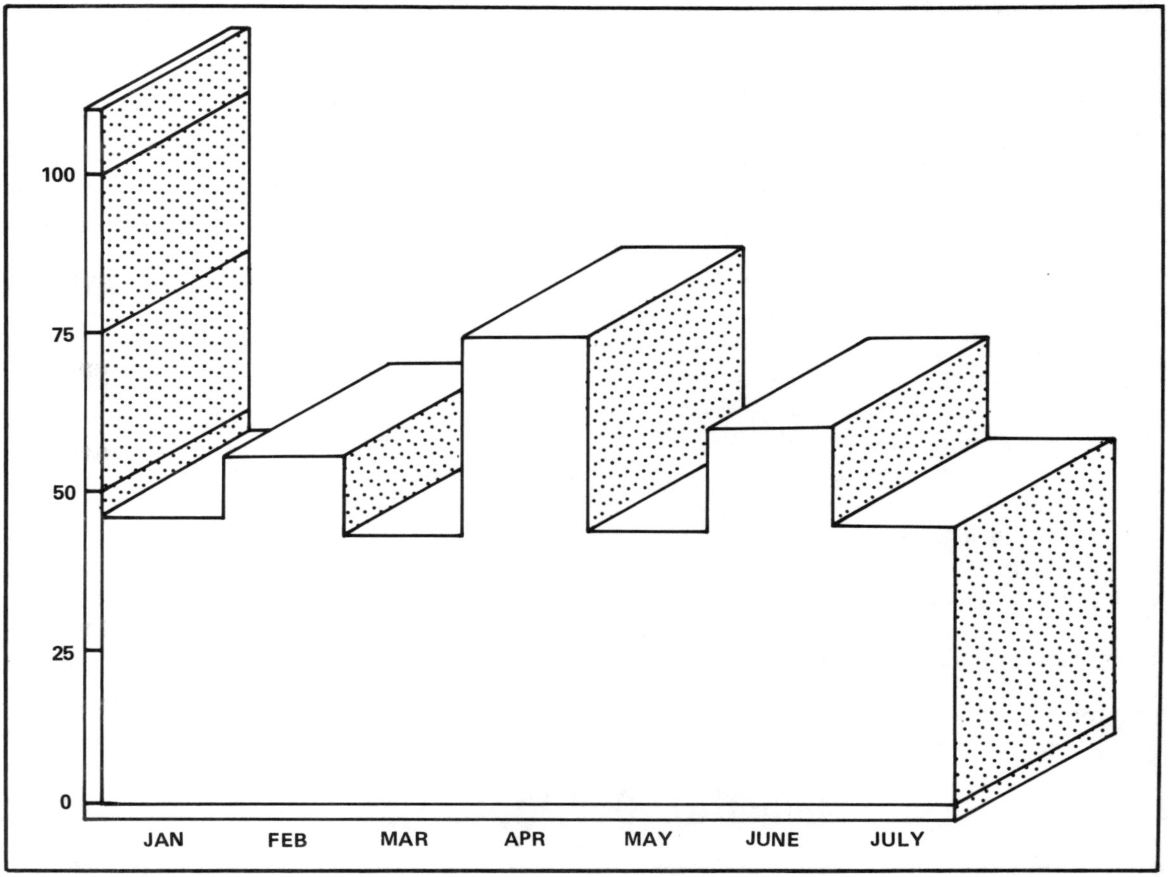

100
75
50
25
0
JAN FEB MAR APR MAY JUNE JULY

Fig. 4-21. The three-dimensional step chart.

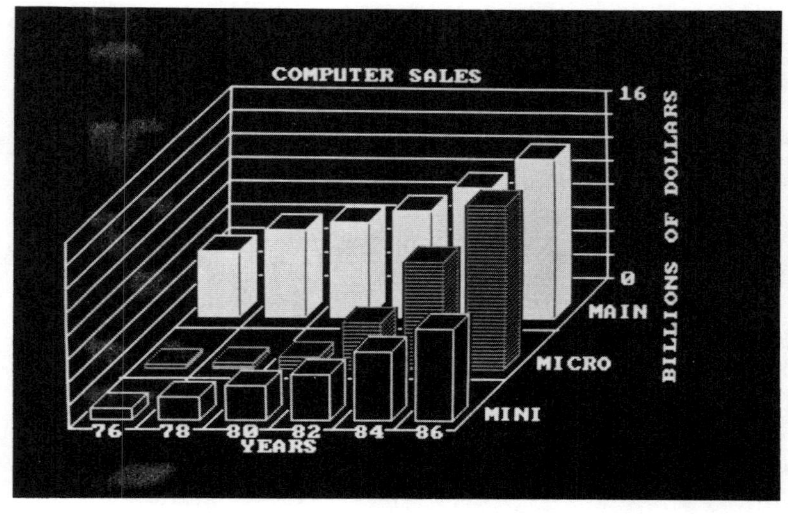

Fig. 4-22. The block column chart.

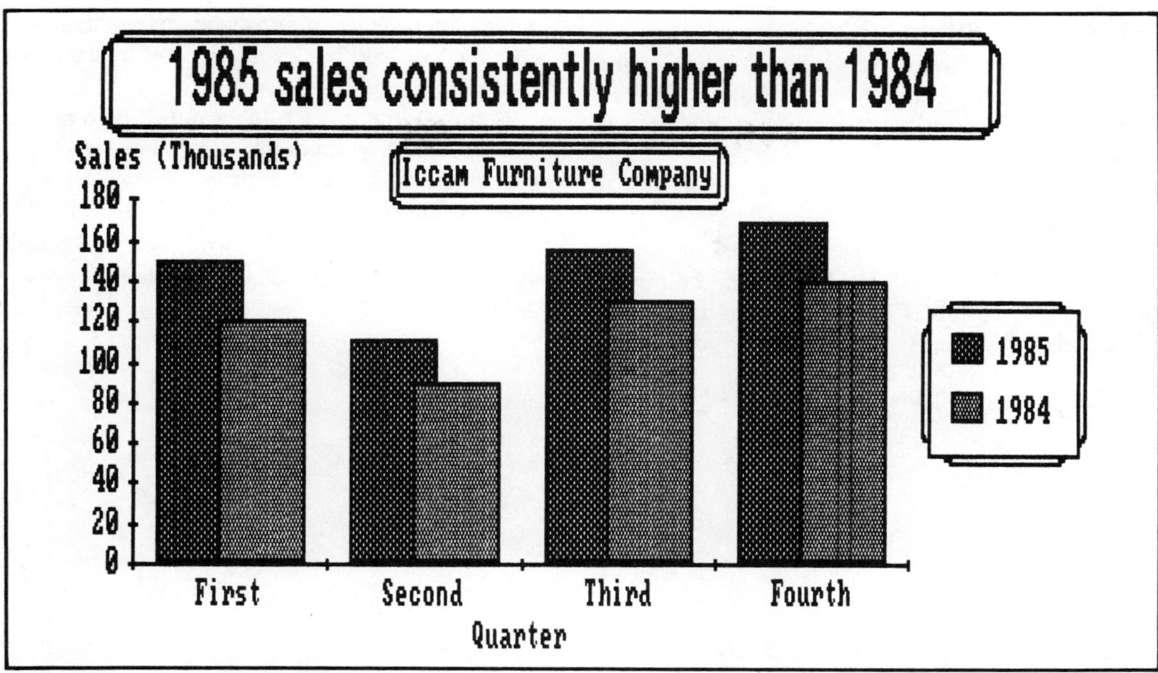

Fig. 4-23. The grouped column chart.

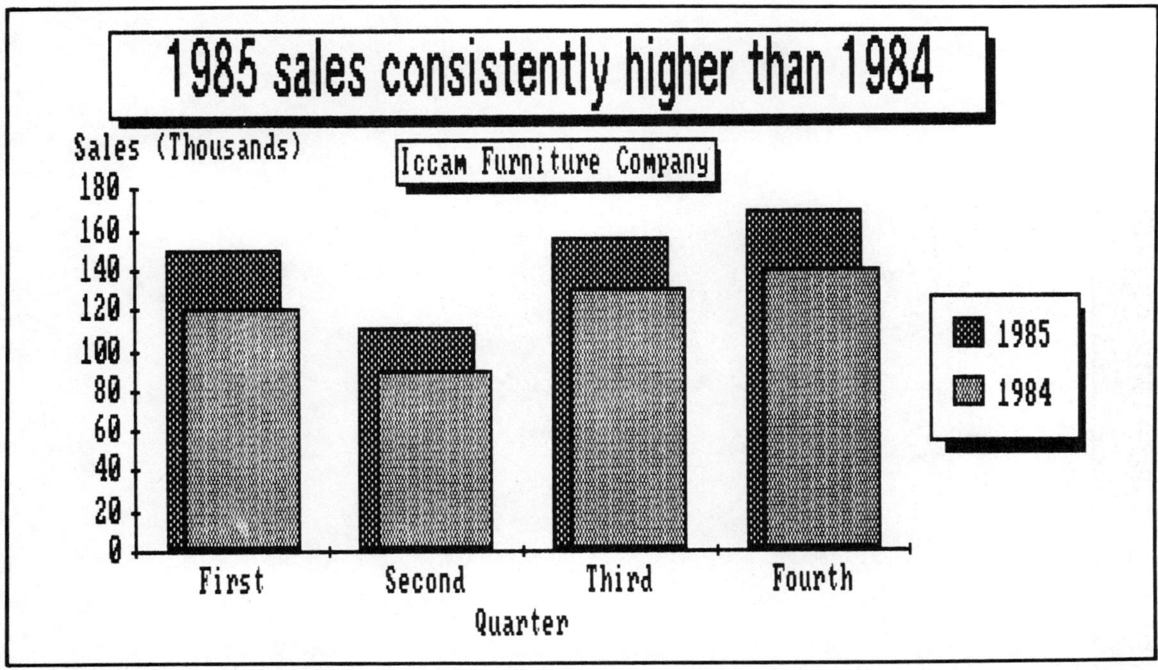

Fig. 4-24. A grouped bar chart emphasizing differences.

GROUPING BARS

Grouped bars are one alternative to the stacked bar chart discussed earlier in this chapter. At each horizontal axis position, there is a group of two, three, or four bars that indicate the subdivisional amounts. The total amount is not obvious, as it is in the stacked bar (Fig. 4-23).

This type of chart is used when the subtotals do not affect the overall total or when the overall total is not important. Grouped bars are used most effectively when there are few groups and few subdivisions to show. Graphing too many of either makes the grouped bar chart difficult to read and analyze.

As shown in Fig. 4-24, the grouped bars can be drawn so that they appear to overlap one another. For example, a bar chart with two bars in a group can be used to plot income and expenses. The difference in the height of the bars will be emphasized because of the overlap; in this case, the difference is profit (or loss).

Chapter 5
Walking the Line

I always avoid prophesying beforehand, because it is a much better policy to prophesy after the event has already taken place.

Sir Winston Churchill

Line charts are used to show trends over a series of time periods. The amount for each time period marked on the x-axis is plotted by a dot, and then the dots are connected by a trend line. As shown in Fig. 5-1, this chart format is used to indicate the direction of the data being plotted.

The plot line can be smooth or jagged, depending on the amount of information available. Sharp, angular trend lines indicate that some intermediate data is not displayed between the plotted points. A rise from one major time period to the next may not include a dramatic fall and rise in the interim.

The advantage of using a line chart is that there can be many time periods on the x-axis. In fact, when more closely spaced time periods are used to plot data the trend line will be smoother. The chart will also be more usable as a forecasting tool because of increased accuracy.

One disadvantage of the line chart is that the actual plotted value may be difficult to determine for any single period. This can be alleviated by using grid lines, as shown in Fig. 5-2, but the point of the chart is to show trends, not precise values. If necessary, a label including the precise value for a given point in time can be added to the graph.

Line charts may have one or more trend lines to plot the trends of one or more variables. Multiple lines are most effective when the data items are measured in the same units. Multiple lines that cross many times, however, are very difficult to read. When multiple lines are used, labels must be included to help the audience analyze the meaning of the chart. Some charts will have different symbols at the plotted points to denote different lines. Others differentiate the lines by patterns or colors, as shown in Fig. 5-3.

To show the trend plots of two items of data measured in different units, a second vertical axis must be used. The second axis is placed at the right side of the graph, with the unit-of-measure labeled horizontally above the new axis.

A line chart may be drawn in three dimensions, turning the line into a rolling plane or a net strung between the axes. Three axes are needed for this

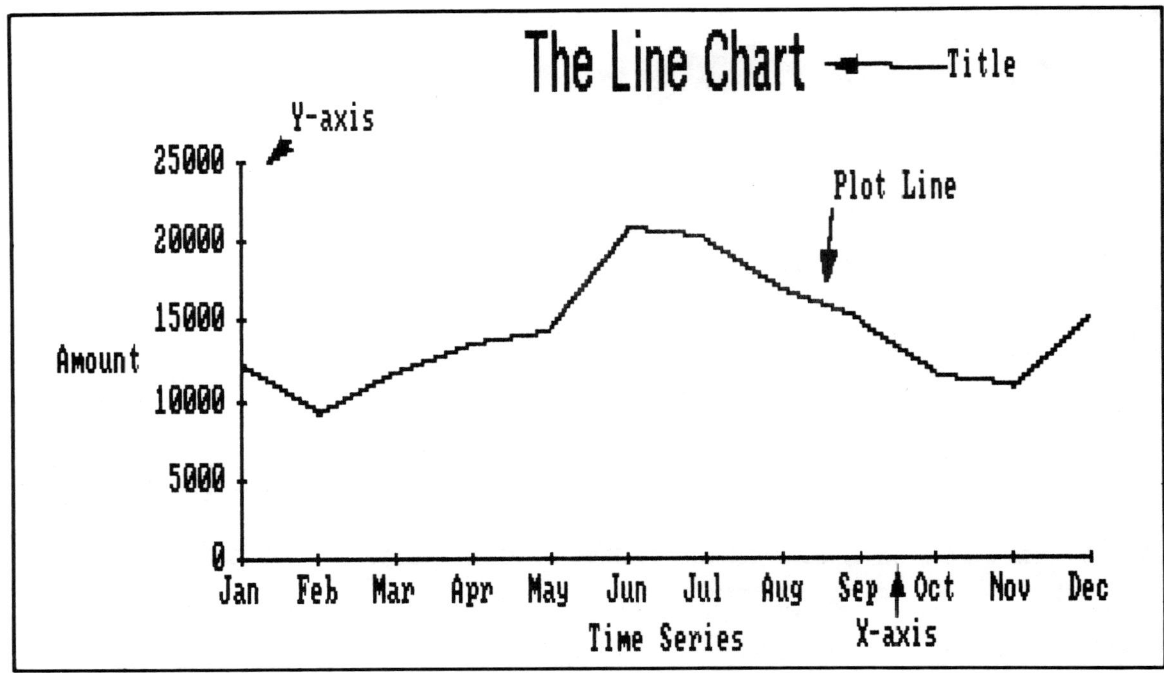

Fig. 5-1. The line chart.

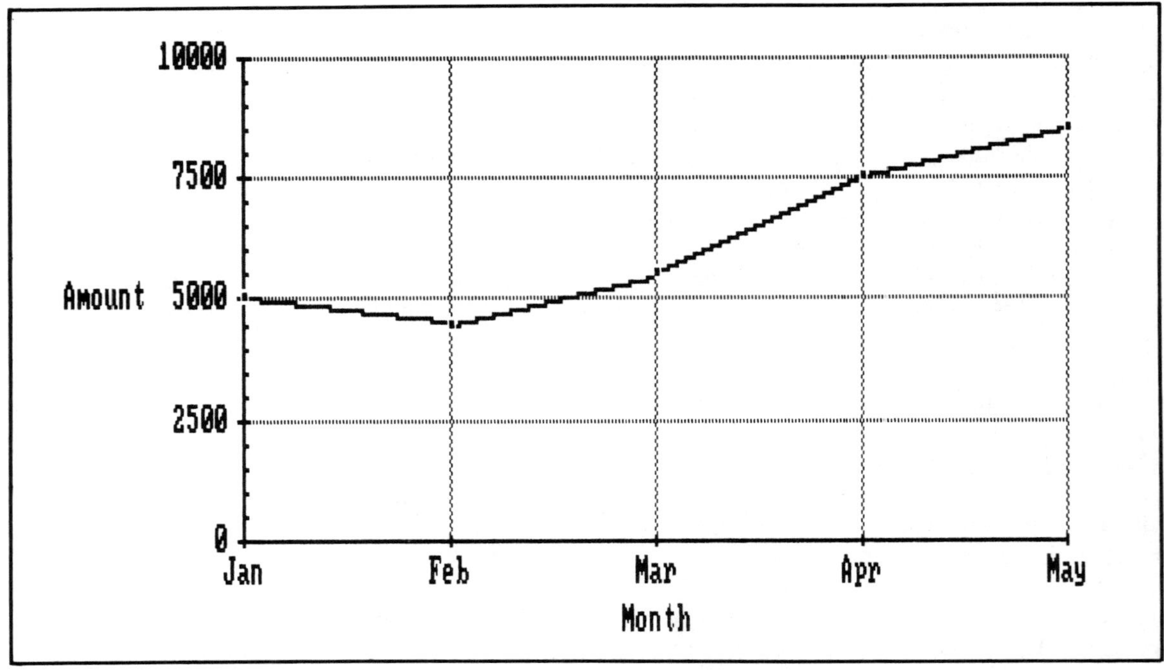

Fig. 5-2. A line chart with grid lines.

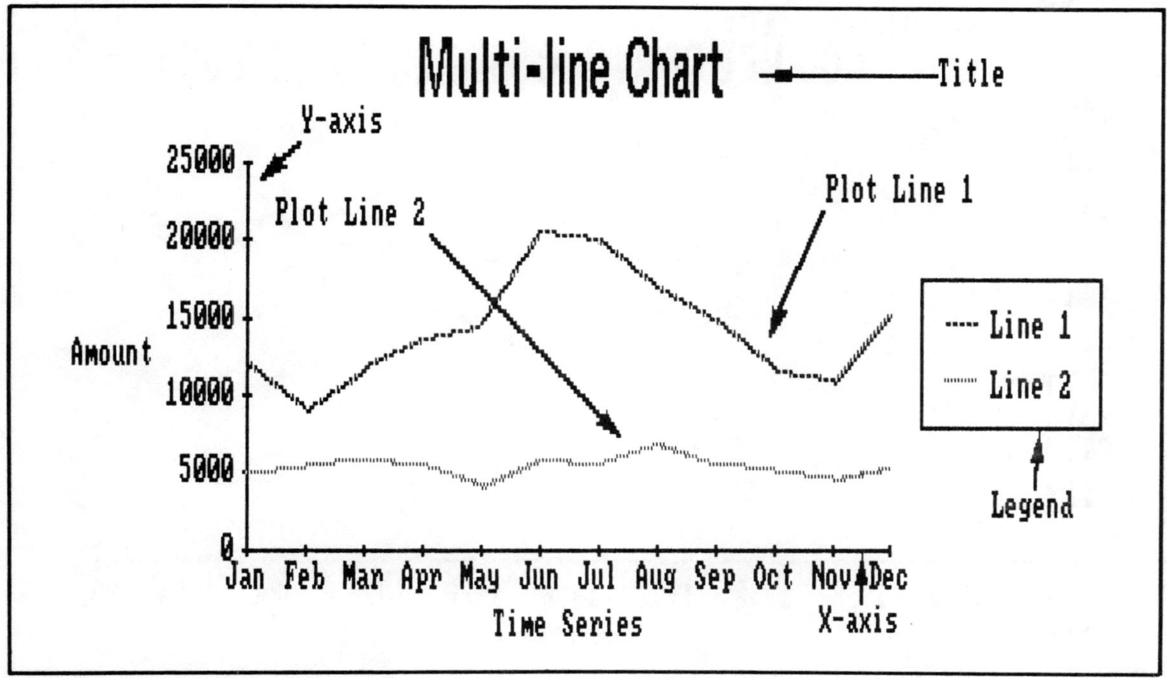

Fig. 5-3. A multiple line graph.

type of graph. The new axis appears (by artistic perspective) to be at right angles to the other two. This axis is called the Z-axis in the Cartesian coordinate system.

Multiple lines can also be used to show high and low values for a data item in a single time period. A third line can be used to show the median or average value of the item. This chart format could be used to compare retail prices of a product by different suppliers, for example.

The surface chart is another variation of the line chart. Surface charts are shaded below the plot line, giving the impression of a hilly surface. A line chart produced in 3-D can also be called a surface chart.

The needle chart is very similar to the surface chart. It is a cross between the line chart and the column chart in that the plot line is a diamond-shaped tip on a line rising from the horizontal axis. This type of chart is also called a *spear* chart. Sometimes the trend line is drawn, and then connected to the horizontal axis by vertical lines at the plotted points.

SINGLE LINES

The single line chart is used to show a trend in the amount or volume of a data item over many time periods as shown in Fig. 5-4. The rise and fall of the line across the time periods specified shows the trend of the item being tracked. If you are plotting consumer prices over a 10-year period, the curve of the line can be associated with world events or used to project the current trend into the future.

The plot line should be darker than the other lines on the graph because it is the area of emphasis. The other lines of the chart should not interfere with the impact of the trend line on the audience.

Grid lines can be used to aid the viewer in analyzing the graph. Light, neutral lines can be projected from the axes to form a grid as shown in Fig. 5-5. Figure 5-6 shows what happens when the grid lines are too dark. The grid lines may be used at any unit value, although common usage would put grid lines at the major divisions with tick marks at half and quarter sub-units.

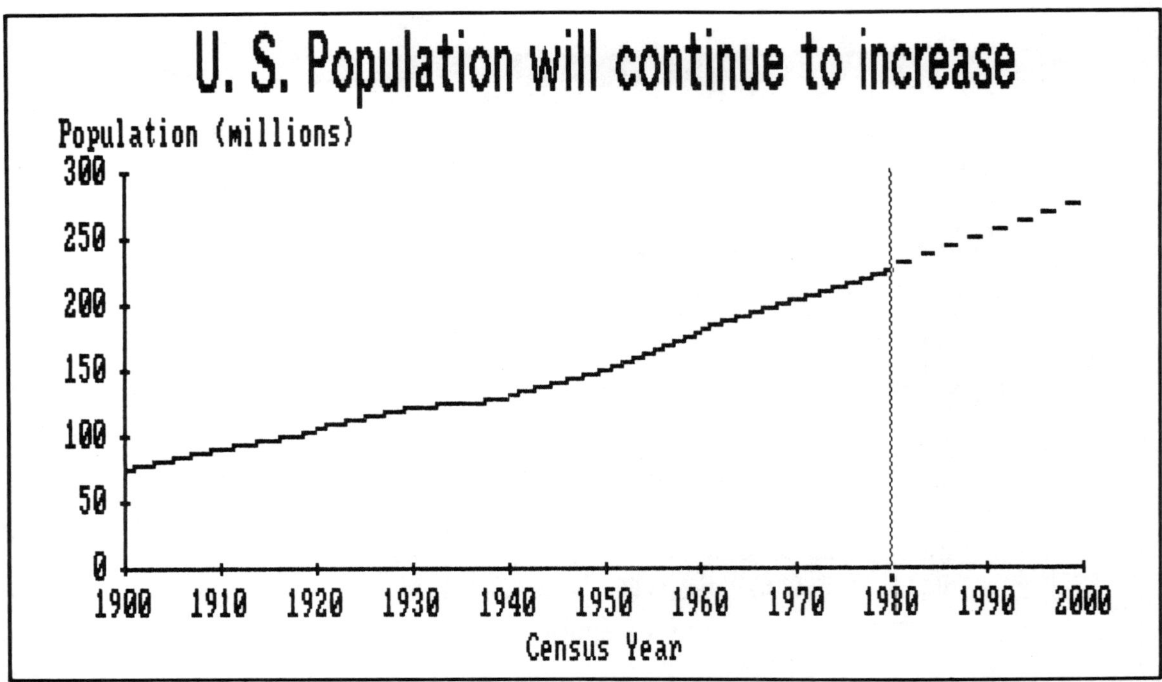

Fig. 5-4. A line chart with a projected trend.

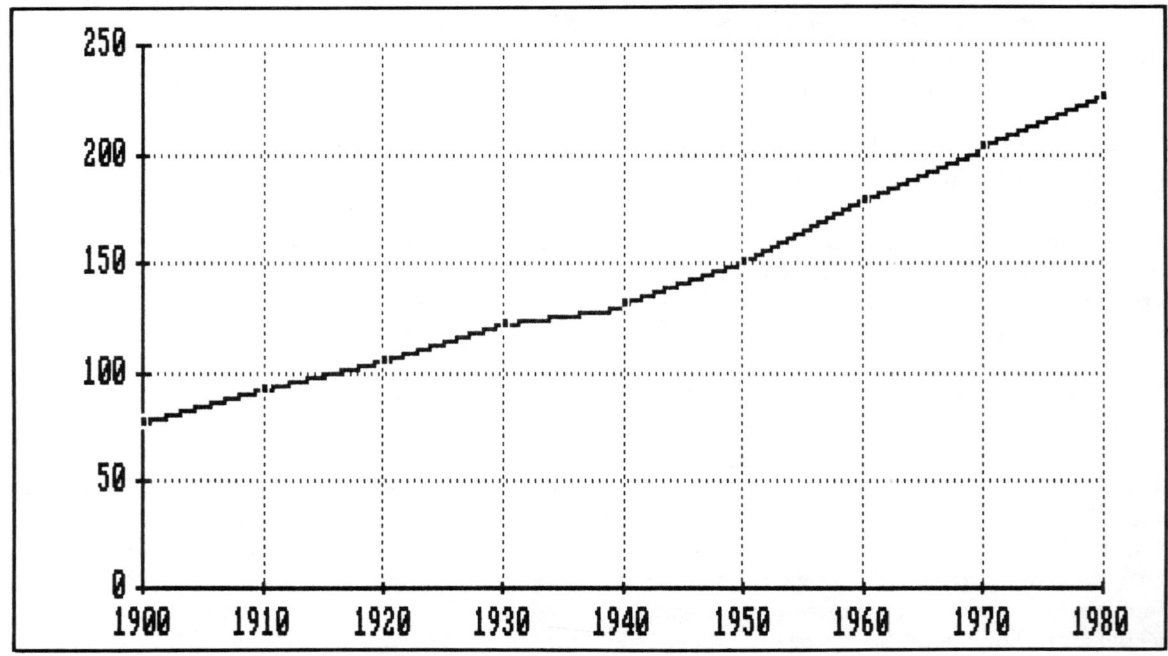

Fig. 5-5. A line chart with light grid lines.

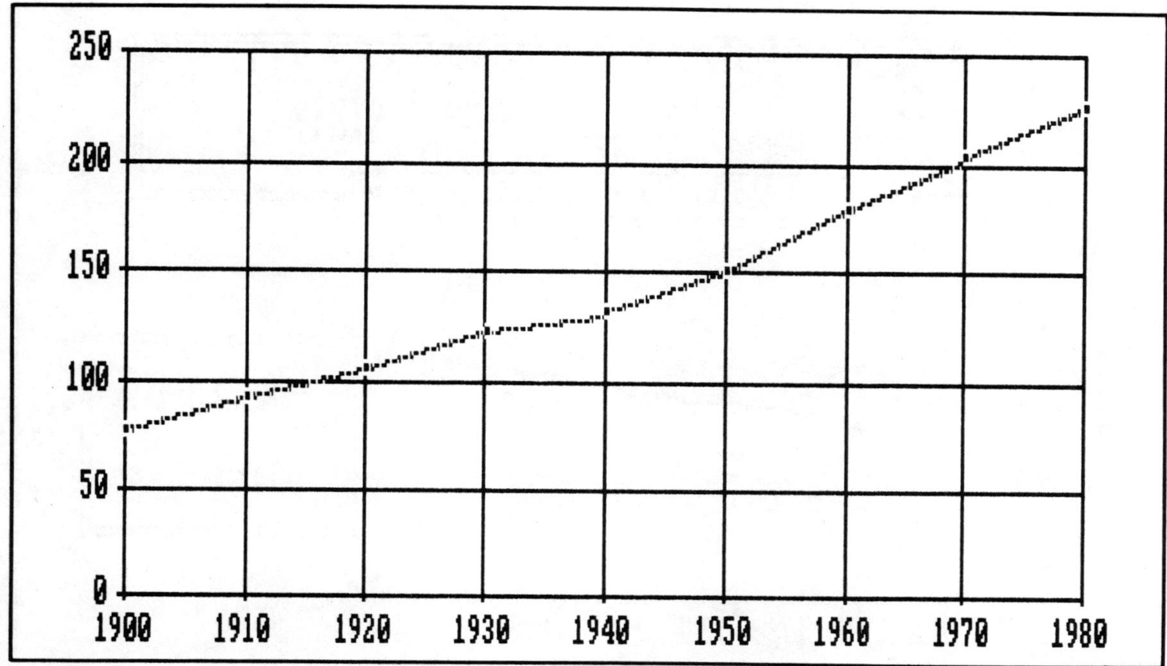

Fig. 5-6. A line chart with heavy grid lines.

The plot line should be a solid, dark line. Dark blue is a good choice for color, if color reproduction is available to you. Red lines, especially on income reports, should be avoided because they can have negative connotations to people of the management persuasion.

Patterned lines, or dot-and-dash lines should be avoided on the single line graph, except where a dashed line is used to show a projected trend. The dashed portion should be clearly marked as a projection.

MULTIPLE LINES

Two or more lines can be shown on a line chart when you are plotting a number of variables over the same time period, as shown on Fig. 5-7. The unit-of-measure for each of the items should be the same, especially where more than two lines are used.

Multiple-lines are used to plot two or more related items. When the items are related, the difference, that is, the area between the lines, is also an important piece of information. For example, two trend lines can be used to plot the income and the expenses of a company through a series of months. The area between the plot lines can be shaded or colored to show profit and/or loss. Labels can be placed directly in the shaded area for ease of analysis.

Multiple-line charts are reproduced best in color. On a black-and-white printout, it is almost impossible to produce a good multiple line chart without using patterned lines. As shown in Fig. 5-8, lines plotted with patterns may be confusing, especially when the trendlines are close together or constantly crossing. This problem is avoided in a color graphic because the lines can be solid in different colors, with a legend to identify the value plotted by each line.

Too many lines on a multiple line graph can be confusing, as shown in Fig. 5-9. The plots will be difficult to read, especially if the chart is reduced using a copier or a photographic technique.

When you are comparing two trend lines of data

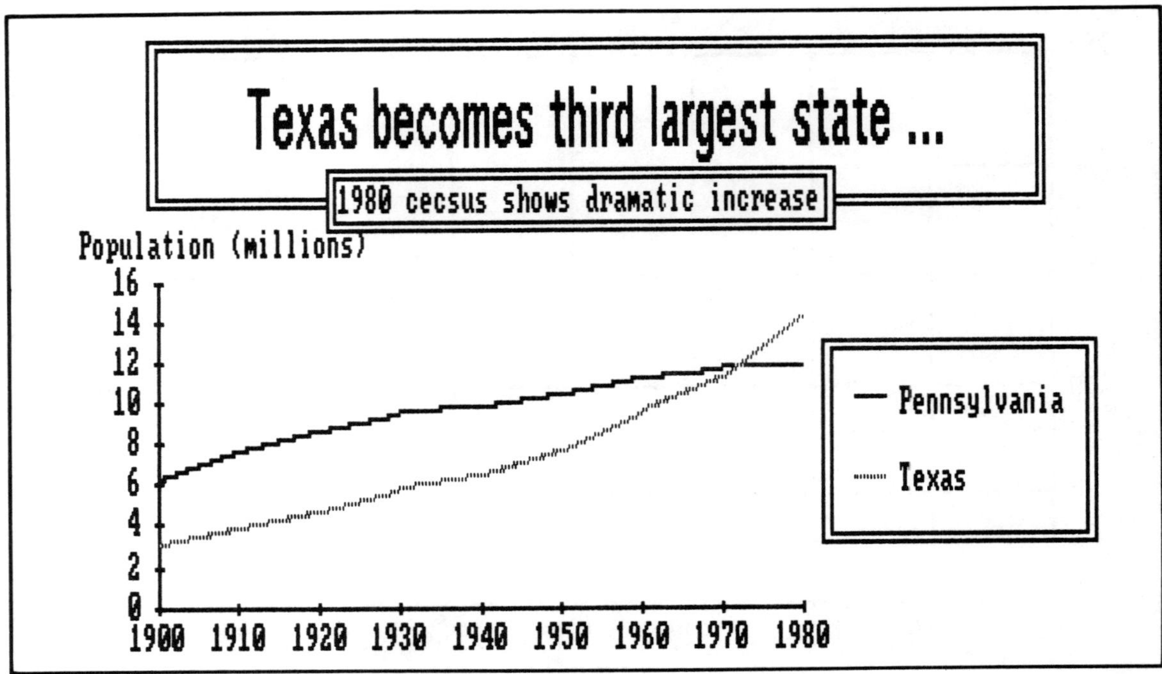

Fig. 5-7. A multiple line chart.

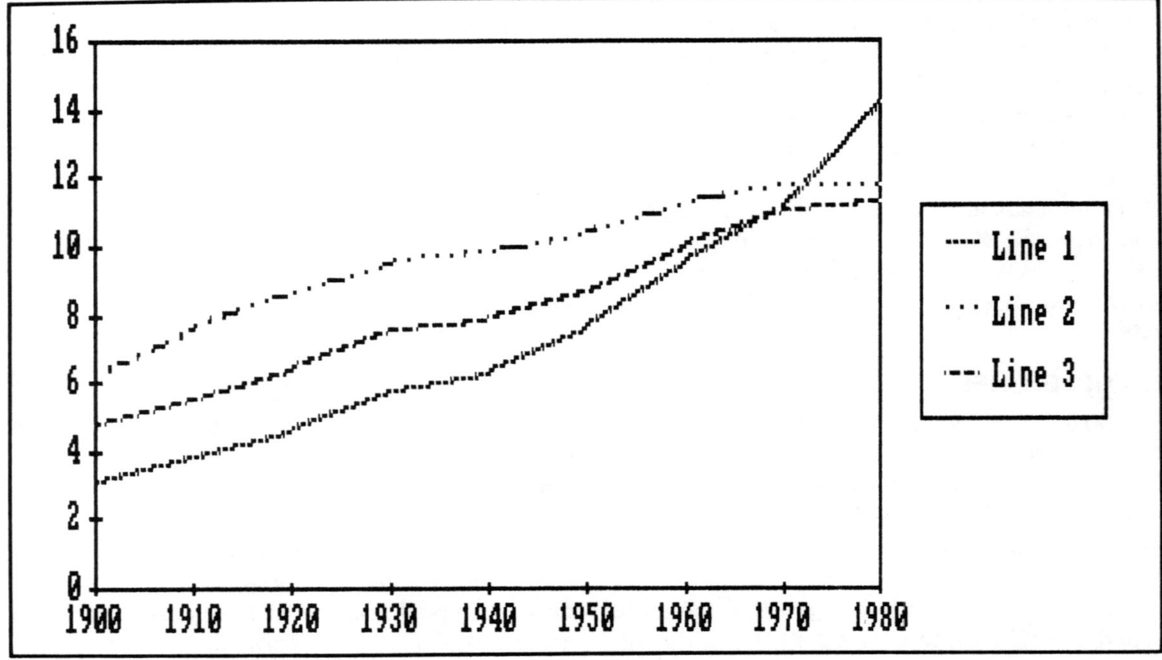

Fig. 5-8. A chart with patterned multiple lines.

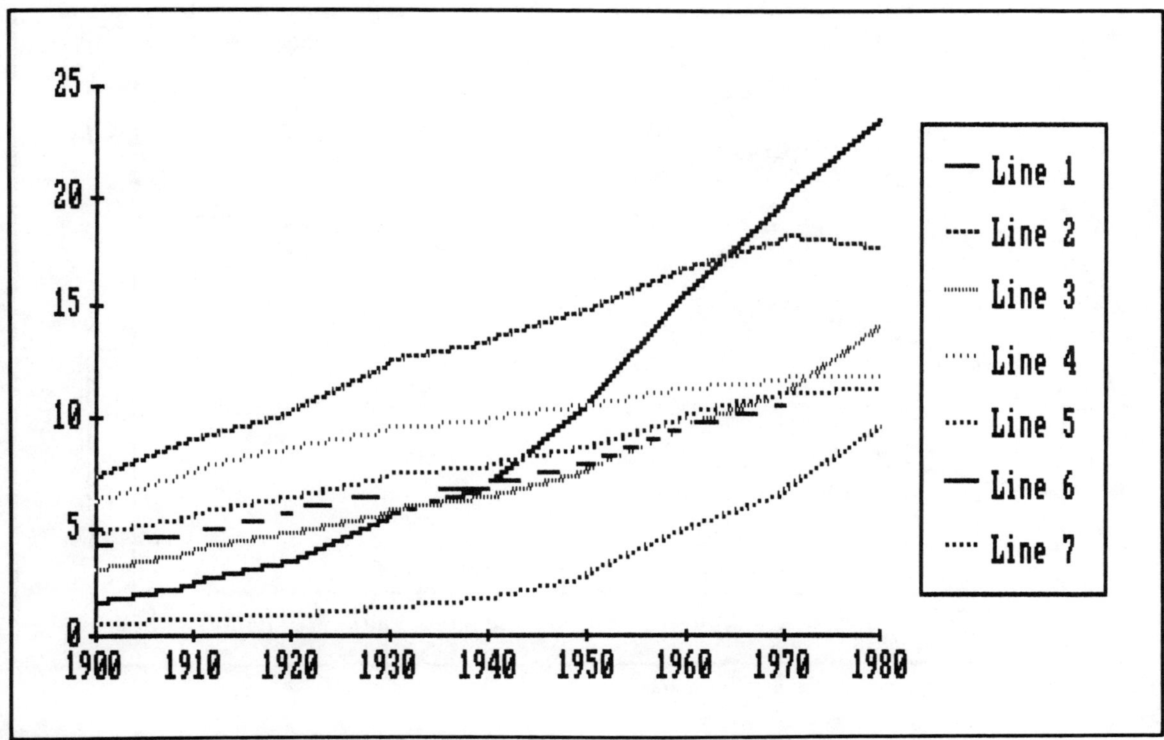

Fig. 5-9. A chart with too many lines.

items with widely varying values, a second vertical scale can be added at the right side of the chart.

MULTIPLE AXES

A graph may have a second vertical scale, which would appear as a third axis on the right side of the graph. This second vertical scale, or "right y-axis," is used when there are two plot lines that differ in their unit of measure. For example, a trend line measured in billions of dollars can be compared to a trend line measured in millions of dollars on the same chart, as shown in Fig. 5-10. The scale on the left side of the graph would be labeled as "billions of dollars," while the right scale would be labeled "millions of dollars." When a second scale is used, be sure to make the use of the second axis clear to the viewer or audience. The trend line should be either colored or labeled in such a way that the viewer instantly knows which scale goes with each line.

3-D LINES

Line charts can be drawn in three dimensions by the use of the third, or Z-axis, and a little artistic perspective. The third axis is drawn at an angle to the other two as shown in Fig. 5-11, even though a true Z-axis would rise perpendicular to the page.

Chapter 3 discussed the use of the horizontal and vertical axes (x-axis and y-axis) to plot data on a Cartesian coordinate system. This coordinate system can include a third axis, the Z-axis, at right angles to both the other axes. The third axis would be impossible to draw on a two-dimensional piece of paper without the use of artistic perspective.

By drawing the Z-axis at an angle on the page, the artist can give the *impression* of depth. Such a graph may look impressive, but it will not be very accurate, especially in the third dimension. Because the position of the Z-axis is approximated by artistic perspective, all points plotted for that scale must also be approximated. As shown in Fig. 5-12,

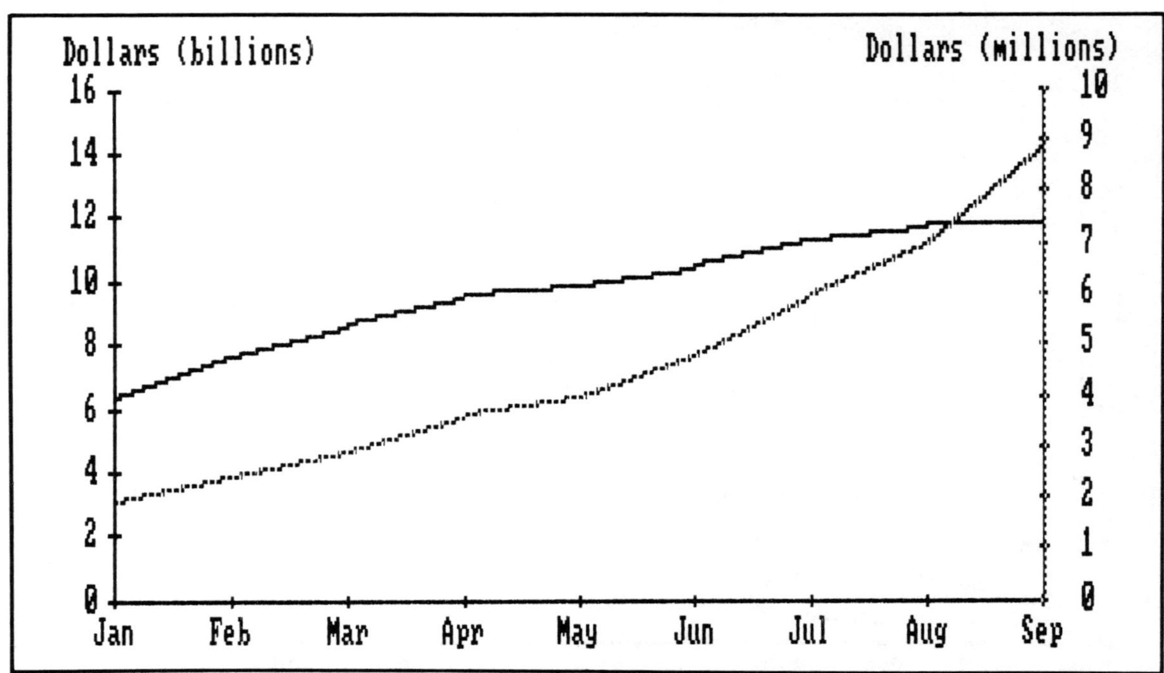

Fig. 5-10. A chart with multiple scales and multiple lines.

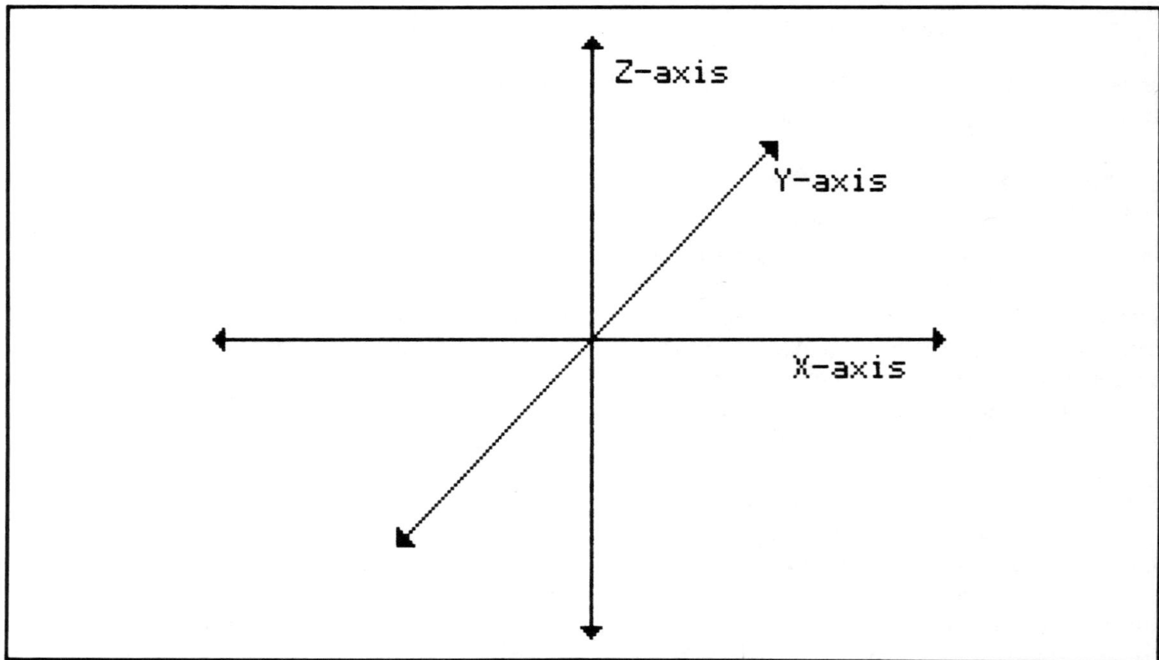

Fig. 5-11. The third axis.

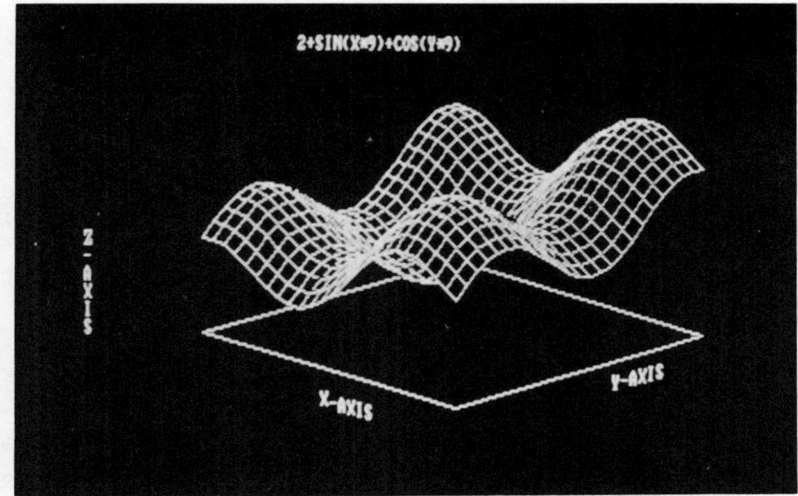

Fig. 5-12. A three-dimensional (net) line chart.

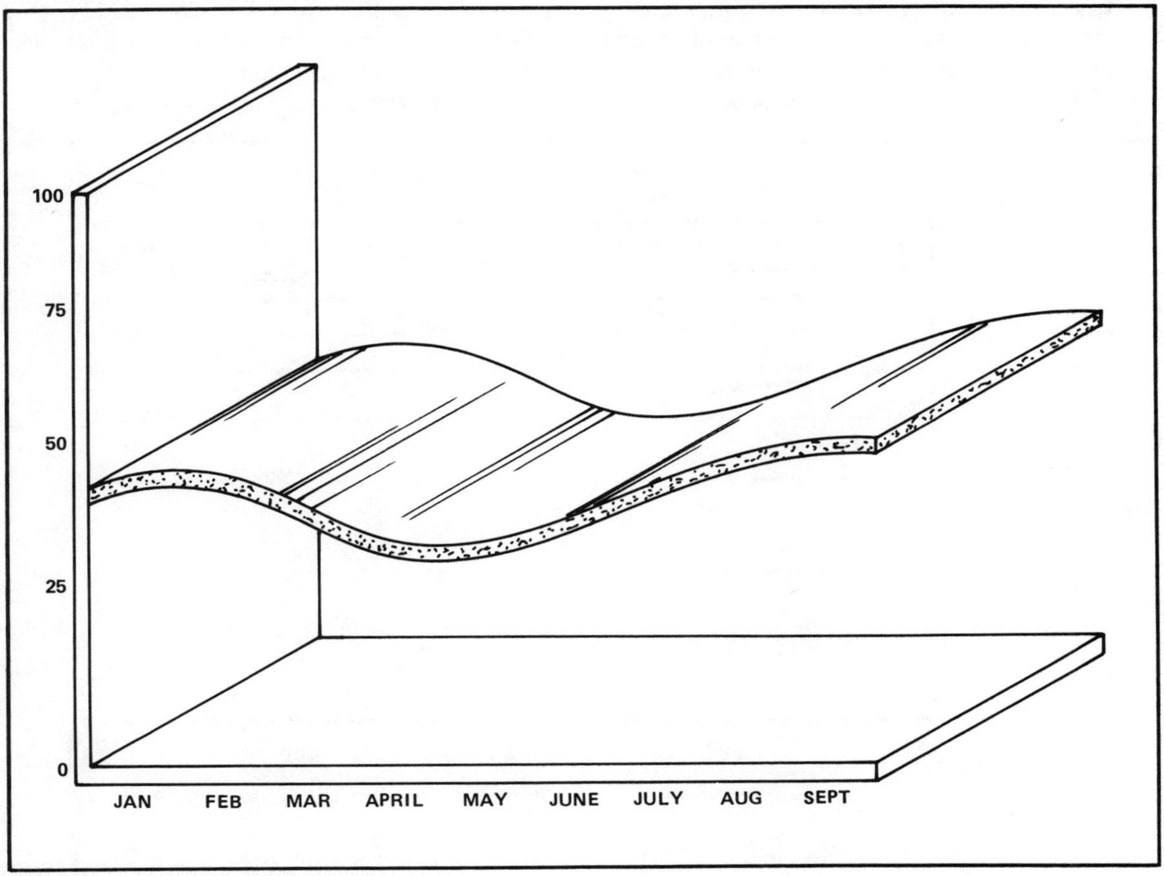

Fig. 5-13. A three-dimensional plot line chart.

microcomputer graphics packages tend to do this sort of calculation very well.

As with other forms of pseudo-dimensionality, the plot produced with artistical perspective techniques will not be easy for most audiences to interpret. The plot line will approximate the values on the Z-axis, rather then really represent them.

Another way of producing a 3-D line chart is to lend perspective to the line itself, as shown in Fig. 5-13. This will make the chart appear like one of the giant slides at an amusement park. This is done with shadowing techniques; this type of format is used more for artistic expression than for actual information exchange.

LOGARITHMIC LINES

Logarithmic line charts have a "semi-log" vertical scale. The plot represents the *rate* of change, rather than an amount or percentage. As shown in Fig. 5-14, this can mislead business audiences, because even a rapid change will look as though the trend is about to start falling.

The logarithmic chart is not usually used for business graphics. The information on such a chart is often very technical or esoteric, and therefore will need more explanation than can be properly provided in either a business report or a presentation.

HIGH-LOW LINES

A multiple-line chart can be used to show high and low values of a data item during a time period. For example, the value of a stock fluctuates between a high and a low value for a single day. The value reported in television newscasts and in the newspapers is really the price that the stock sold for at the last sale of the day, the closing price. As shown in Fig. 5-15, a three-line plot could be used to show the high value, the low value, and the closing price of the stock for the period.

High-low charts can also be created by cross-

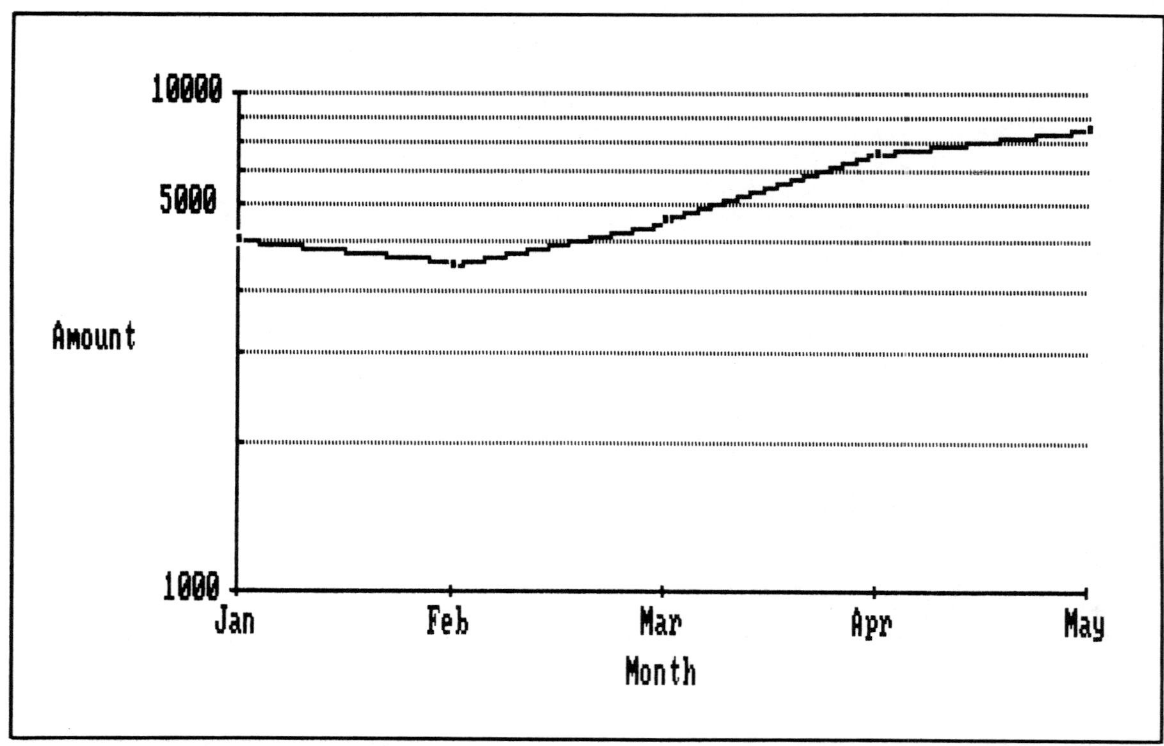

Fig. 5-14. A line chart with a logarithmic scale.

ing a line chart with a bar chart. The bars/columns are partial, that is, they do not reach to the horizontal axis. The top of the bar represents the high value of the item, while the bottom of the bar represents the low value. A line plot is then added to the chart to show the average value of the item.

Stock prices are not the only data that can be tracked using a high-low chart. The prices of various commodities can be tracked this way, as well as temperatures, rainfall, and other climatic information.

SURFACE CHARTS

Surface charts are line charts that are filled in with shading patterns, as shown in Fig. 5-16. The shading gives the impression of a mountain or hill in cross-section. The shading pattern is filled between the plot line and the horizontal axis; in charts with more than one plot line, different shading is filled in between each pair of lines starting with the topmost line and ending with the x-axis.

Surface charts are used to show the difference between two plots when that difference is itself an item of information. The most common example of this kind of chart is the profit/loss chart (Fig. 5-17). The upper line represents the gross income for the company, while the lower line is the total expenses plot. The area between them is the profit realized. If the lines ever cross, a different shading pattern must be used to identify the loss. This type of chart is also known as an area chart.

One variation of the surface chart is a chart in which the subdivisions of the total amount charted are identified. The total amount is the uppermost plotted line in the chart, while the totals for each subdivision are plotted below it and shaded differently. This gives the graph a look of being a pile of different-colored materials. Each shaded area represents the actual contribution of the subdivison.

Another variation is the 100% surface chart, as shown in Fig. 5-18. This type of graph is used to show the proportional contribution of various sub-

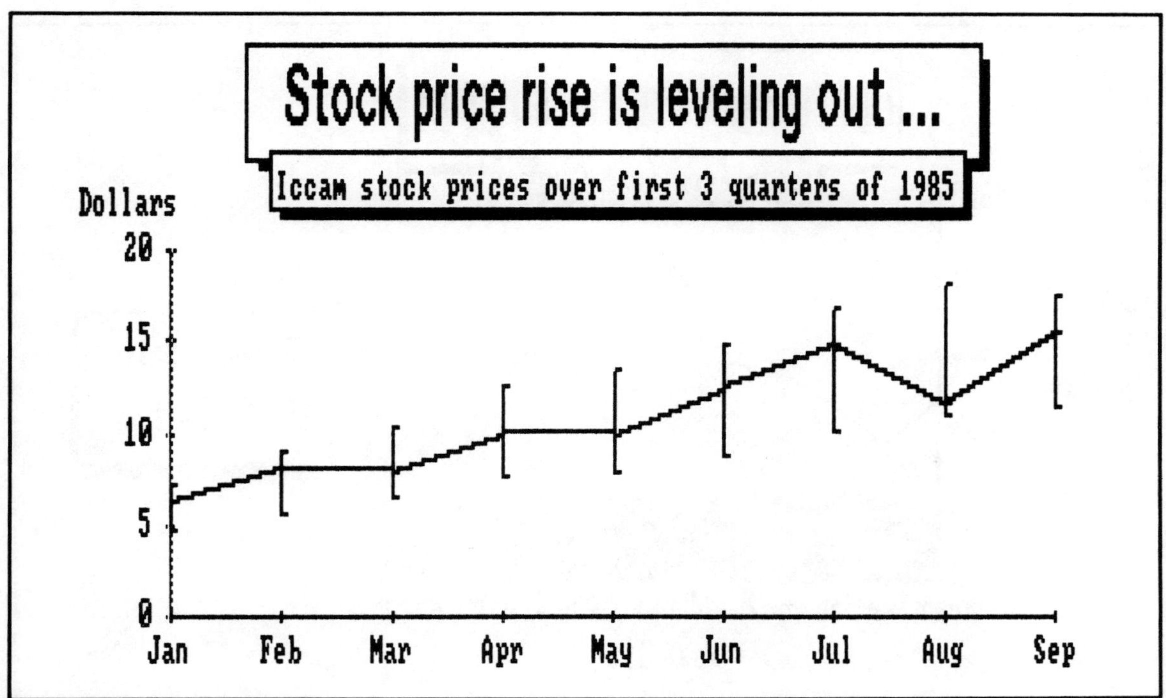

Fig. 5-15. A high-low line chart.

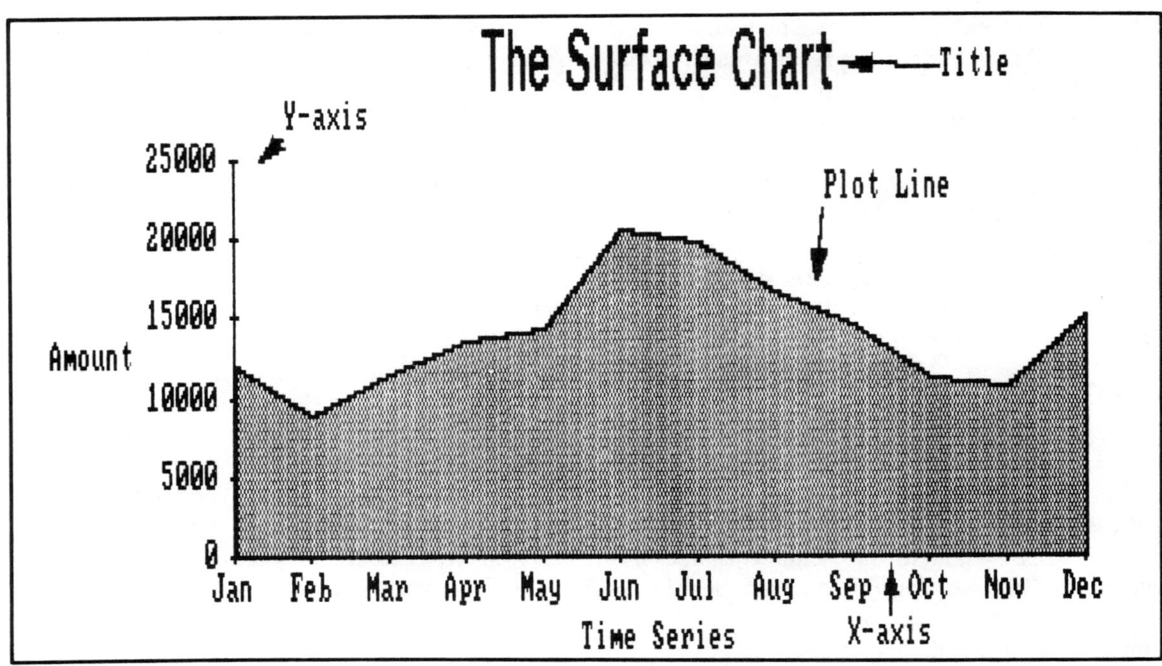

Fig. 5-16. The surface chart.

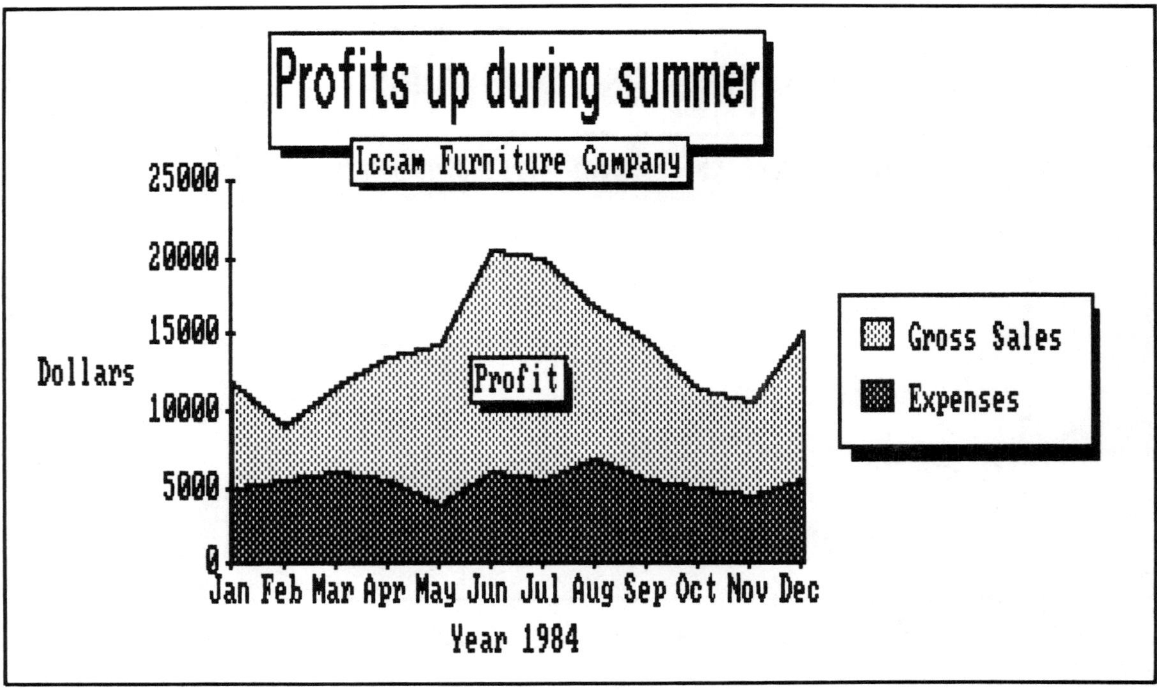

Fig. 5-17. A profit/loss chart.

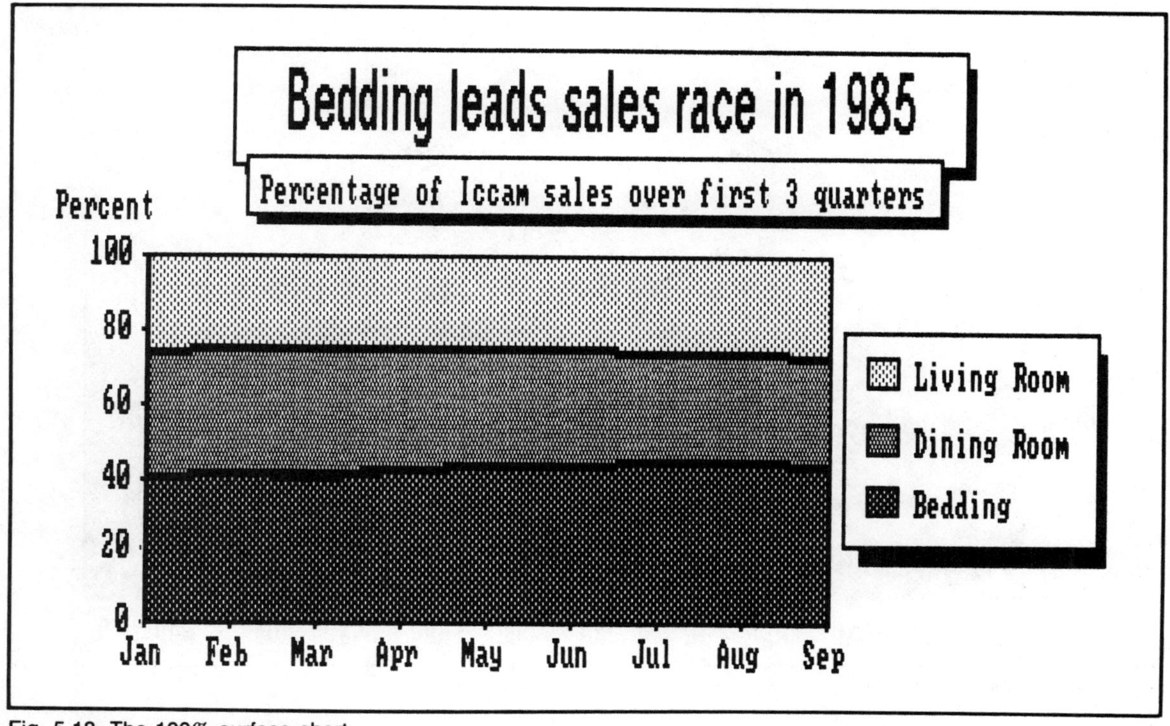

Fig. 5-18. The 100% surface chart.

divisions to a whole. The entire graph is shaded, because the uppermost amount will always be the total. Each subdivision has a different shade or color to represent the ratio of the subdivisional amount to the whole. Most often, pie charts are used to show this type of information, since the 100 percent surface chart and its relative, the whole-bar chart, can cause viewer confusion; it is possible that one subdivision is increasing at a good rate, while other departments are increasing more quickly. This will cause the plot for the particular subdivision to appear to be shrinking, while the department itself is growing.

The shading and/or the coloration of a surface chart should start with the darkest shading or color at the bottom. The patterns should be graduated from darkest at the bottom to the lightest at the top. The background color should not be used as a surface color, because this gives the impression of a hole in the graph.

Surface charts have the advantage of lending solidity to your data by inference. One disadvantage to their use is that not more than four subdivisions can be shown without causing viewer confusion.

One final variation of the surface chart is the three-dimensional surface chart, or net chart. There is no shading on this type of chart; the many plot lines appear as a net strung between the axes. The disadvantage to using this format is that plotted points are not very easy to analyze. The pseudo-depth added by artistic perspective can make it difficult to see what any one particular plot value is.

It is important to remember that when you are producing a subdivided, or *stacked*, surface chart that the angularity of the lowest line will be reflected in the other lines above. this is because the next subdivision's actual total is added above the plot for the first. To avoid misinterpretation, the smoothest or least angular plot should be the closest to the horizontal axis. This can be done by looking at a surface chart of each subdivision separately, and ordering the surface chart according to degrees of

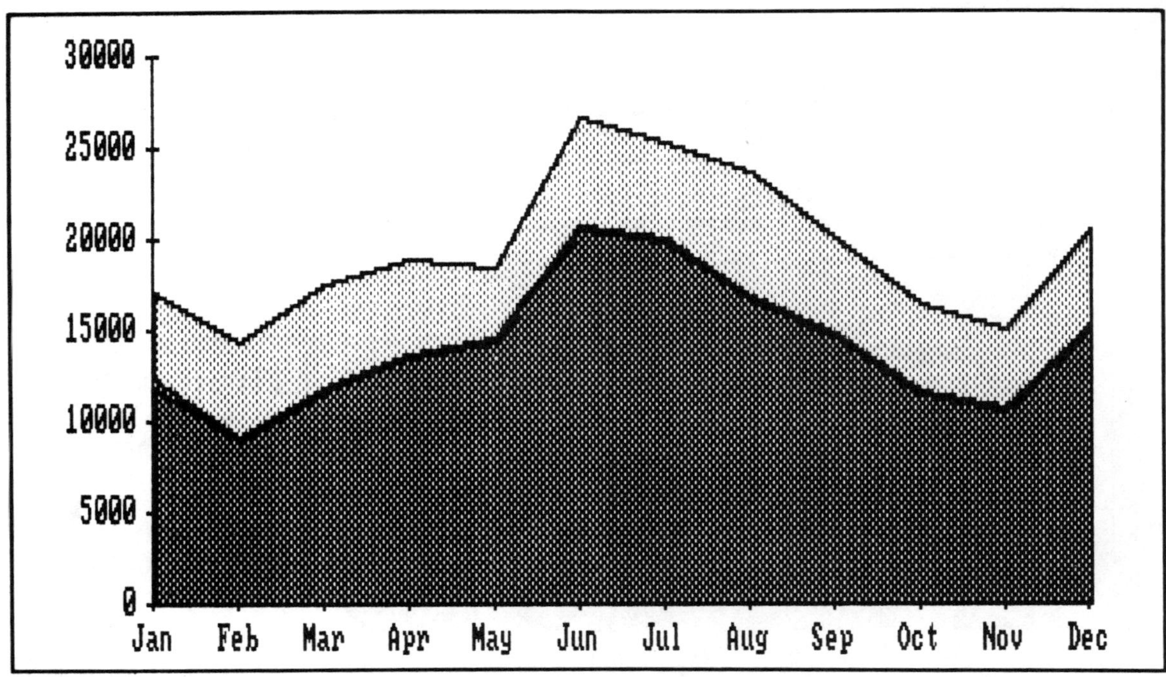

Fig. 5-19. The surface chart with the most angular plot at the bottom.

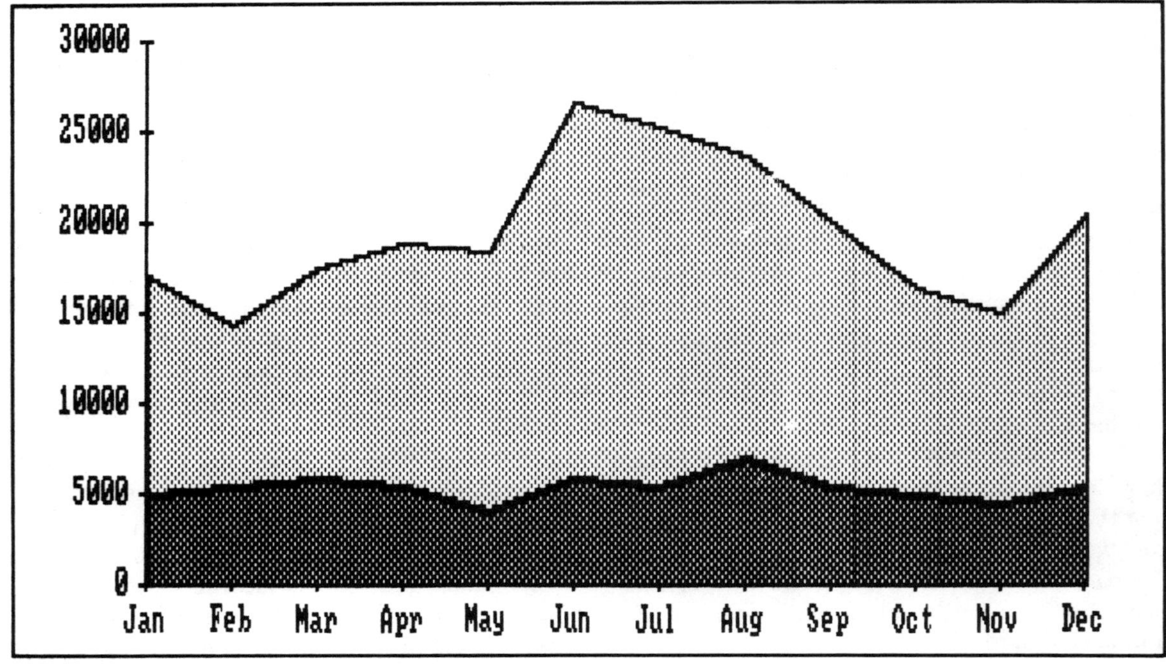

Fig. 5-20. The plot shown in Fig. 5-19 with plots reversed.

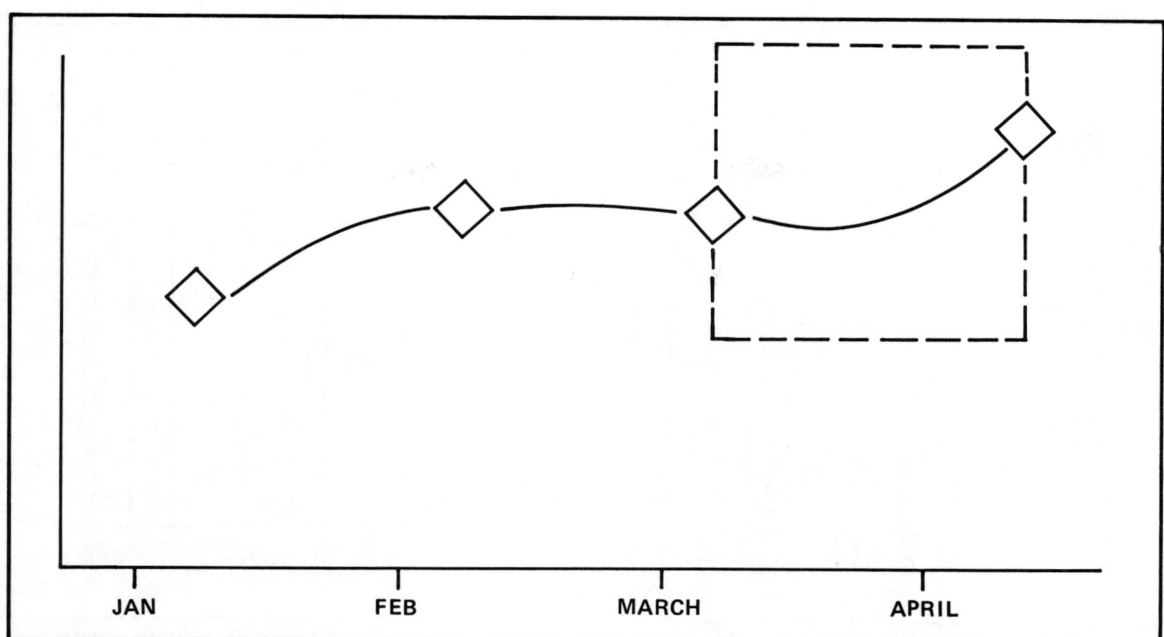

Fig. 5-21. A false rising trend.

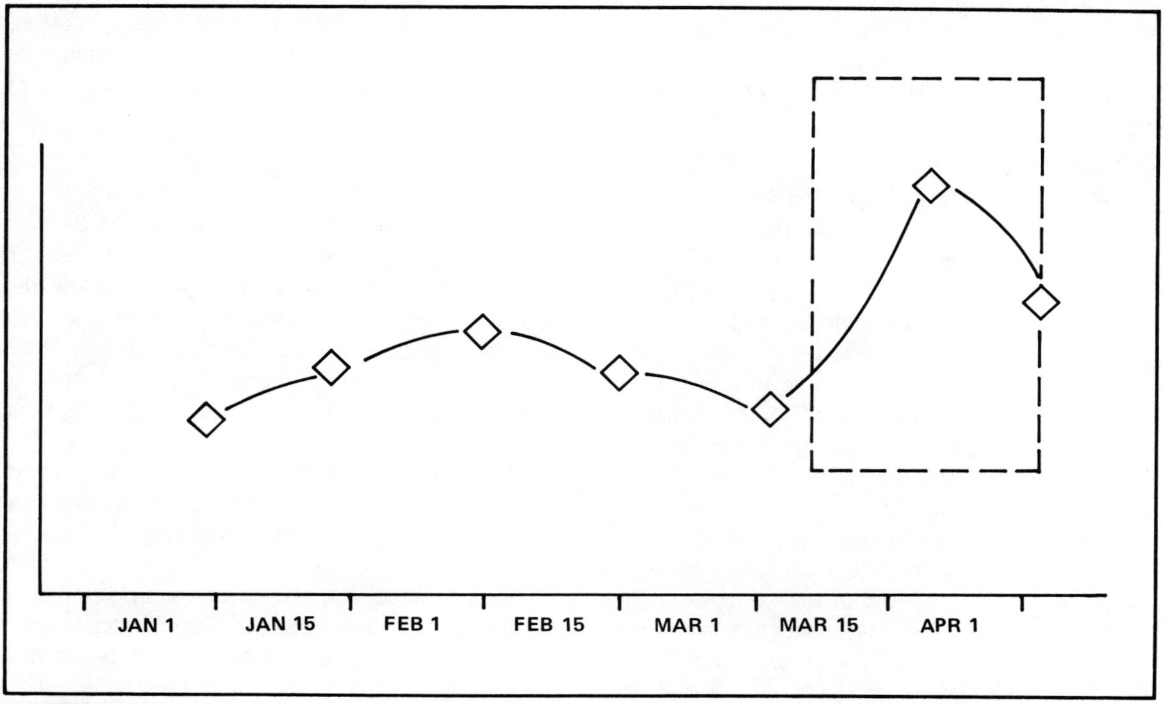

Fig. 5-22. The true trend.

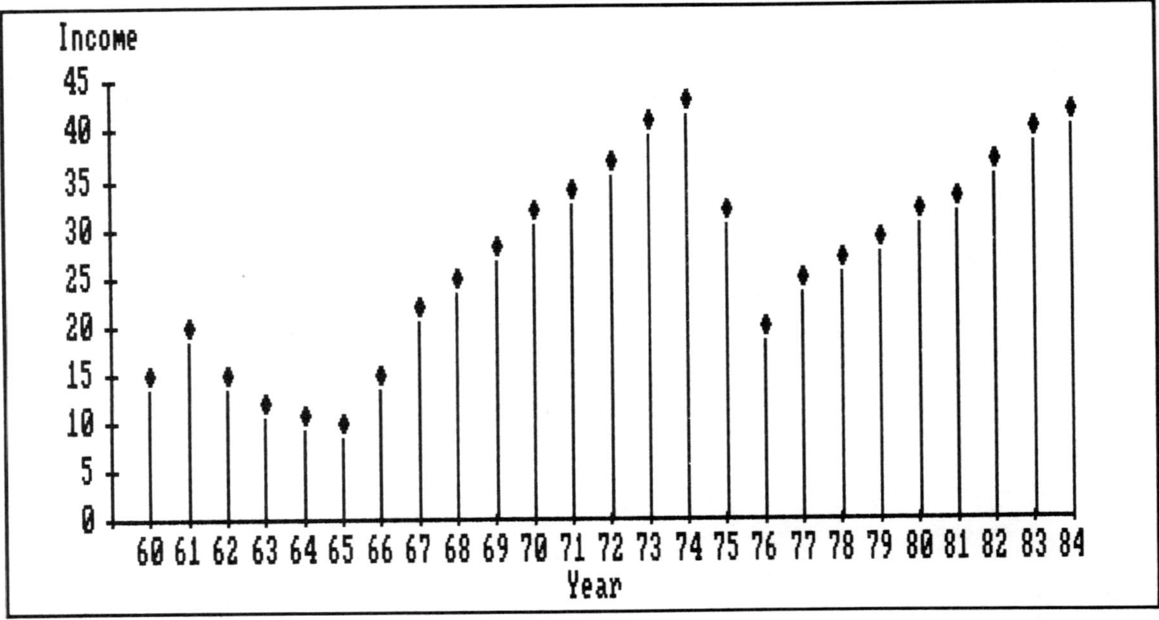

Fig. 5-23. The needle chart.

angularity. The chart should be graduated from the least angular plot at the bottom to the most angular at the top. Figure 5-19 shows a poorly-planned surface chart, and Fig. 5-20 shows a well planned chart.

CURVING THE LINE

When data points are plotted for a line graph, the dots are connected by straight lines. This is because exact data figures are not available for every point between the plotted points. Straight lines indicate this to the viewers of the chart.

With an increase in statistical frequency, that is to say, with more data points available for plotting, the line will be smoother. As the number of available points grows and the spacing between the series decreases, the plot line will cease looking angular and become a curve.

Curving the lines between plotted point without available data can mislead an audience. A falling trend can be made to look as if it was rising, depending whether the curve was toward or away from the horizontal axis. When seen with finer plotting points, the true trend is seen (Figs. 5-21 and 5-22).

Curving the line between the dots gives the impression that more data points have been plotted. To avoid misrepresentation of information, use straight lines where there are few plotted data points.

NEEDLE CHARTS

A needle or spear chart is a variation of the surface chart. As shown in Fig. 5-23, the plotted points are represented by diamond-shaped arrowheads, connected to the horizontal axis by a line. This format is reminiscent of the column chart, with a large number of narrow columns. The plot line is formed by the arrowheads, while the shaft appear like shading below.

Another variation of the needle chart is a chart in which the vertical lines extend to a plot line. This gives the appearance of a very sparsely shaded surface chart.

This type of graph is effective in showing a great many horizontal axis divisions (time periods). Where a bar chart becomes ineffective after six columns or so, the needle chart only *becomes* effective after 15 or 20 spears.

Chapter 6

Pie in the Sky

Man built most nobly when limitations were greatest, and therefore, when most was required of imagination in order to build at all. Limitations have always been the best friends of architecture.

Frank Lloyd Wright

Pie charts are used to show the relation of various items to a whole. As shown in Fig. 6-1, each sector or division of the pie shows the relative proportion of an amount to the total. Pie charts are also known as circle charts, sector charts, and sectograms.

One way of analyzing the pie chart is to imagine the face of a clock superimposed on the circle. The first line is drawn at the twelve o'clock position. Each hour position on the chart would represent 8.3 percent of the whole. A sector that has its boundaries drawn at twelve o'clock and three o'clock would represent 25 percent of the total.

Pie charts can be a very effective way of showing partial contributions to a whole. Some variations of the pie chart can be used to emphasize specific sectors or the impact of the chart as a whole. For example, if you are graphing the destination of each portion of a dollar of income, the circle could, by addition of artistic perspective and shading, become a coin, as shown in Fig. 6-2. The circle could become a clock face, showing the portions of each day devoted to certain activities.

Another variation shows the sectors of the circle divided and separated. This exploded pie can be used to emphasize one or more individual sectors. One pie slice can be separated from the others to emphasize that particular sector.

When a sector is itself comprised of several subdivisions, a whole bar can be added to the pie chart to show the relative contributions of each subdivision of a sector to the sector. In this case, the bar represents 100 percent of the sector, not of the entire pie.

THE BASIC PIE CHART

The total amount of whatever you are graphing is represented by the circle or pie. This can be 100 percent of something, or a total number of dollars, people, or items. Each sector of the pie represents a component of the whole.

Each sector of the pie chart should be labeled with the name of the subdivision. A legend can be used to identify the subdivisions by the pattern of shading used. Additional labels can be used to show

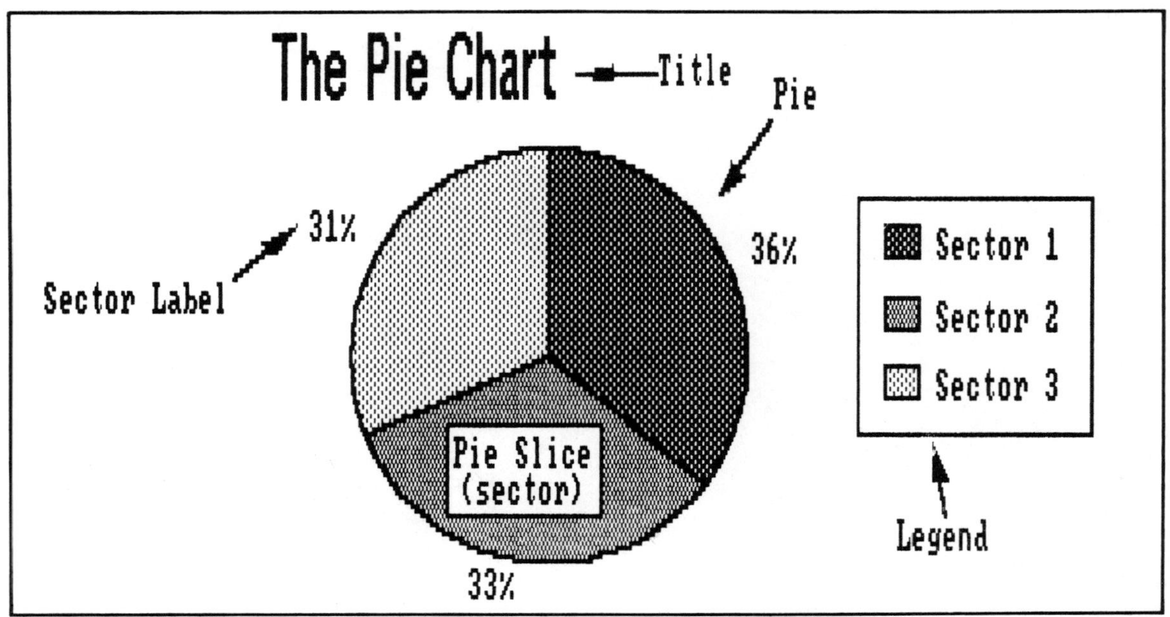

Fig. 6-1. The pie chart.

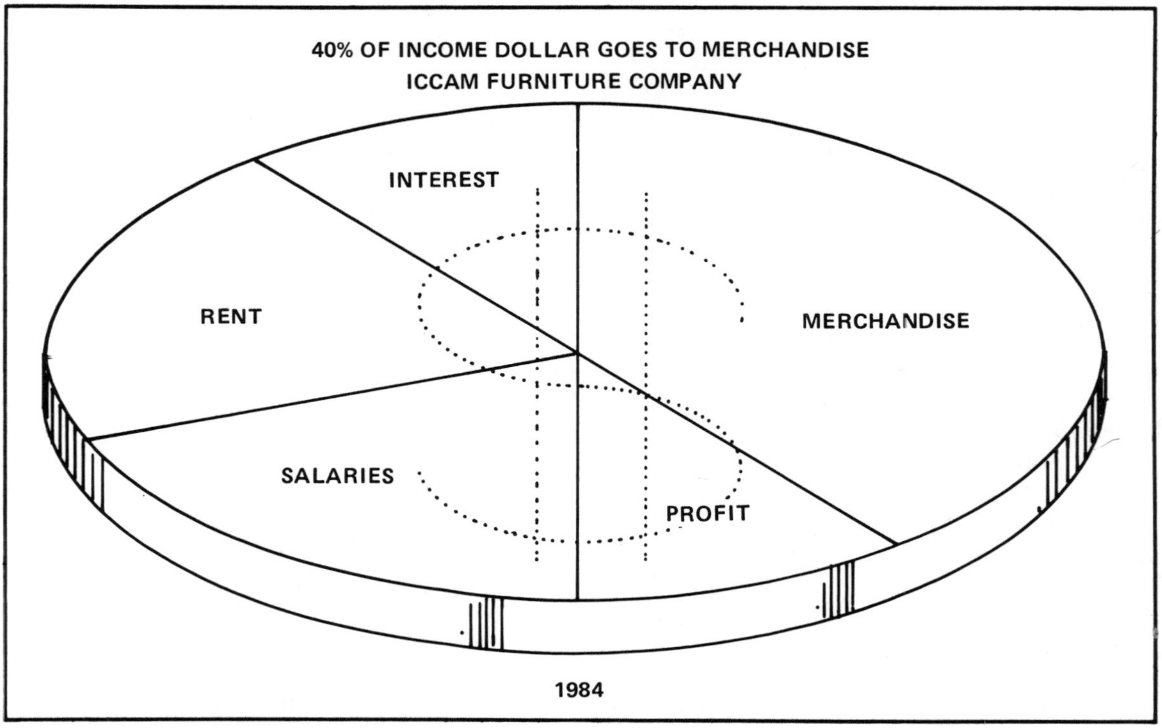

Fig. 6-2. The coin chart.

the percentage or amount actually represented by each sector. Additionally, when you are showing amounts, the total amount represented by the pie can be placed at the center of the pie or below the pie.

For example, a presentation on affirmative action might include a pie chart showing the ratio of male to female employees of a company. The amounts can be represented as percentages, 45 percent women to 55 percent men (Fig. 6-3); the proportions can also be represented by the actual numerical amounts, 49500 women to 60500 men yields 110,000 total employees (Fig. 6-4).

Most pie charts have three, four, or five divisions. Too many slices can cause the chart to look cluttered, and make the relative proportions unclear.

One method of avoiding the too-cluttered pie chart is to combine several minor subdivisions into one slice labeled "other" or "miscellaneous", as shown in Fig. 6-5. If necessary, the minor subdivisions can be broken out using a whole-bar representation of the slice.

Generally speaking, the largest sector of the pie should be the first slice clockwise from the vertical. The sections are graduated from largest to smallest as you proceed clockwise. The exception to this rule occurs when a "miscellaneous" or "other" slice is used to represent several minor subdivisions. The "other" slice is always the first slice counterclockwise from the vertical, or the last slice as you proceed clockwise.

When you need to show the proportional growth or shrinkage of a subdivision, several pie charts may be used. Each pie may be labeled with a time period, such as a year, or may represent the relative proportions of the same data items across companies or departments (Fig. 6-6).

Several pies can appear on the same page. While all pies are usually the same size, it is possible to use proportional sizing techniques to emphasize differences in the amounts that the pies represent. For example, a company presentation might include a pie chart showing the proportion of income from various sources ten years ago, and

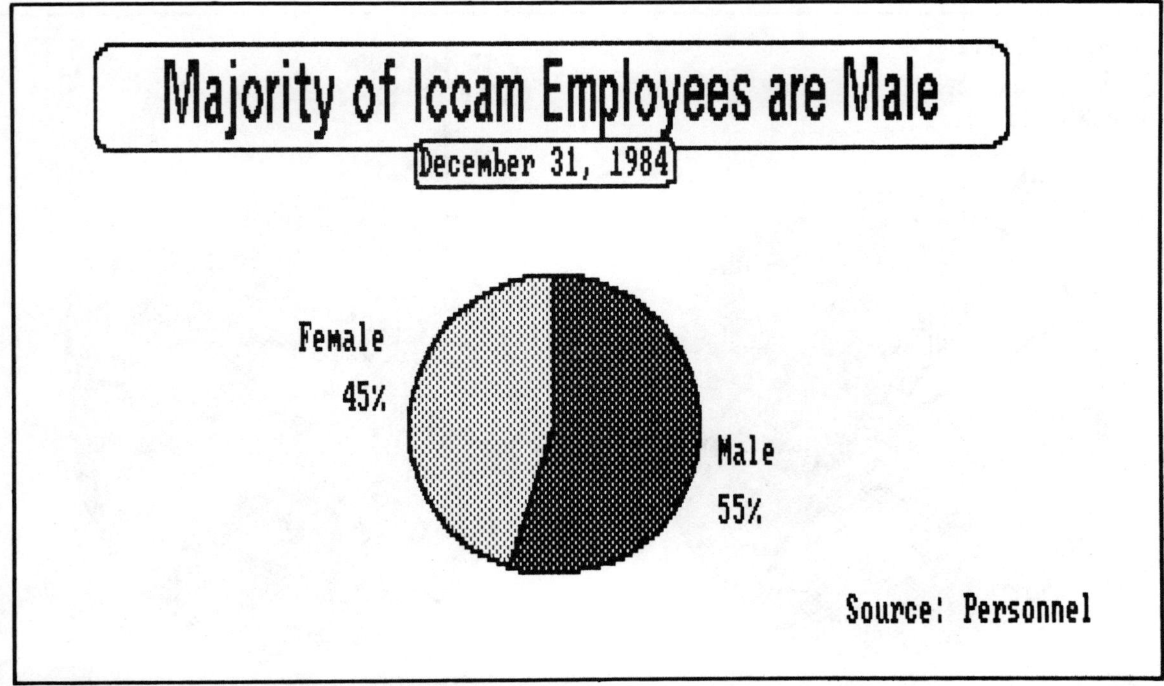

Fig. 6-3. A pie chart with totals represented as percentages.

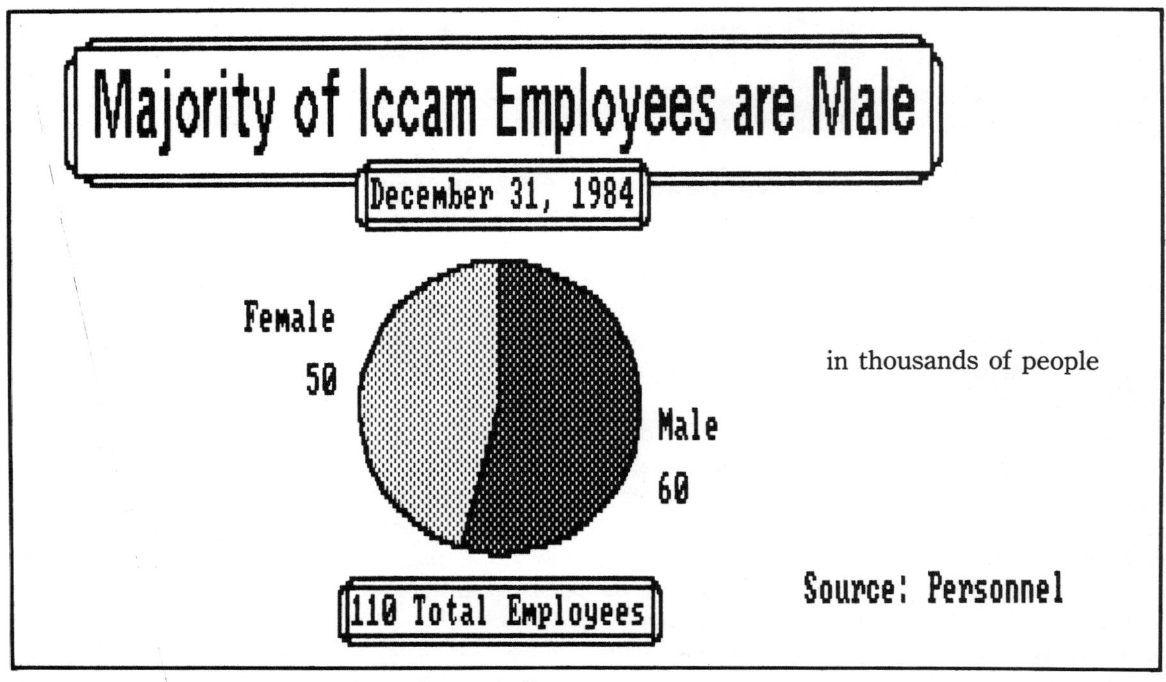

Fig. 6-4. A pie chart with totals represented as amounts.

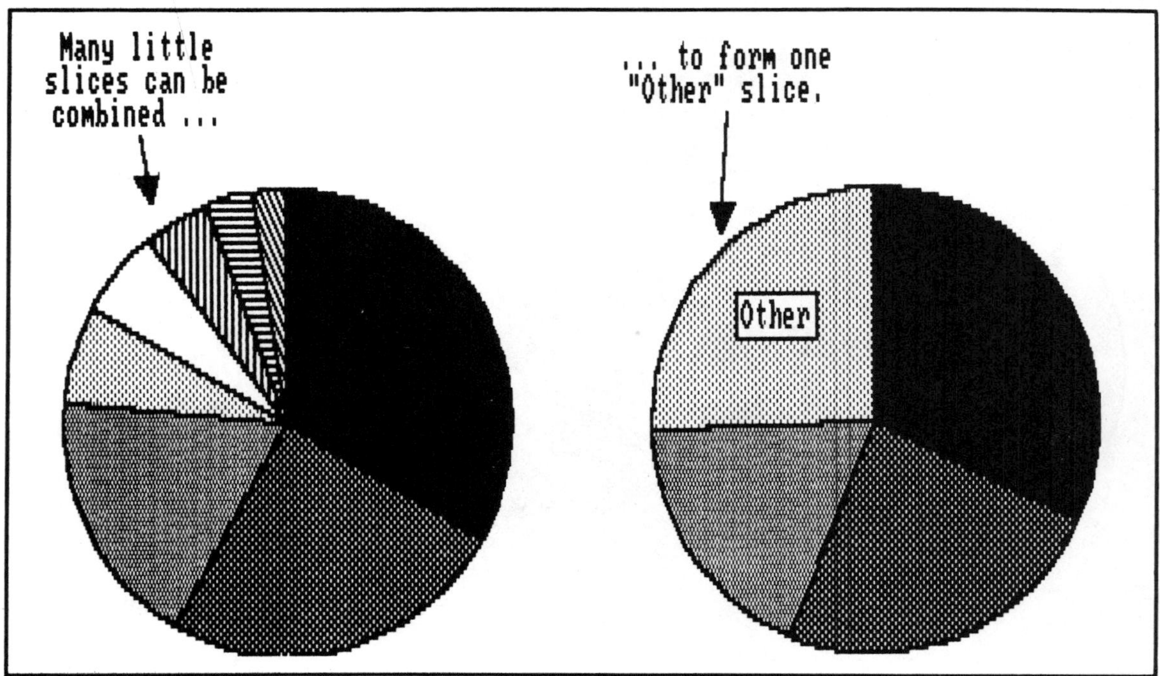

Fig. 6-5. The other slice.

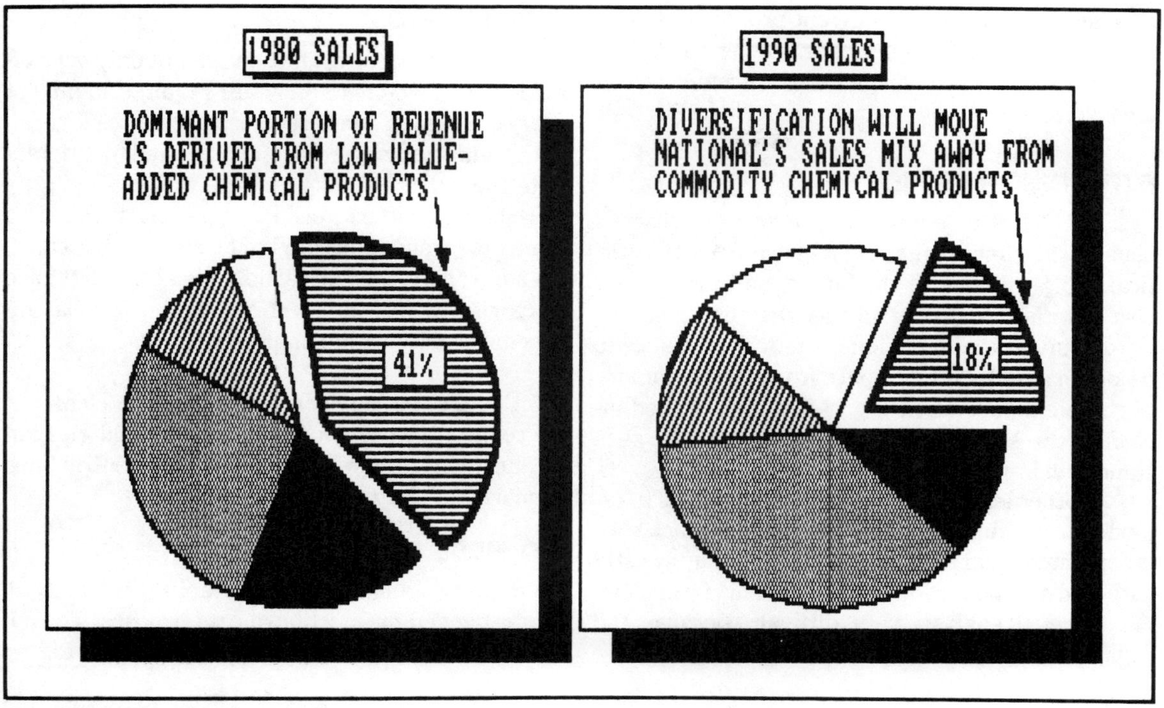

1980 SALES
DOMINANT PORTION OF REVENUE IS DERIVED FROM LOW VALUE-ADDED CHEMICAL PRODUCTS
41%
1990 SALES
DIVERSIFICATION WILL MOVE NATIONAL'S SALES MIX AWAY FROM COMMODITY CHEMICAL PRODUCTS
18%

Fig. 6-6. Multiple pies.

Sales show dramatic increase since 1970
$115,000
1970
$325,000
1980
Bedding
Dining Room
Living Room

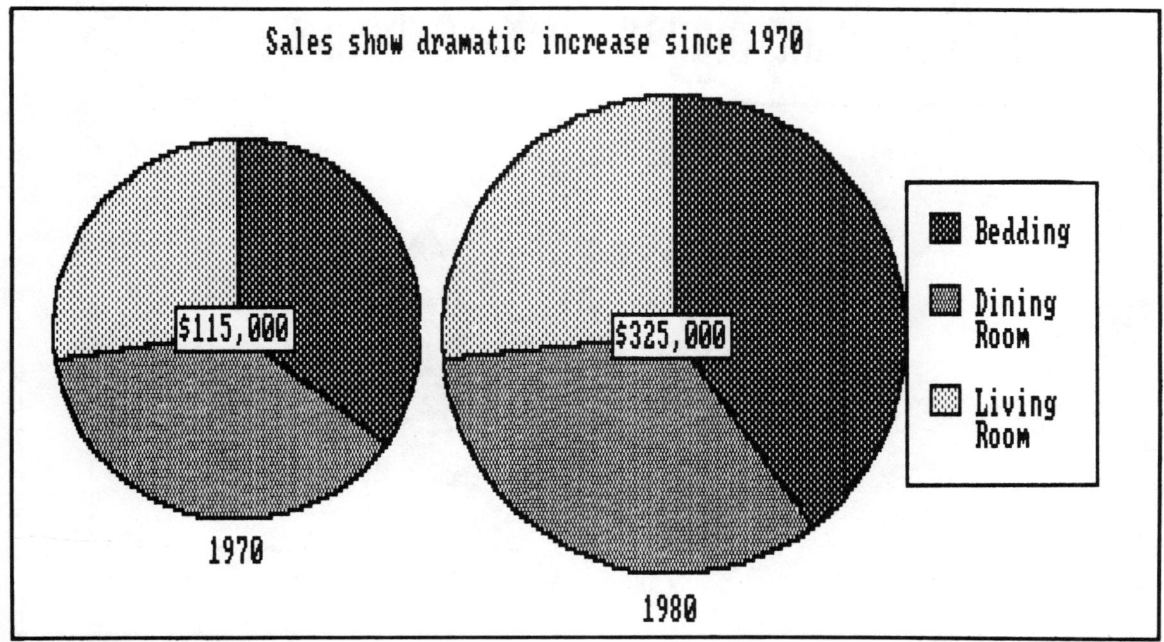

Fig. 6-7. Proportional pies.

another pie showing the current proportions. The second pie can be sized larger or smaller depending on whether the actual amount of income has increased or decreased for current period. (Fig. 6-7).

EXPLODING THE PIE

The "slice of emphasis" for the pie chart is usually the first segment clockwise from the vertical. This will also be the largest and the darkest slice, as discussed later in this chapter.

An often-used technique is moving the slice to be emphasized slightly apart from the remainder of the pie as shown in Fig. 6-8. This is called *exploding* the slice. The separation makes the slice stand out in the eyes of the viewer.

Another less commonly used technique is to explode the entire pie, as shown in Fig. 6-9. Each slice is separated from the others, although they are still gathered around a common center. This format can make visual analysis very difficult, because the separation inhibits comparisons.

RICH FILLINGS

Shading and/or coloration are not only very effective on a pie chart, they are required in almost every case. Each sector represents a unique division of the whole, so some way must be used to differentiate the sectors.

Shading patterns used on a pie chart should be graduated from darkest to lightest as on a bar chart. On a pie chart, the dark shading is at the first slice clockwise from the vertical, and the shading becomes lighter as you proceed clockwise, as shown in Fig. 6-10.

Boundaries between sectors will be clearer if the colors are well matched. Unclear boundaries can be alleviated somewhat by using dark neutral lines to mark the sectors.

3-D PIES

Flat, two-dimensional pie graphs are usually all that is needed for most business purposes. The addition of a little perspective, however, can add an

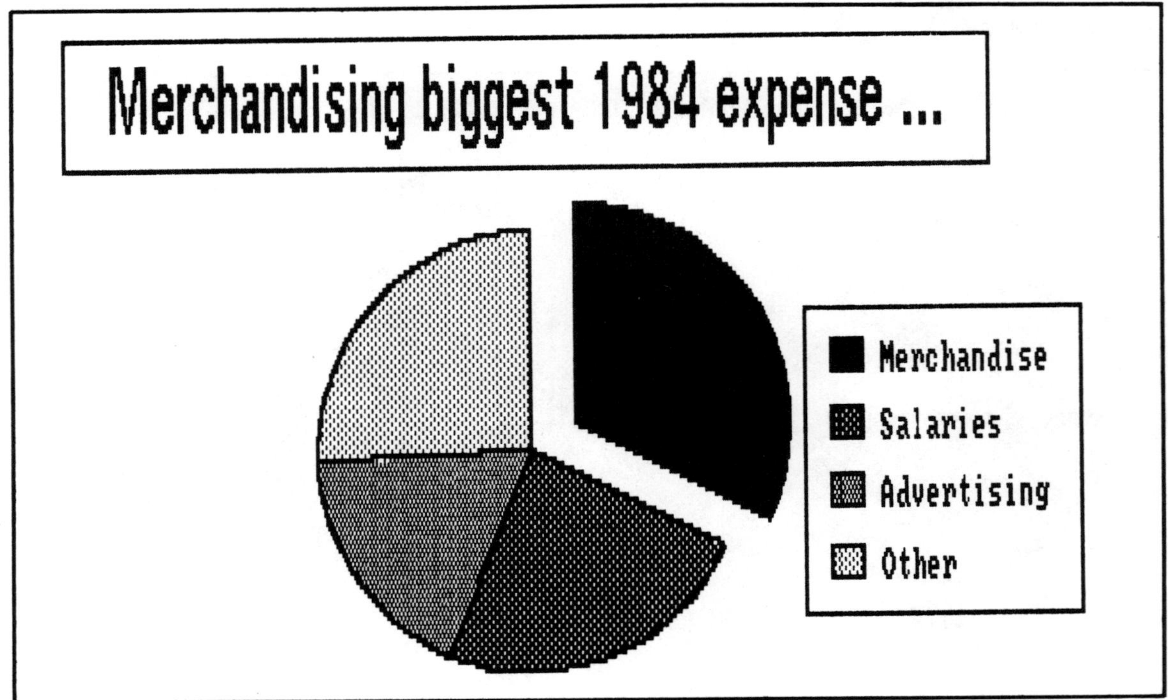

Fig. 6-8. The exploded slice.

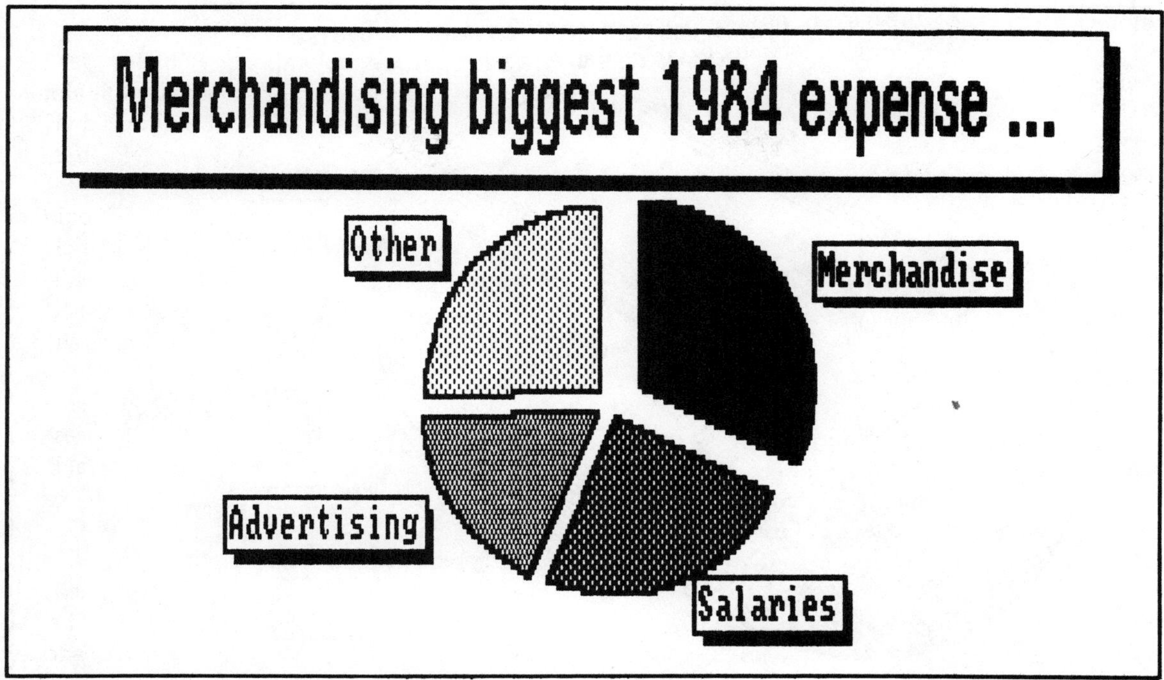

Fig. 6-9. A pie chart with all slices exploded.

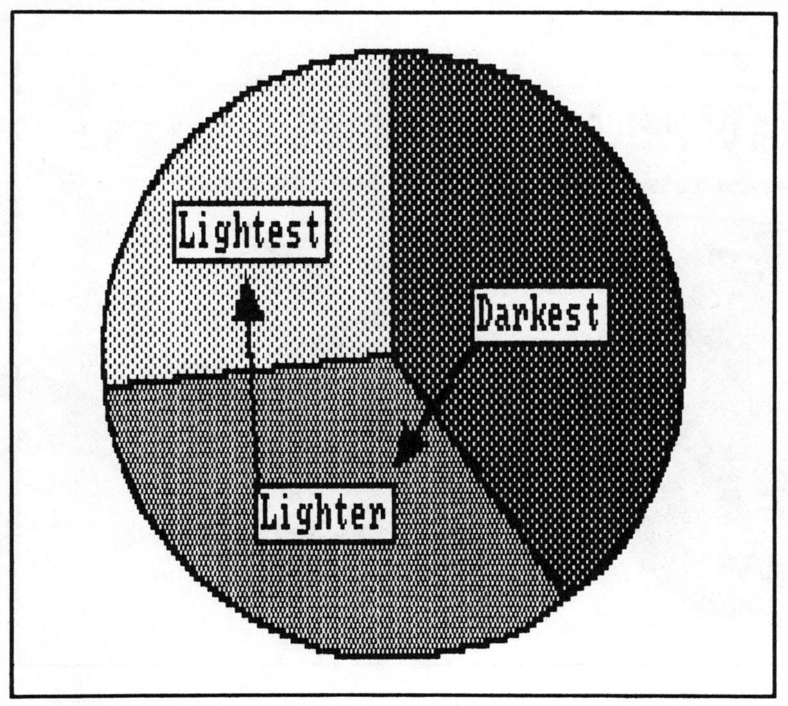

Fig. 6-10. Shading the pie chart.

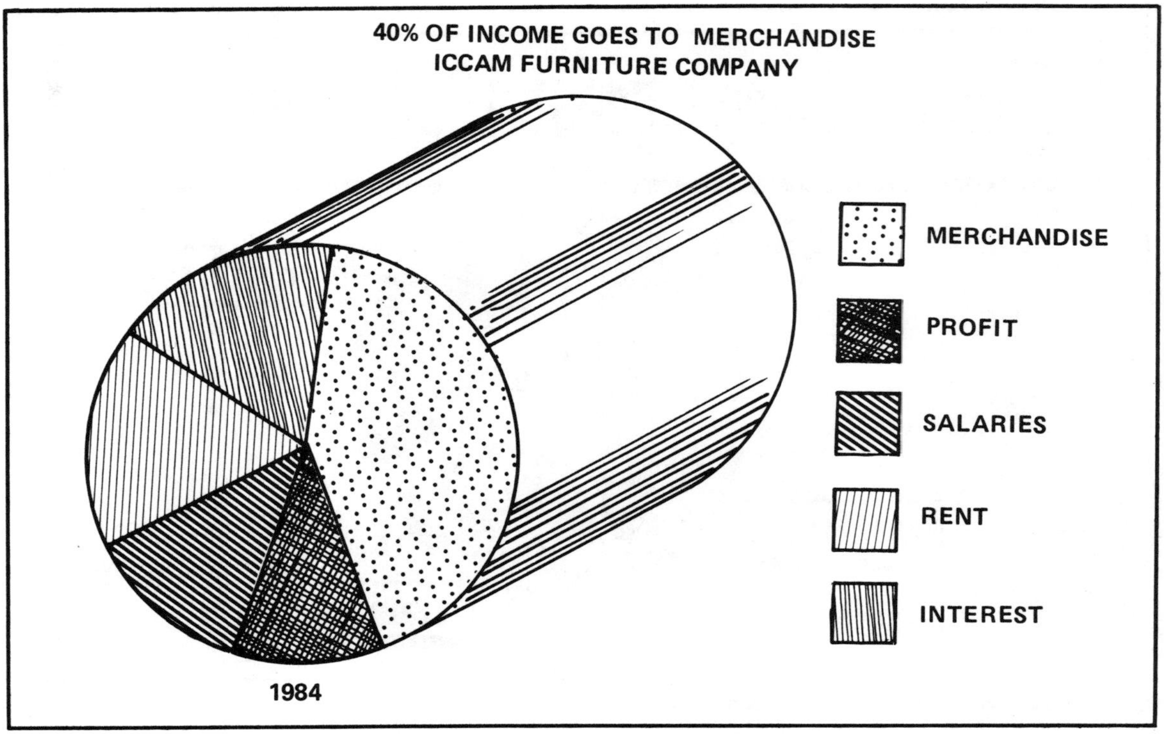

40% OF INCOME GOES TO MERCHANDISE
ICCAM FURNITURE COMPANY
MERCHANDISE
PROFIT
SALARIES
RENT
INTEREST
1984

Fig. 6-11. The three-dimensional pie.

Division of Merchandising Expenses
Other
Merchandise
Advertising
Salaries
Misc.
Living Room
Dining Room
Bedding

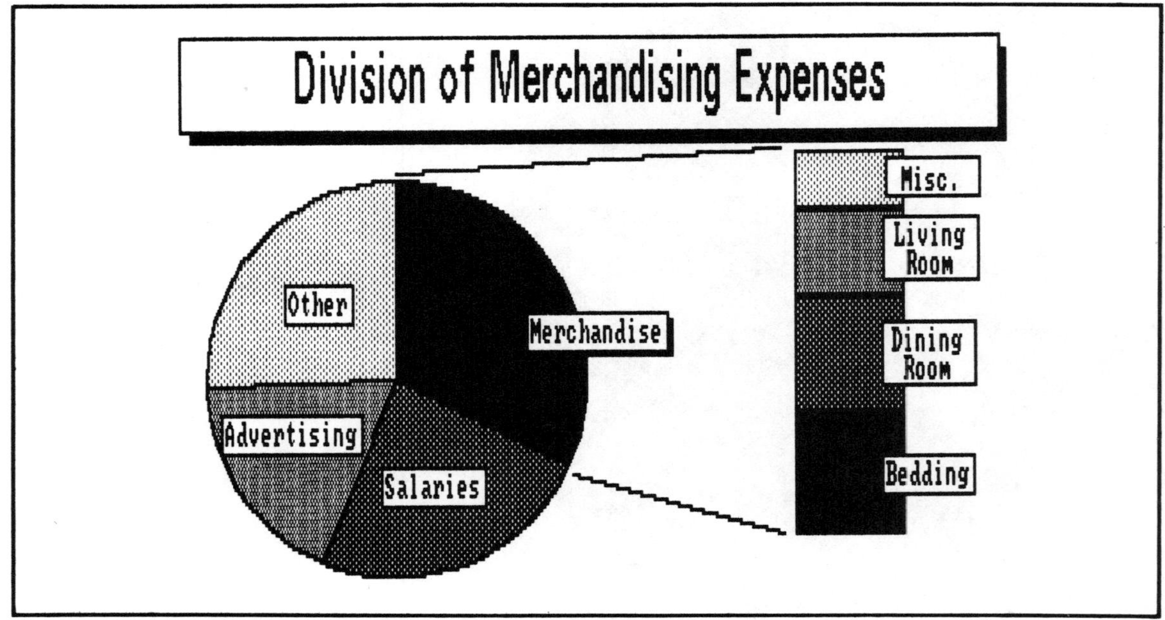

Fig. 6-12. A pie chart with a bar.

artistic flair to a pie chart when needed, as shown in Fig. 6-11.

The addition of shadow can give the pie an illusion of depth. This can be used with vertical shading to make the pie appear like a coin, to enhance "division of a dollar" pie charts.

BARS WITH PIES

Sometimes, a major section of the pie chart must be broken into further subdivisions. Rather than adding more sectors to the chart, a whole bar can be shown projecting from the subdivided slice by drawing dashed lines from the corners of the sector to the top and bottom of the bar, as shown in Fig. 6-12.

The whole bar shows 100 percent of the sector, with proportional subdivisions to show the relative percentages of the subdivisions within the slice. This chart format may be slightly confusing to an audience, but it can be invaluable in reducing the number of sectors on the chart.

A slice with a projected whole-bar attached to it will be emphasized by the bar. This technique should only be used with sectors that you wish to emphasize.

Chapter 7

Mapmaker, Mapmaker, Make Me a Map

There are three kinds of lies—lies, damned lies, and statistics.

Mark Twain

Using geographical maps to show statistical data has been a popular graphic technique since the beginning of the post-World War II business boom.

History and geography textbooks have used maps of countries to describe the distribution of population, conditions of climate, and regional production.

One technique used to chart by map is the *choropleth* map, where areas are shaded in to show the location of certain conditions. For example, a map of the United States can be used to show which states have certain laws or are considering passing those laws. The chart could also be used to show relative population by state or any information that can be expressed at a state level.

Another use of maps is to show relative proportions of subdivisions within a data item, for example, population. This is done by placing a pie chart in each state. This is a variation of the block map.

A block map may also be formed by crossing a map with a column chart. A single column or stacked column can be shown rising from each geographical subdivision, turning the map into a variation of the block chart. This way, the top of the column would represent a total, which could be compared to other regions' bars.

The prism map is a column chart variation made possible by the use of computer graphics technology. Each geographical subdivision is raised or lowered from the horizontal plane in relative proportion to the amount being charted for that subdivision.

Finally, surface maps are another variation made possible via computer technology. In the surface map, sharp peaks rise above the horizontal plane of the map to plot amounts. This is useful in presenting information that could be presented using a block map in a more modern-looking format.

GEOGRAPHICAL MAPS

Geographical maps of any region can be used as a backdrop for conveying a graphic message. Either a chart can be added to the map, the map itself can be come a graph, or a graph can be superimposed over a background map. Maps can be used to show the locations of company offices across the country. A map might also show just a group of states or even counties where the company has offices or sales personnel.

A map of the United States can be divided into major regions, time zones, or states, depending on the information to be included. Most U.S. maps are divided into states, this being the most easily recognizable subdivision. If larger divisions are being used, the larger regions are bordered with a heavy line, while state boundaries are marked with lighter lines. This way, the viewer, who is familiar with the state boundaries, can see which states fall into the larger regions.

Individual state maps can be divided into counties or regions in the same manner. The regions should be easily identifiable by the viewer, but should not be so pronounced that the message of the chart is muddled. Counties can be further divided into towns, townships, boroughs, or wards. Foreign countries can be divided into geographical regions or provinces.

The major reason for using geographical maps is that they are easily recognizable. The message of the map should be a breakdown of quantities or amounts by the regions shown, except when a map is used as a background.

The subdivisions of the map should be clearly defined and distorted as little as possible, although distorted maps are used from time to time to show relationships by the area of the subdivision. If the relative populations of the New England states are shown in proportional areas, Connecticut would appear very large, and Vermont would shrink; when in fact, they are almost the same land area.

DRAW A MAP

Before computers, a map to be used in a chart would have to first be obtained or drawn using the standard materials of an artist: pencil, paper, a map to trace from, sweat, a ream of tracing paper, and a large wastebasket. Once drawn, the outline map would be photocopied for every map-chart needed from then on.

Computers have made the use of maps in charting easy and accurate. Available software packages contain maps of the United States down to the county level, and even foreign countries and their provinces. Also available are world maps that conform to the contours of the earth. All of these maps can be reproduced any number of times. Moreover, when an amount is to be plotted, the computer can accurately plot values in three dimensional perspective that would require a skilled artist to draw. Geographical subdivisions such as states and counties can be distorted to compare volumes between the subdivisions, a feat that is almost impossible to accomplish by hand.

If your particular situation requires the use of map-charts, the best course of action would be to purchase the software package that will produce the type of chart you want, without needless effort.

Some software packages can draw the usual two-dimensional map, while some can add artistic perspective to produce a three-dimensional map. Shading can be added to make the map appear to be a solid layer, as if the land had been peeled from the globe. Still other packages can produce various global projections. Most of the software packages available for microcomputers, however, use only two-dimensional maps.

CHOROPLETH MAPS

The most common map-charting format is the choropleth map. The map is subdivided into either geographical or political areas, which are shaded to represent the information being charted, as shown in Fig. 7-1. This type of map is used to show areas where certain conditions prevail; for example, areas where certain laws are in effect, areas where a political candidate has taken a majority, or areas that have certain climatic conditions.

Another method of using a choropleth map is to shade areas to show ranges of values or percentages. For example, you could produce a map showing the percentage of population growth between the 1970 and 1980 censuses. States with a 25 percent growth between those years, like Alaska, would be shown in a dark shading, those with 20 to 25 percent growth in a lighter shading, and so on. This type of map could be used to show increases or decreases of any value or volume.

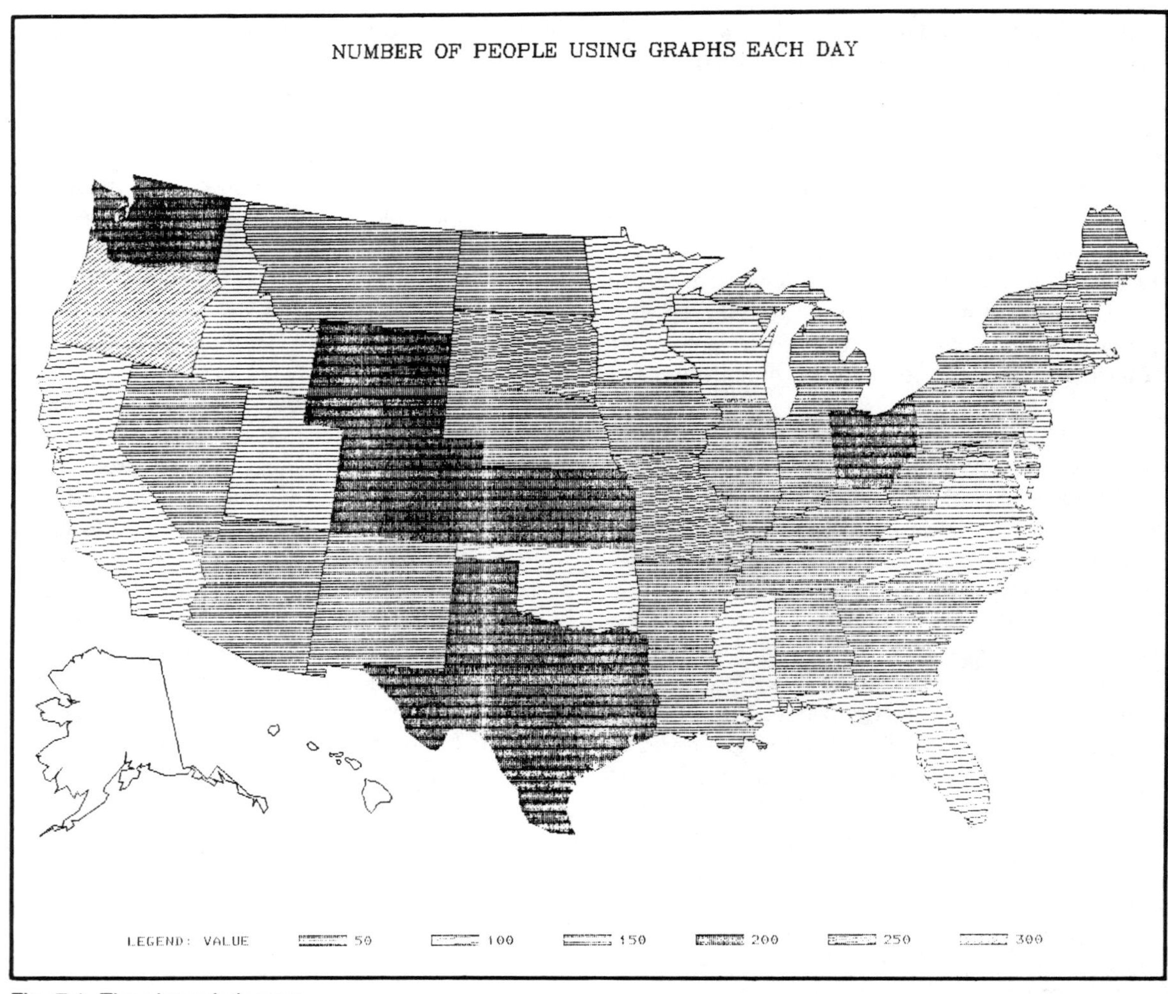

Fig. 7-1. The choropleth map.

Choropleth maps should *not* be used to show proportions across the entire map area. Different areas can slant the information. For example, a map of the United States shows that the eastern states are much smaller than the western states, even though 80% of the population resides in eastern states. Consider the statement:

> 11 states in both the eastern and western United States arrest a lot of people for drunk driving.

In this case, it would be proper to shade or color those states that have made these arrests. If, however, you were to shade 11 western states, almost one-third of the continental land area would be taken. If 11 eastern states were shaded, the information would look less impressive (Fig. 7-2).

Most maps will not attempt to show the actual relative size of Alaska. Alaska would take up most of the available space; having almost one-sixth of the total land area of the United States, it is *2.2 times* larger than Texas and would stretch from coast to coast. If you are producing a map for a company that has interests in Alaska and/or Hawaii, they should be included in insets at the edge of the map.

BLOCK MAPS

When a map is used as the backdrop for a block chart, it is called a block map. Each geographical area's information to be graphed becomes the "block" where the graph will reside. Each area's individual graph will convey information about that area in comparison with the other areas of the map.

Any chart format can be used in the block map; the most common format used is the column chart. Columns on a block map can be used in a variety of ways. One way is to produce a standard column chart, where the base of all the columns is at zero. This way, stacked or grouped bars can be used to show the makeup of the total or comparisons of the same area in different time periods (Fig. 7-3).

Another way that columns can be used in a block map is to have the map surface become some base value from which the columns either rise or fall. This can be produced effectively only by using three-dimensional artistic perspective. For example, to show the rise and fall of state populations between the 1970 and the 1980 census, the plane of the map becomes the 1970 value, while the columns that either rise or drop from the plane indicate

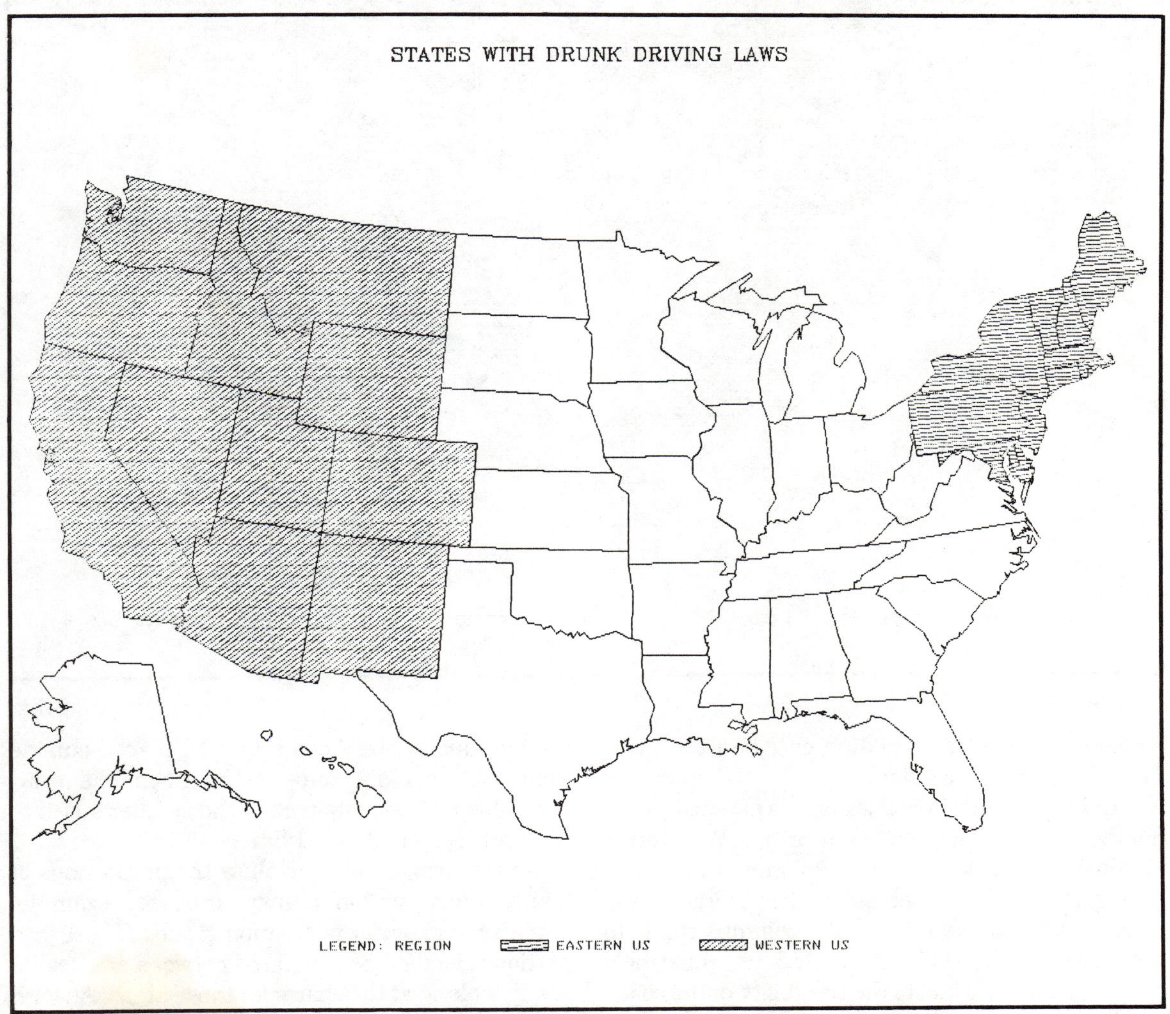

Fig. 7-2. A misleading map.

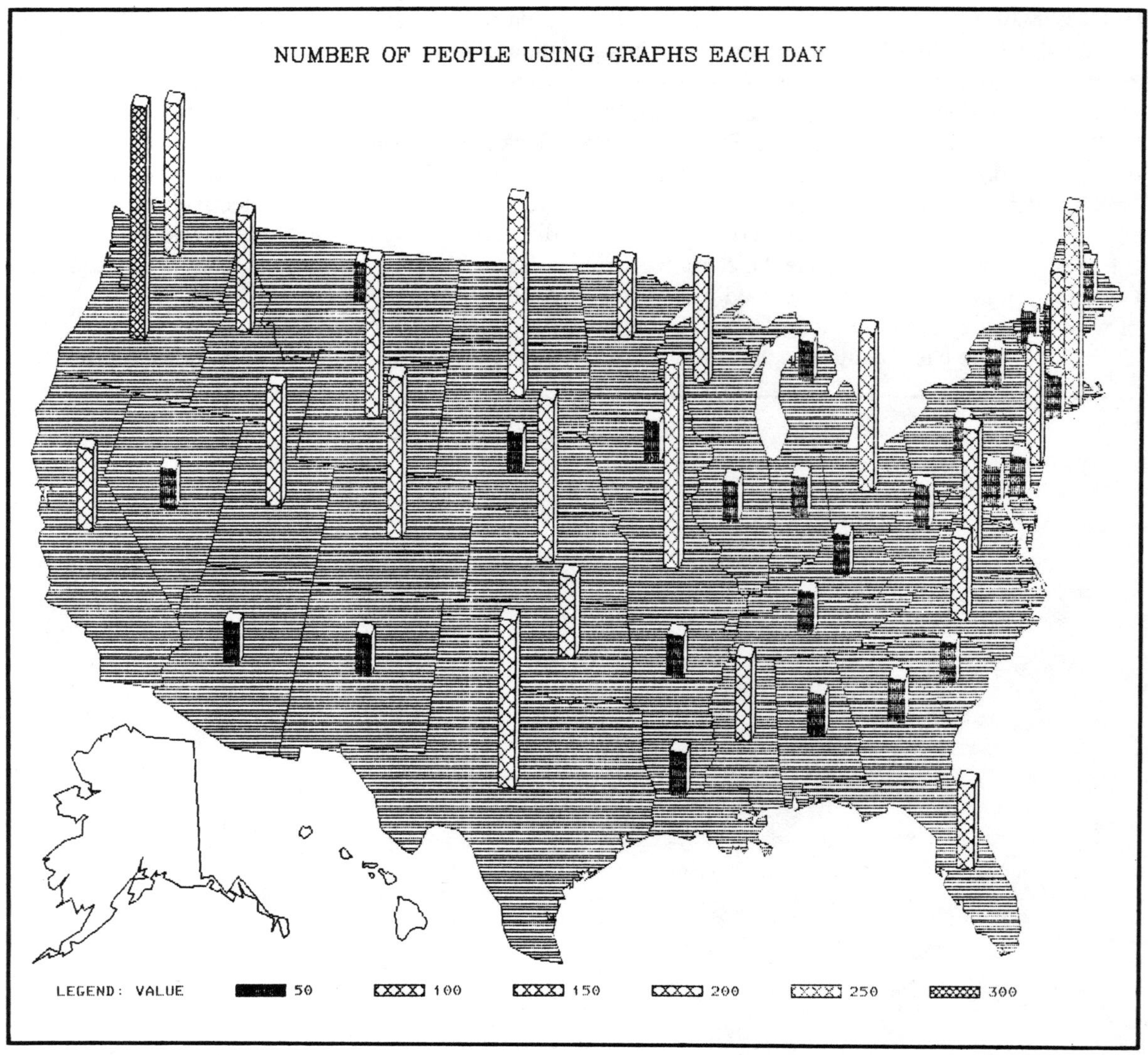

Fig. 7-3. The column block map.

amounts or percentages of difference between those figures and the 1980 figures.

Using columns in block maps is effective if the number of bars is limited to one or two. With three-dimensional block maps, one column is the limit. The columns will not necessarily be accurate to the exact value, but the sizes of the columns can help the viewer see the differences. Adding value labels to the columns will add to the credibility of the chart.

Pie charts can also be placed in the states, although, due to size, they might be placed outside the actual area and connected to it by a line or arrow. This is especially true of the smaller states in the northeastern United States.

Pie charts are used to show the proportions of two amounts within a map area, for example, minority to majority population groups. These proportions can then be compared between areas, simply by looking at the charts for those areas. As with the column charts, the pie charts should only have two sectors, or three at the most. The small size of the pie charts will affect the readibility of the chart; value labels should be used, but sparingly.

Each pie or column should be shaded or colored to enhance the viewer's understanding. The message of the map should be "this is the difference between these areas." Areas of particular emphasis could have their charts projected from the map or darker in shading than others.

PRISM MAPS

A *prism map* is produced by raising or lowering entire subdivisions of a map from a plane, thus turning the entire map into a column chart, with each subdivision becoming a column. The term "prism" comes from the appearance of the exposed edges of the subdivision, which are smooth with sharp angles, as shown in Fig. 7-4. Prism maps can be made accurate and practical only by using computer technology and software.

Three-dimensional perspective techniques must be used to display a prism map. The map area, for example the United States, becomes a flat or partially shadowed plane, with the appearance of lay-

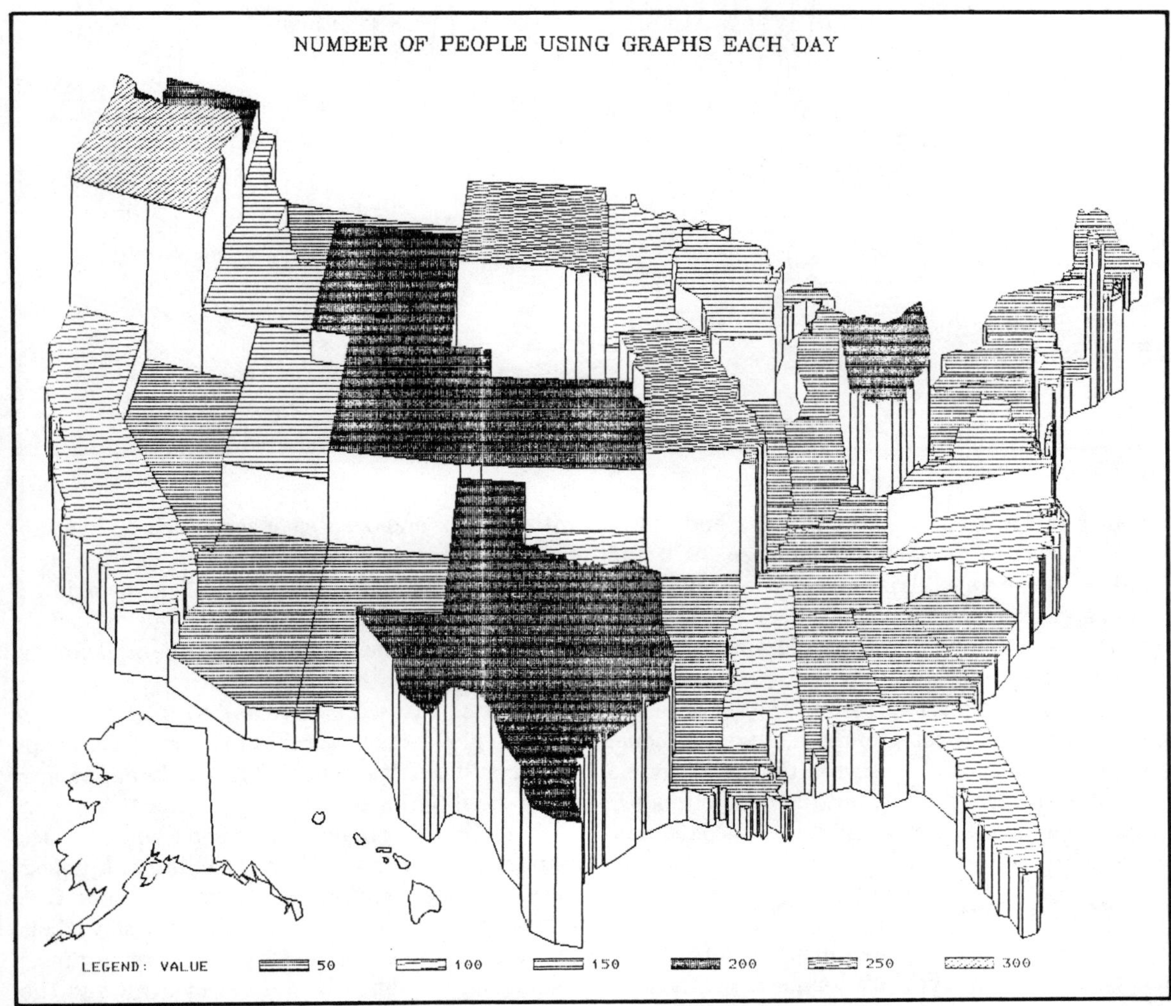

Fig. 7-4. The prism map.

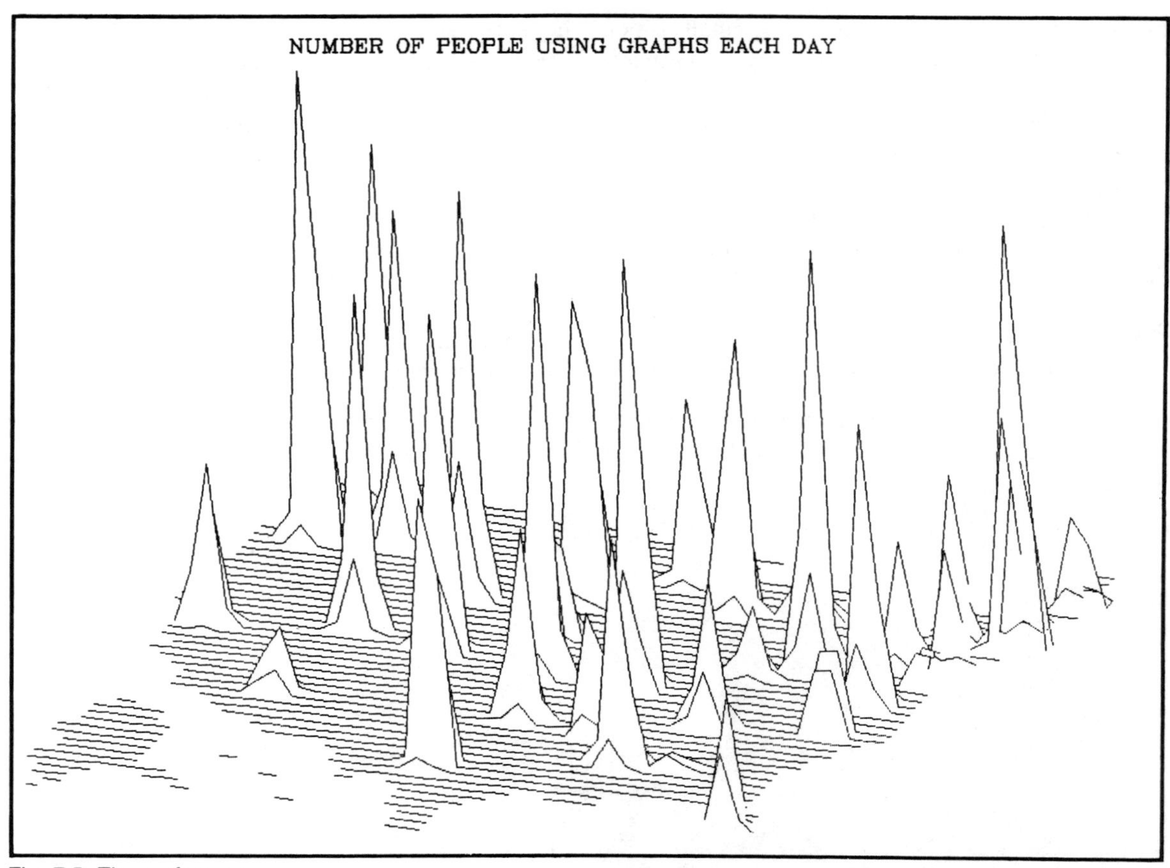

Fig. 7-5. The surface map.

ing flat. If you were to chart the rise and fall of individual states' populations between 1970 and 1980 as a percentage, Arizona, Nevada, and Alaska would appear to rise high above the surface, while Rhode Island and New York would appear to sink slightly below.

The prism map is impressive in appearance, but not very accurate because of the three-dimensional perspective. The actual values of the area/columns are not easily identifiable, but the differences are emphasized by the relative heights of the columns.

SURFACE MAPS

Surface maps are another mapping format that has been made practical by computer technology. A surface map is a cross between the block map with columns and the area or surface chart. In a surface map, the map area is drawn like a three-dimensional plane and shaded with horizontal lines. Values are charted by peaks and valleys in this plane, which appear in the middle of each subdivision, as shown in Fig. 7-5.

Surface maps are not easy to read or to accurately plot data on, but they are impressive in appearance. The relative sizes of the peaks and valleys show the differences between the charted areas.

Subdivisions are not always shown on a surface map, making precise comparisons difficult unless the viewer has a good knowledge of geography. One way of enhancing the surface map is to apply labels and amounts to the areas of greatest importance, connecting the labels with lines or arrows to the peak or valley referred to.

Chapter 8

Management Miscellany

A decision is the action an executive must take when he has information so incomplete that the answer does not suggest itself.

Sir Arthur William Radford

ORGANIZATIONAL CHARTS

A hierarchical chart, sometimes called an *organizational chart,* is used to show the relationships of functions within a corporate structure. Each level represents a controlling management function, while each symbol represents a controlling group or person, as shown in Fig. 8-1.

Hierarchical charts are also used to show relationships of functions in a system of functions within a company or computer system. They can also be used to show any hierarchy where one level is comprised of one or more subsections.

Each office in the management hierarchy is denoted by a symbol, usually a rectangular box. This box should contain the name and/or title of that office. The highest level box is the office of control for the function shown. The next level shows all the offices or functions that are the responsibility of the highest office. The third level would contain the functional breakdown of each block at the second level, and so forth.

Lines are drawn between the rectangles to show the chain of command. Lines rising from lower-level blocks are gathered into a single line by connecting them with a perpendicular line. The perpendicular collecting line is drawn only across paths to collect them into a single path. Blocks subordinate to different superior blocks are never connected in this manner.

Computer systems are designed to handle various functions required by a company. Each major function is divided into smaller subfunctions, until the lowest level of detail is reached. The computer function chart details the hierarchy of functions within the computer system (Fig. 8-2); organization charts used in the same way are called *module* or *function* charts (Fig. 8-2).

Organization charts can be used to describe the workings of government bodies, civic and military organizations. They can be very effective in showing any hierarchy, from the management of a cor-

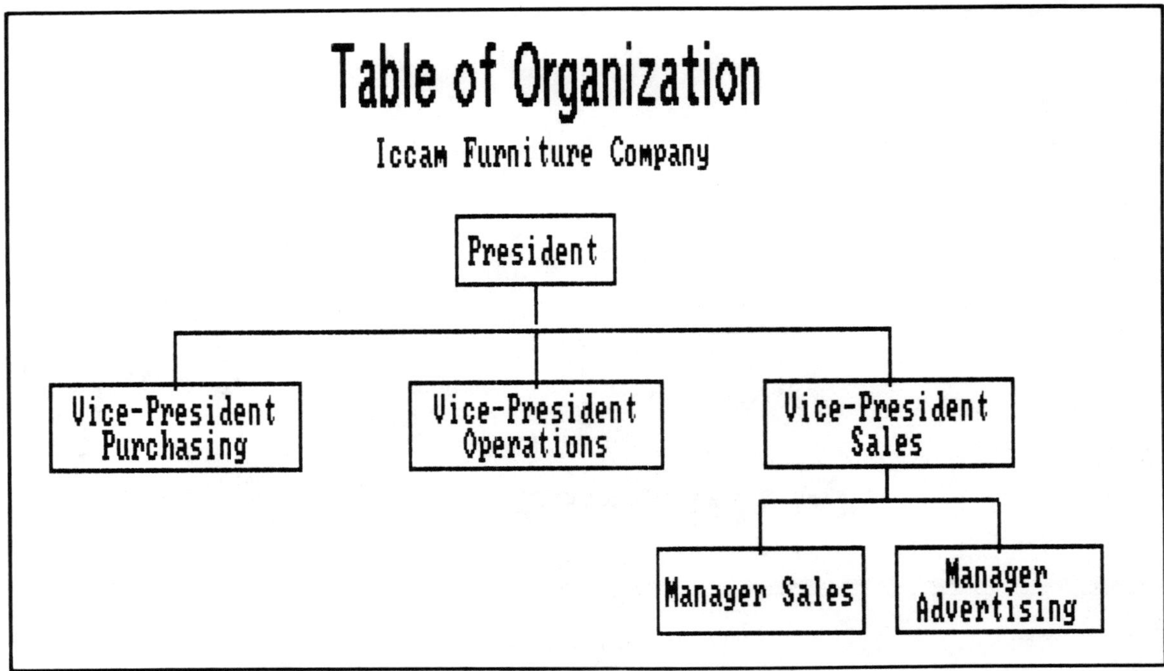

Fig. 8-1. The organization chart.

poration to the arrangement of books in a library.

CALENDARS

Calendars are charts that show a physical relationship between days, weeks, months, and years. Everyone is familiar with the standard wall calendar; charting by calendar can sometimes require a few changes to the standard format.

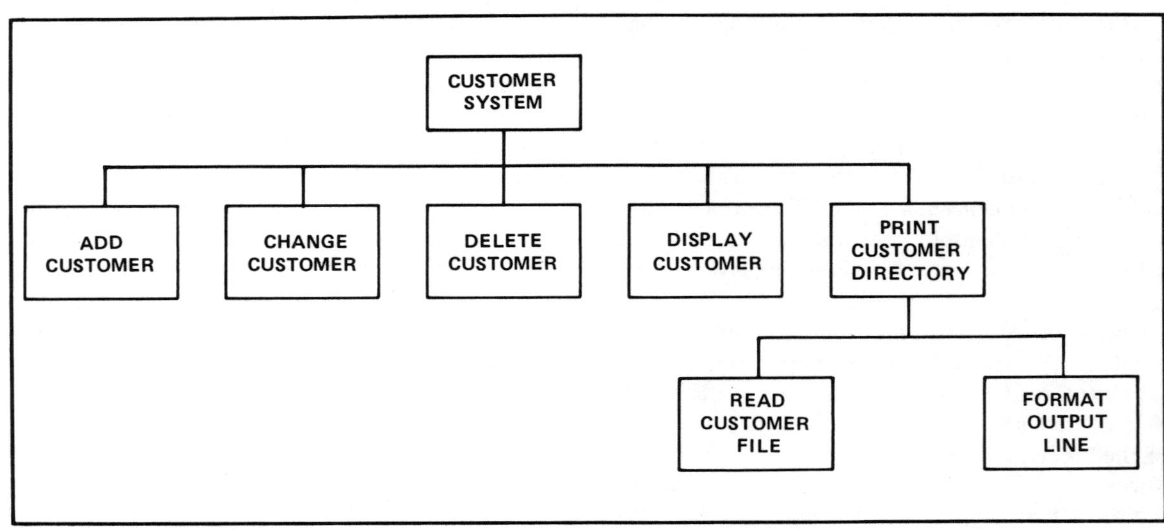

Fig. 8-2. The function chart.

One technique is to lay out the days, weeks, or months in a straight line, as shown in Fig. 8-3. This is the same concept used in a time-series graph, where the time periods are listed on the x-axis. In a scheduling chart, however, the time periods are the value axis. Data points plotted on such a chart represent the beginning date, the ending date, and the duration of the task or project.

Scheduling functions are shown best with this type of calendar. The Gantt chart, which will be presented later in this chapter, is a very common scheduling chart format that uses the time-line form of a calendar.

Standard calendars can be used to show the duration of a project, class, or meeting that is at least one day long. The name of the activity is centered between its start and end dates, and arrows are extended from the name to those dates, to show the duration of the activity (Fig. 8-4).

Standard calendars can also be used as block charts. If an amount, volume, or total is to be plotted on a day-by-day basis, a column, a column can be placed in the center of each square (day). This format would emphasize the difference of the amount from day to day, and would be most effective when the differences are large. Also, the exact value should be printed within or below the column because placing a value axis in each block can be nearly impossible.

Pie charts could also be placed directly on a standard calendar to show the day-to-day change in the proportions of some whole. Each pie chart should look identical insofar as shading and placement of slices is concerned. As with the calendar-column, the value or percentage of the slices should be present if space allows.

Block charts can be created with other calendar units. A row of four blocks might represent the quarters within a year, with as many rows as there are years to chart. As with any block chart, columns, pies, grouped columns, 100 percent bars, or stacked columns can be used in the blocks.

SCHEDULES

Schedules presented in tabular form have the same drawbacks as numerical data displayed in that format. Names and dates can become confused and confusing.

One method of straightening out the confusion is to use the calendar as a backdrop to scheduling. The scheduled activities can be represented by lines that cross day-blocks on the calendar, marking the number of days that each activity takes.

Another alternative is to place daily schedules inside of the day blocks where the activity occurs. While this is not totally effective, it does aid in sorting out the activities.

Scheduling activities and personnel to perform them can be aided by use of the various chart formats. This, however, is only part of the scheduling problem.

Activities must be ordered by their level of importance to you and to the company. Most likely, some activities will require the completion of other activities before they can be started. The overall goal should be broken down into the tasks that need to be performed before that goal is reached. The tasks

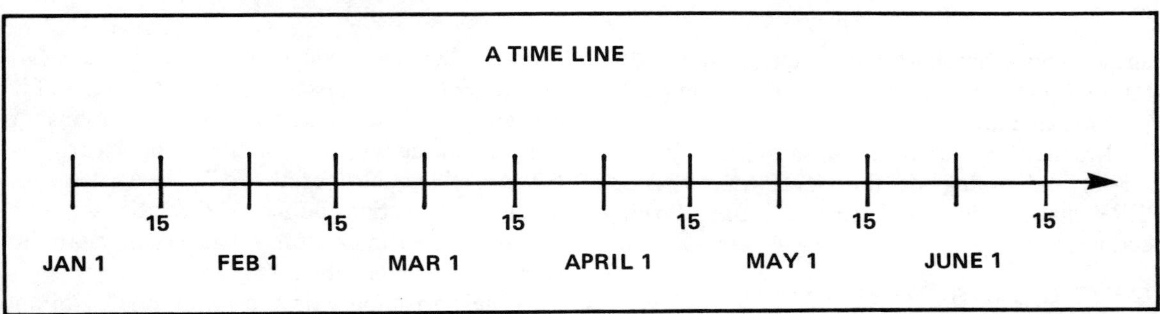

Fig. 8-3. The time line.

MARCH 1985				
MONDAY	TUESDAY	WEDNESDAY	THURSDAY	FRIDAY
				1 +NATURAL/VSAM+
4 +===============SAS BASIC=================+	5	6	7 +=VSAM FOR AP. PROGRAMMERS==+	8
11 +=========SPF BASIC=========+	12 +============NATURAL (ADVANCED)============+	13 +GOLD KEY CLU+	14 +SPF OFF-SITE+	15
18 +=========SPF BASIC=========+	19	20 +===============SAS BASIC================+	21	22
25 +=======SPF ADVANCED========+	26 +=========SAS GRAPH=========+	27	28 +=======EASYTRIEVE I========+	29

Fig. 8-4. The schedule calendar.

can be divided among the different people on the staff or among groups of people, depending on the level of management.

Two methods of ordering activities by their priority and timing are the Gantt chart and the PERT chart, which are discussed in the following sections.

GANTT CHARTS

Gantt charts are a variation of the horizontal bar chart used with a calendar axis. Bars mark the start, end, and duration of each activity, as shown in Fig. 8-6. Once laid out in this manner, the relationships between the activities can be seen more clearly, but they are still not obvious; the *PERT* chart, described in the next section, defines the relationships between activities more clearly than a Gantt chart, but it is less clear on scheduling and duration.

The horizontal axis can be graduated in any time period, but the most common format is to use

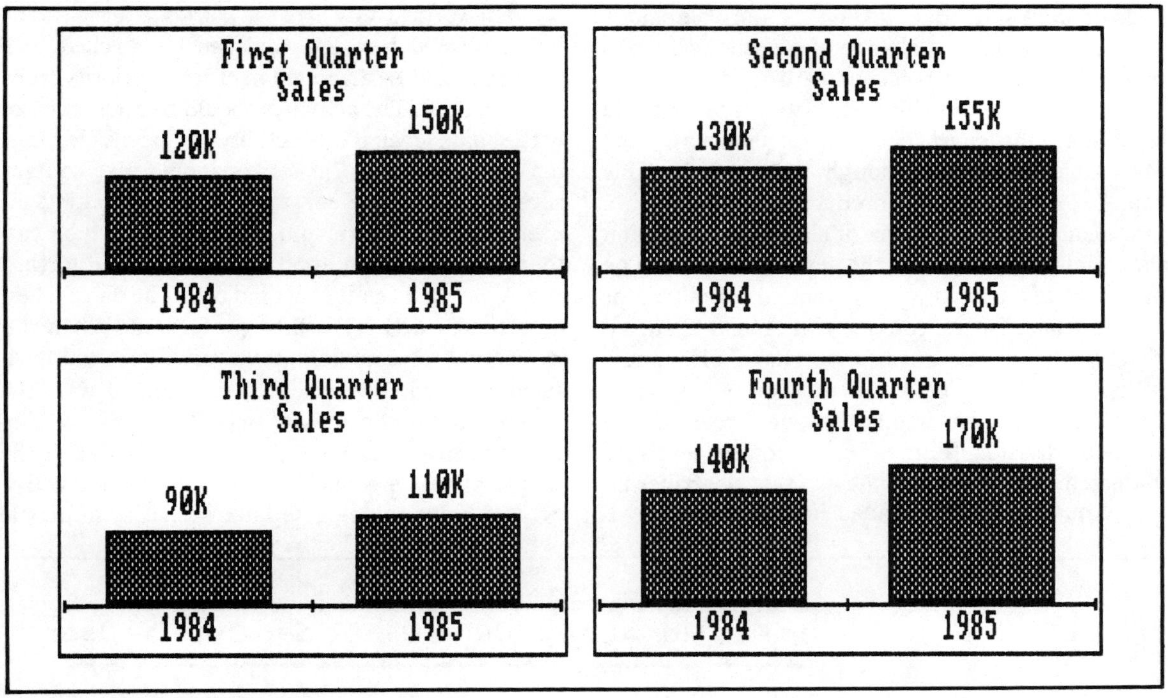

First Quarter Sales
120K
150K
1984
1985
Second Quarter Sales
130K
155K
1984
1985
Third Quarter Sales
90K
110K
1984
1985
Fourth Quarter Sales
140K
170K
1984
1985

Fig. 8-5. The quarter block chart.

ABC CORPORATION
NEW PRODUCT INTRODUCTION
JAN
FEB
MAR
APR
MAY
JUN
DEVELOPMENT
ROLLOUT
MATURITY
CASH FLOW
PROGRAMMING
PACKAGING
MARKETING

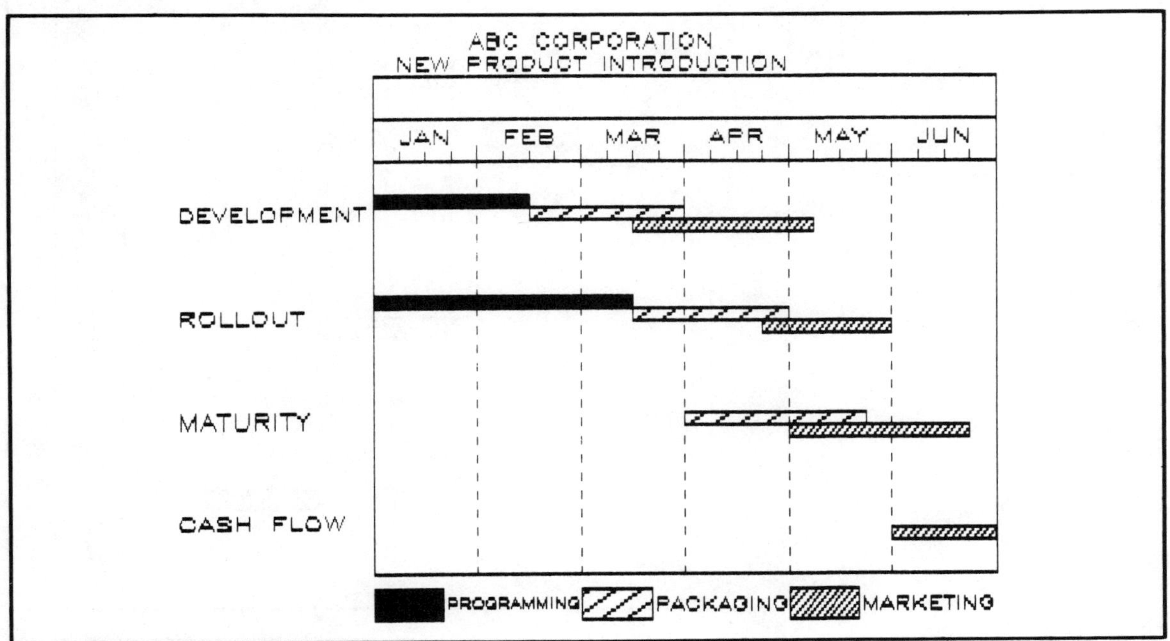

Fig. 8-6. The Gantt chart.

days or weeks. Graduations on the horizontal axis should also mark the change of months and years when the project is so scheduled.

As you can probably tell, it would be possible to have a Gantt chart that would stretch across the manager's wall, given enough time periods. This can be alleviated by producing charts for a month, a quarter, or a year, at a time depending on the smallest division of the horizontal axis. The president of a company may want an overall major activity chart for the coming year (Fig. 8-7) such a chart would be laid out in months or half-months rather than days. The lower levels of management would require charts in quarters, with weeks as the smallest division (Fig. 8-8); the lowest levels of management might want a chart that describes an entire quarter, but is divided into days.

The vertical axis lists the names of activities to be performed before a goal can be reached. Activities should be arranged in order of priority from top to bottom. The activities should be approximately the same level; if one activity can be divided into ten subtasks, then the others should also contain several subtasks. Keep it simple by breaking an overall project down into major tasks, which can then be detailed on another chart, and so forth.

A bar on a Gantt chart indicates the dates when a particular activity will be performed. When the last activity is complete, the overall goal will have been reached. Each bar can be labeled with the ending date of the activity once it is complete. Another device is to label the activity bar with the names of the personnel that will perform the activity; this helps to delegate later activities to people

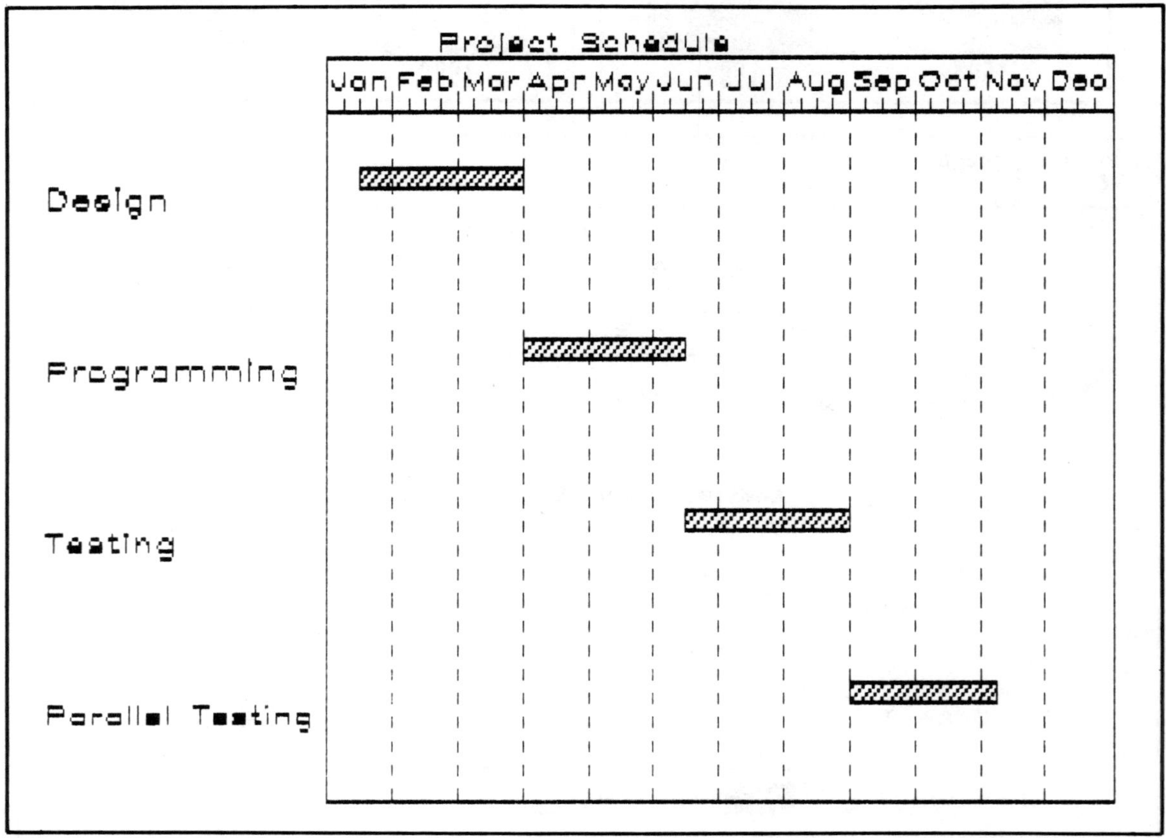

Fig. 8-7. A high-level Gantt chart.

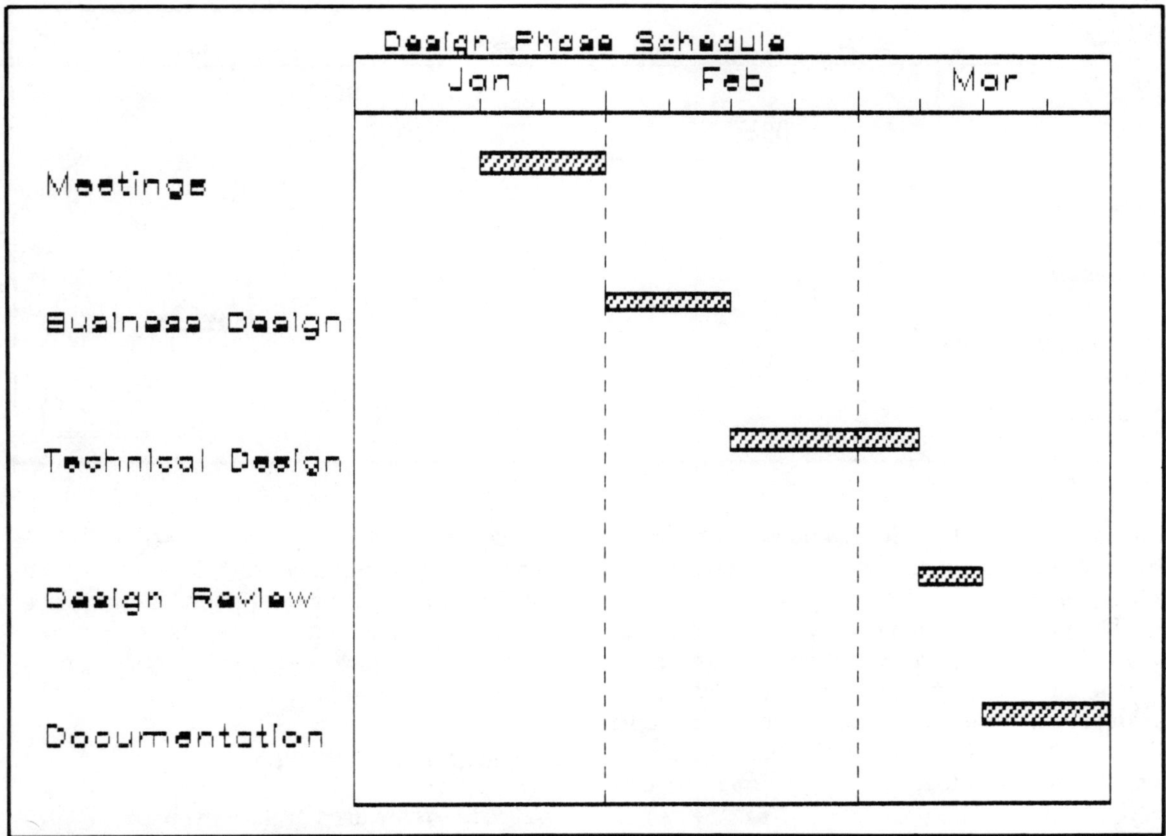

Fig. 8-8. A lower-level Gantt chart.

who will have finished an activity and can be placed on another. Labeling the bars with the names of the responsible personnel can also indicate where a person is being over-used.

Traditionally and logically, the time axis of a Gantt chart proceeds from left to right. The bars denoting activities near the beginning of the time period are at the top of the chart, while the later activities are closest to the bottom. Activity dates can overlap, although the bars will not. When an activity takes longer than estimated, the bar can be extended easily without use of a computer, once the chart is on paper. Rescheduling the project based on over- and under-estimates requires redrawing of the chart.

One variation on the Gantt chart is a chart on which the bars are labeled with the activity names instead of the vertical axis. This eliminates the need for a vertical axis at all, except as to denote the starting point in time (Fig. 8-9).

PERT CHARTS

PERT (Program Evaluation and Review Technique) charts are used to analyze the network of activities necessary to reach a specified business goal. Where the Gantt chart is more of a scheduling too, the PERT chart is a prioritizing tool because it examines the relationships of activities to each other.

Each activity is plotted in its relationship to other activities occurring at the same time or later in the project. The goal of each subtask is represented by a bubble, or circle, drawn on the chart (Fig. 8-10). Lines connecting the goal bubbles are called *paths*.

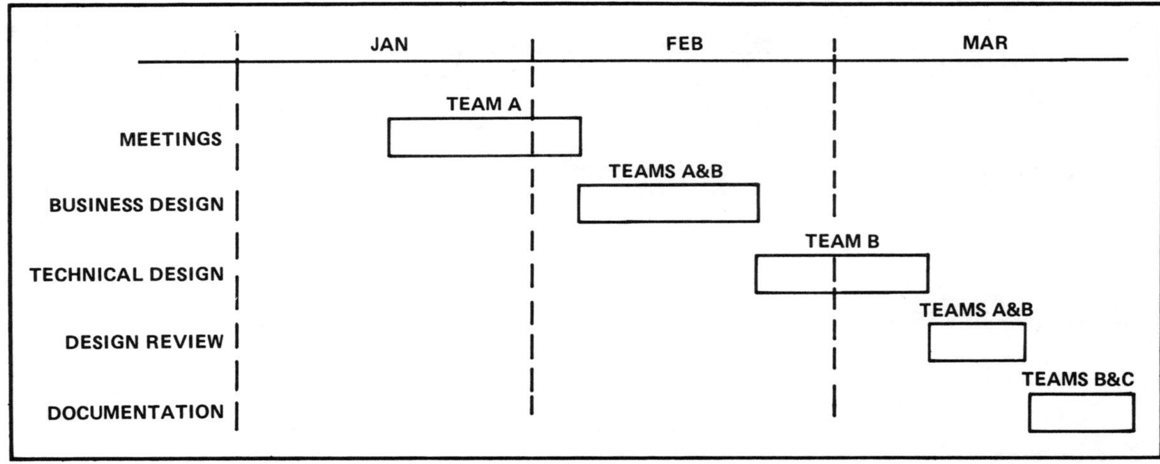

Fig. 8-9. A Gantt chart with labeled bars.

The paths are labeled with the number of person-days necessary to complete the task, as well as what activity is to be carried out to reach the goal.

The priorities of activities is immediately apparent, because the first activity on any path must be completed prior to preceding to the next activity, and so on to the end of the project. Slide paths can branch out from any particular bubble to describe activities that can be performed concurrently.

The *critical path* is the path representing the greatest amount of time, and therefore, the path that will hold up any concurrent activities (Fig. 8-11). If two branching paths, one 14 days long and the other 10 days long, both converge on the same goal bubble, then the ten-day path will have been completed before the fourteen-day path, making the entire crictical path 14 days.

PROCESS FLOWCHARTS

Flowcharts are used to chart the path of control through a process. Where Gantt charts and PERT charts show relationships between activities, the

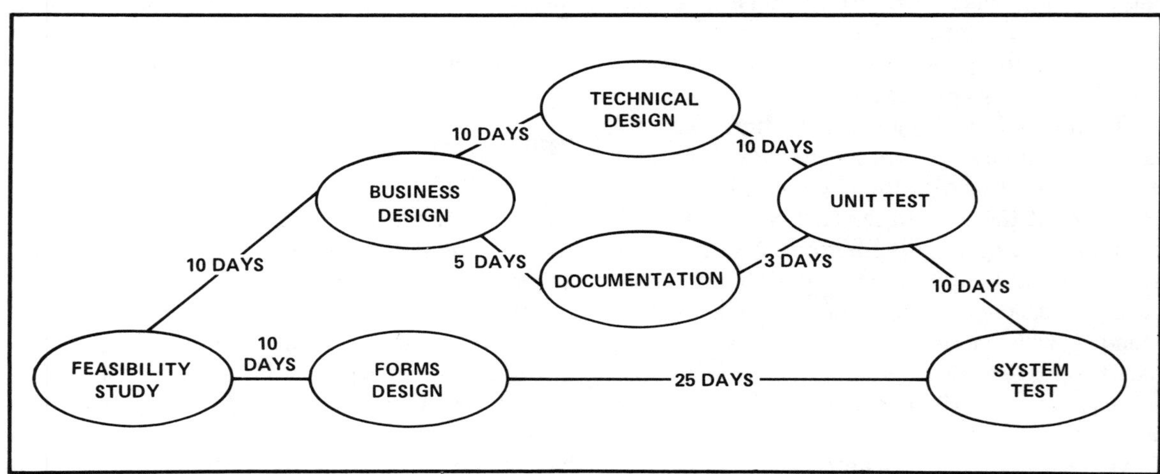

Fig. 8-10. The PERT chart.

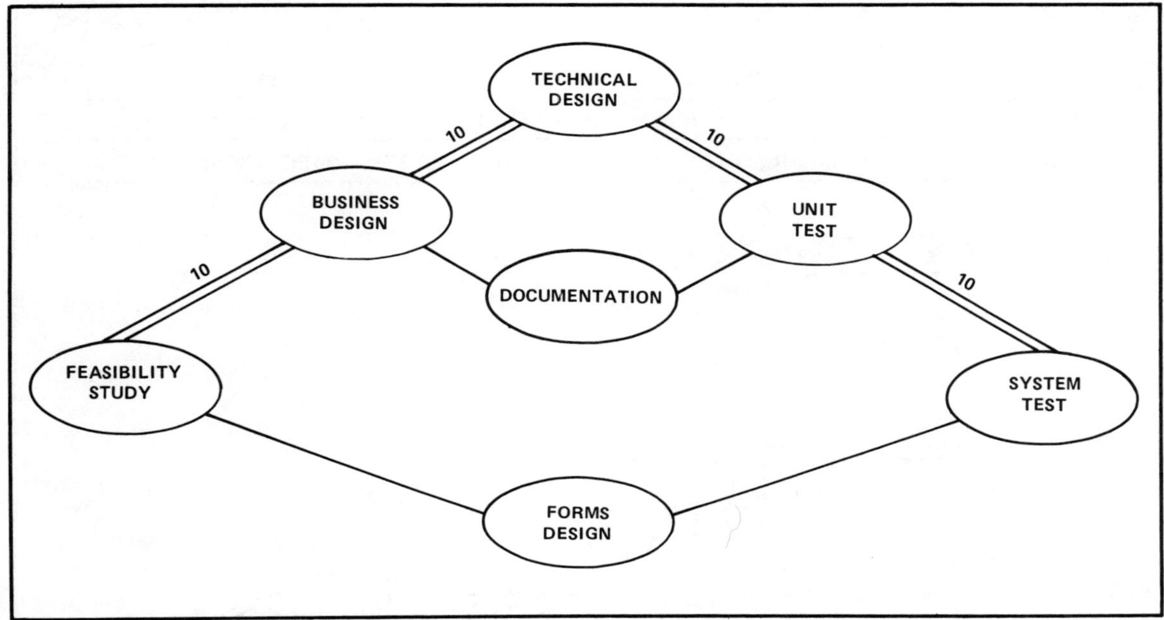

Fig. 8-11. The critical path chart.

flowchart shows the exact steps to take to perform the activity. Each decision point, activity, operation, and iterative loop is drawn using the symbols of flowcharting to produce a road map of a process that shows its most intricate details (Fig. 8-12).

The idea of a flowchart is to show the flow of control through a system, whether the system be a computer program, a manufacturing process, or even the flow of office paperwork. This flow of control is denoted by a line. The line branches to or around activities, but there is only one path that is active at any one time. Control can branch because of a decision, but only the one path is followed.

Each activity on the line is performed as it is reached. The next step cannot be started if the previous step is unfinished. This is sometimes described as *linear processing*. Musical melodies are an example of this type of process; each note in a melody must be played before the next note can be started, one at a time, one following another, until the end is reached.

The activities are denoted by symbols, called *nodes*, that have various shapes depending on the type of activity to be performed. Each symbol has one flow line entering it, and one exiting it, with the exception of collector nodes, terminal nodes, decision nodes, and device symbols. Each process (rectangle) and decision (diamond) are reached through a single line of flow; however, a decision can have two outcomes, *Yes* or *No*, each represented by a line of flow. *Terminal nodes* (ellipses) start and end the flowchart; *collector nodes* (small circles) gather many flow lines into one; *device symbols* denote input or output (one-way operations) (Fig. 8-13).

Flowchart symbols also include those for manual processes, sorting and collating, and other processes that are not common within computer programs. These symbols can be used to describe the physical system of procedures of which a program is part. Flowcharts that depict this level of activity are called *system* flowcharts.

Flowcharts can also be used to describe processes that are not computer-related. One large use of flowcharts is in product servicing and repairs. An automobile mechanic will ask you what you think is wrong with your car, examine it himself for symptoms, and consult a manual on the intricacies of the car. This manual will include a flowchart that the

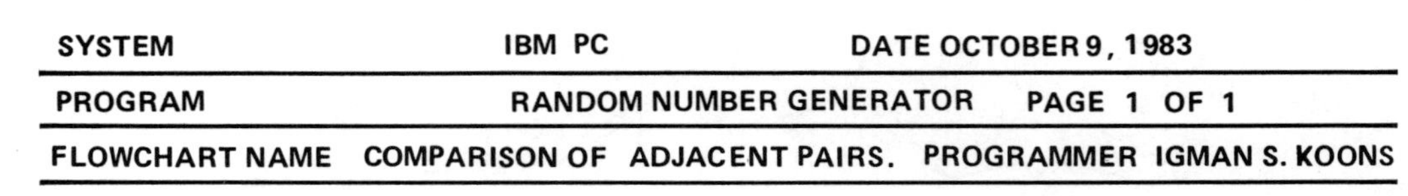

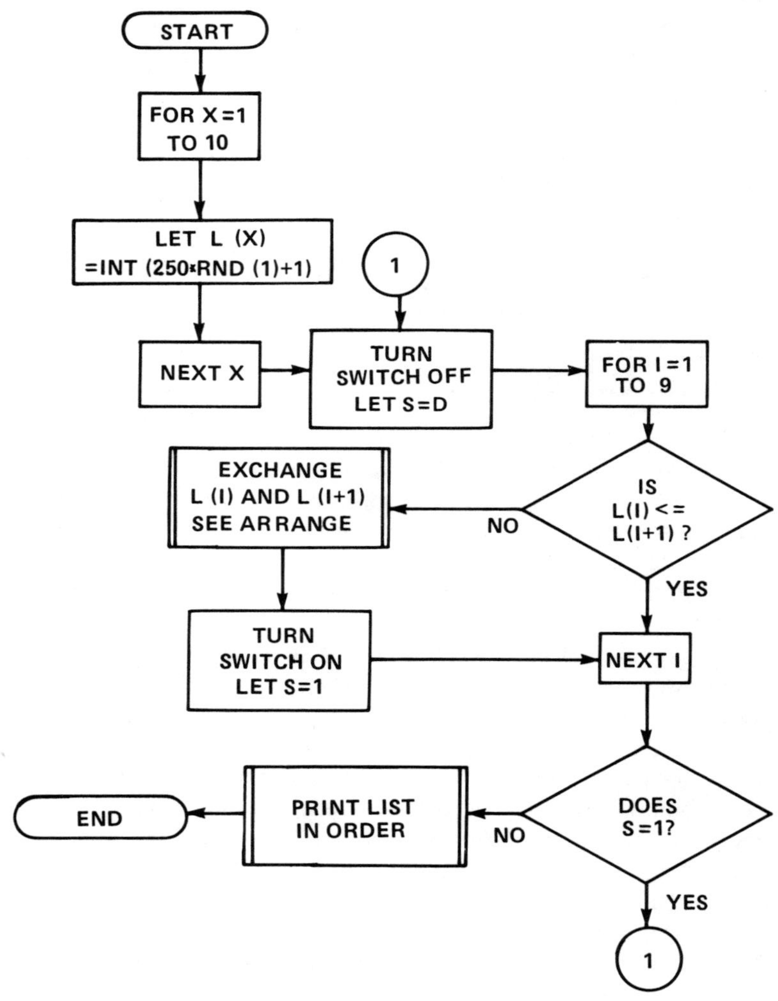

NOTE- FLOWCHART FOR ARRANGING A LIST OF NUMBERS ASSIGNED FROM RND( ) USING COMPARISON OF ADJACENT PAIRS

Fig. 8-12. The flowchart.

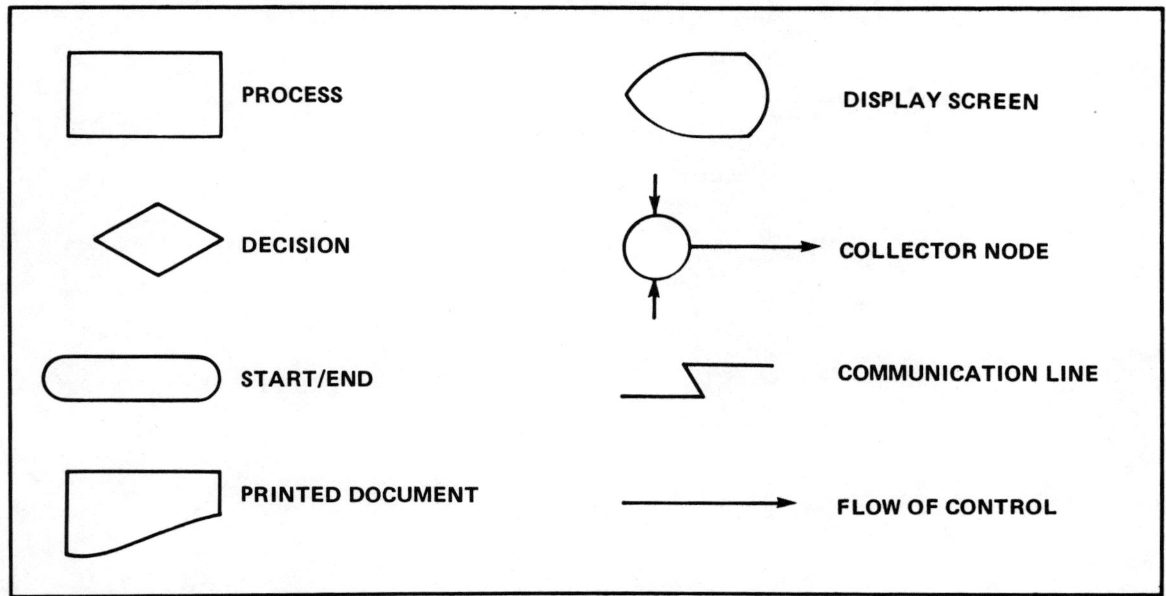

Fig. 8-13. The flowchart symbols.

mechanic can follow based on the noted symptoms.

MANAGEABLE GRAPHICS

Managers need to report their activities to their companies in a way that is concise and precise. Graphs and charts can aid the manager in presenting his accomplishments and problems to upper management. Their use can mean the difference between upper-management enthusiasm and upper-management indifference.

Microcomputers allow managers to prepare these graphics more effectively than ever before. The microcomputer has brought professional typesetting, graphic arts, and reproduction into the reach of almost everyone. A manager can produce a chart, revise it as new information becomes available, and present it to higher management in a very short time. As with any microcomputer software, however, the choice of package must be the decision of the person who must use it.

The second half of this book will introduce you to the most popular graphing software available today. You can use this book to identify the packages that are worth considering and to get a preview of the facilities that they provide.

Section 2

Using Todays Graphics Packages

The second section of this book is devoted to the best known graphics software and output devices on the market. This section has several purposes. It can serve as a review of each of the packages presented. If you are planning on purchasing a graphics package, you can "look" at many of the top selling packages before you choose one.

The chapters in this section represent many of the different types of graphics packages found on the market today. Graphics packages come in an assortment of different types and are not limited to the traditional business graphics of the past. Some software companies are even inventing new types of graphics.

The chapters in this section present the following types of graphic packages.

Standalone Graphics Packages
Integrated Packages
Text Slide Packages
Picture Processors and Graphic Enhancers
Highly Specialized Packages
Little Known Packages That Do Wonderful Things

There is a final chapter on hardware devices.

Standalone Graphics Packages have been around since the beginning of the computer revolution. These exist solely to produce graphs. Each one is somewhat different than the other. Integrated software is fairly new. Since Lotus introduced 1-2-3, which combined spreadsheet, data management, and graphics, there have been many other integrated packages that include graphics as one of their modules.

Corporate America is joining the computer revolution in large numbers. Most corporate presentations are *bullet* slides. Because of this, "Text/Slide" packages that allow text charts in different fonts, colors, and sizes were invented.

The most significant activity today is in the *picture processing* area. Ever since Prentice Hall published VCN EXECUVISION, picture processors have been introduced at a rate of several a month.

The Apple LISA pioneered another type of drawing package called LISA DRAW. This concept has now been enhanced by many manufacturers; the resulting products are called *painting* packages. Also in this area are the *graphic enhancers.* These are packages that exist to modify graphics that were created by another program. They capture what was on the screen in the other package and then allow you to make changes. Many of these will be demonstrated in the Picture Processors and Graphic Enhancers chapter as well as the Little Known Packages That Do Wonderful Things chapter.

The chapter's in this section can also serve as overviews of how different packages handle business graphics. When you are comparing business graphics, you must keep in mind that each package is designed to take care of a certain set of problems. This author personally uses three different packages all the time to meet certain needs. You must look closely at each package and determine which packages will most nearly meet all your needs.

Another factor that influences a software package's usability is the number of different options that are available. Often there is a direct correlation between price and performance, as can be expected. A $95 software package probably will not do all a $695 software package does. As a minimum, a standalone package should offer two types of bar charts, a line chart, a pie chart, and an area chart. There are many other types of charts, as you saw in the first part of the book, but these are the minimum that should be expected. The number of line connections, type fonts, shading patterns, titles and labeling options usually increase as the price of the package increases.

As the number of options increase, the complexity of the program and the size of the manual will also increase. Some powerful packages are extremely easy to use; other packages do almost nothing and are difficult to use.

Documentation is extremely important. A manual does not have to be large to be good, but it should be well written and contain easy to follow examples with many pictures including some in color. If the manual doesn't make the product look good, chances are that it isn't.

A good package usually has a manual in two parts. Generally the first part is a guide to getting started and includes some type of self-study tutorial. The second part of a good manual is a reference guide to all the menus or commands. It should detail the capabilities of each option or command and be full of examples. A good index is also essential to a good manual.

On-line help is also the sign of a good software package. On-line help allows the user to hit a key (usually F1) and instantly receive some explanation about the function or menu they are trying to use. A help index and the ability to see other help screens without returning to the program are also desirable.

No matter how well the package performs, if the output is not legible, it can not be considered a good package. Some packages are designed to have excellent quality screen displays, while some do a very poor job on the screen but make up for it on a printer or plotter. Some software packages can produce hardcopy output only on a plotter. This is fine as long as you have a plotter.

Generally a package should do a fair job of producing screen output but do an excellent job of printer and plotter hardcopies. Some of the better software packages automatically adjust to take advantage of the maximum print quality of your output device. Others are merely screen dumps whose resolution (numbers of dots per inch), will be no better than it is on the screen. A package that lets you choose where the output will be placed on the paper, what size it will be, and what horizontal or vertical rotation will be used can be considered a superior package. Some packages even allow you to split the screen and display several graphs at once.

The newest display technology today is the Polaroid Palette. This device allows you to take color slides and instant prints from your screen. It can take screen images in the same resolution as your monitor, and if the software has a built-in device driver for the Polaroid Palette, it can display images at a far greater resolution. Several of the products described in this section have Palette interfaces. The

Polaroid Palette is described in detail in Chapter 15.

The final and probably the most important consideration when you are analyzing a graphics package is its speed and error handling capability. A software package that *bombs* or does not work properly is worthless. While some packages can produce a graph instantaneously, some take several minutes to place a graph on the screen. Depending on your needs, speed may be important.

As you read these overviews of each package, keep in mind what your needs are. Your specific needs and desires are as important as the packages cost and reputation. The best known package is worthless if it doesn't do what you want it to do.

The first few packages in each section are reviewed in more detail than the last ones. All the packages in each section are there because they do what they are supposed to well. After reading about the first several packages in each chapter, you will read about only the highlights and unusual features in subsequent packages.

The software and hardware are not reviewed; rather they are demonstrated and explained. The facts given are gathered through ten to fifty hours of use of each package. Each package's manual was read from cover to cover, each feature was tried, and every manufacturer questioned at length about any questions that could not be answered using the manual.

More important than the final product is the method of producing the graph. Most of the screen photos demonstrate how a graph is created; they are not merely photos of the different graphics the package can create.

The appendix at the end of the book lists all the hardware and the software programs, including manufacturer's name, address, and phone number, and the cost, and present version.

Chapter 9

Standalone Graphics Packages

MICROSOFT CHART
CHART-MASTER
GRAPHWRITER
BPS BUSINESS GRAPHICS
DR GRAPH
PFS GRAPH

Standalone graphics packages are those packages whose primary function is the creation of business graphics. These include bar, line, pie, text, area, and other charts primarily used by businesses. Packages that create business graphics as an auxiliary function are discussed in later chapters. Some of the packages in this chapter have their own database or spreadsheet interface. Some allow you to use data created in other programs or in other forms such as standard ASCII files, dBase II DBF files, DIF files, Lotus 1-2-3 files, or files in other standard formats.

There are two types of standalone graphics packages: menu driven packages and command driven packages. *Menu driven* means that to use the package, you merely have to fill in menu screens. There are several types of menu systems as described in this chapter. Each has its own quirks and differences. Some require filling in more menus and some less, but all depend on menus that function in the same manner.

A command driven package is one that is controlled by individual commands, much like a programming language. These packages can be very powerful as they allow a multitude of combinations that some menu driven packages do not allow. They are generally more difficult to learn initially, and logic must be employed to structure the individual commands. Once a command driven package is mastered, however, results are usually achieved in less time than with a menu driven package.

The following information is presented for each software package discussed in this chapter.

1. An introduction to the basic philosophies of the package and a discussion of what it is intended to do and who its intended audience is.
2. A presentation of the best or most unusual features that set this product apart from all others.
3. Discussions of the *boot* or first screen, the documentation, the expected learning time, and the tutorials that may be available.
4. Discussions of how the program handles and

changes input data and how it handles data created outside the workings of the program.

5. A discussion of the types of graphs produced and the program's ability to use the same data for different types of graphs without requiring that the data be reentered.
6. A discussion of the available formatting commands including the ability of the software to control the placement and type of text, legends, titles, labels, and tick marks.
7. A presentation concerning the separation of data and formatting commands.
8. A discussion of the output quality on the screen, dot matrix printer, Polaroid Palette, and plotter.
9. An evaluation of the overall performance, speed, and error handling, and general comments about the ease of use of the package compared to the results achieved.

There are several features that generally make a standalone graphics package better than another. The most important is the ability to share data between different types of graphs. Most packages will allow you to create a set of data. This data can then be shown on bar, line, or pie charts (as well as any other graphs that the package allows) without changing the data. Some packages require data to be reentered for each type of graph. This concept of *data independence* is an important one in computer graphics and will be examined carefully throughout the evaluation of each package.

Another concept equally important is how a format is stored. A *format* is usually defined as everything except the data and possibly the type of graph. This includes titles, labels, patterns, colors, scales, tick mark placement, legends, line connection, and possibly the type of graph. If you are producing graphs with different sets of data, you should be able to use the same format even with different types of graphs. Since you probably do not want to redefine the format each time, you should be able to store your favorite formats separately from the data. This *formatting independence* is also the mark of an exceptional computer graphics package.

Standalone graphics packages are the bread and butter in today's graphic world. As you read about each standalone package, remember, that the more a package can do in the shortest time, the more time you will have for preparing other aspects of your presentation.

MICROSOFT CHART

Microsoft Chart is one of the most versatile packages on the market today. The basic purpose of Chart is to provide a graphics environment that not only lets you quickly and easily redisplay your data in a wide variety of chart types, but also provides you with unparalleled flexibility for preparing effective business graphics.

Its best feature is the ability to move and restyle any part of the chart. Legends, titles, labels, and added chart notes can be moved anywhere on the chart and displayed in many different formats. Anything can be resized or restyled to fit individual tastes. Customizing the display is just one of Microsoft Chart's amazing qualities.

Another unique feature is the concept of the picture gallery. As shown in Fig. 9-1 there are eight basic different chart types that can be produced using Microsoft Chart. Each of these chart types has up to eight variations of each chart. Not including charts that you can customize there are over 40 different chart types.

Essentially Microsoft Chart is a menu-driven graphics package. It uses the same approaches that have contributed to the popularity of Microsoft's other products, such as its spreadsheet Multiplan and its project scheduler Project. Microsoft Chart uses horizontal selection menus. This type of menu is also found in other best selling spreadsheet packages such as Lotus 1-2-3 and Sorcim's SuperCalc3. Microsoft is the only company to have successfully adapted them to a graphics package. Because of this, anyone who has used one of the popular spreadsheet programs can instantly become familiar with the workings of Microsoft Chart.

Chart is being used by many groups of people that need graphics support, but its true value is for the person who needs graphs that must not only show the business graphics correctly, but must show the labels, axis, shading patterns, fonts, and even

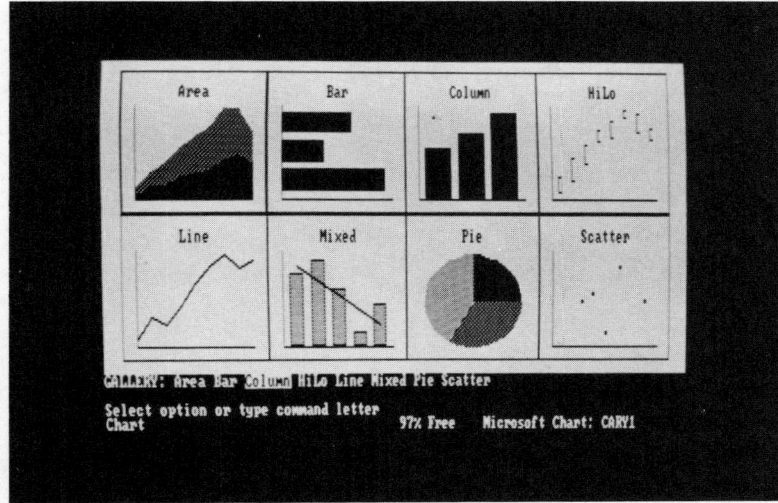

Fig. 9-1. The Microsoft Chart main menu.

arrows pointing to chart items and special chart notes. This complete on-screen customization is not found in any other package today.

Chart comes in a clear plastic library case. This device keeps the manual protected from dirt or any liquids that might be spilled. It also serves as a holder so that it can be read in several comfortable positions. The manual itself is 472 pages composed mostly of text and diagrams. It comes in a three-ring binder in traditional small, IBM PC-size pages. The manual is divided into several sections including a short tutorial, a section on using the more advanced features of Chart, and a command reference guide. There are also several appendices that explain file formats and the variety of fonts available. Microsoft Chart comes on two disks. One is the main system disk and the other is the font disk. Fonts from the font disk are copied onto the system disk as you need them. Generally, one disk is all that is needed to run Microsoft Chart.

Chart does not come with an interactive training session on a disk, but it has an adequate tutorial section that demonstrates the basics as you follow the instructions. Help is available at any moment by hitting <Alt-H>. Whatever is selected at that moment is the subject that the help panel will cover. There is also a help index, and Chart gives you the ability to go between help screens. The essentials of Chart can be learned in just a few hours; the advanced features will require about half a day to master. Several sample charts demonstrate some of the advanced features of Chart.

Creating a chart begins with entering the data. Because Chart allows you to share data between all its formats, you might think that understanding the techniques of data input is difficult. It is not. Two panels control the entire data input. Figure 9-2 shows the screen that allows you to define a data series. Microsoft Chart thinks of a data series as the data that would make up a single line. The x and y values are defined later. When you start the package this screen is displayed, ready for data input.

In Fig. 9-2, the third data series has just been defined. The name, which will be shown on the legend is "Trucks." The category name is the name of the x-axis, and the value name is the name of the y-axis. The category type is defined as a sequence that is a year starting in 1980 and being incremented one year at a time. This information is used when the actual data is entered.

Three data series have been defined. The Entry command found on the main panel allows you to define the data for a specific data series. Whichever series the cursor is on is the series that the data will be entered or edited for. As shown in Fig. 9-3, the first year that was defined in the series panel is shown first. As each data value is entered the year

```
Incl.(*) Name              Source of data      Type     # pts.

1  *   Tools               Entry               Sequence 5
2  *   Ladders             Entry               Sequence 5
3  *   Trucks              Entry               Sequence 5

NAME define series name: Trucks
         category name: Year            value name: Amount Sold
         category type: Date Number(Sequence)Text
         category start: 1980           increment: 1
         increment period: Day Month Weekday(Year)
Enter text
L3   List                          98% Free    Microsoft Chart: CARY1
```

Fig. 9-2. The Microsoft Chart defining a data series panel.

field is incremented by one. This is how data is entered into Microsoft Chart. Data is edited in the same way. A data series is chosen, and the previously entered data is displayed. You can edit any of the data or add more data points to it.

Once you have entered your data you can choose how you want to see it. This simple method of choosing different chart types is one of the best features of Chart. Chart gives you a gallery of different chart types. These types include Area, Bar, Column, HiLo, Line, Mixed, Pie, and Scatter. After you have input your data, you can choose the way you wish to see it displayed.

All chart types are available without changing your data. This is the most preferred method of handling data. No matter what form your data is in, Microsoft Chart can show it using any of the more than 45 chart types, which are variations of the eight basic types of graphs.

Figure 9-4 shows the different variations of the column chart. There are eight types of column charts available. Each chart can have many bars and is not limited to the number that are shown in the column gallery. You have your choice of seven types of bar charts, six types of line charts, six types of pie charts, seven types of area charts, and seven

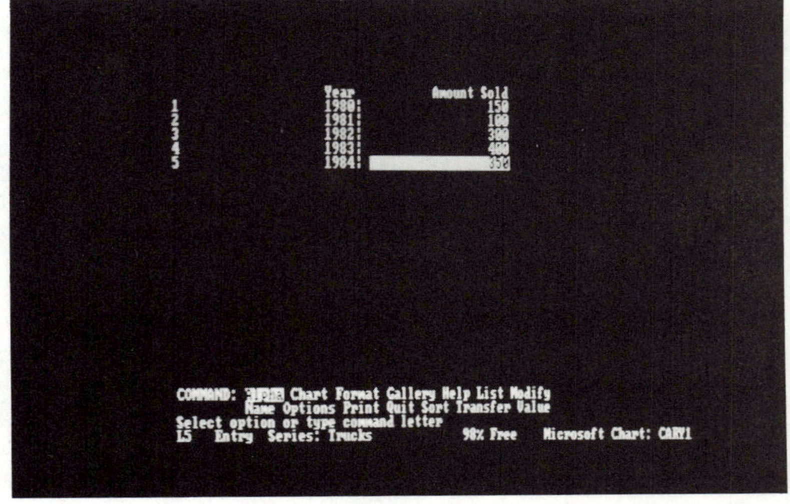

Fig. 9-3. The Microsoft Chart data entry panel.

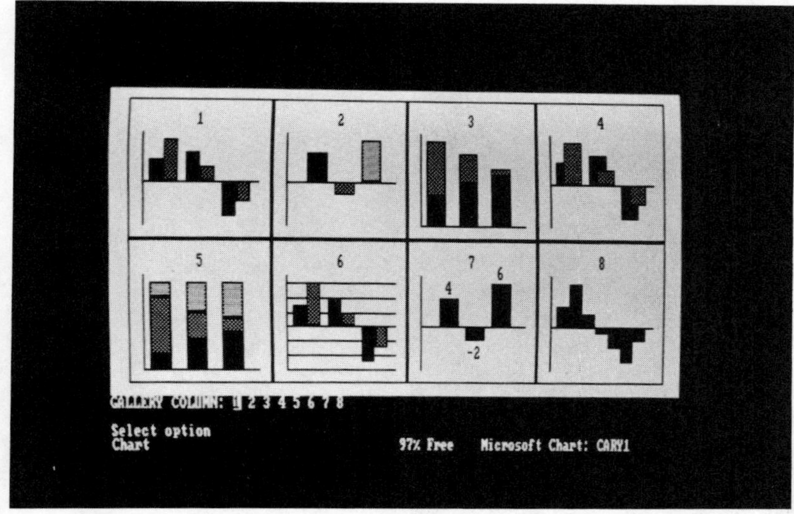

Fig. 9-4. The Microsoft Chart column gallery.

types of mixed charts, as shown in Fig. 9-5.

Once you have selected the type of chart from the main gallery (refer back to Fig. 9-1) and then selected the specific variation of the chart, the graph will be drawn to fit all of your data. Figure 9-6 shows the effect of selecting <Gallery Column 1>. A simple column chart is displayed on the screen.

The gallery is a user-friendly and quick way of letting you select different type of formats. However, the galleries are simply a guide. You can select different types of graphs without using the galleries at all. Instead you could use several different menus to create complex graphs. The graphs in the galleries are merely suggestions of the most common types of graphs you might want. Figure 9-7 shows the Format Type menu that is used for changing chart types without using the gallery. The type of graph can be selected. You can also define which series are to appear in the graph. This allows you to create graphs that don't use all your data. "Vary by categories" option allows you to select different patterns or colors for the bars and can be set to one pattern if you desire. The stacked bar option and the amount of space between columns can also be

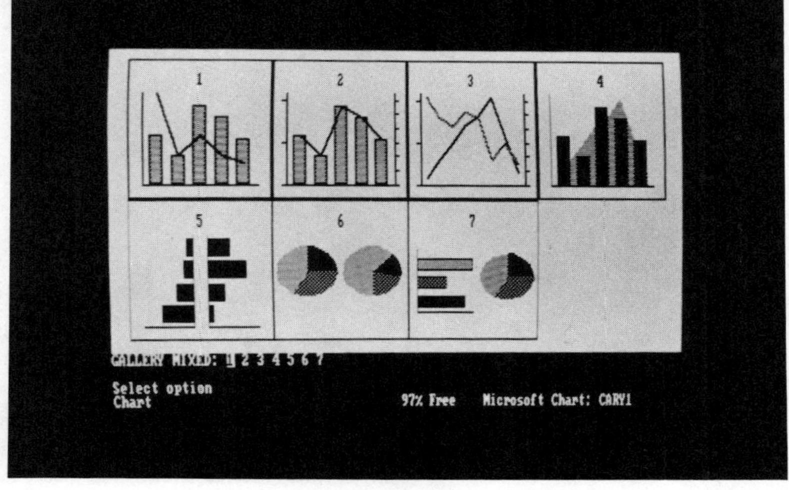

Fig. 9-5. The Microsoft Chart mixed gallery.

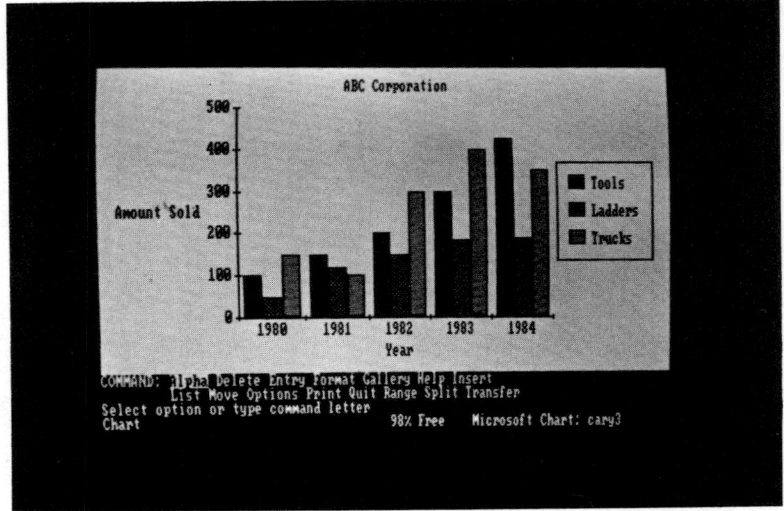

Fig. 9-6. The Microsoft Chart simple column chart.

controlled from this menu. Zero percent spacing will place the bars adjacent to each other as in a histogram. You can also overlap the bars to create an unusual effect as shown in chart number four in Fig. 9-4. A frame can also be drawn around the whole graph with the Format command.

The true power of Chart comes from its formatting commands. These commands allow almost everything to be styled in some way. Chart allows you to first select the object or part of a chart to be formatted and then lets you use many selection menus to format the item down to the tiniest detail. Figure 9-8 shows a chart after the legend has been moved and formatted,the title has been formatted, and new labels were added along with arrows pointing to the desired bars. At the bottom of Fig. 9-8 are some of the sample format commands used to format the title. The options have been selected using an arrow that can be moved from item to item. In this case, the title label was selected. Now, when you begin to use the formatting commands, you have the option of changing the item you have selected to format without leaving the menu itself. Features like these save valuable keystrokes and make

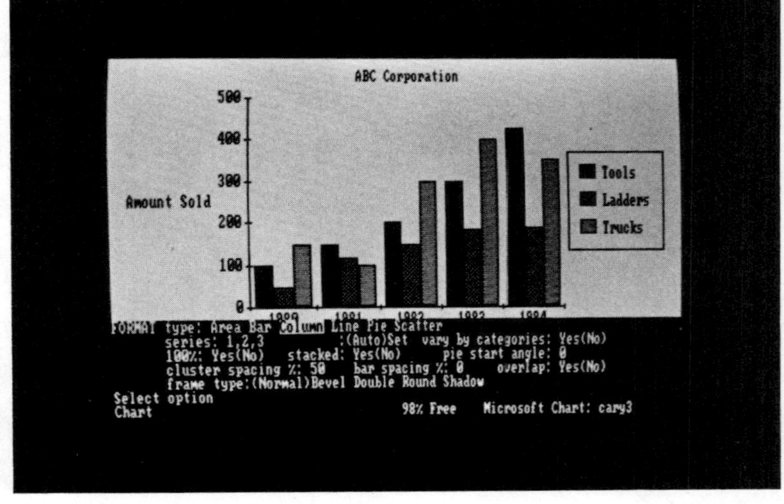

Fig. 9-7. The Microsoft Chart format command.

Microsoft Chart a truly productive tool.

A label can be customized by changing its text or by adding one of several types of borders (the title has a double border while the legend was styled with a shadow effect). Any text can be placed either vertically or horizontally. As you can see from the menu at the bottom of the screen, you can change the font type and size, realign the label (or whatever you are working on) at the top, bottom, middle, left, right, or center of the screen, and change the size and shape of the border.

The text fonts include Modern, Roman, Script, Decor, Foreign, and Symbols. There are *raster fonts,* which are used with raster devices such as screens and dot-matrix printers and are available in fixed sizes. There are also stroke fonts in any size for plotters and such devices. Fonts can be bold, italic, and underlined as well. With the fonts provided and the ability to add additional fonts, the text handling capabilities of Chart are limitless.

These are just some of the formatting commands available for legends, titles, and chart notes. Even more amazing is the ability to move any part of a Microsoft Chart around on the screen. Using the arrow that appears on the screen when you press any of the cursor keys, you select the object you want moved. Once you choose the object, you have two choices; you can input the x and y coordinates to which you want to move the object, or you can use the cursor keys to move the object. Once you move the object, the screen is redrawn to take advantage of its movement. Figures 9-7 and 9-8 illustrate how this happens. Note how the legend has been moved to the center of the screen and the graph has been expanded to fill the void.

Not only can you move legends, titles, and labels, but after drawing the borders around them, you can resize them. If you wanted Tools, Ladders, and Trucks to be on one horizontal line, you could grab the legend and stretch if lengthwise and shrink it vertically. The text inside the border would be redrawn to fit inside the border.

Unlike many graphics packages, Chart enables you to add notes anywhere on the screen in any font or size. Arrows can be drawn from the chart notes or any other label to any series point. In Fig. 9-8 arrows help explain the chart. The arrows themselves can be formatted to have different sized heads, and open or closed arrowheads; even the width of the head can be controlled. The color of any object can be controlled. When you are dealing with bar charts and any chart that requires patterns, the pattern, color, border, and even weight can be carefully controlled. Tick marks can be controlled to be inside, outside, or centered on the axis lines.

Another major feature is the ability to place the actual values of the points above, below, or on the

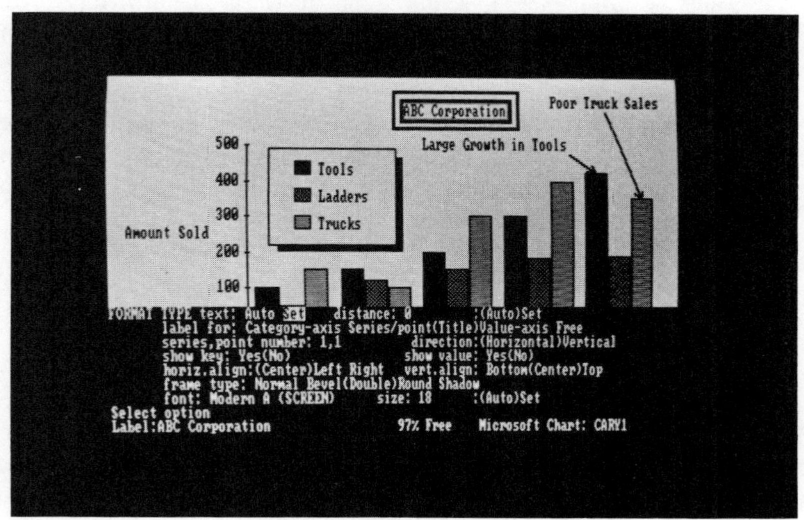

Fig. 9-8. The Microsoft Chart style format command.

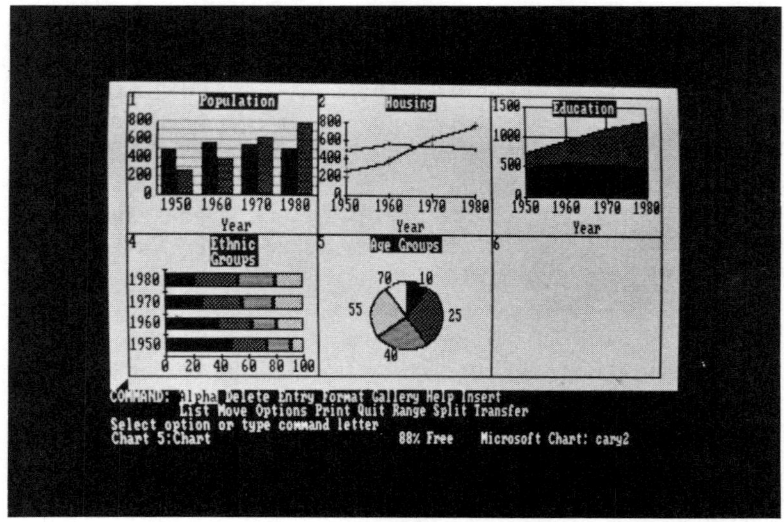

Fig. 9-9. The Microsoft Chart multiple graphs screen.

point itself. A rule of thumb we quickly learned was that anything can be formatted. There is little doubt that Microsoft Chart's true power is in its formatting commands and its excellent quality graphs.

The formatting commands can be stored separately from the data. This allows many graphs with different data and even different labels and titles to be styled in the same manner for a consistent look. The "Transfer Load" and "Transfer Save" commands allow you to choose to load and save the "Data," the "Format," or "All" (both the data and the format).

Another useful feature is the ability to work with several graphs at the same time. Figure 9-9 shows a screen that has been split into six areas in which different graphs were created. Each graph can be blown up to full size and styled accordingly.

Multiple graphs can share one set of data, and you can select which data series you want to display on each individual graph. Figure 9-9 was created using one set of 11 data series. Graph 1 used two of them, while graph 4 used four different sets of data. You do not have to have separate data storage for different graphs. You can tell Chart which data is applicable for each graph. By removing the border lines, moving three graphs around the screen, and adding and moving titles, you can create the dazzling effect shown in Fig. 9-10.

Microsoft Chart can be run in high resolution black and white or in medium resolution color. You cannot readily switch between the two. Whatever you specify when booting Chart will be in effect until you leave the program.

The output quality of Microsoft Chart both on the screen and on printer or plotter is fascinating. Sometimes labels do not appear exactly where you want them when you are using hardcopy devices. These instances are rare and can be corrected easily because you can set your screen view to a *printer view.* This means that what you see on the screen will be as it appears on the printer. The text will be difficult to read and the graph slightly blurred, but the exact alignment and placement of labels and arrows is achieved.

Microsoft Chart supports the "complete" array of graphic printers and plotters available today. It is very easy to switch between devices by using the cursor keys. Resolution on a dot matrix printer is high quality and brings desired results. The plotter yields its usually excellent quality and range of colors. The Polaroid Palette is not directly supported at this time, although you can capture screen images.

Overall this package is among the best on the market. It is fast, error free, and supported by one of the leading microcomputer product corporations. It is very easy to learn to do simple graphs and moderately easy to learn to do even the most ad-

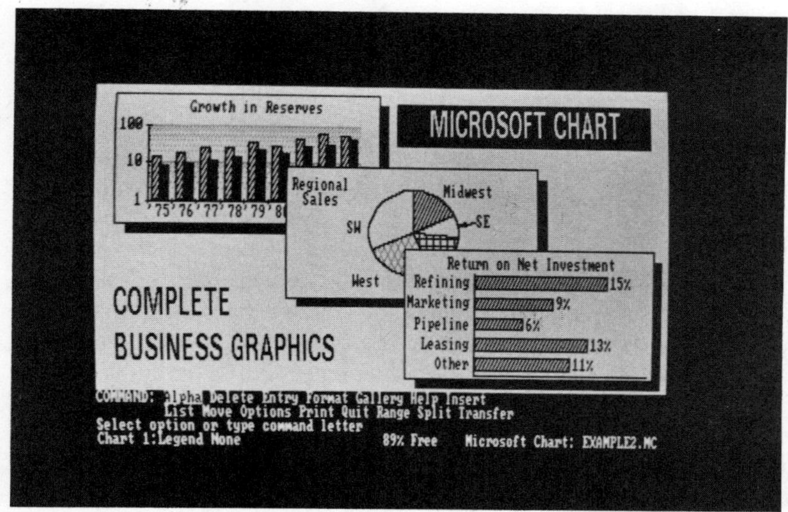

Fig. 9-10. The Microsoft Chart dazzling effect.

vanced charts. A full day with Microsoft Chart would make you an expert with the only limit being your knowledge of graphics. After reading this book, that shouldn't be a problem either.

If you need a package that must do a large variety of the basic charts, provide completely customized charts, and produce excellent output, Microsoft Chart is for you!

CHART-MASTER

Chart-Master is a menu-driven standalone graphics package produced by Decision Resources of Westport, Connecticut. This company was founded in June of 1981 and was started in order to design, develop, and market quality software tools for use by business professionals. Decision Resources produces and markets three graphics products: Chart-Master for business graphics, Sign-Master for text slides and tabular data, and Diagram-Master for organization, and gantt charts.

From the very first screen, pictured in Fig. 9-11, Chart-Master leaves no doubt that it is a high-quality graphics package.

Chart-Master is one of the easiest to use

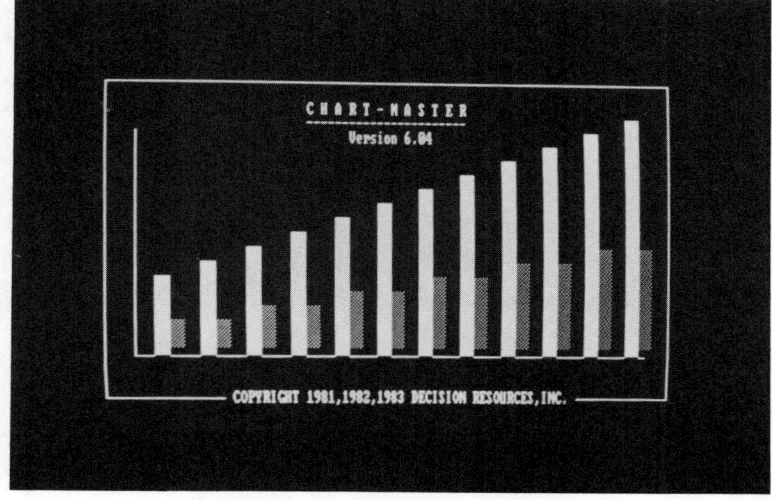

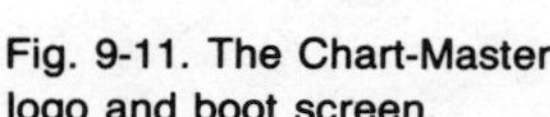
Fig. 9-11. The Chart-Master logo and boot screen.

packages on the market today. Its simple menu structure makes it simple to create a chart without ever opening the manual. Though it is menu driven and very simple to operate, it provides the user with a high degree of control throughout the graph creation process. One of the unique features of Chart-Master is its ability to work with a plotter. Using the IBM PC's cursor keys you can control the plotter pen to precisely determine where to put the graph and how big to make it. This allows multiple graphs to be placed on a page with a degree of control unmatched by any other package on the market.

Chart-Master is for the person that needs to produce a large number of high-quality plots or prints and doesn't need complete customization. It is not as powerful as other packages but its ease of use and very high quality output make up for it's lack of features.

Chart-Master comes in a single IBM type binder and slipcover. Two hundred pages of documentation complete with a book tutorial make it easy to get started. Fortunately a lack of pictures and diagrams doesn't hurt the manual because the package is very easy to use. The package also contains an excellent library of sample charts along with full color plot samples. A demonstration guide provides excellent help in getting started. Chart-Master comes on one disk along with a pie chart disk and a sample charts disk. You should be able to learn to create your first graph in less than five minutes.

Chart-Master begins with its main menu, as shown in Fig. 9-12. From this menu you can choose to create, verify, plot, edit, store, retrieve, or delete a chart; to change the options that are available; or to use a set of miscellaneous options.

You begin by creating a chart. Menu item one will guide you through a series of steps to create a graph. When you create a graph, the first screen you will see is the title screen. As shown in Fig. 9-13, you must first enter title lines. You can enter none, if you want, or as many as four. You can style each line or even each letter by going to the bottom of the menu and changing some of the defaults. Chart-Master has six fonts including standard, bold standard, roman, bold roman, script, and gothic. Each line, word, or character can also be sized from size one to size sixteen (actually identified as sizes 1 through G) with the default being seven. You can also choose to underline the selected text or to make it italic. You can choose to left-or right-justify the item, or to center it. The last item you can select is the pen number to be used when working with a plotter. These options may not be as powerful as those offered by some of the other packages, but they will do the job 90 percent of the time.

After you enter the titles, you can deal with the axis labels. Up to two x- and y-axis labels can be

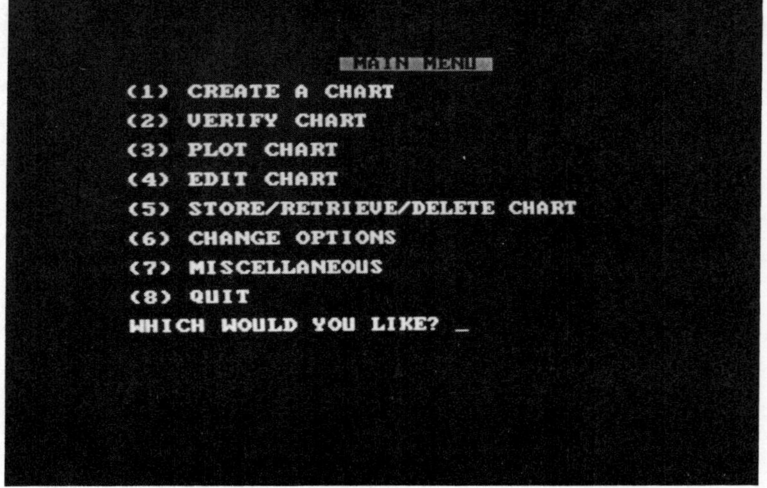

Fig. 9-12. The Chart-Master main menu.

TITLES

ENTER TITLE LINE 1 : BC CORPORATION
ENTER TITLE LINE 2 : OTAL SALES
ENTER TITLE LINE 3 : 1980-1984)
ENTER TITLE LINE 4 : _

FONT STD
SIZE 7
ITALICS NO
JUSTIFY CENTER
PEN 1
UNDERLINE NO

Fig. 9-13. The Chart-Master titles screen.

entered. The same styling features that apply to the titles can be applied to labels.

Chart-Master then forces you to decide how many variables or data series there will be and how many observations or x-axis points there will be. A screen that displays each question is used for this.

You can either type in your data, or retrieve it from any standard DIF file from Lotus 1-2-3, SuperCalc, or VisiCalc. After you choose the number of variables and the number of observations, the variable label screen appears and then the observation label screen is displayed. Both screens allow you to restyle the labels according to your tastes. Figures 9-14 and 9-15 show these screens.

Finally, you get to entering data. Figure 9-16 shows a typical data entry screen after it has been filled in. For each variable there will be a screen that allows you to enter as many observations as you have chosen. The labels for each are shown, and only the y value is input in each case.

Once the data is entered, you are automatically returned to the main menu to choose your next course of action. Data is shared by all graph types. Before you display your chart you can verify the data

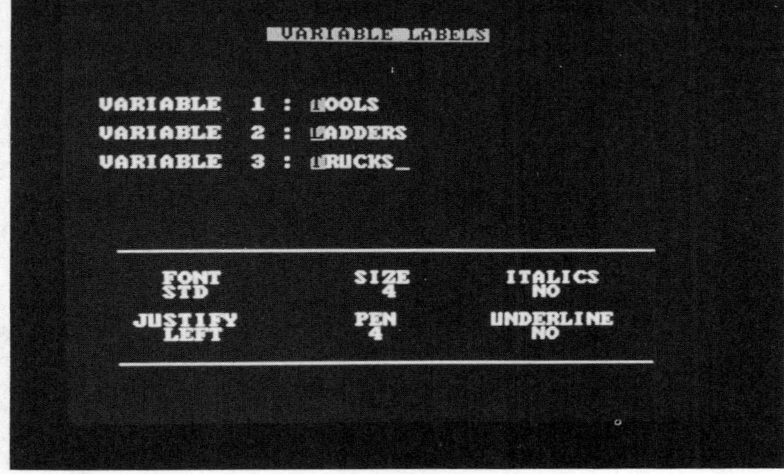

Fig. 9-14. The Chart-Master variable label screen.

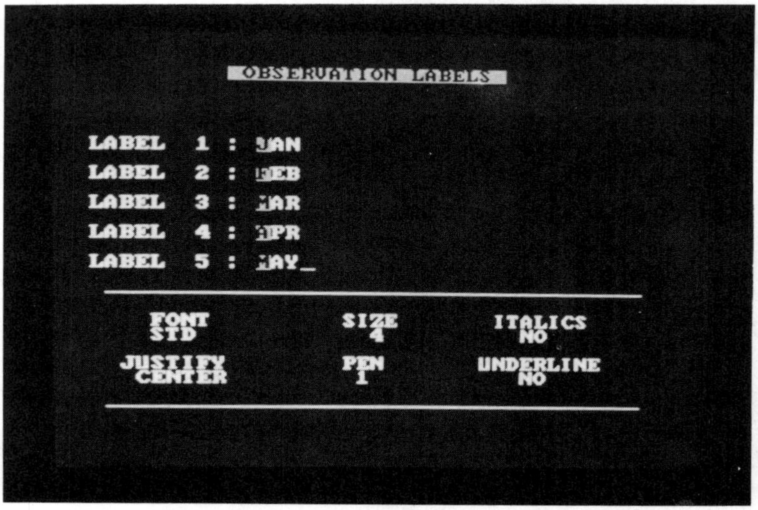

Fig. 9-15. The Chart-Master observation label screen.

using main menu selection number two. If you don't usually make mistakes, you will probably want to display your chart without verifying the data. Choosing option number three on the main menu will cause the plot menu to be displayed. As shown in Fig. 9-17, this menu allows you to choose from two types of bar charts, scatter charts, line charts, pie charts, and area charts.

You can choose the type of chart that you want to produce. After you choose the chart type, the main menu appears on the screen. You can then display the graph. Graphs are displayed through the produce chart on ... menu. This menu, as shown in Fig. 9-18, allows you to choose between a variety of output devices including the screen, printers, plotters, and the Polaroid Palette.

There are three different options for the screen; high resolution black and white, or medium resolution in green, red, and brown or in cyan, magenta, and white.

As shown in Fig. 9-19, the screen images are fair at best. Chart-Master is not strong here. Its plots on dot-matrix printers are not much better. Chart-Master's strong points are on the Polaroid Palette and especially on the Hewlett-Packard line of plotters.

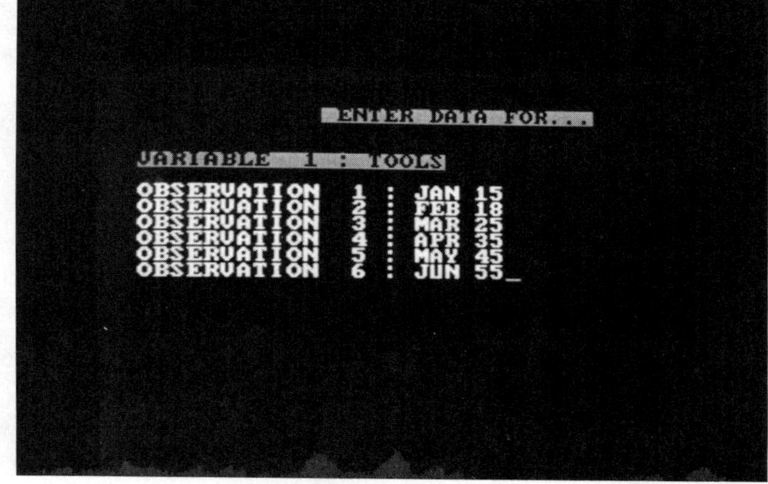

Fig. 9-16. The Chart-Master data entry screen.

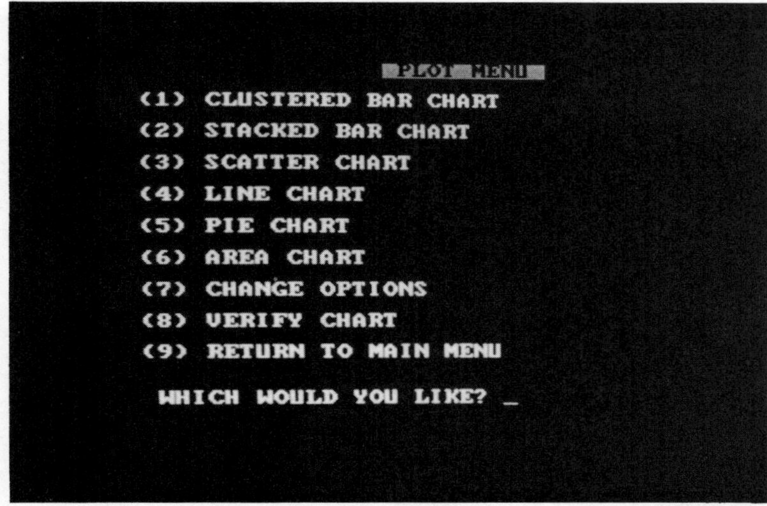

Fig. 9-17. The Chart-Master plot menu screen.

Making changes in your chart is easy. The main menu features an "Edit Chart" option. As shown in Fig. 9-20 you can edit the titles, labels, or data that you have entered. Once you choose the section to be edited, the same menu that you entered your data with is displayed. At this point, it contains the values that you have entered and allows you to change them.

After your chart is entered, you can customize it to a very high degree. There is a separate customization menu for each chart type.

Bar charts can be styled as shown in Fig. 9-21. Both clustered and stacked bar charts are styled here. The actual data value can be placed atop the bars. Hatching means that each bar will contain a different hatch pattern for each variable. You can select the hatching pattern from a list of eight hatch patterns. The legend heading does not have to say "Legend." You can change it to anything you want. The legend can be placed anywhere on the screen. Regression can be applied to the bars and can produce a trend line. Subsequent menus prompt you for more information on each of the bars. Normally the bar chart is a vertical one, but you can specify

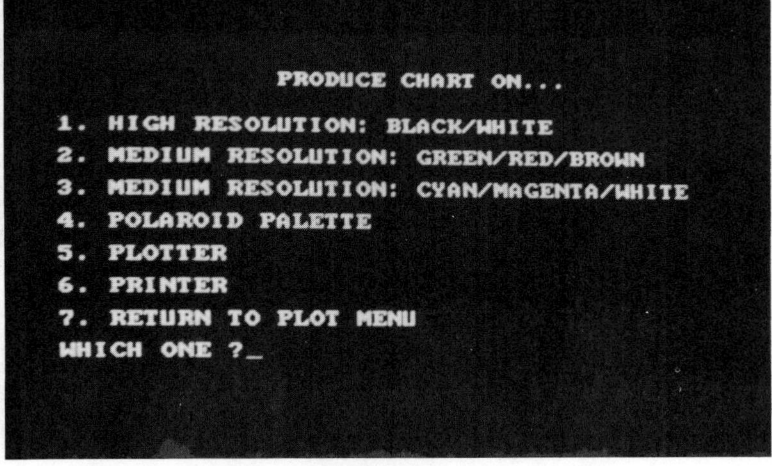

Fig. 9-18. The Chart-Master produce chart on . . . screen.

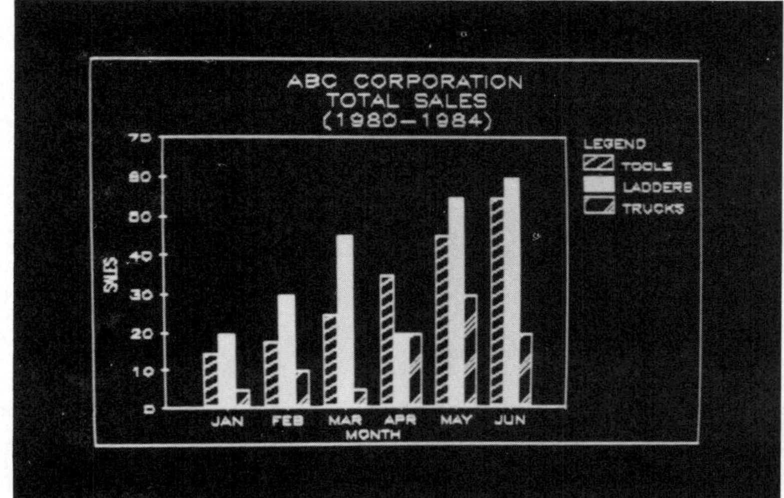

Fig. 9-19. The Chart-Master screen image.

horizontal bars on this menu.

There are also option menus that apply to a chart regardless of its type. These allow you to define the plot size on hardcopy or on the screen and to select the orientation of the graph. You can also choose whether the graph will take up the whole page or be drawn in a small area of the screen or paper. You can select the pen speed when you are using a plotter. Slower speeds are necessary when you are creating a transparency. The frame option is used to determine whether or not a border should be drawn around the graph. Outer means that a border will be drawn around the entire page or screen. Inner is a unique type of border that puts the chart itself inside a box and places all axis markings and labels outside of the inner box. In effect it is an unlabeled x-axis on top of the graph and an unmarked y-axis on the right side of the graph. A footnote can also be defined for any graph.

Line charts can also be styled using an options menu. The actual data value can be placed atop the points. You can specify the line type from a list of eight line types. The legend heading does not have to say "Legend." You can change it to anything you

Fig. 9-20. The Chart-Master edit screen.

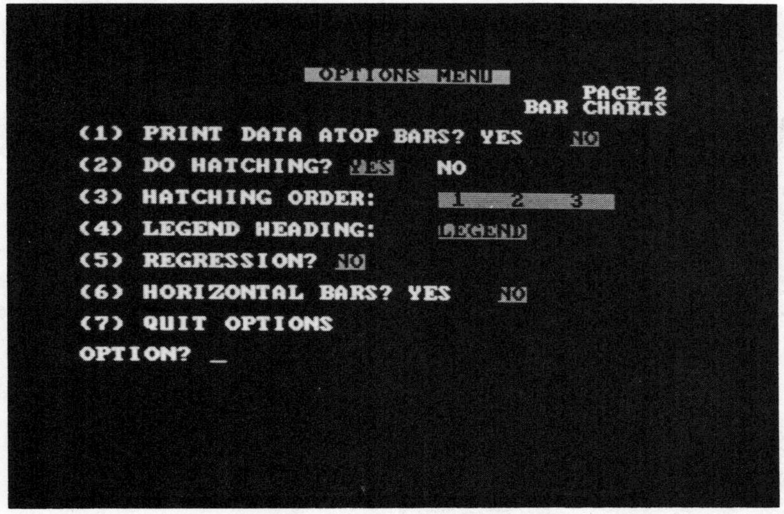

Fig. 9-21. The Chart-Master bar charts option menu screen.

want. The legend can be moved to anywhere on the screen. Regression can be applied to the points and can produce a trend line. Subsequent menus prompt you for more information on each of the lines. The lines can have symbols if you desire, and you can choose from a list of eight symbols.

There are also options to control the left and right y-axes. You can decide which variables will be plotted against each axis and whether the scale is logarithmic or linear. You can also specify the minimum and maximum y values and the units between this range. Grid lines can be added through this menu, and different line types can be used for the grid lines. The right axis menu is the same as the left axis menu, except the options apply to the right y-axis. Using a right y-axis, you can plot different scales on the same graph, as shown in Fig. 9-22.

Pie charts are the last menu option available. Multiple pies are produced for each set of data if

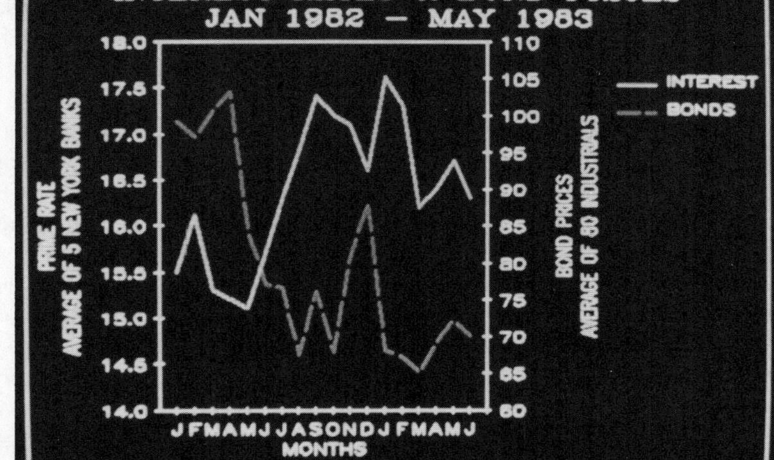

Fig. 9-22. A Chart-Master graph with a right axis.

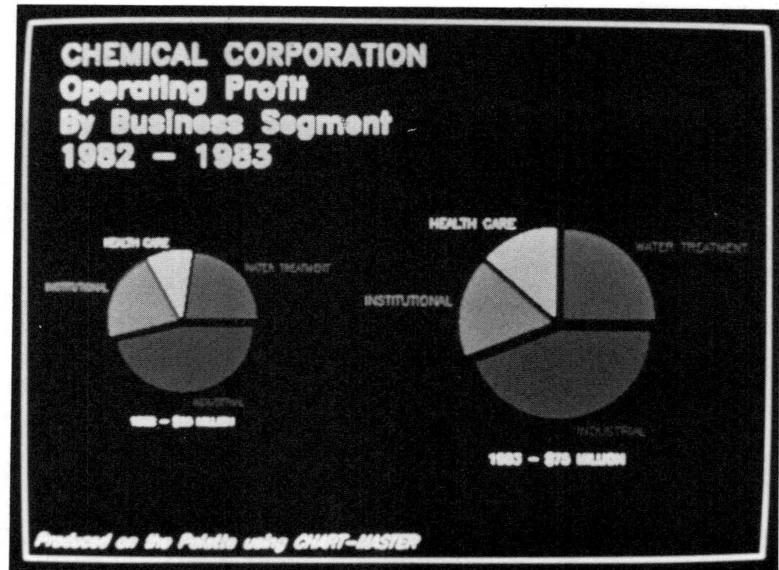

Fig. 9-23. The Chart-Master proportional pies.

there are more than one variable. The data can be used in absolute terms or as a percentage with the Data option. You can place the percentage or actual value inside each pie slice. You can also control how the pies are produced from the data. Each pie can be an observation or a variable. The maximum is four pies and twenty slices. You can choose to plot any or all of the four pies if you have at least four data items. You can also control the type of filling and the order of the hatching patterns. Pie chart explosion is also available. Another very important feature is the ability to create proportional pies. As shown in Fig. 9-23, this allows you to have several pies whose actual size is in proportion to the total of the actual values in each pie itself. This means that three pies shown together for several years where sales are increasing would show several different size pies with the largest pie representing the total sales.

Storing and retrieving charts is easy. You can get a catalog of all your charts. Each one has a number beside it and can be retrieved by the number only. The data and formatting commands are stored together. If you wish to save a graph with the same data in different formats you will be saving the data automatically each time.

As discussed earlier, one of the unique features of Chart-Master is its ability to work with a plotter. Figure 9-24 demonstrates the quality of the plotted output. This output is actually two charts, one overlaid on the other. What is unusual about this is the ease with which it was done. With most packages, you would have to plot the larger chart, measure the offset from the left and top sides, and calculate the space available for the smaller graph. If you measured right and were lucky, the second graph would fit inside the first. If you were wrong both graphs would have to be replotted. With Chart-Master, there is no guesswork. After you have drawn the first graph with your plotter, Chart-Master can place the second graph anywhere on the same paper. By using a very friendly interface, you can use your IBM PC cursor keys to touch two points inside the first plot. These two points become the corners of the graph frame and the new plot is drawn within those boundaries in perfect proportion. This allows a multitude of graphs to be placed inside another graph or anywhere on a piece of paper.

Chart-Master is free of errors and very quick. This has helped the Chart-Master package get to the top of the graphics package market. Chart-Master is a simple menu driven package that lets you create excellent quality plots and Polaroid pal-

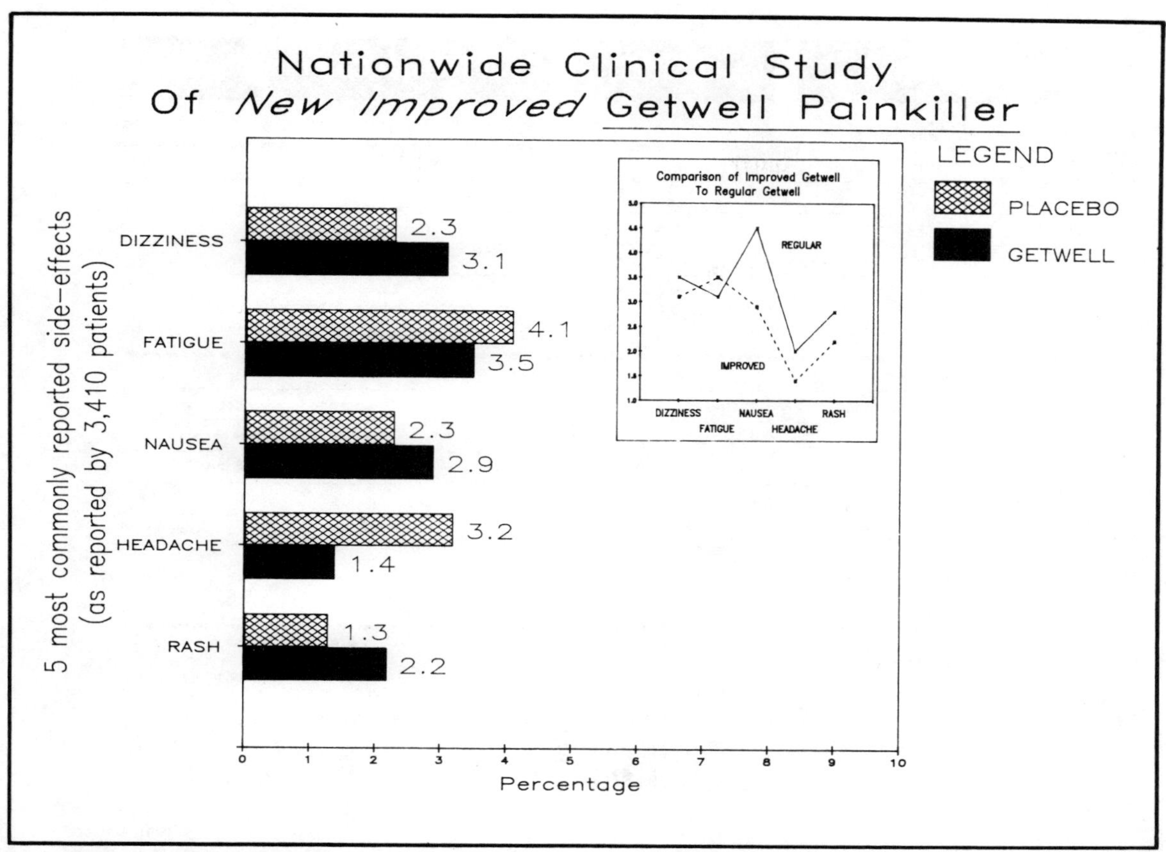

Fig. 9-24. Chart-Master plotter output.

ette images. It is extremely powerful, yet easy to use. If you need extremely high quality graphics and want to do as little work as possible, Chart-Master is for you.

GRAPHWRITER

Graphwriter by Graphics Communications Inc. of Waltham, Massachusetts is another outstanding package. It features more types of graphs than any other package on the market today. Graphwriter works on the IBM PC and the DEC Rainbow.

Graphwriter is essentially a menu driven product. It uses selection menus to let you choose the next course of action and then asks questions one line at a time to derive the desired inputs to produce the graph. Graphwriter comes with a set of input sheets that allow you to fill in the information that will be required. This includes the chart data and the formatting specifications. Figure 9-25 shows a sample Graphwriter input form for the Pie-Bar Chart. When you are actually creating a Pie-Bar Chart, the menus look very much like the input sheets.

Graphwriter enables you to produce an amazing array of charts. There is a basic set of 11 totally different types of charts, and an extension set of 12 more types, including mixed charts, pie/bar charts, Gantt charts, Organization charts, and the little known bubble charts. Even text charts can be created using Graphwriter. Graphwriter also has many formatting options that allow you to make very presentable charts.

The number of types of graphs produced is tru-

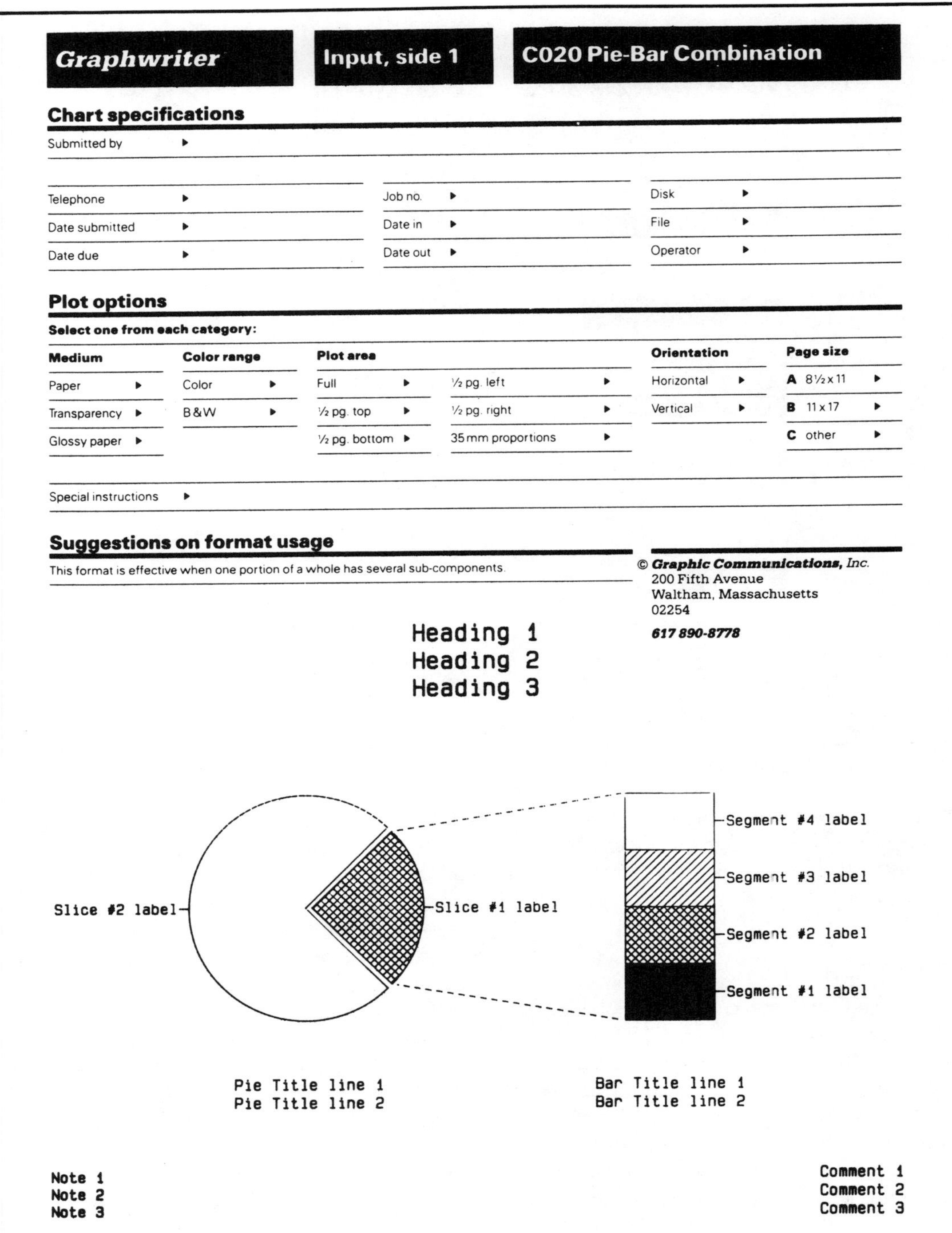

Graphwriter | Input, side 1 | C020 Pie-Bar Combination

Chart specifications

Submitted by ▸

Telephone ▸
Date submitted ▸
Date due ▸

Job no. ▸
Date in ▸
Date out ▸

Disk ▸
File ▸
Operator ▸

Plot options

Select one from each category:

Medium	Color range	Plot area		Orientation	Page size
Paper ▸	Color ▸	Full ▸	½ pg. left ▸	Horizontal ▸	**A** 8½ x 11 ▸
Transparency ▸	B&W ▸	½ pg. top ▸	½ pg. right ▸	Vertical ▸	**B** 11 x 17 ▸
Glossy paper ▸		½ pg. bottom ▸	35 mm proportions ▸		**C** other ▸

Special instructions ▸

Suggestions on format usage

This format is effective when one portion of a whole has several sub-components.

200 Fifth Avenue
Waltham, Massachusetts
02254
617 890-8778

Fig. 9-25. A Graphwriter sample input form.

Graphwriter | **Input, side 2** | **C020 Pie-Bar Combination**

Titles

Print exactly as desired; observe character count maximum.

Heading 1 ▶		48
Heading 2 ▶		48
Heading 3 ▶		48
Note 1 ▶		48
Note 2 ▶		48
Note 3 ▶		48

Pie title	Line 1	32	Line 2		32
Bar title	Line 1	32	Line 2		32

Data

Use additional forms for slices/segments 9–16.

Pie **Which slice expanded into bar?**

Slice (1–16)	**Slice label** 20	**Slice value**	**Color**	**Pattern**
1				
2				
3				
4				
5				
6				
7				
8				

Bar

Seg. (1–16)	**Segment label** 20	**Seg. value**	**Color**	**Pattern**
1				
2				
3				
4				
5				
6				
7				
8				
9				
10				

Color codes

1 Black	6 Brown
2 Blue	7 Violet
3 Green	8 Turquoise
4 Red	9 Gold
5 Orange	10 Lime green

Pattern codes

1, 2, 3, 4, 5, 6, 7, 8

Comments

Comment 1	Location
Comment 2	
Comment 3	

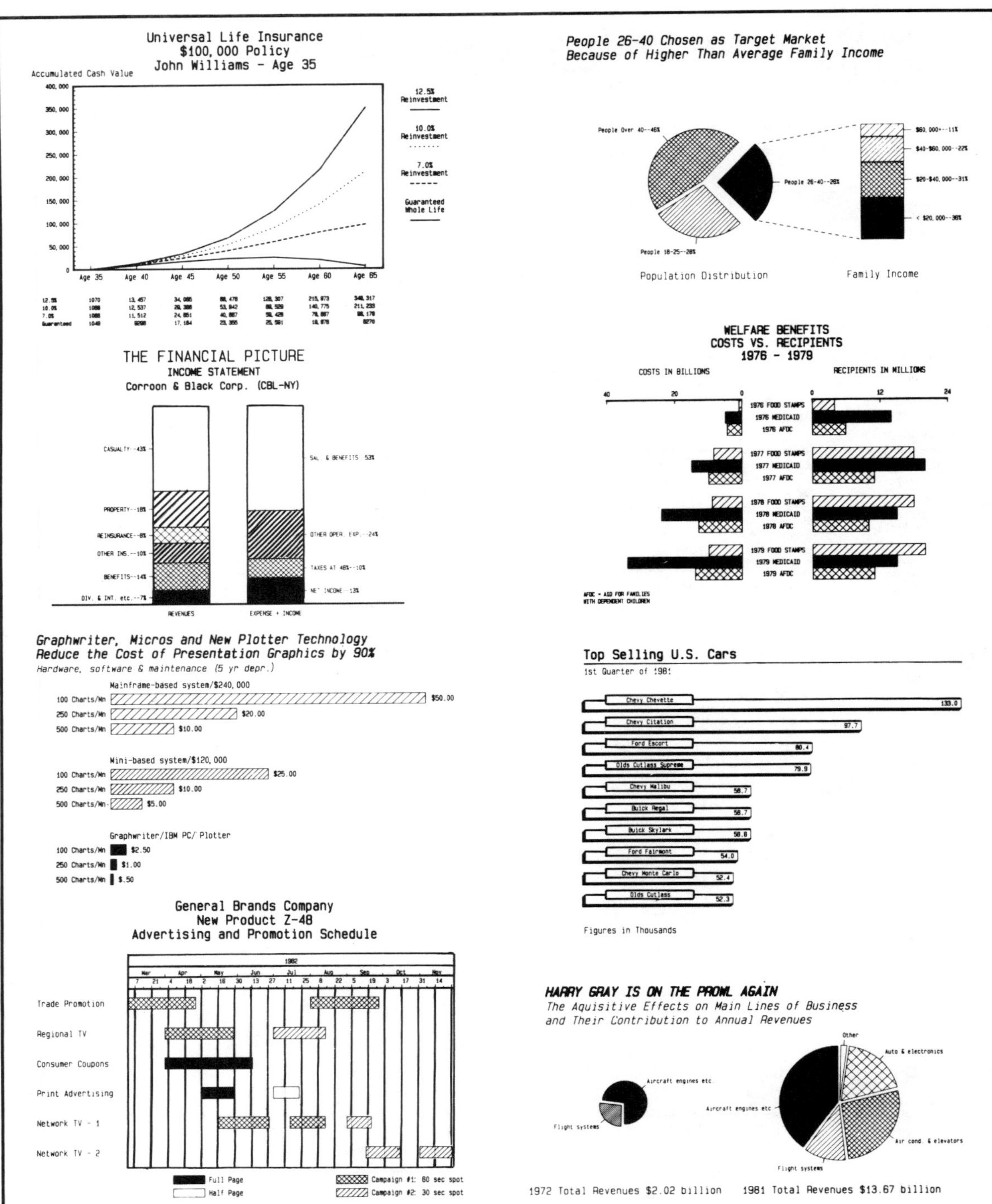

Fig. 9-26. Graphwriter Sample Chart Formats.

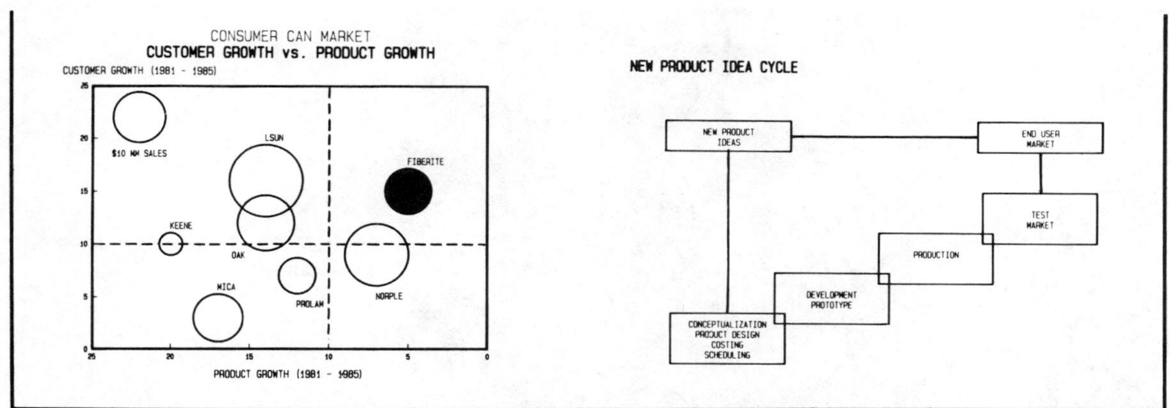

ly amazing. Figure 9-26 is a sample of the format selection guide.

Most of the graph types cannot share data. This restriction doesn't seem to hurt Graphwriters performance because "families" of graph types can share data. Certain bar charts can share data, for example. This forces you to decide what kind of chart you want before you begin, but it results in a better first chart.

Graphwriter comes in a single manual in an IBM size binder and slipcover. The manual contains about 500 pages and is chock full of examples, diagrams, and graphic displays. The package comes on 10 disks with the extension set and occupies almost 4 megabytes of a fixed disk. Disk swapping is not really a problem because you only have to change disks when you change chart types. There also is some minor disk swapping for some of the options. There is an excellent book tutorial. Graphwriter also comes with two excellent pocket reference guides; one is a format selection guide, and the other is a demonstration guide. The manual itself is well written and expertly indexed.

There are literally hundreds of menus in Graphwriter. You only see them as you use the product and request more detailed charts. Often a menu asks for information. If you have never seen the menu before, you would normally be scrambling for the manual. Graphwriter, however, provides excellent on-line help at all times. Whenever something that you don't understand is displayed, you simply hit the <F1> function key, and the possible responses and an explanation are shown. You can then input the desired response and continue.

Learning time is fairly long, but you only need to learn about the menus you use. Graphwriter is not hard to learn once you get over being intimidated by the size of the product.

Graphwriter can handle manually input data or data from other popular programs.

It is very easy to create your first chart. After starting with the main menu, which allows you to create a chart, you are placed in the "Select Graphwriter Format" menu, as shown in Fig. 9-27. This menu allows you to choose one of the basic format types from either the Basic or Extension set.

Once you have selected your format you will be instructed to insert the proper disk and choose your method of data entry. You can enter new data or edit previously saved data. Most charts begin by prompting you to enter the headings. A sample headings menu is shown in Fig. 9-28. After the headings are entered, another screen that lets you enter chart notes appears.

Once your headings are entered, you are instructed to enter the x-axis titles, the y-axis titles, and the range values. Depending on the type of chart, you may then be asked how many variables or bars there will be, along with how many observations or segments there will be. If there are more than one variable, a legend screen is next. Each screen is made up of standard 80 column text. Legends can have multiple lines. After the legends

```
Select Graphwriter Format
------------------------------------------------------------

   Basic Set                              Extension Set
   ---------                              -------------
1. B010 - Column chart (vertical)      13. S020 - Gantt chart
2. B011 - Bar chart (horizontal)       14. S030 - Organization chart
3. B020 - Segmented bars (vertical)    15. S040 - Bubble chart
4. B021 - Segmented bars (horizontal)  16. S050 - Table chart
5. B030 - Clustered bars (vertical)    17. C020 - Pie-Bar combination
6. B031 - Clustered bars (horizontal)  18. L020 - Surface Line chart
7. P010 - Pie chart (1-4 pies)         19. L030 - Line-Table chart
8. L010 - Line chart                   20. B022 - Double stacked bars
9. S010 - Scatter plot (regression)    21. B032 - Grouped bars
10. C010 - Bar-Line combination        22. B040 - Range chart (bars)
11. T010 - Text/Word chart             23. B050 - Paired bars
12.      - Unused                      24. B060 - Horiz. bars (inset labels)

Select one: _
```

Fig. 9-27. The Graphwriter select format screen.

are entered the bar or x-axis labels are entered. Figure 9-29 shows these labels being entered.

Once the labels have been entered, Graphwriter will guide you through the data entry screens. There will be one screen for each variable (or more if there is a lot of data). The labels that you entered are displayed along with a space in which you can enter your data for each value. Once your data is entered, there are several more menus. The next menu is a styling menu. Figure 9-30 shows this menu. You can change styles of different parts of the chart including the headings, titles, colors, shading patterns, and text.

Graphwriter allows much formatting. Graphs can be horizontal or vertical. Graphs can be placed anywhere on the paper. Multiple graphs can easily be placed on a page. Graphics can also be plotted without any text to allow for later typesetting. Graphwriter can adjust the location of all headings, footnotes, and legends to allow for transparency frames. The chart elements are separated to prevent color bleed, and the pen speed and fill type are automatically altered to handle the transparency pens and material. Graphwriter also contains a special format for plotting 35mm slides.

Graphwriter features a variety of patterns, line

```
Enter headings
------------------------------------------------------------

Heading 1 is ....... unspecified                          :
Enter new heading 1: ABC CORPORATION

Heading 2 is ....... unspecified                          :
Enter new heading 2:

Heading 3 is ....... unspecified                          :
Enter new heading 3: _
```

Fig. 9-28. A Graphwriter sample heading screen.

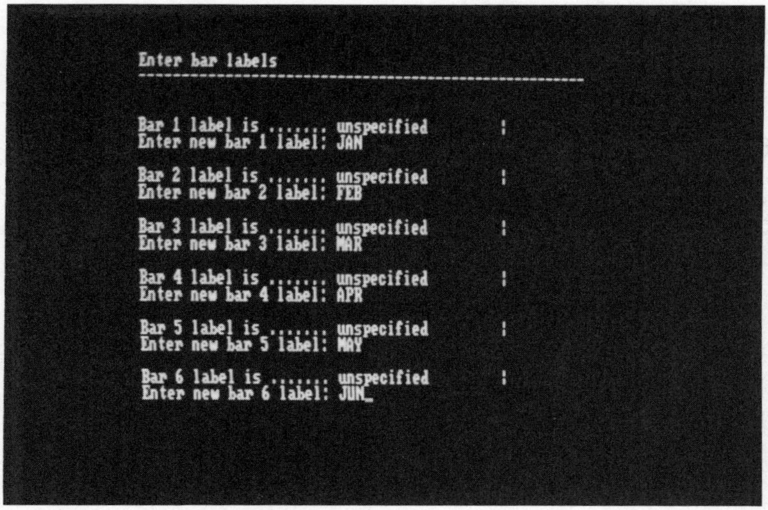

Fig. 9-29. A Graphwriter sample bar labels screen.

types, and plotting symbols. You can control the formatting of grid elements, labels, tick marks, the x- and y-axes, the text, legends, headings, and data values on lines or bars. There is also a complete array of fonts including both vector and raster fonts. Through the formatting commands, you can place any of the objects anywhere on the graph and can place a frame around the entire graph.

Data and formats are generally saved together. When you save the data, the format is stored along with it. A series of menus controls this phase of Graphwriter.

Once you have chosen your styles it is time to plot a graph. Figure 9-31 shows the plot menu.

Graphwriter, like most packages does not do a tremendous job on the screen. Its true worth is on a color plotter or on a Polaroid Palette with its higher resolution. A complete interface to the Palette means that it's unnecessary to leave the program to use the Palette. The slides are produced with resolution far greater than that of your monitor. Graphwriter also works with most black and white printers. Graphwriter features a batching facility that plots one graph after another on your

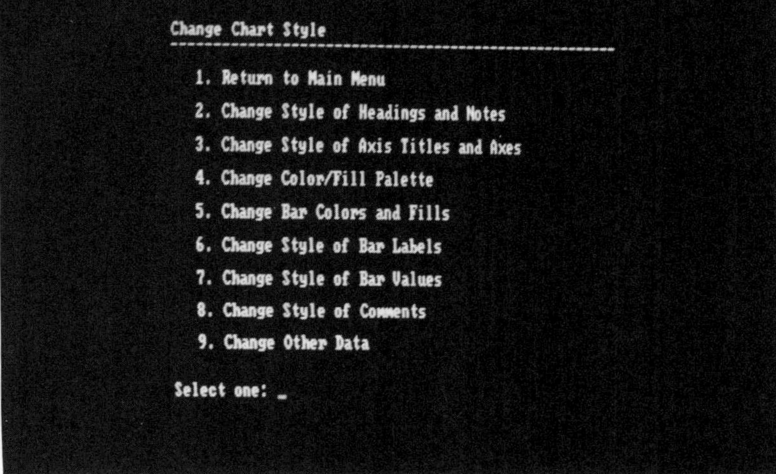

Fig. 9-30. The Graphwriter styling screen.

```
Plot
------------------------------------------------------------

  1. Return to Main Menu

  2. Fast Plot on Plotter/Printer

  3. Full Plot on Plotter/Printer

  4. Preview on Screen

  5. Store Composed Chart in File

  6. Graphics Only on Plotter/Printer (no text)

  7. Change Plot Options:
       Color Range..... color plot      Page size........ A (ANSI 8.5x11 in.)
       Medium/Pen set.. plain paper     Orientation...... horizontal
       Plot area....... full page       Graphic Device... HP 7470A

  8. Polaroid Palette Menu

 Select one: _
```

Fig. 9-31. The Graphwriter plotting menu.

hardcopy device without operator intervention. This is especially useful with the Polaroid Palette.

A sample Polaroid Palette plot is shown in Fig. 9-32.

Graphwriter is fairly fast, and speed is only limited by the fact that many menus are required to perform certain functions. Its lack of ability to share data between graph types may not meet some users requirements. Nevertheless Graphwriter is one of the best packages on the market, and for the person who needs many types of graphs from different data sources, Graphwriter makes an excellent addition to their graphics collection.

BPS BUSINESS GRAPHICS

BPS Business Graphics is completely different from any other package described in this section. It uses almost no menus and is a command driven program. This means that single commands are given in order to use the product. "Edit" is used to add or change data. "Draw Bar" is used to draw a bar

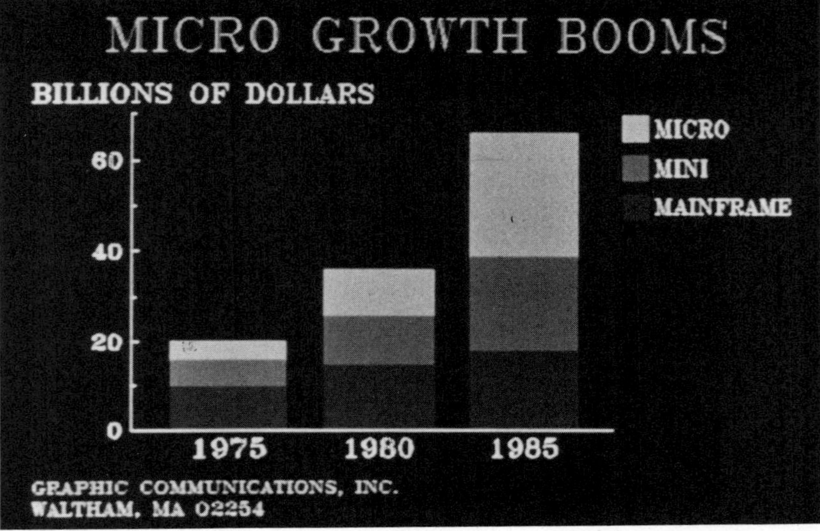

Fig. 9-32. Graphwriter sample output.

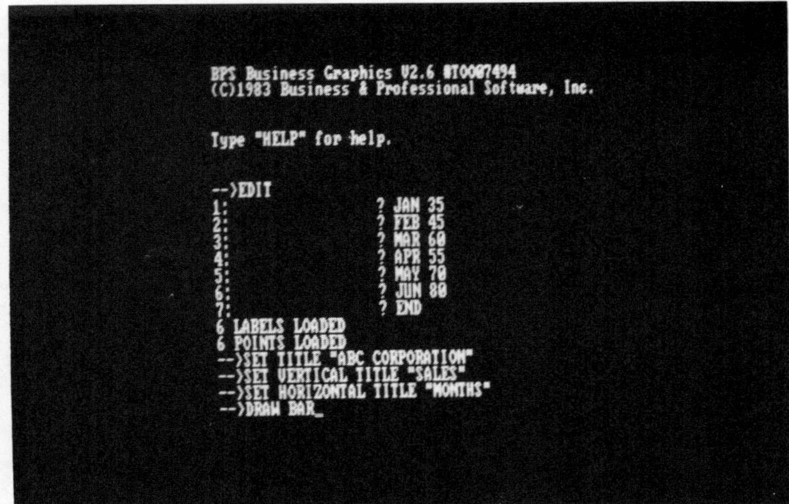

Fig. 9-33. The BPS Business Graphics main screen.

chart. "Title" is used to create a title. There are over 100 different commands to learn in order to use BPS Business Graphics. In this age of menu driven software, you might wonder why anyone would sell a package that produced graphics through commands similar to those in a programming language.

Actually, a command driven package is usually faster to use than a menu driven package. BPS Business Graphics is no exception. Once the various commands are mastered, you merely have to give the commands you want to create the graph. This can be as few as one or two commands once the data has been loaded, or as many as a few hundred for extremely complicated graphs.

BPS comes is a three-ring IBM style binder with slipcover. It features an excellent computer based demonstration and a lengthy colorful book tutorial. Its manual is divided into several sections, which include the tutorial and a complete reference section. Charts and graphs in the manual are in several colors. The manual is clearly written and easy to understand. An on-line help feature is always available to give you more information about a certain topic.

Figure 9-33, shows the first screen that BPS Business Graphics displays. The --> symbol is where the various commands are entered. The first command to learn is Edit. This command lets you enter the data that is the basis of any chart. A sample editing session is shown in Fig. 9-33. These commands would produce the chart shown in Fig. 9-34.

Data is entered through the Edit command. Each line becomes an observation in a single data series. The first entry is the x-axis label while the second is the y-axis value. Multiple data series are entered and stored separately. After the data has been entered some title and label statements are entered along with the Draw command, which produces the graph.

Though this is very different than most other packages, the results are not different from those produced by a menu driven package. Once you understand the commands, you can create graphs and charts with greater speed and flexibility than you can with a menu driven package.

BPS can produce all of the standard graph types including bar charts, line charts, pie charts, area charts, and combined charts. Because each command you give BPS is applied to the existing graph unless the graph is cleared, multiple effects are easy to accomplish. Data can be added, deleted or changed with the editing commands.

Normally as you type in data and commands, they are not saved. You can save the existing data but not the formatting commands unless you create a special type of file. This file lets you save the formatting commands as well as the data. The data and formatting commands are saved separately and

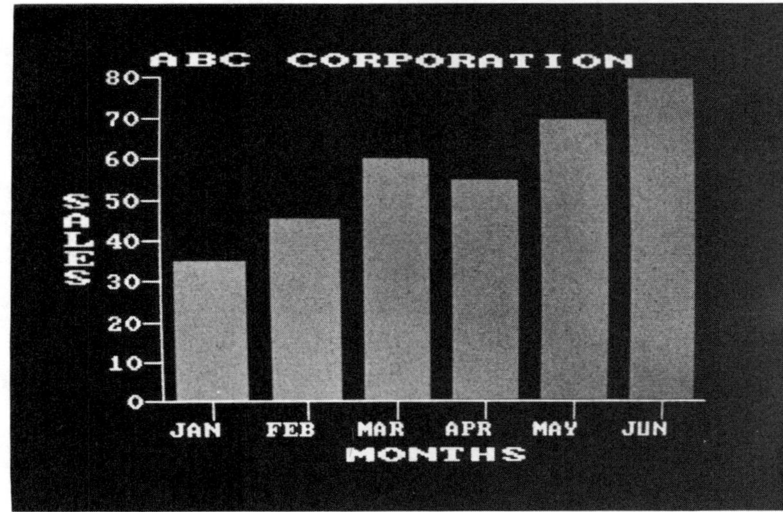

Fig. 9-34. A BPS Business Graphics sample graph.

can be used with different data by retrieving each file individually. You can also save the finished screen and later redisplay it, but you cannot make changes to the saved screen.

BPS contains extensive formatting commands that allow you to format everything including legends, grid lines, axes, titles, patterns, colors, and text fonts. Data can even be divided by constants to make multiple data series constant. Multiple graphs can be displayed in a variety of ways. Regression and curve fitting lines can be added, along with mathematical relationships and formulas.

When you save formatting commands, they can include commands that load in data. These files are then used to completely reload and draw graphs. You can save as many as you like. The true value of this is the ability to save a *template*. A template is a starting point or a standard set of commands. By varying only the data, all your graphs can look a certain way. BPS gives you extensive formatting capabilities while keeping data and commands completely separate.

BPS Business Graphics works with the printer or plotter. It uses several Set commands to set the device and the device type for printing or plotting. Placement on the page can be controlled.

If you re looking for a quick way to produce graphics and don't mind learning a few commands, you should consider BPS Business Graphics, it is the choice of thousands of companies for their graphic needs. Its versatility and power make it an excellent standalone graphics package.

DR GRAPH

DR Graph is a standalone package by Digital Research Corporation, the people who brought us CP/M, Concurrent DOS, and now the GEM operating system. They are widely known for some of the best software in the world, and this package is no exception. DR Graph is a well designed product that combines the traits of several of the best selling packages.

The DR Graph boot screen, shown in Fig. 9-35, shows some of the power behind this little gem.

DR Graph comes in an IBM style three-ring binder and slipcover. Its manual is only about two hundred pages and contains reproductions of all its menus that control the creation of graphics. Several different versions are available. You can get disks that run in 128K, 192K, or 256K, or with in 8087 Math Chip. Each of these versions runs a little faster than the other. Only one of these versions are ever used but its nice to know the others are available. The package also comes with several device driver disks for whatever peripherals you wish to hook up to it.

DR Graph contains several unique features that

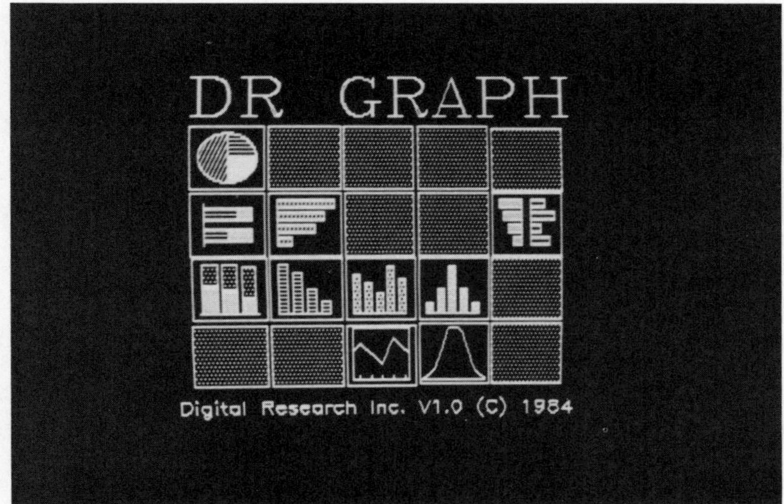

Fig. 9-35. The DR Graph boot screen.

make it worthy of inclusion in this book. DR Graph allows you to place several graphs on the same page through the use of a multiple graph menu. You can place multiple graphs (up to four) in a multitude of ways. You can change formats and redisplay the graphs as you see fit within the graph boxes that you select.

DR Graph also provides an annotate feature for adding text anywhere on your graph and then moving it later to other locations. The text can be added in a variety of fonts, colors, and sizes.

DR Graph supports several chart types including line, clustered bar, stacked bar, pie, step, stick or needle, scatter, and text only. These graph types are simple and can be overlaid on the same chart.

Charts are created through a series of easy to follow menus. DR Graph begins with a main menu that features the usual functions of creating, recalling, and displaying graphs. The main menu is shown in Fig. 9-36.

Once you decide to select Create New Graph, the chart types are listed as shown in Fig. 9-37.

When you create the graph, the display refers

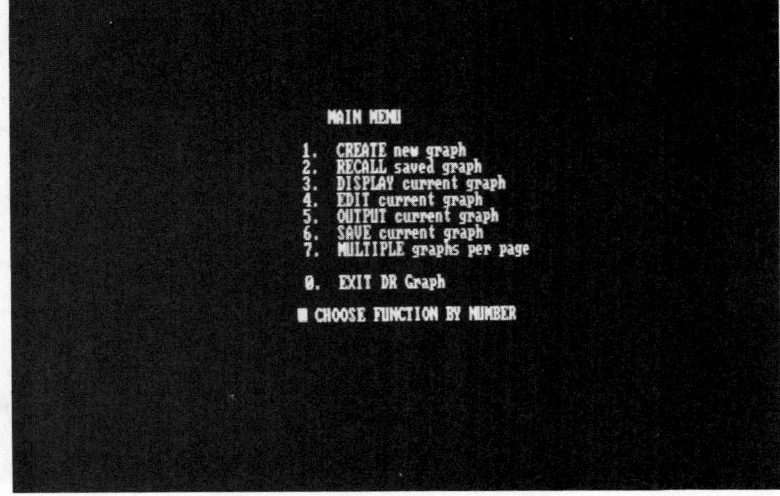

Fig. 9-36. The DR Graph main menu.

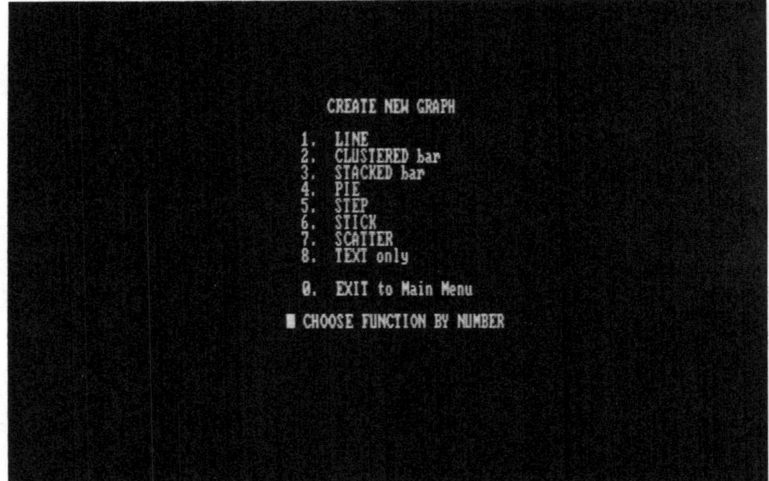

Fig. 9-37. The DR Graph graph type menu.

to the sets of data as *curves*. The curve menu is shown in Fig. 9-38. DR Graph requests that the data be entered first, even before the headers, labels, or any formatting commands are entered. Many different data series can be entered. Each data series occupies a vertical column on the data entry screen. The rows represent tick marks that will be defined on the x-axis.

Once the data is entered, you can begin to enter the headings. As shown in Fig. 9-39 a menu controls this entry. At the top of the menu is a place for the headers to be entered. The axis labels are also entered here. The axis type will determine what type of labels you can enter later. Legends for the various data series are entered from this menu. This menu also allows you to select options for each data series, including the type of line or bar, the color, pattern, or line style, the marker symbols, and the line width. You can display your graph at any time.

Before displaying your graph you may want to do some additional styling. Figure 9-40 demonstrates the additional curves edit menu. This menu lets you style the headers and axis labels for

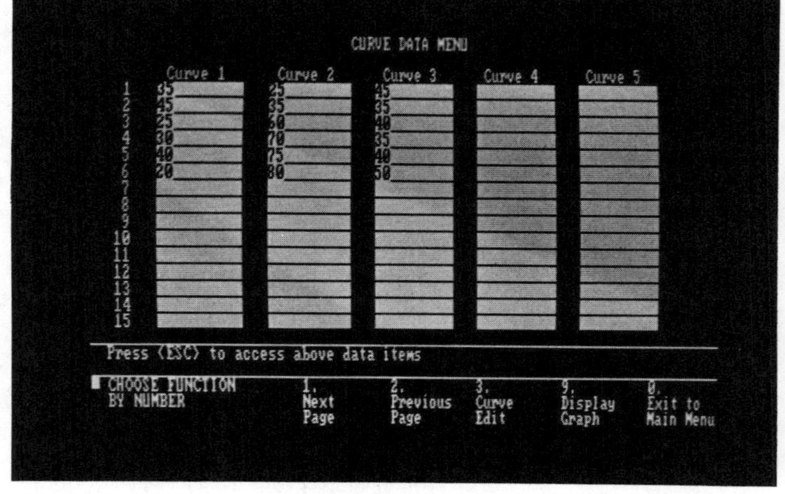

Fig. 9-38. The DR Graph curves data entry menu.

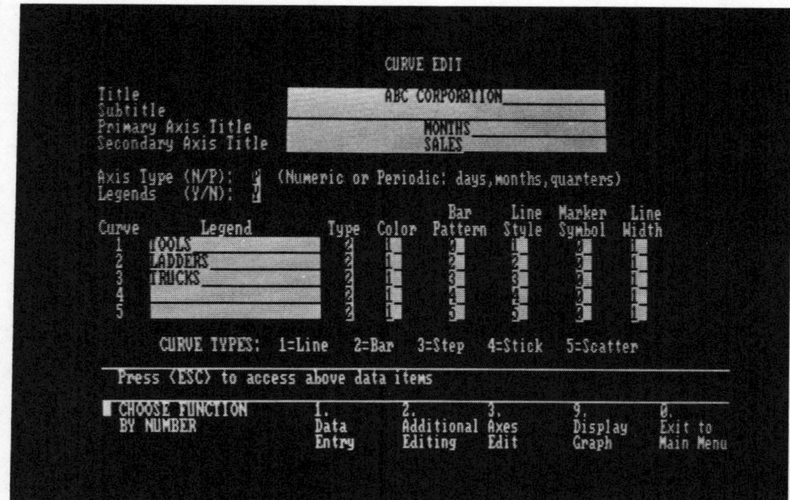

Fig. 9-39. The DR Graph curve edit menu.

color, font, and size. A border and frame around the axes can also be drawn. This menu also allows you to define the type of bar or pie chart and the horizontal or vertical orientation of the chart.

Figure 9-41 shows the Axes Edit menu. This menu allows you to control the way the axes look and how the x-axis is labeled. Instead of having to type many labels, you only have to enter the label type, the starting period, and number of periods. If the values are not periodic, you can enter any data you want. Whether or not the data was periodic was determined in the curves edit menu. The y-axis scale and range are also controlled from this menu. The axis can be a linear or a log scale. Grids are controlled from this menu.

Once you have filled in these menus you can plot your graph, as shown in Fig. 9-42. Data and formatting commands are saved together and recalled together. You can recall a saved graph and then change its format or data.

Another nice feature of DR Graph is its ability to let you add chart notes in what it calls an Annotate Session. Figure 9-43 shows the graph after a label has been added to emphasize the large

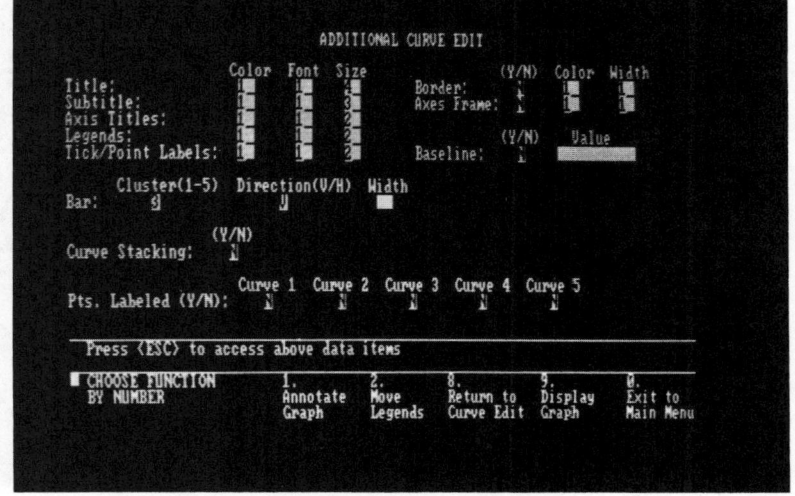

Fig. 9-40. The DR Graph additional curve edit menu.

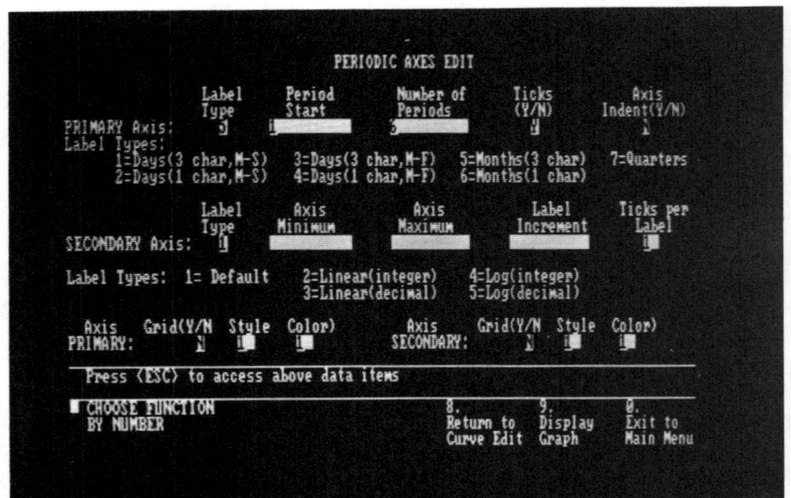

Fig. 9-41. The DR Graph axes edit menu.

growth in sales. Text can be added, changed, moved, styled, or deleted anywhere on the screen.

Another interesting feature that sets DR Graph apart from others is its ability to allow you to create multiple charts. Figure 9-44 shows the multiple graph menu. You can select multiple graphs from five different formats. You can also select up to four different graphs for one display. After the charts are selected, the screen automatically places and draws your charts. Figure 9-45 shows three different charts.

DR Graph supports all the popular printers and plotters, and even the Polaroid Palette. Digital Research also sells a package that contains DR Graph and the Polaroid Palette hardware. This allows you to get started with both the hardware and the software necessary for the creation of beautiful graphics. Included in this package is DR Draw, which is a drawing tool used to enhance charts and create pictures or graphics. Figure 9-46 shows the DR Draw main screen. This package is essentially a picture processor similar to the others in the picture processor section. It is integrated very well into the DR Graph family.

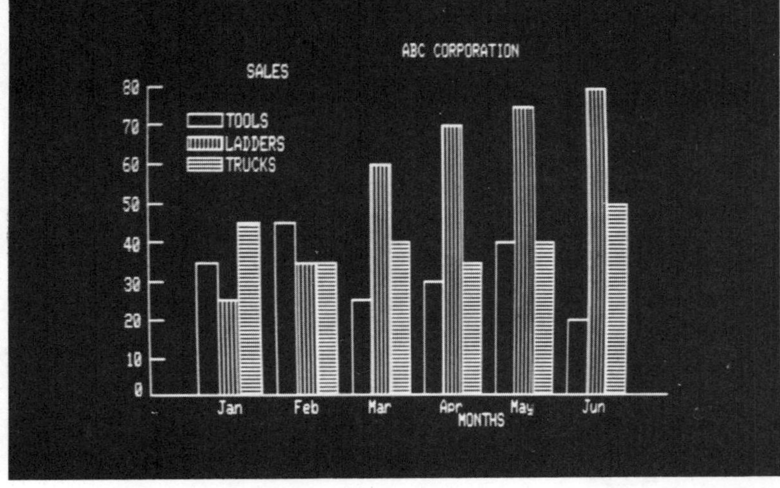

Fig. 9-42. A DR Graph bar graph.

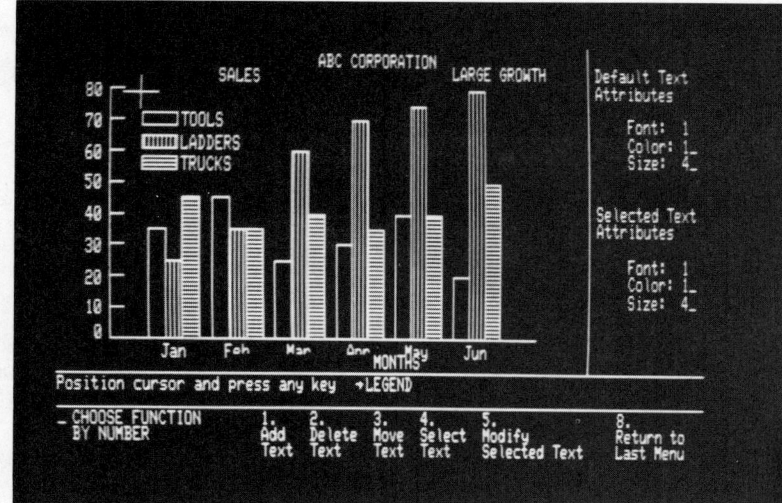

Fig. 9-43. The DR Graph annotate menu.

If performance and ease of use are important to you, DR Graph and DR Draw may be what you are looking for.

pfs: GRAPH

pfs: graph is one of the simplest packages available today. It is also one of the least expensive. This package and the entire pfs: series were chosen by IBM to become the Assistant Series now being marketed by IBM. The Assistant Series includes pfs: graph, pfs: file, pfs: report, pfs: plan, pfs: access, pfs: write and pfs: proof. Each of these packages retail for about $125. Inexpensive packages usually give you inexpensive results. This is not true of the pfs: series.

pfs: graph and the IBM Graphing Assistant deliver every bit of quality that you would expect from a low-end package endorsed by IBM. Not meant to compete with the $500 packages, pfs: graph is meant to suit the person who has an occasional need for graphics. The package is very simple to use and yet produces excellent results. Learning time for this package is no more than a few minutes.

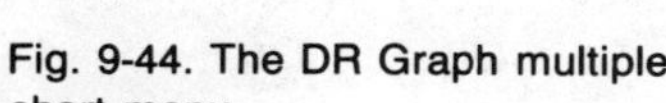
Fig. 9-44. The DR Graph multiple chart menu.

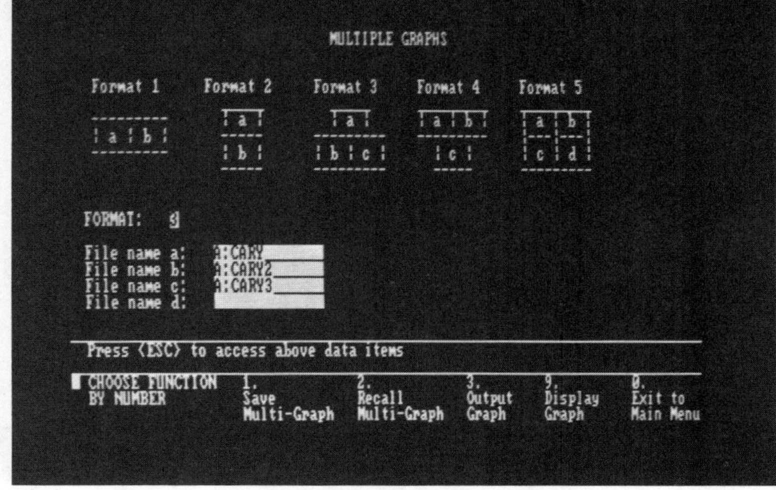

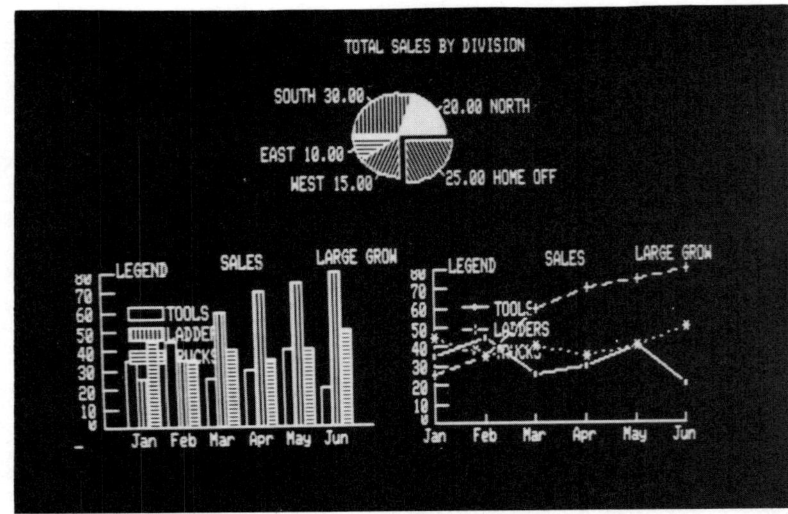

Fig. 9-45. DR Graph multiple charts.

pfs: graph comes in a small box that contains an excellently done spiral-bound manual of several hundred pages. The package is so simple, however, that you will probably only use the manual in rare instances. The manual is full of pictures that make learning very easy. The book contains an excellent tutorial and a sampler of charts to get you started. Within minutes you will be able to create your first pfs: graph. pfs: graph comes on one disk and there is a second disk of sample graphs and data.

This package is a standard menu-driven package. Figure 9-47 shows the pfs: graph main menu. It features eight menu items that allow you to retrieve or input data, define the chart, display the chart, save and retrieve charts, print or plot charts, clear the definitions and data, and exit.

The first selection allows you to retrieve or input data. As shown in Fig. 9-48, data can be retrieved directly from any other pfs: package, or from a standard DIF file from 1-2-3, SuperCalc, or VisiCalc. Most data would probably be input directly as the first selection allows. You must also select the graph that the data will belong to. Data is

Fig. 9-46. The DR Draw main screen.

PFS:GRAPH MAIN MENU

1 GET/EDIT DATA 5 PRINT CHART
2 DEFINE CHART 6 PLOT CHART
3 DISPLAY CHART 7 CLEAR CHART
4 GET/SAVE/REMOVE 8 EXIT PFS:GRAPH

SELECTION NUMBER: _

(C) 1983 Software Publishing Corporation

F10-Continue

Fig. 9-47. The pfs: graph main menu.

entered one series at a time, with four series being the maximum allowed. You can also merge new data with old data if you wish.

The data entry menu shown in Figure 9-49 prompts you to enter the x and y values and the x data format. The x data format is a single letter to tell pfs: graph what type of data is being entered on the x-axis. The choices include Identifiers for non-numeric labels; Numeric labels, which can only be used for line charts because numeric values imply a continuous range of values; and dates, which can be in several forms including Days, Months, Years or Quarters. Sample data is also shown in Fig. 9-49. The data was defined as Identifier even though months were used.

Once the data has been entered, you can go to the define chart menu, which is option number 2 on the main menu. This is where you will determine what the graph will look like. Figure 9-50 shows the define chart menu. The menu is divided into three parts. The upper most section is where you will define the type of chart, the legend (what the data series represents), and whether or not the series should be treated cumulatively (added to the

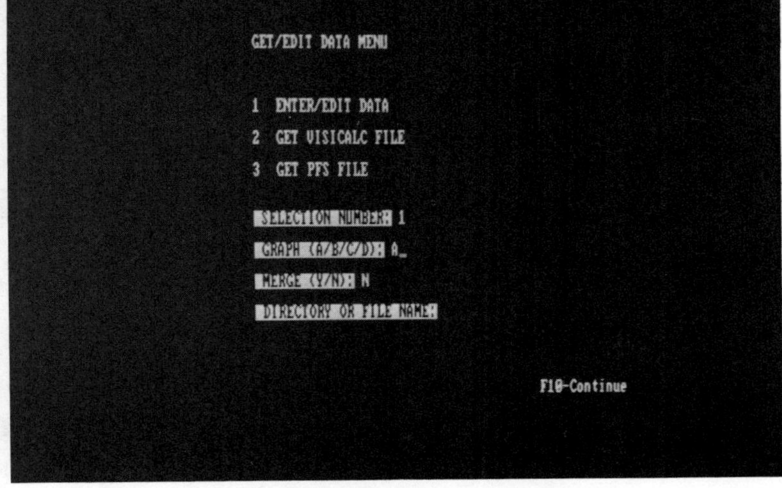

Fig. 9-48. The pfs: graph GET/EDIT DATA Menu.

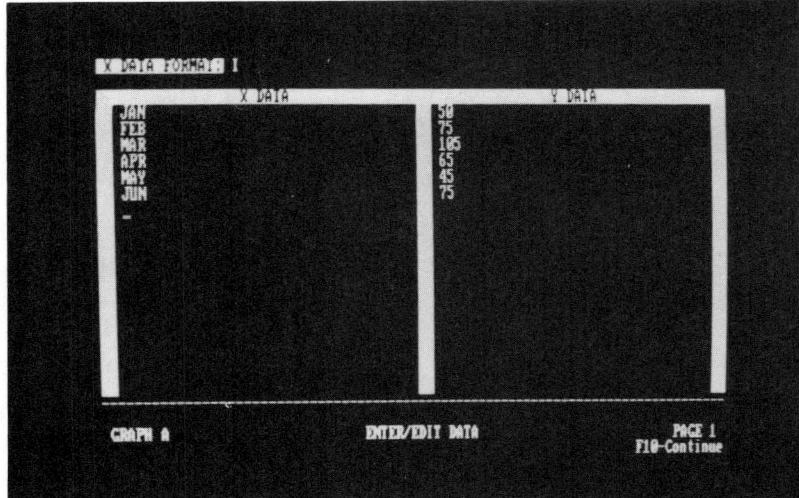

Fig. 9-49. The pfs: graph Data input menu.

preceding values).

pfs: graph lets you define three basic types of graphs: line, bar and pie charts. You can also stack a bar chart and create an area chart by stacking line charts. Bar charts and line charts can be mixed by defining each data series differently.

Once the basic charts are defined you can define titles for the chart and the axes. The final portion of the menu will let you decide whether or not the data series should be stacked, whether or not there should be grid lines, and whether the graph should be in color or monochrome.

There is only one text font and nothing can be moved or styled in this package. This limitation however is part of the simplicity of the program and should not be considered a deficit.

The y-axis range and intervals can also be defined. This is actually the extent of the formatting commands. A single title, axis labels, a legend, the y data range and interval, and grid lines are all that can be controlled. If this simplicity is enough for you, this is the package that meets your needs.

pfs: graph does a good job of outputting the graph to both the plotter or printer. Many standard printers and plotters are supported through a menu interface. On dot-matrix printers you can select

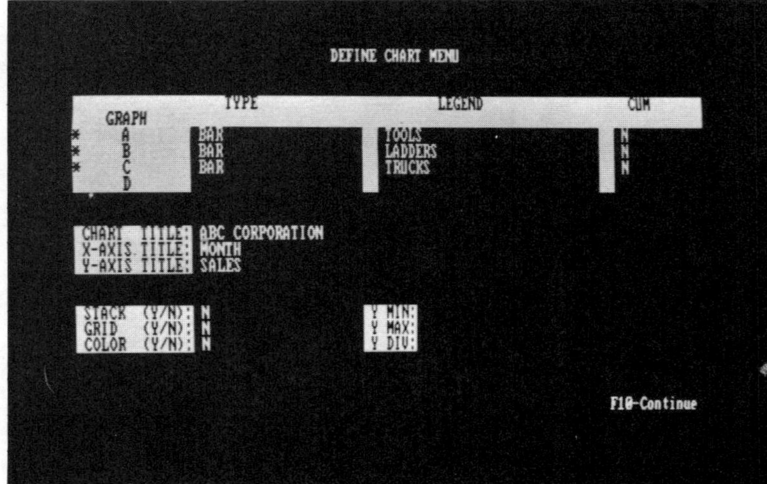

Fig. 9-50. The pfs: Define chart menu.

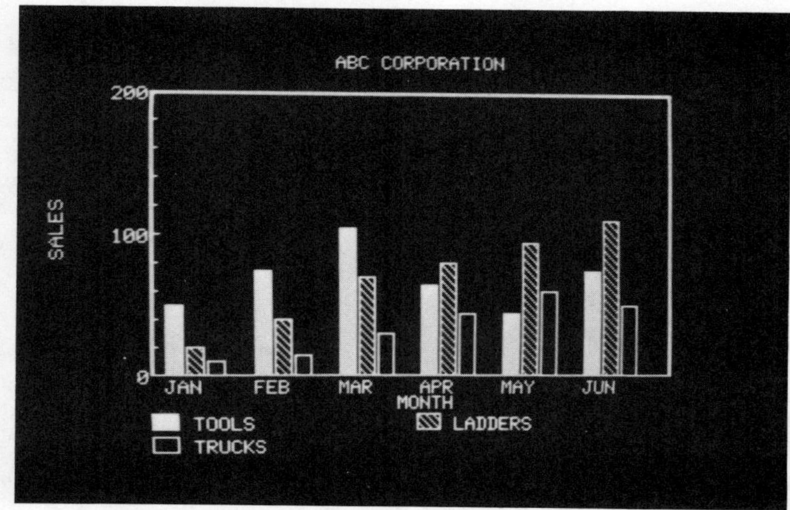

Fig. 9-51. A pfs graph bar chart.

whether the chart is to be printed vertically or horizontally and whether or not the data points are to be printed. The plotter options allow you to select a pen speed for transparencies and to decide whether or not to stop for pen changes.

Overall, pfs: graph is a fine package for anyone needing simple but high quality graphs. It does not contain a large number of formatting commands, but it is simple to use and produces excellent results. It draws graphs very quickly on the screen and on paper and has no known errors. It is an excellent package for those in need of simplicity and ease of use.

Figure 9-51 shows a sample pfs: graph.

When you are retrieving or saving charts, there are excellent submenus that display the names of your files. You can save your data and format together, or you can save the actual output as a picture. When you save a picture, however, the data and formatting commands are not saved. Saving the picture simply lets you redisplay the picture at a later time.

pfs: graph is known for its simplistic approach and ease of use. It is one of the best selling graphics packages and offers enough features to fill the needs of many business people.

Chapter 10

The Integrated Packages

1-2-3
SUPERCALC3 RELEASE 2
FRAMEWORK
SYMPHONY
SMART SYSTEM

Integrated packages are those software packages whose main function is not graphics, but which include graphics as one of the many functions that the package performs. Some integrated packages contain just a few *modules*, such as a spreadsheet and graphics capability, while others contain many modules including a spreadsheet, a database, a word processor, a communications module, and a graphics module.

Because an integrated package is not designed primarily to produce business graphics, the quality of the graphics portion is rarely as good as that of a standalone graphics package. The graphics functions in typical integrated software consist of the bare minimum expected from a standalone system—the bar, stacked bar, pie, and line charts. Some include high-low-close charts and scatter diagrams.

Usually, the same data can be used to produce each type of chart. Some of the better integrated packages also allow more than one graph on the screen at a time through a *windowing* approach.

Generally, there is little you can do to change format style in an integrated software package. The better ones allow the use of titles, axis labels,and y-axis scaling. Generally, these packages don't let you move labels around, select legend types, add text anywhere, or save the format separately.

The following information is presented for each software package discussed in this chapter.

1. An introduction to the basic philosophies of the package, and a discussion of what it is intended to do and who its intended audience is.
2. A presentation of the best or most unusual features that set this product apart from all others.
3. Discussions of the *boot* or first screen, the documentation, the expected learning time, and the tutorials that may be available.
4. A discussion of the general integration of the package including how well the graphics are integrated into the whole package and how easy

it is to enter graphics from the spreadsheet or the database.
5. Discussions of how the program handles and changes input data and how it handles data created outside the workings of the program.
6. A discussion of the types of graphs produced and the program's ability to use the same data for different types of graphs without requiring that the data be reentered.
7. A discussion of the formatting commands available including the ability of the software to control the placement and type of text, legends, titles, labels, and tick marks.
8. A presentation concerning the separation of data and formatting commands.
9. A discussion of the output quality on the screen, dot matrix printer, Polaroid Palette, and plotter.
10. An evaluation of the packages ability to print graphics in the middle of a word processing document or with the spreadsheet.
11. An evaluation of the overall performance, speed, and error handling, and general comments about the ease of use of the package compared to the results achieved.

General integration is a key factor in these packages. You must be sure that a graph can be defined quickly and easily from your data, whether it is in spreadsheet or (if the package has one) in database form. Data selection should be easy. Some packages only allow you to select data from contiguous areas. This means, that the data for the graph must be placed in adjacent cells of the spreadsheet. Some packages force you to place all the labels in the spreadsheet itself and do not allow you to change the labels and titles externally. There are good and bad aspects of this, but it is desirable to have both options.

Output quality, both on the screen and on hardcopy printers and plotters should be in no way diminished because you are using an integrated package. Most packages allow a full range of printers and plotters to be used.

A package that can print a graphic in-stream (on the same page) as a spreadsheet, word processing document or database, should also be considered superior. You are probably using an integrated package because you want your output integrated as well.

The integrated packages described in this section range from an integration of the "standard" three modules of spreadsheet, database, and graphics to the more elaborate concoctions of today, which also include word processing and telecommunications. Though none of these packages handle graphics as well as any good standalone graphics package, each has something to offer from ease of data selection to some excellent graphics output and display.

LOTUS 1-2-3

Lotus 1-2-3 is the best selling software package in recent times. It consists of the most powerful spreadsheet and macro language on the market and also has data management and graphics capabilities. Its graphics functions are simple and easy to use and produce simple results. Lotus uses menus on the top of the screen to accomplish its purposes. The graphs are built right in to the main menu, and selection is consistent and easy. Lotus uses single line menus with a submenu line at the top of the screen as shown in Fig. 10-1.

The spreadsheet is the best part of Lotus 1-2-3. It is well known as being one of the largest and fastest spreadsheets on the market. It also is extremely easy to use and features an excellent macro programming language that is designed to save repeated keystrokes and allow fully programmed models. In the "Little Known Packages That Do Wonderful Things" section, you will see some other products that make Lotus graphics even better.

Lotus 1-2-3 comes in a single binder with an IBM type slipcover. It is distributed on several disks, including a system disk, a utilities disk, and a print graph disk. A separate module is required to print the graphics. Lotus 1-2-3 also comes with an adequate on-line tutorial and a small book tutorial. Because Lotus 1-2-3 is one of the most popular programs on the market today, there is a tremendous aftermarket of training available. 1-2-3 also features an excellent set of help menus. A sample help menu

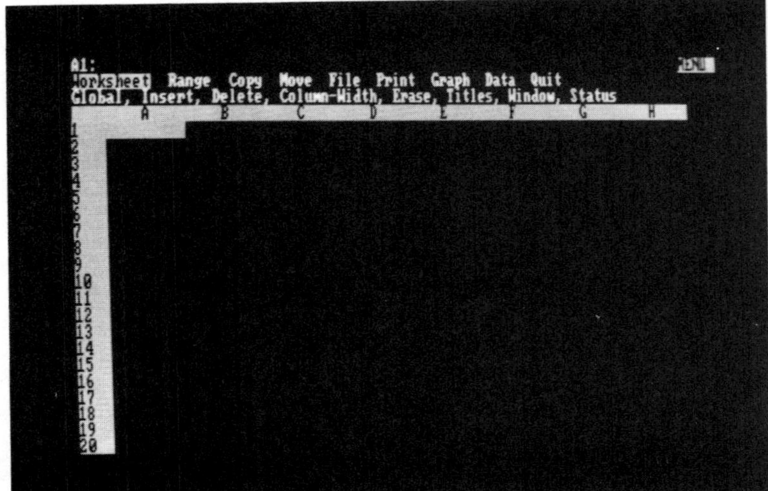

Fig. 10-1. The Lotus 1-2-3 main screen.

is shown in Fig. 10-2. Lotus uses standard graphics characters to display its help menus.

It is very easy to enter data from the spreadsheet. The cursor is a reverse video block that is moved about by the cursor keys. As data is entered, it is displayed on the top of the screen where the menu line is normally displayed. When the Enter key is pressed, the data is placed on the spreadsheet. Where it is placed is dependent upon the location of the cursor when the entry began. The left side of most spreadsheets contain numbers, while the top contain letters. Hence, in Fig. 10-1 the cursor is in cell A1.

Usually when you are working with spreadsheets, your data will tend to be contiguous. This means that it will be in cells that are next to each other. A sample data entry for a graph is found in Fig. 10-3.

The data is actually a table. Each piece of data is resting in a single cell. Each label and title also takes up a single cell. The label TOOLS, for example, is in cell B5.

After entering your data, you can start creating your graph. This is done through a series of menus that appear on top of the status line at the top of the screen. Figure 10-4 shows the menu line that

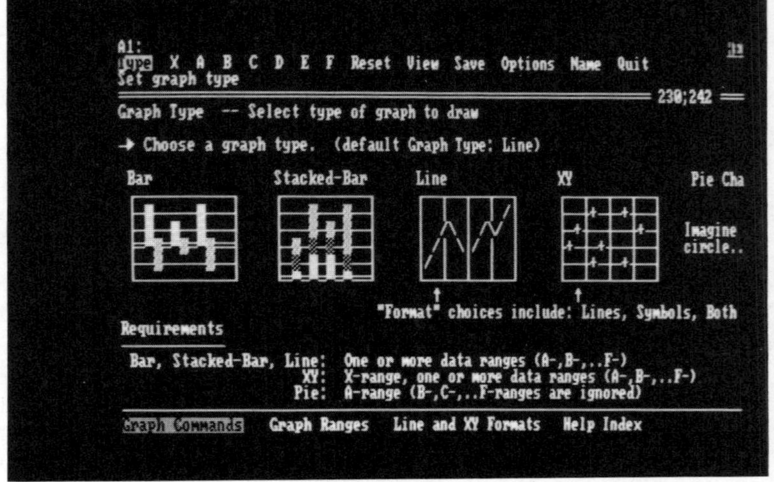

Fig. 10-2. The Lotus 1-2-3 help screen.

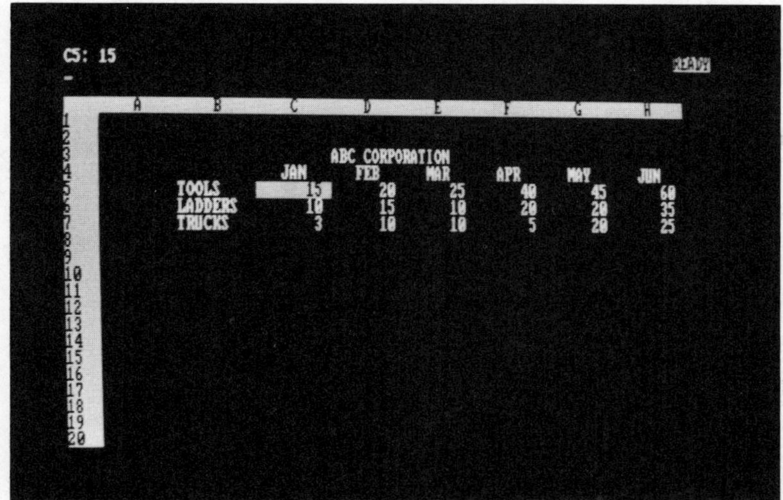

Fig. 10-3. Lotus 1-2-3 with data entered.

appears after Graph is selected on the main menu. The options include setting the graph type, entering the x-axis labels and up to six different data series, and selecting the output format.

First the graph type is selected. The choices are line, bar, xy, stacked bar, and pie. Next the x-axis labels are selected, as shown in Fig. 10-5. The range appears at the top of the screen. In this example the x-axis labels are found in cells C4 to H4. Lotus 1-2-3 shades the area to indicate selection. The x-axis labels and data selections are done in this fashion. If the data is not contiguous, there would be no way to select it as only one data range is allowed.

Figure 10-6 shows the Graph Options menu. This menu works totally differently than the data selection menu did. The options menu allows you to input legend labels, titles, grid lines, scaling factors, color choices, and *data-labels* (the data value that will be displayed on top of a bar or next to a line).

When you select one of these options a submenu appears. If you choose "Titles," you would see a submenu that lets you enter a main title, a subtitle, an x-axis title, and a y-axis title. After choos-

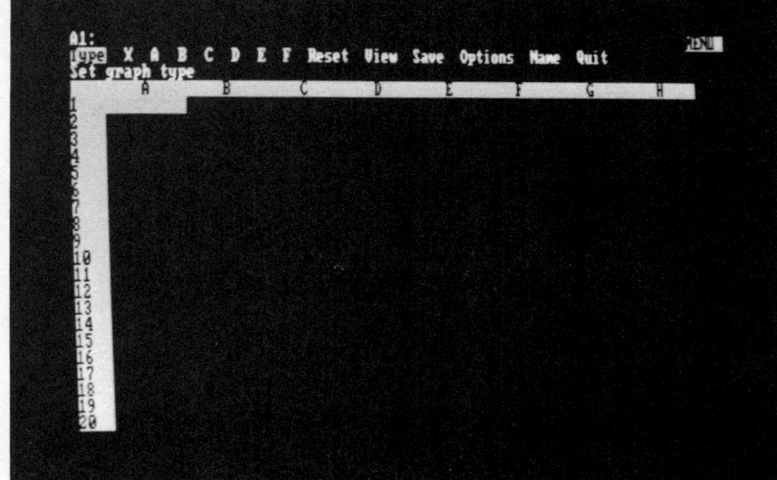

Fig. 10-4. The Lotus 1-2-3 graph menu.

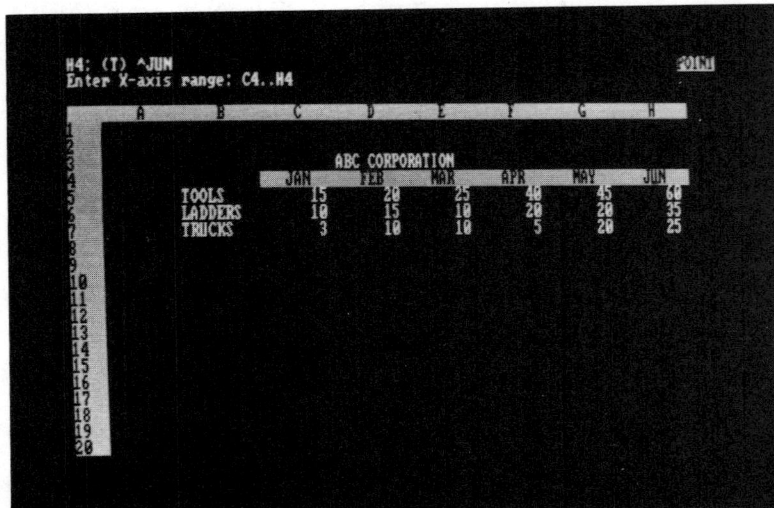

Fig. 10-5 Lotus 1-2-3 x-axis selection

ing the main title, you could type "ABC Corporation." Even though this information appears on the spreadsheet, Lotus 1-2-3 has no way of retrieving it and will make you type it in again. Legends, axes, and grid lines all work this way.

After making your selections, you can display the graph, as shown in Fig. 10-7.

Printing the graph is a two step process. First you must save the graph. Graphs and their options are stored separately. Graph data and graph formats are stored separately so they can be later retrieved and used with other data or other formats. The graph image itself must also be stored if you want to print it. Lotus 1-2-3 features its own graphics printing subsystem that requires you to change disks. Figure 10-8 shows the Lotus PrintGraph menu.

There is a complete set of options including print densities, colorations, device selection, placement on the page, and sizing of the print or plot. Even font selection is controlled at print time. Once you make your selections, Lotus 1-2-3 will print a high resolution image of your graphic on the printer or plotter.

Lotus 1-2-3 has been known as the king of the

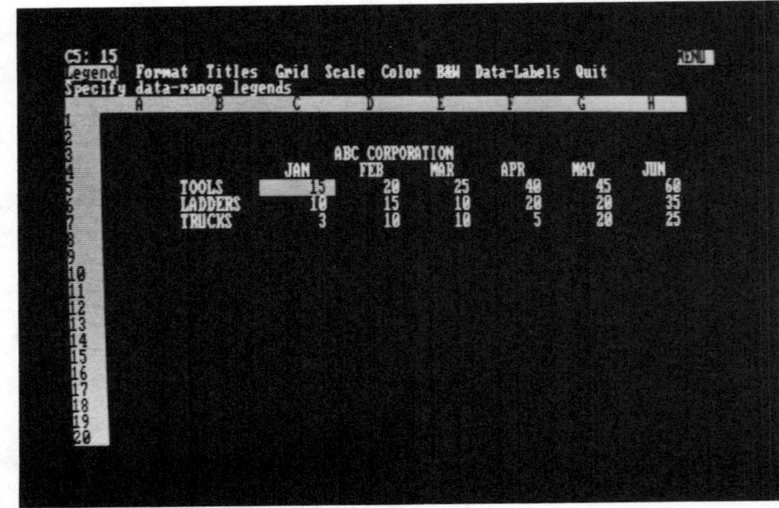

Fig. 10-6. The Lotus 1-2-3 graph options menu.

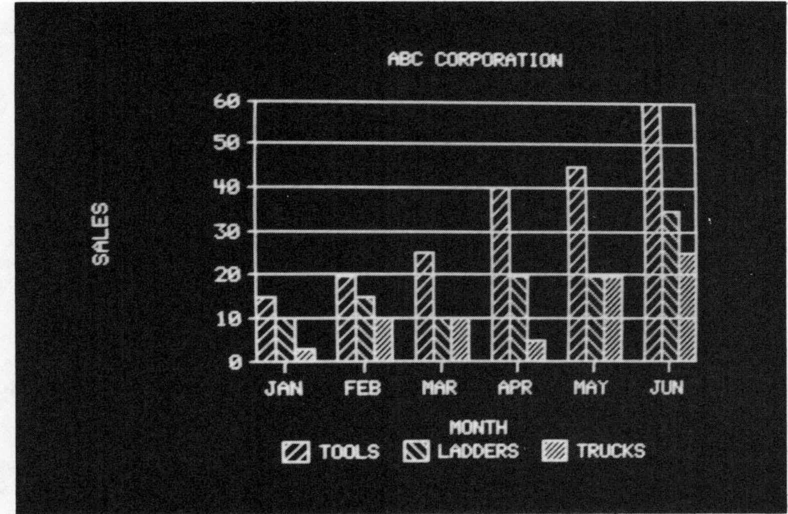

Fig. 10-7. A Lotus 1-2-3 bar graph.

spreadsheets. Its graphics capabilities are somewhat lesser than the other packages in this chapter, but it is still by far the most popular spreadsheet available today.

SUPERCALC3 RELEASE 2

SuperCalc has been around as long as microcomputers have been productively used. First built for CP/M machines and now available in popular 16 bit MS-DOS formats, this package has undergone a radical transformation from a simple spreadsheet to a powerful integrated package. Built by the SORCIM company (thats MICROS spelled backwards), it is now part of SORCIM/IUS, a powerful company that sells the SuperCalc line as well as EASYWRITER and the IUS accounting line of software. SuperCalc3 Release 2 is now the current version and competes head on with Lotus 1-2-3. Spreadsheet, graphics, data management, and a powerful macro language give users everything they might want. The graphics portion is probably one of the best available in an integrated package. It

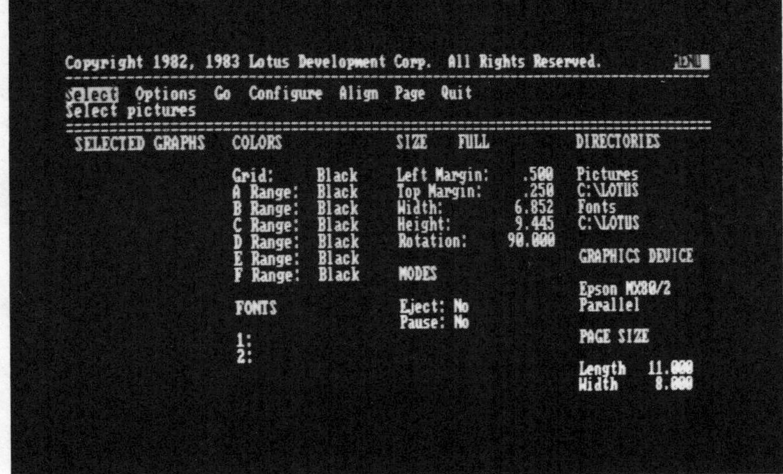

Fig. 10-8. The Lotus 1-2-3 printgraph menu.

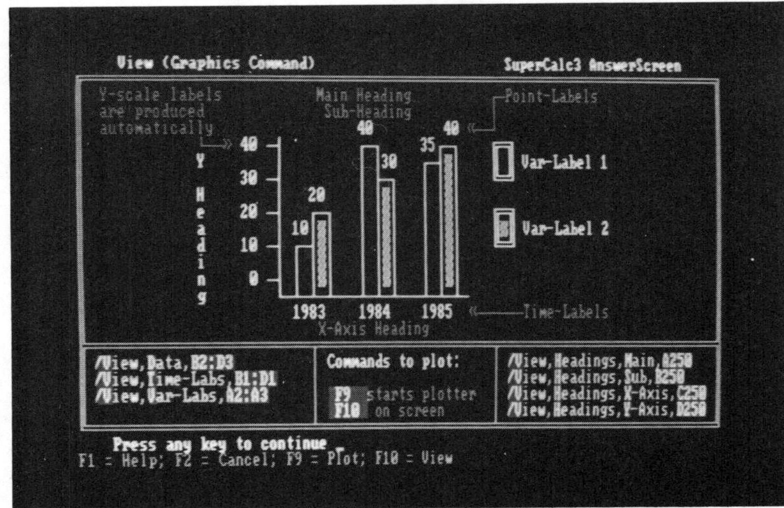

Fig. 10-9. The SUPERCALC3 help screen.

allows an enormous number of options and gives the best screen displays and printouts of the integrated packages.

SuperCalc3 Release 2 is distributed in an IBM type slipcover and a three-ring binder. It features several hundred pages of colorful pictures and diagrams. It includes a graphics answer card, an enjoyable book tutorial called "10 Minutes to SuperCalc3," and even a sample disk with some of the most unusual macros you will ever see, including a functioning blackjack game complete with pictures of cards. It also includes some very interesting templates to get you started. SuperCalc3 comes on only two disks. One contains the necessary printer and plotter drivers, which are loaded onto the main disk, and also contains the sample and tutorial files. The main disk is all that is needed to run the program, including displaying and plotting all the graphs. On-line help is available at any moment by pressing the standard F1 key. Figure 10-9 shows a sample help screen.

SuperCalc3 is a *first generation* integrated package. It is essentially a spreadsheet with graphics and is not really an integrated package by

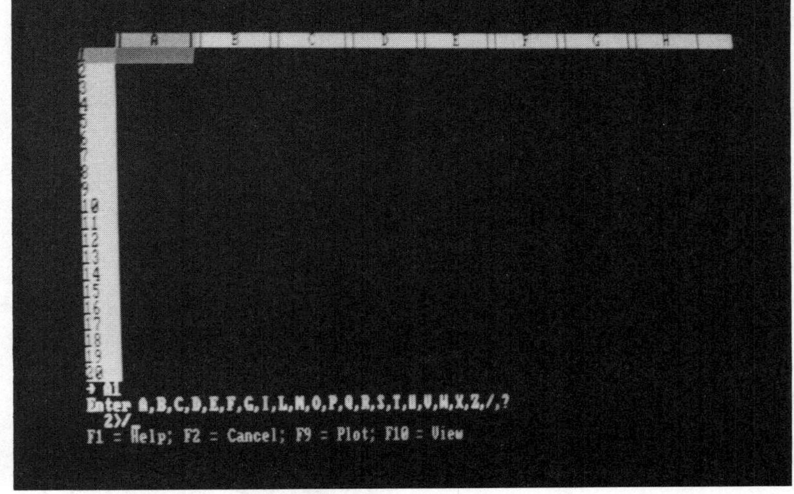

Fig. 10-10. The SUPERCALC3 main screen.

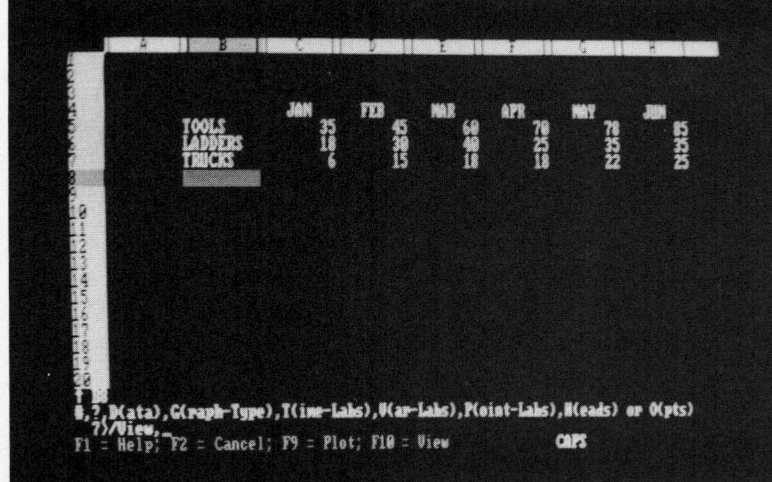

Fig. 10-11. The SUPERCALC3 spread sheet and view command.

today's definition. Its graphs are simply another module in the package.

As shown in Fig. 10-10, SuperCalc (as it will be referred to in this description) begins with a blank spreadsheet. It has standard rows and columns that can be resized or styled. A list of commands is displayed along the bottom of the screen as shown in Fig. 10-10.

Before you can create a graphic, you must create a spreadsheet. The data will be selected later, but it must be in contiguous blocks. As shown in Fig. 10-11 the data is in a block that runs from C5 to H7. The spreadsheet has labels, which indicate what each row represents, and headings above the columns. The spreadsheet also has a title.

This information is all that is needed to produce graphics in SuperCalc3. SuperCalc is very well thought out and allows you to specify as little or as much as you want.

The *slash* commands are shown at the bottom of Fig. 10-11. The /View command is used to create the graph. This command has several options that will be explained in detail. The "#" lets you select a number to assign the graph to in memory. Up to

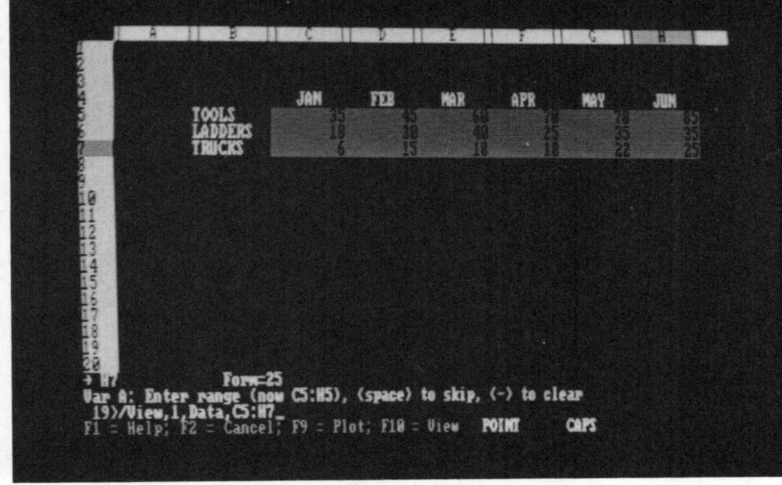

Fig. 10-12. The SUPERCALC3 view data command.

10 graphs can exist in memory at the same time. The "?" is another way to obtain help. The rest of the options are used to create the graph and select among options.

Figure 10-12 shows the /View,Data command. The number in the command indicates that the graph is assigned the number 1. The Data option lets you specify the range of the data for the graph. In this example the range is C5:H7. This includes all the data in the contiguous block formed by the intersection of rows five through seven and columns C through H. Unlike other packages, you cannot control the row or column specification of the x- and y-axes. This block of data will yield three lines with six data points on each line. If you were to graph the data right now, the data would be graphed without any labels or titles.

The /View Graph command is shown in Fig. 10-13. The graph type is chosen here. The options include Pie, Bar, Stacked-Bar, Line, x-y, Area, and Hi-Lo graphs. You can easily create many graphs by typing /View,1,Graph,Line, then/View,2,-Graph,Bar, and then/View,3,Graph, Area. Later you can show all three graphs in quick succession.

The /View Time-Labels command is used to select the labels for the x-axis. In this example, the time labels are C4 through H4, or JAN through JUN. This technique will allow you to select many graphs from one spreadsheet.

After choosing the x-axis labels, you should choose the data series labels. These are known as Variable-Labels. When these are chosen, a legend will be created and displayed. If they are not chosen, there will not be a labeled legend. The variable labels chosen in this example are B5 through B7, which are "Tools," "Ladders," and "Trucks." A column will usually contain the variable labels.

Point labels can also be chosen. Usually these would be the same as the data command range. If these are selected, the data value will be displayed above the actual plotted point.

There are four type of headings that can be entered, as shown in Fig. 10-14. There can be a main heading and a second main heading or subheading. There can also be x-axis and y-axis labels. The labels themselves are not entered here; instead the name of the cell that contains the label is entered. Cell B3 contains the title of this graph.

The /View,Options command allows you to set a few other options including the format of the y-axis values, y-axis scaling, and pie chart explosion.

Once the graph is set up to your satisfaction, it can be displayed by pressing F10 after selecting the number of the graph with the /View,# command. Figure 10-15 shows a sample Supercalc graph.

Once the graph is created there are a number

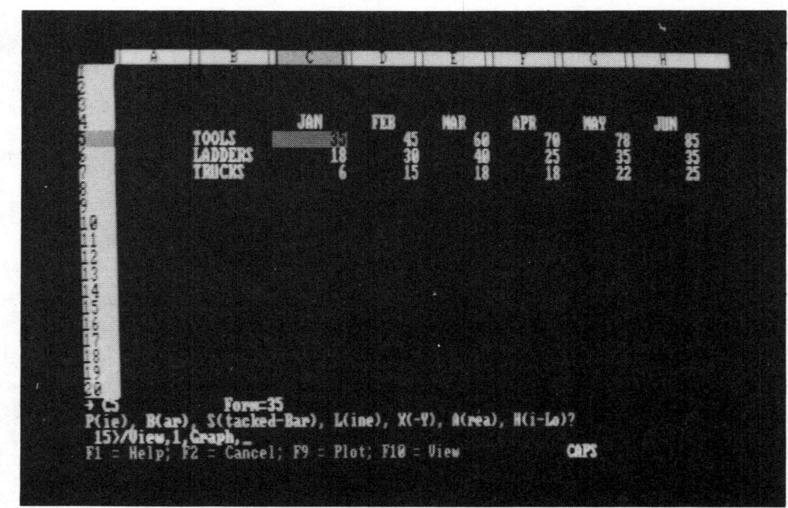

Fig. 10-13. The SUPERCALC3 view graph command.

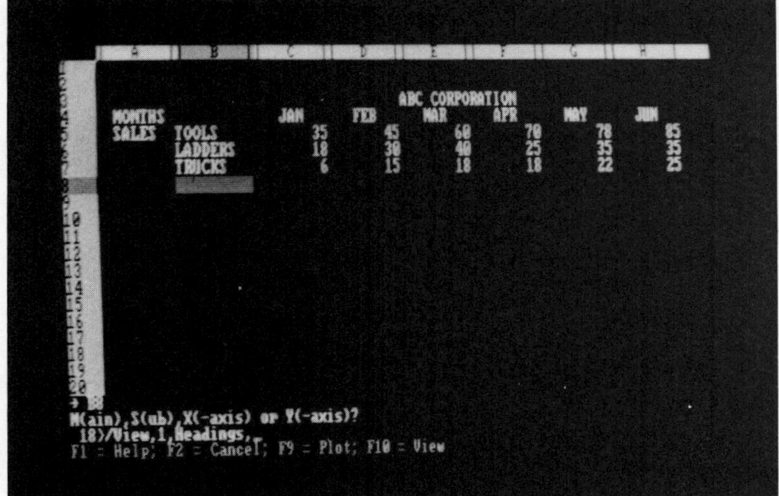

Fig. 10-14. The SUPERCALC3 view headers command.

of options available with the /Global,Graphics commands. These options include Colors, Fonts, Layout, Options, and Device.

The Colors panel allows you to set different colors when you are displaying the graphs in color on the monitor. They also let you set the pen number for color plotters. You can set the colors for each variable, label, heading, and axis, and even for the grid lines and tick marks.

The Fonts menu lets you select the fonts for each heading and label. The fonts include block, roman, italic, and script in several densities.

When you are plotting or printing a chart, the output can be precisely controlled by the Layout menu as shown in Fig. 10-16. When you selected a paper size the width and length of the chart are adjusted appropriately. The graph size allows you to select the size of the graph on the paper chosen. You can choose to place many graphs on a piece of paper. A graph mode of Full, Half, Top, Bottom, Left, Right, Quarter (1-4), or Manual is allowed. In any mode but manual, the graph size, rotation, and offset are automatically calculated. In the manual mode, the graph can be rotated and can be placed

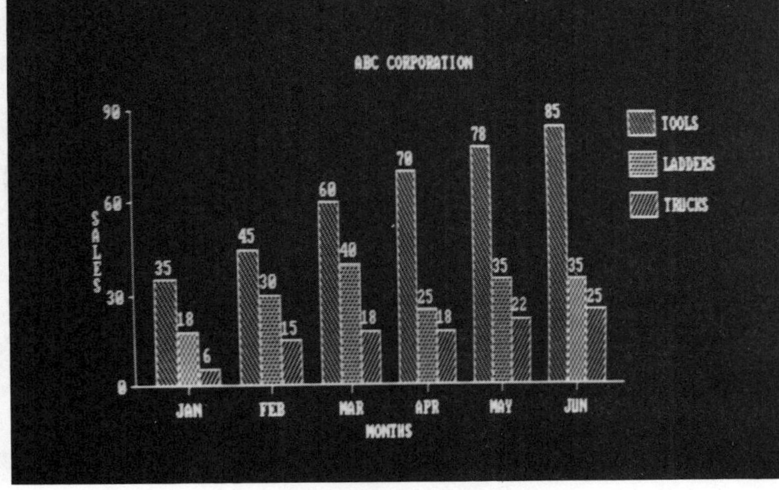

Fig. 10-15. A SUPERCALC3 bar graph.

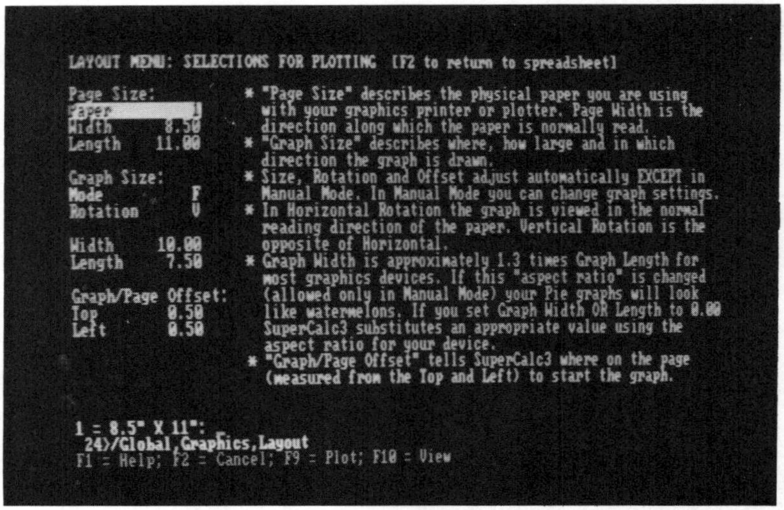

Fig. 10-16. The SUPERCALC3 global graphics layout panel.

anywhere on the page in any size.

The Global Graphics Options menu controls much of the final graph appearance. As shown in Fig. 10-17, you can control the existence of grid lines, axis lines, and tick marks, and determine whether or not the graph appears in a box. You can chose between solid and hatched fill. Line charts can have only lines or only symbols, or can have the symbols connected by lines. The grid lines can be horizontal, vertical, neither, or both.

You can change whether the display is shown in high resolution black and white or medium resolution color. Dot matrix printers can be set to single, double, triple, or quadruple density. When quadruple density is used on a dot matrix printer, the output begins to resemble plotter output in terms of quality. The number of plotter pens can also be specified.

For plotting or printing the type of interface (parallel or serial) is specified, as well as the LPT or COM number. Plotters can automatically be set up without the mode command, and two monitors are supported.

There is also a panel that allows you to choose

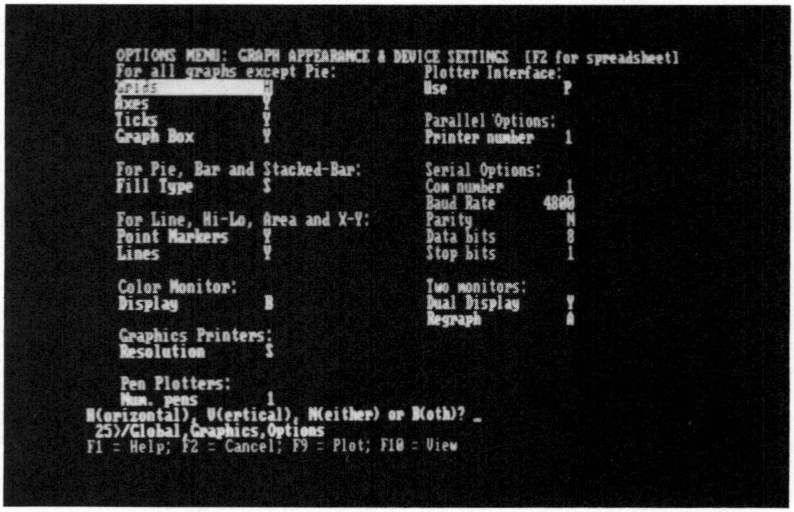

Fig. 10-17. The SUPERCALC3 global graphics options panel.

from a list of over fifty printers and plotters.

As shown in Fig. 10-18, the screen images are excellent. The charts produced by dot matrix printers and color plotters are also excellent.

SuperCalc3 is one of the most powerful spreadsheet packages in existence today. Its spreadsheet capabilities are as good as any other package on the market. Its graphics are a superb example of the capabilities of modern graphic packages. This package is for anyone who needs extensive spreadsheet capabilities and graphics.

FRAMEWORK

Framework is a product of Ashton-Tate, the makers of dBASE II, dBASE III, and Friday! Framework is an integrated package that has six modules including a spreadsheet, a database, a word processor, an outlining module, a communications module, and a graphics module.

Framework is designed for people whose primary duties are creating management reports and word processing documents. Its outlining features allow the user to quickly and easily create and manipulate reports. Spreadsheets and database files can be inserted into reports along with graphics that are created from the spreadsheet or from the data management system.

The graphics in Framework are among the better of the graphics included in integrated packages. Framework allows the selection and display of graphics with just a few keystrokes. Pull down menus control graph selection and graphic options.

Framework allows the standard graph types, such as bar, stacked bar, pie, line, and scatter charts. It also allows overlaid charts through manipulation of the formula that Framework automatically creates to draw the graph. Through the use of these formulas, known as the "Fred" programming language, you can add anything to the screen, including chart notes, and even make the display reverse video.

Perhaps the most unusual feature of Framework is its ability to integrate text, numbers, and graphics on the same page. Through the use of *outlining* you can control the positioning of text and graphics. Outlining is a new function available in the computer industry today. It quickly lets you organize your thoughts and move sections or subsections of your material around with just a few keystrokes.

Framework begins with its boot screen as shown in Fig. 10-19. This is the empty *desktop* where all your work will take place. The Framework desktop is where all the work of Framework is performed. Windows, known as frames, are displayed on the desktop. Framework comes in an IBM type slipcover and two large manuals. One manual is the tutorial manual, while the other is the reference

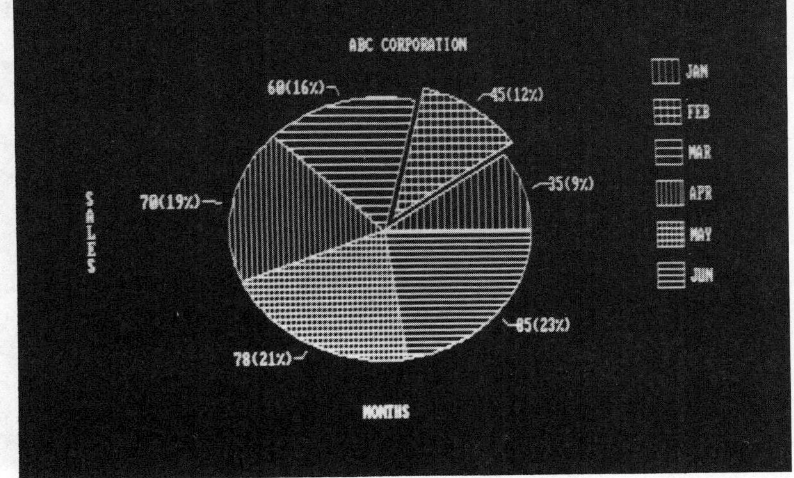

Fig. 10-18. The SUPERCALC3 sample screen output.

Fig. 10-19. The Framework empty desktop.

guide. Framework comes with an excellent computer based tutorial that makes you an honorary member of the Spy Academy. The package is distributed on two disks, along with a utilities disk and a tutorial disk. This well-written tutorial is supplemented by an excellent book tutorial. Framework also features an extensive help menu library. Two of these are displayed in Figs. 10-20 and 10-21.

Learning the entire Framework system will take several days. This is reasonable for an integrated package that provides as much as Framework does. The tutorial and computer based training make learning Framework as much fun as using it.

The various modules in the Framework are well integrated. Data can be easily moved from the spreadsheet to the database. Word processing documents can be cut and pasted anywhere in another document. The graphics are easily integrated into the entire package and can be accessed with almost unheard of ease. Once a spreadsheet is created, a graph can be created in as little as five keystrokes.

Creating a graph begins with creating a spreadsheet. Just two keystrokes instantly create a spread-

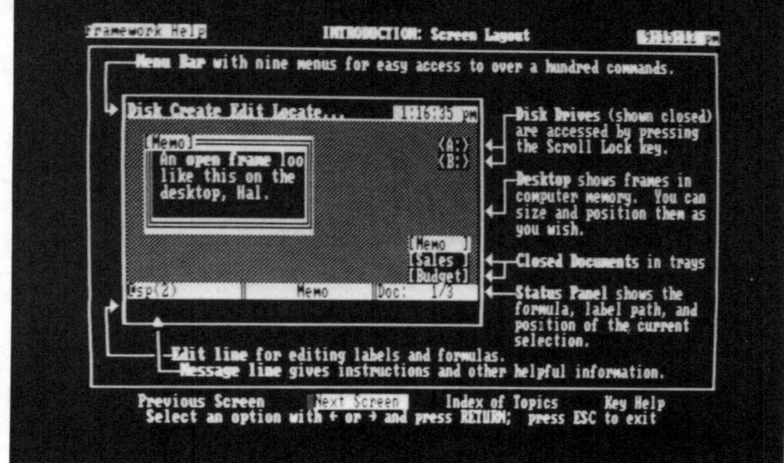

Fig. 10-20. The Framework screen layout help menu.

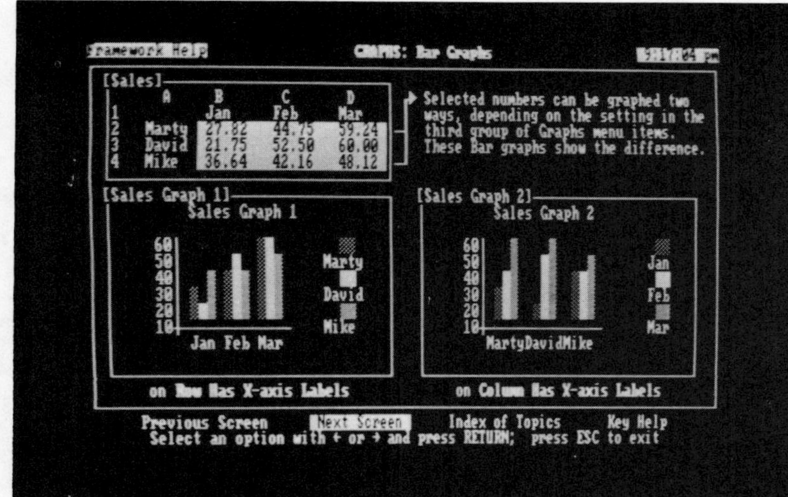

Fig. 10-21. The Framework bar graphs help menu.

sheet on the desktop.

The spreadsheet occupies its own frame on the desktop. The spreadsheet in Fig. 10-22 has been filled in to show three variables over a period of six months. In order to create a graph the data must be selected. This spreadsheet has had the range B2 to G4 selected. Framework will automatically use the first column to determine the x-axis labels and the first row to determine the variable names that will appear on the legend.

Once the data has been selected, the graph type and any necessary options can be selected. The Graphs pulldown menu consists of two sections. The main section pulls down from the Graphs option of the main menu along the top of the screen. The graphic option menu slides out from the Options section of the Graph menu. Together they allow the user to create the graph and to specify any options.

The Graphs pulldown menu is broken into four sections. The first section allows you to create a new graph or add to an existing one. Adding to an existing graph will create an overlaid or mixed graph. The second section of the menu lets you choose the graph type from the six types listed in the display

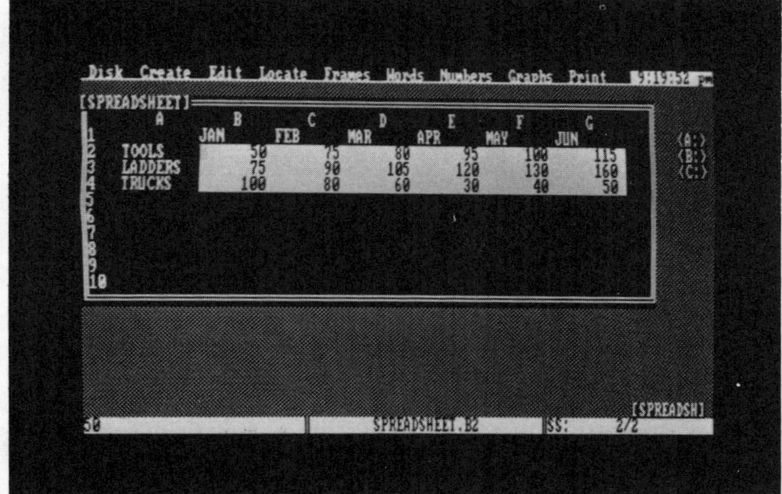

Fig. 10-22. The Framework spreadsheet frame.

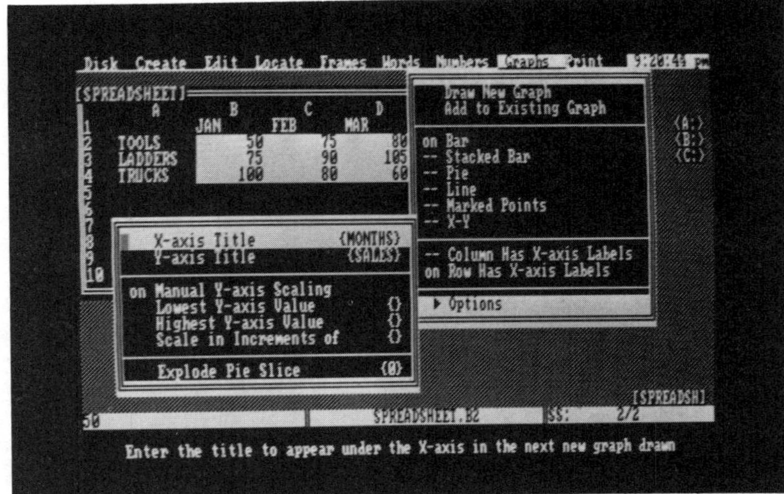

Fig. 10-23. The Framework graphs pulldown menus.

shown in Fig. 10-23. A bar is moved up and down the menu to select the type of graph. Data can be in any format. Framework allows complete data sharing with its graphics. You can also tell Framework whether the rows or columns contain the x-axis labels. In the data shown in Fig. 10-22, if "Row" is selected, the months Jan through JUN will be along the x-axis and "TOOLS", "LADDERS" and "TRUCKS" will be the three lines or bars in the graph and will be identified in the legend. If "Column" is selected, the months JAN through JUN will create six lines or bars and "TOOLS", "LADDERS", and "TRUCKS" will be x-axis labels.

The Options submenu of the Graphs pulldown menu lets you choose the various options that you might want to use when creating the graph. As shown in Fig. 10-23, these include x- and y-axis labels, y-axis range and intervals, and pie chart explosion.

A typical Framework graph is shown in Fig. 10-24. The graph is drawn in its own frame. Framework frames can be resized and moved anywhere on the screen. The unusual aspect of this graphing process is the ability to display the graph in a variety of sizes. Normally, Framework displays

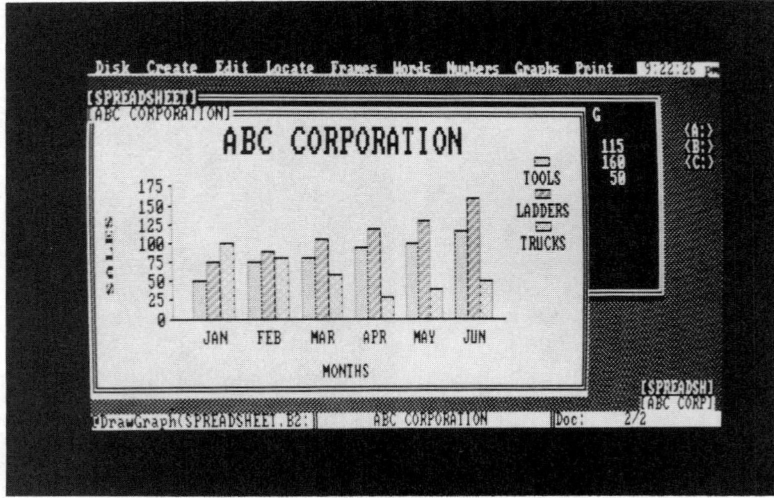

Fig. 10-24. The Framework bar graph.

the graph in a standard size frame in black on white. The *Zoom* key lets you see the graph in fullscreen view in medium resolution color.

The graph is actually produced by a formula known as the "@DrawGraph" formula. This formula allows the customization of any Framework graph without respecifying the graph. This formula also allows you to change any label or title, resize and change fonts, and even display chart notes. The graph can also be displayed in reverse video.

Figure 10-25 shows the effect of changing the formula to add a line to the bar chart. This overlaid graph is actually made up of two "@DrawGraph" formulas. Notice the spreadsheet has also been restyled to add a totals row and some necessary underlining. The graph now reflects the added totals line, and totals appears in the legend. The graph frame has also been resized and moved.

A Framework graph is never really saved. The formula is saved, and when the frame is redisplayed the graph is redrawn. If the spreadsheet changes, the graph will change when recalculated. The graph can also be *linked* to the spreadsheet to automatically change when the spreadsheet is changed and recalculated. The formatting commands become part of the graph formula, which is saved. Since the data is determined by the spreadsheet (or a database), the formatting commands and data are actually saved separately.

Framework does a good job in outputting to any dot-matrix printer or plotter. Its screen display is also excellent. Framework comes with an installation program to connect to most of the known printers and plotters on the market today.

Framework lets you place your graphics anywhere on a printed page. Placement within text or spreadsheets is controlled by the outlining process. You can place a graph in the space allotted between other documents and you can control the exact size of the graph, but these procedures require a lot of trial and error.

Framework is this authors choice of the ultimate package for word processing and outlining. This text of this entire book was created using Framework. Its graphics are good and very well integrated with the rest of the system. Framework is fast and virtually bug-free, and is an extremely useful tool for producing graphics, or handling other chores.

SYMPHONY

Symphony is Lotus's second attempt at integrated software. Like 1-2-3 it features a spreadsheet, graphics, and a database. Like other integrated packages, it also features word processing and communications modules. This package is a very complex and powerful package. It handles graphics very differently than its companion Lotus 1-2-3.

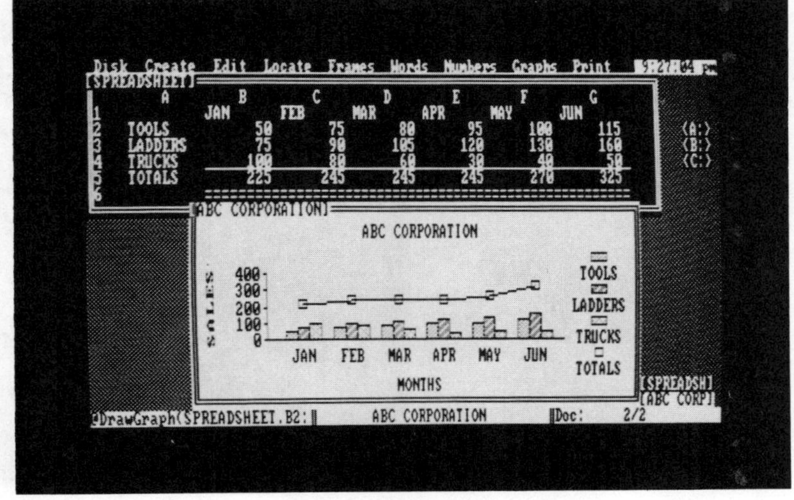

Fig. 10-25. The Framework bar/line graph.

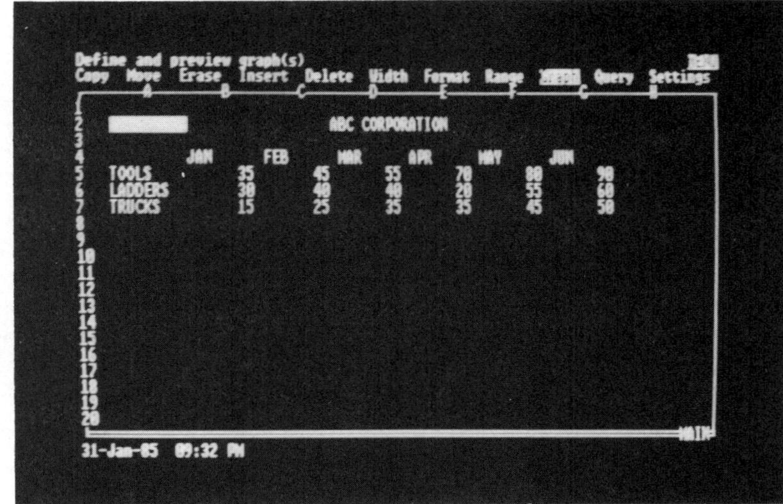

Fig. 10-26. The Symphony spread sheet.

Symphony comes in a large plastic case. It features the best and probably most costly documentation you will see for a long time. Three separate multicolor spiral manuals comprise the Symphony documentation. These include an introduction, a how to manual, and a reference guide. There is a computer-based tutorial along with reams of book tutorials and examples.

Symphony is very well integrated. It can run in one of two modes. Graphs can be integrated with text or they can be displayed separately. Symphony features windows much as Framework features frames.

The basis of Symphony is a spreadsheet. Figure 10-26 shows a Symphony spreadsheet. The standard Symphony commands including "Graph" are shown at the top. The data is arranged as it would be in most spreadsheet packages.

Once the data is entered into the spreadsheet, the graph can be created. The Graph command displays a submenu as shown in Fig. 10-27.

There are two menus for creating the graph.

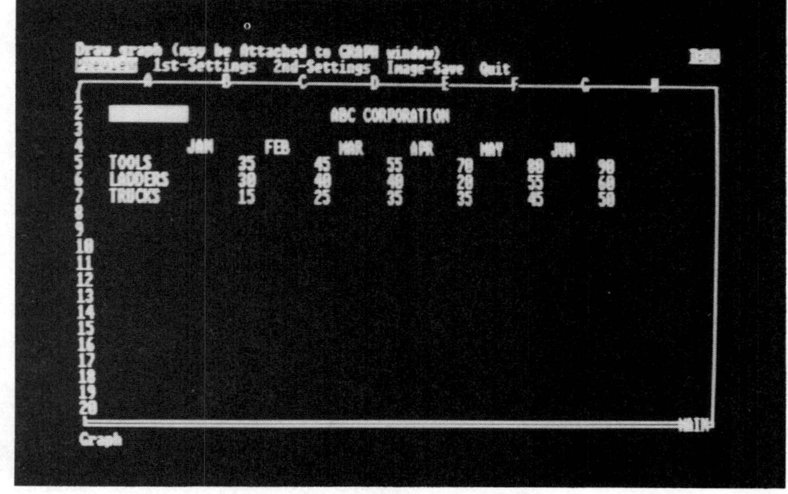

Fig. 10-27. The Symphony graph menu.

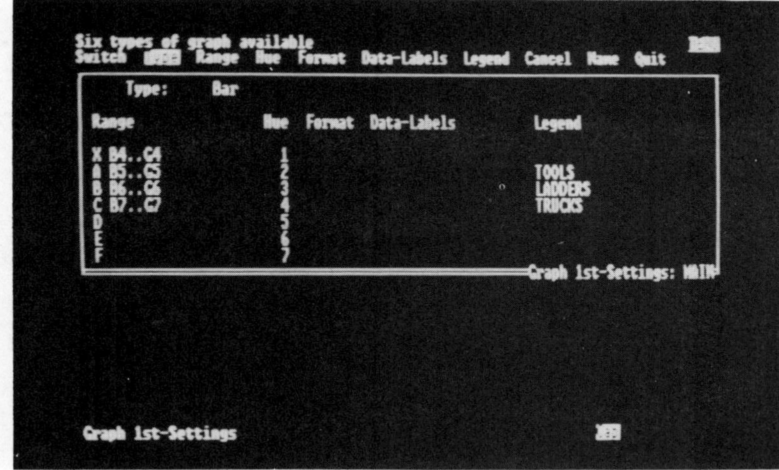

Fig. 10-28. The Symphony 1st-settings screen.

The first, called 1st-Settings, lets you specify the x-axis and data values. It also lets you specify the graph type, data labels and legend labels. The 1st-Settings menu is shown in Fig. 10-28.

The 2nd-Settings menu lets you specify the graphic options that are necessary to format the graph. In Fig. 10-29 you can see they include titles and axis labels, y-axis range and scaling, grid lines, and other options. Once this is done you can preview the graph.

The bar graph in Fig. 10-30 looks good on the screen. The same data is shown as a pie chart in Fig. 10-31.

Symphony can print and plot to a large number of hardcopy devices.

It can place graphics in the middle of a document. Formats and data are saved separately for ease of changes.

Symphony is one of the most popular integrated packages on the market. If you are looking for a well rounded package that has all the integrated functions and produces relatively good graphics, Symphony is for you.

SMART SYSTEM

The SMART system by Innovative Software

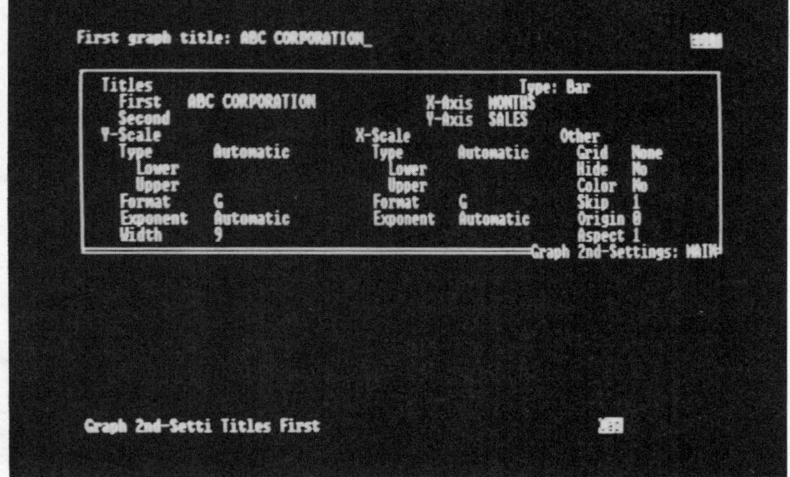

Fig. 10-29. The Symphony 2nd-settings screen.

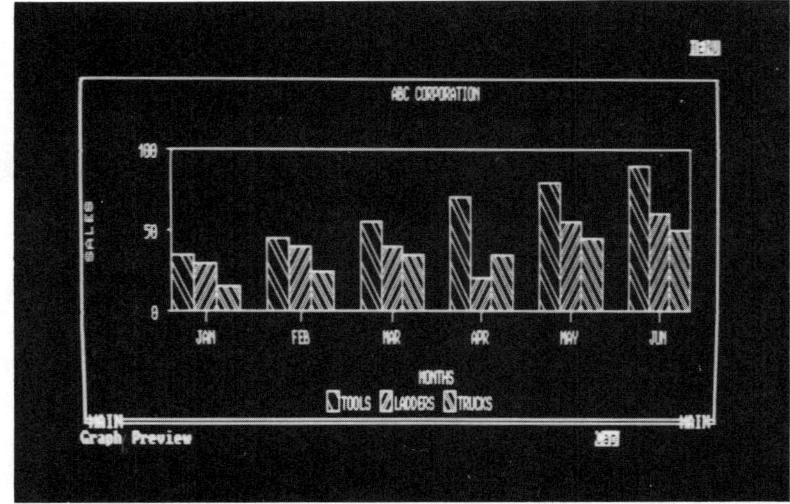

Fig. 10-30. A Symphony bar chart.

has been largely overlooked by the software industry. This is a shame because within the package is one of the most powerful software creations ever created. The package not only features spreadsheet, a database manager, a word processing module, and a very powerful language, called Project Processing, but also contains one of the most powerful graphics packages available. To top it off, it also has an appointment calendar and a calculator that are always available for use.

The SMART package was developed as an integrated package with standalone modules. Each module is a very powerful standalone package that is well integrated with the other modules.

The SMART system comes in a large plastic library case. It includes three IBM sized looseleaf binders. One contains the word processing and general operations manual. The second contains the Data Manager, while the third contains the SMART spreadsheet with graphics. Each section comes with a computer-based tutorial as well as an excellent book tutorial. Each module is on a separate disk, and there is also a main system disk that contains memory-resident code. There is a tutorial disk for

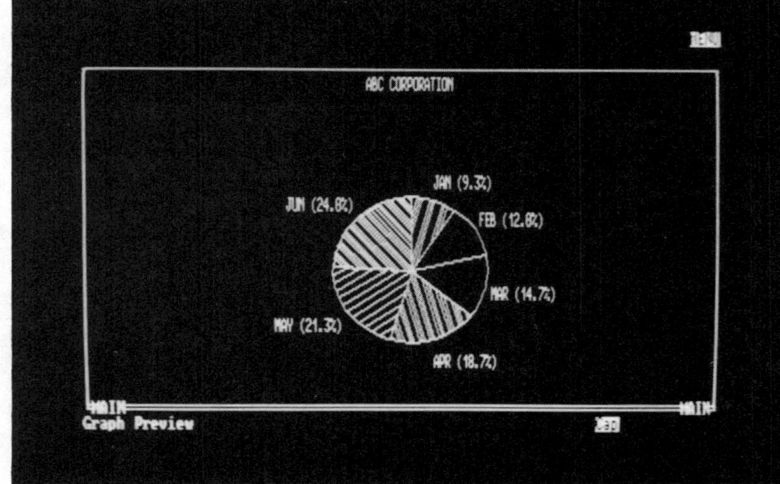

Fig. 10-31. A Symphony pie chart.

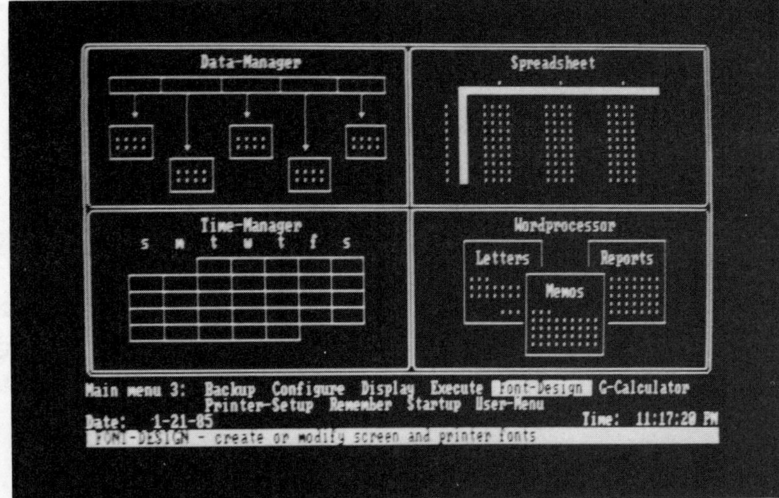

Fig. 10-32. The SMART System main menu.

each section, and on-line help is available. As you would for any integrated package, you should allocate a few days for learning this package.

Unlike most integrated software systems, the SMART system allows you to control the overall functioning of the package. You can set the foreground and background colors of the panels. You can also set the confidence level. This is a parameter that controls the number of menu items that appear in the menu line. As you are learning, you might only want a few options, but as you become more proficient or need more power you can change the confidence level. The command line shown on the main menu is that from confidence level 3. This package even lets you create your own fonts for use in all modules. It also contains one of the more powerful macro and programming languages called Project Processing.

Figure 10-33 shows a SMART system spreadsheet. At first glance it looks like any other spreadsheet except that its rows and columns are numbered. SMART refers to cell "A1" as R1C1. Once the data is entered the graph can be defined.

A menu option lets you define the graph. The

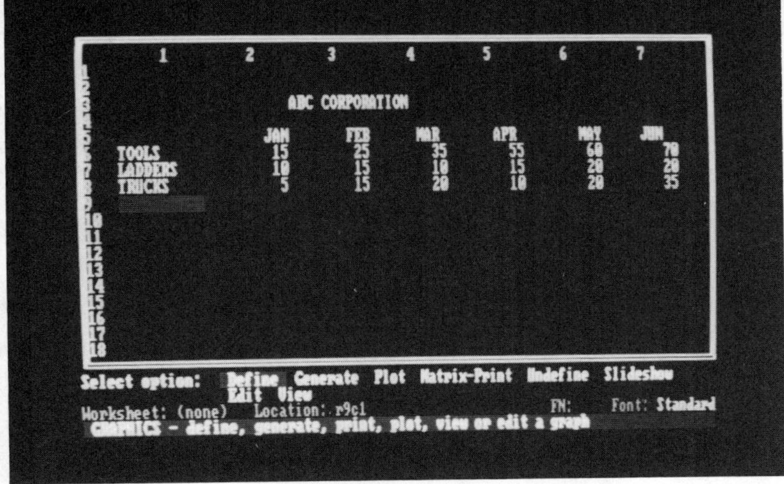

Fig. 10-33. The SMART System spreadsheet.

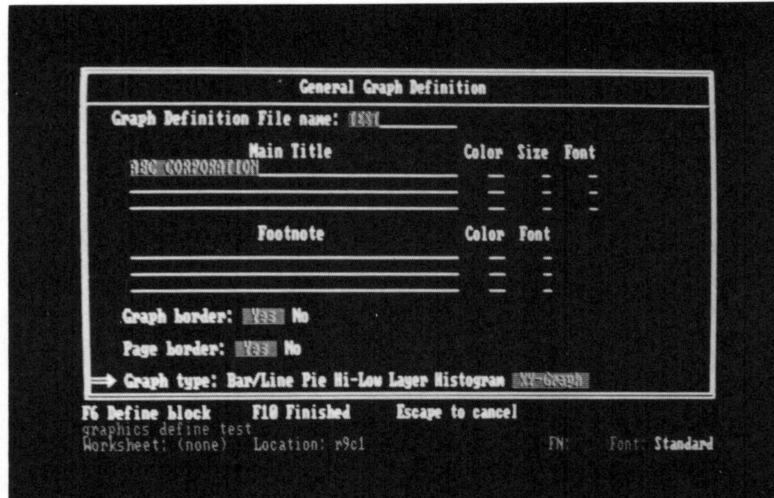

Fig. 10-34. The SMART System graph definition menu.

first menu to use is the General Graph Definition menu, shown in Fig. 10-34. If you have previously stored a format, you can retrieve it using this menu. This menu also lets you enter and style titles and footnotes. The graph type and the border defaults are defined at the bottom of the menu. All graph types can share data.

If you choose the Bar/Line definition, meaning that either a bar or line chart will be created, the menu in Fig. 10-35 is displayed. The menu is broken up into independent and dependent regions. The independent regions contain the x-axis labels, while the dependent regions contain the data series that will make up the chart. As each dependent region is selected, the spreadsheet replaces the menu. The data selected is highlighted, and the menu automatically displays the rows and columns that were highlighted. You can add a legend label to be displayed later. The x-axis or independent region is retrieved the same way. X- and y-axis titles are also controlled from this menu.

The last menu you must use to produce a graphic is the Options menu. This controls how the graph looks. One graph type that only SMART can

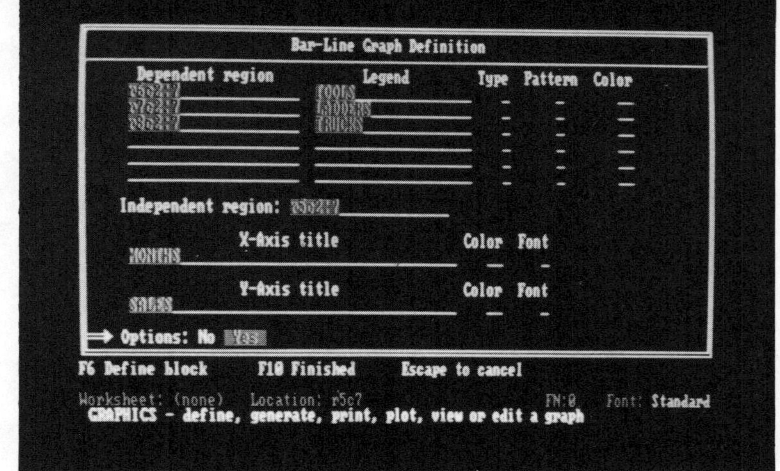

Fig. 10-35. The SMART System data definition menu.

```
Bar-Line Graph Options

→ Bar dimension: 2-dimensional 3-dimensional Line
  Bar orientation: Vertical Horizontal
  Values on top of bars: None Horizontal Vertical
  Legend position: None Bottom 1 2 3 4
  Point type: Dots Symbols

  Divisions: Color Font Tics/Div.
    X-Axis:    _     _     _
    Y-Axis:    _     _     _

  Grids:     (y/n) Color  Style
    X-Axis:    _     _     _
    Y-Axis:    _     _     _

  Scaling:   Type  Minimum  Maximum  Increment
    Y-Axis:    _   _______  _______  _______

F6 Define block     F10 Finished     Escape to cancel
Worksheet: (none)   Location: r5c7        FN:0   Font: Standard
GRAPHICS - define, generate, print, plot, view or edit a graph
```

Fig. 10-36. The SMART System graph options menu.

do is a three dimensional chart known as a *block* chart. The Options menu controls many options. You can choose two or three dimensional bars, or a line chart. You can then decide whether orientation should be horizontal or vertical. Values can be placed on top of the bars, legends positioned, and marker points defined in this menu. The format of the axes including division and scaling is controlled here, along with color, and font. Grid lines are also controlled in this menu.

Once the graph has been defined it can be displayed, printed, or plotted each with excellent resolution. Figure 10-37 demonstrates the quality with which a standard monitor displays a three-dimensional bar chart.

The SMART system is built around a common interface that allows the integration of text, numbers, and graphics. Its graphics capabilities are the best of any integrated package, and its performance and design is also first rate. This package should be considered by anyone who wants to buy one package and get the most out of it. Each module is excellent by itself; but SMART is even better when considered as a complete package.

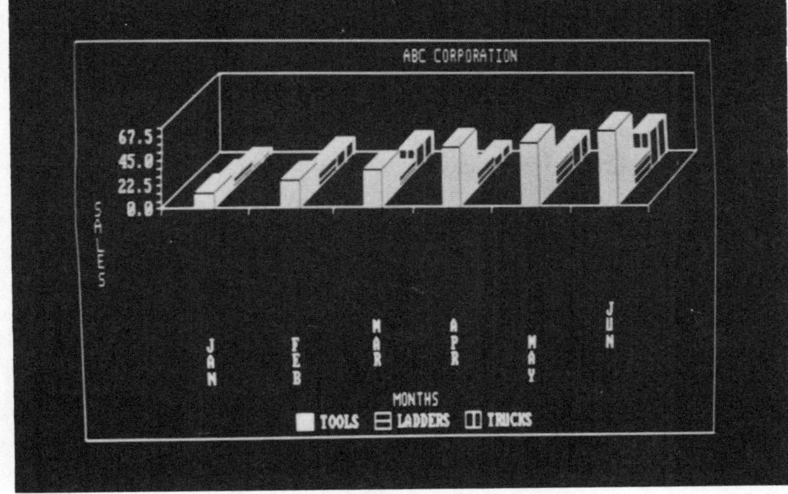

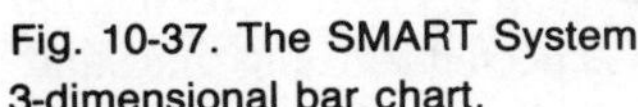
Fig. 10-37. The SMART System 3-dimensional bar chart.

Chapter 11

Text Slide Packages

OVERHEAD EXPRESS
SIGN-MASTER

Text slide packages are those packages whose primary function is to produce text-only slides. These are the mainstay of American business today. Text-only packages should be fairly simple to use. They should offer a multitude of font and font sizes and also contain some special characters. You should be able to place text anywhere on the screen and draw a border around the whole slide.

The better text slide software allows graphic characters to be used to draw boxes around any text and allow flowcharts and process charts to be drawn within the slide. Anything else that needs to fit into rows and columns, such as tables or calendars, can also be produced. These can be adjusted to any size to fit around the text being used.

These packages should allow excellent resolution. It is important in a text-only presentation that the text be readable. When you are displaying a graph, it is permissible to have text that is partially unreadable because the message should be conveyed by the graph itself. When your entire presentation must be read, it better be as legible as possible.

The packages described in this section produce excellent quality output both on plotters and on dot matrix printers.

The following information is presented for each software package discussed in this chapter.

1. An introduction to the basic philosophies of the package and a discussion of what it is intended to do and who its intended audience is.
2. A presentation of the best or most unusual features that set this product apart from all others.
3. Discussions of the *boot* or first screen, the documentation, the expected learning time, and the tutorials that may be available.
4. Discussions of how the program handles and changes input data and how it handles data created outside the workings of the program.
5. A discussion of the types of slides produced. Are they text only, or can the contain special characters? Can a border be drawn around the slide? Can vertical and horizontal lines be placed anywhere on the slide?

6. A discussion of the available formatting commands including the ability of the software to control the placement and type of text, legends, titles, labels, and tick marks.
7. A presentation concerning the separation of text and formatting commands.
8. A discussion of the output quality on the screen, dot matrix printer, Polaroid Palette, and plotter.
9. An evaluation of the overall performance, speed, and error handling, and general comments about the ease of use of the package compared to the results achieved.

The ability to produce high quality text slides easily seen at distances, when projected, or quickly read on paper is prime criteria on which these packages should be judged. Business slides are sometimes put together at the last minute by people with no artistic abilities. The more professional a slide can appear, the better the chances for a favorable decision if the data (or text) makes valid points. Many an argument has been won with good slides as a deciding factor.

The *bullet* slide, that is, a slide that contains lines of text preceded by small solid circles or bullets, is the most popular type of slide today. You should be consistent when you are creating these slides. You should use only two or three colors on each slide, and these colors should mean the same thing on each slide.

Fonts that are clear and readable should be used. Gothic and script are very pretty fonts, but can they really be easily seen? If you choose to use a special font, use it consistently. Size should also be used consistently. A larger title is a good idea, if every title is large.

Some good packages make it easier for you to be consistent by allowing you to use *templates.* Templates allow you to specify formatting instructions for each screen. When you enter the text on a given line, the formatting instructions for that line are used to display the text.

There are two types of text/slide packages: menu-driven and command-driven. Menu-driven means that to use the package, you merely have to fill in menu screens. Most packages today are menu-driven. Some require that you fill in more menus and some less, but all are relatively the same in the way the menus work.

A command-driven package is one that is controlled by individual commands, much like a programming language. These can be very powerful as they allow a multitude of combinations that some menu-driven packages do not allow. They are generally more difficult to learn initially, and logic must be employed to structure the individual commands. Once a command driven package is mastered, however, results are usually achieved in less time than with a menu-driven package.

The packages in this chapter allow only text and a few special characters. Packages that do text and a whole lot more are described in the next chapter.

OVERHEAD EXPRESS

Overhead Express does what its name implies; it enables you to produce overhead transparencies. It also does a wonderful job on the screen and can produce slides or do large monitor presentations. If that is all this package did it would still be an excellent text/slide package; however, it does much, much more.

It has several unique features that set it apart from any other package. While with other text/slide packages, you are lucky if you can change sizes, fonts, styles, and colors of text, with this package, this is just the beginning. Overhead Express features an editor that makes these functions quick and easy.

Figure 11-1 shows Overhead Express' startup screen. The image looks like a screen reflecting a brilliant display. Since text/slide presentations are the bane of the contemporary manager's existence, you need a package that can do brilliant things.

As shown in Fig. 11-2 the main menu of Overhead Express begins to tell you something about its capabilities. It features two editors. One editor uses predefined templates to produce slides. The other lets you define templates to produce your own special effects. The main menu also lets you review a presentation and display the overheads on the screen or printer.

Template is the word used to indicate a

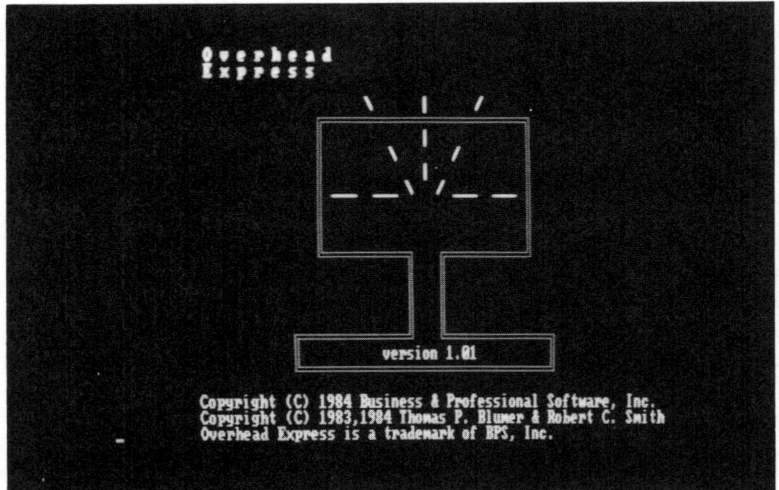

Fig. 11-1. The Overhead Express startup screen.

predeveloped model. In this case the template provides a way to type in the data and have it flow into an overhead layout. The most common layout is a bullet slide. Figure 11-3 shows the express editor screen with a bullet chart template and some data entered. This bullet chart consists of a title, subtitle, and several bullets. The subtitle is underlined. The /U for underline is selected from a submenu that is displayed on the bottom of the screen. The function keys at the bottom of the screen control these menus. The submenus enable you to change fonts, resize letters, and underline, shade, italicize and style the text in hundreds of ways. Mundane text presentations are given new life as they are made interesting for the first time.

The second bullet is styled with an italic font. The \F2 is the indication of this font. The experienced user can key in the \F2; the novice can use the function keys and the submenus to choose the italic font, which automatically places the correct \ symbol in the text. The \F3J F1 before the third bullet indicates that a special symbol, in this case a pointing hand, will be used. At the top of the screen is the line and column count, which tells you

Fig. 11-2. The Overhead Express main menu.

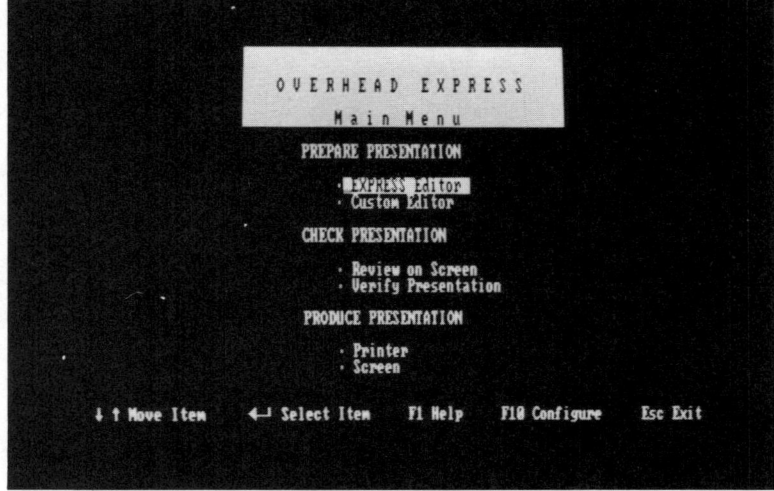

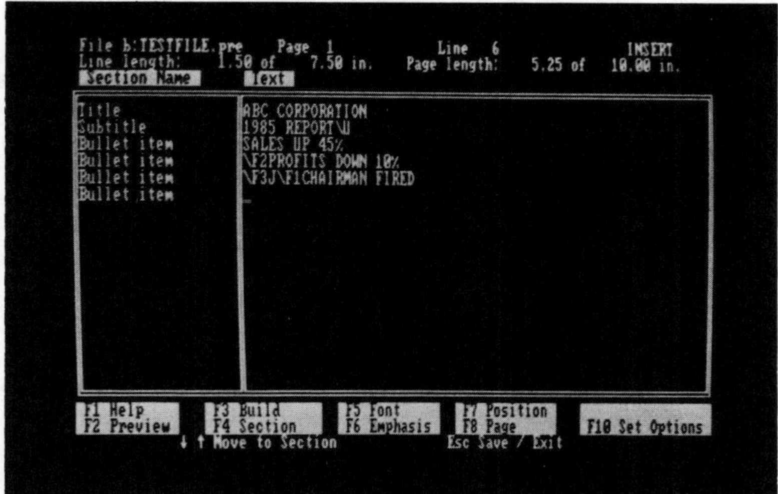

Fig. 11-3. The Overhead Express editor screen.

Fig. 11-4. The Overhead Express printer output.

when a page is full of text. Figure 11-4 shows the printed output from this bullet template. The pointing hand is used to emphasize the item. Overhead Express features a list of symbols that help you make your presentations. Figure 11-5 shows a list of the special symbols, which can be sized and styled themselves.

Templates can be used for far more than the creation of simple symbols and bullet slides. Templates can be used to place horizontal and vertical lines to make a tabular chart. Figure 11-6 shows a sample template and the results. This type of display can easily be created even by the novice through the use of the function key menus.

There are many predefined templates. They can be used to create interesting slides such as boxes that can be filled in, grid lines for hand drawn graphs, outlines, comparisons, and multicolumn tables.

Overhead Express also has a custom editor that can be used with the templates to create some amazing slide shows. An interesting template allows a hand symbol to move slowly down the list of items; when it reaches the bottom, the screen becomes reverse video. Only a couple of statements are needed to produce the effect, as shown in Fig. 11-7.

Figure 11-8 shows some sample slides and the code used to create and display them at five-second intervals.

The final and most unusual feature of Overhead Express is its slide show or marquis feature. In addition to displaying one screen at a time or using a dissolve or curtain effect as many packages do, Overhead Express can actually scroll the screen, as

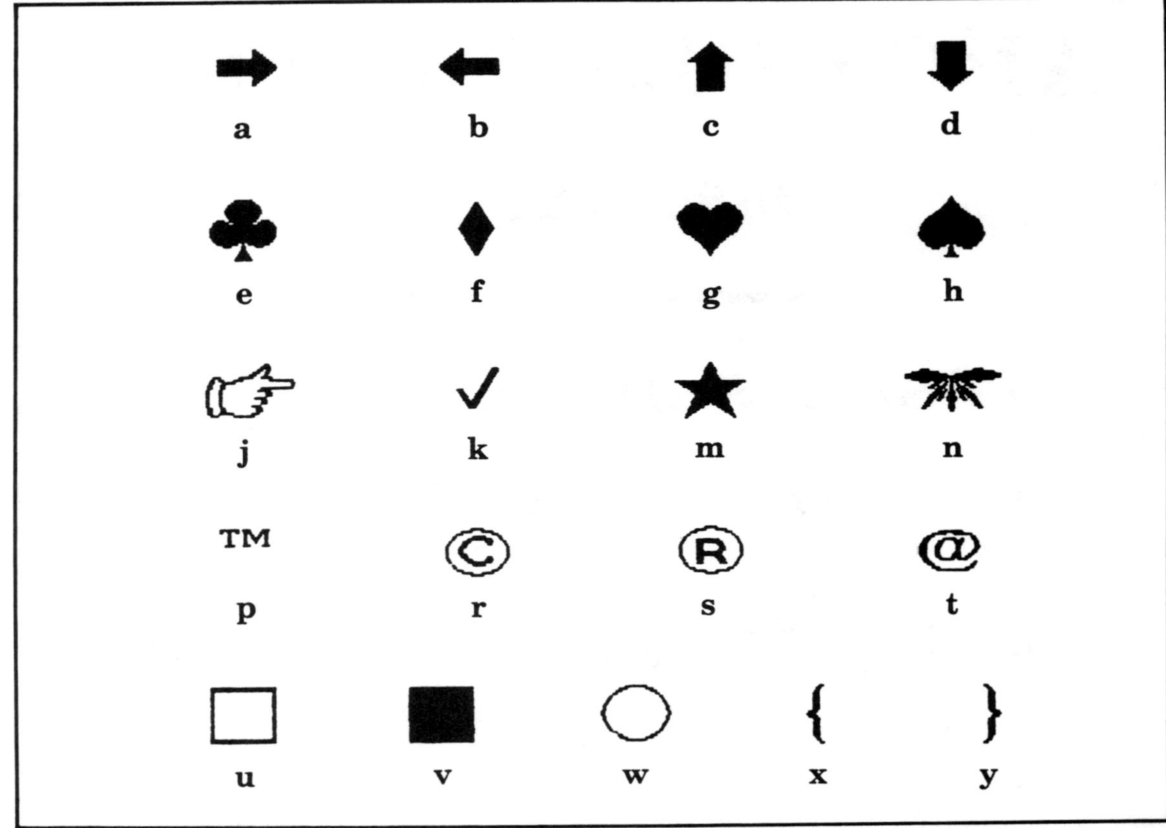

Fig. 11-5. The Overhead Express symbols.

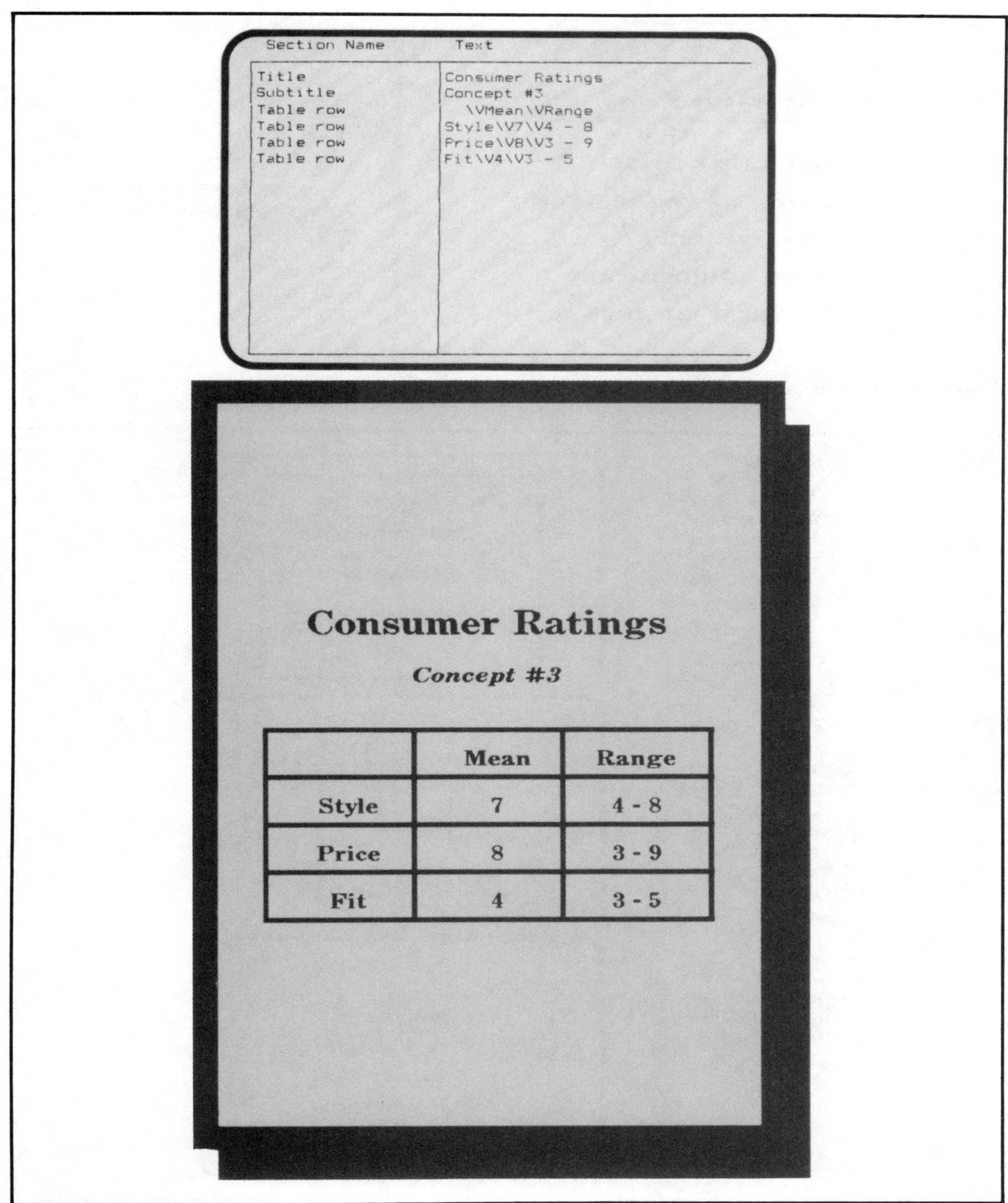

Fig. 11-6. The Overhead Express templates.

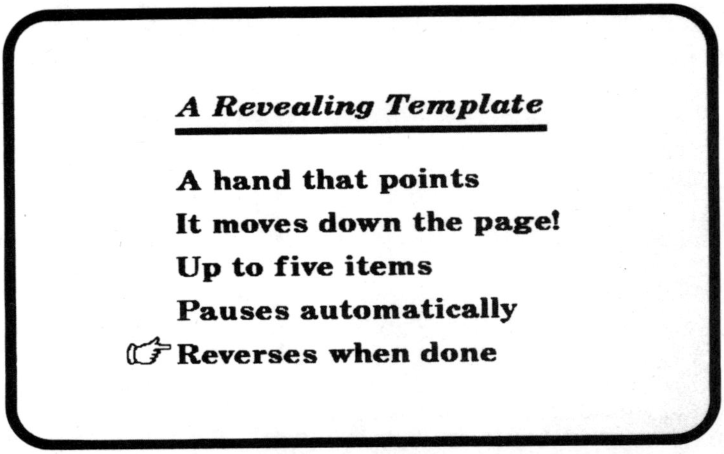

A Revealing Template

A hand that points

It moves down the page!

Up to five items

Pauses automatically

☞ **Reverses when done**

Fig. 11-7. The Overhead Express revealing template.

```
.page screen
.font C24 C40
.box
Welcome to the
2nd Annual
 \F2Somerville
 \F2Accountants'
Convention
.box end
.wait 5
.page screen
.font C40
.elastic
Food and Drinks
.elastic
in the
.elastic
Gold Room
.elastic
.wait 5
.page screen
.font C24I
.down 50
.right
.block
(down the hall
to the right
and up the first
flight of stairs)
.block end
.wait 3
```

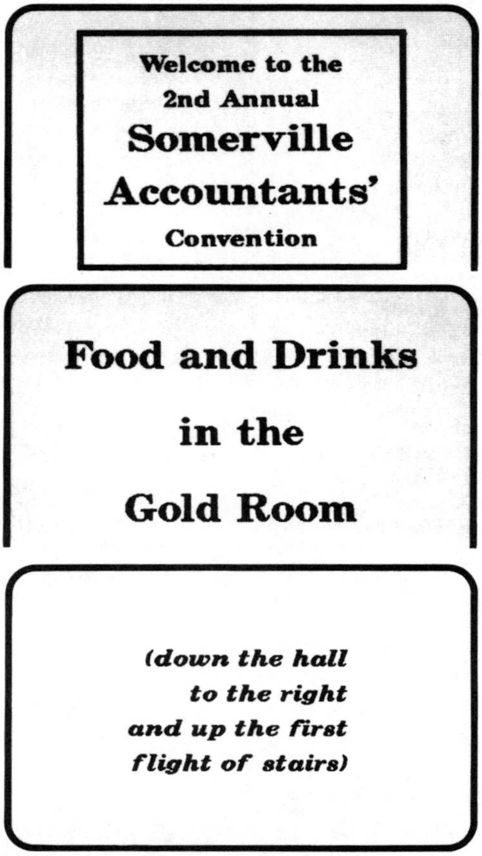

Welcome to the
2nd Annual
Somerville
Accountants'
Convention

Food and Drinks

in the

Gold Room

(down the hall
to the right
and up the first
flight of stairs)

Fig. 11-8. The Overhead Express marquee display.

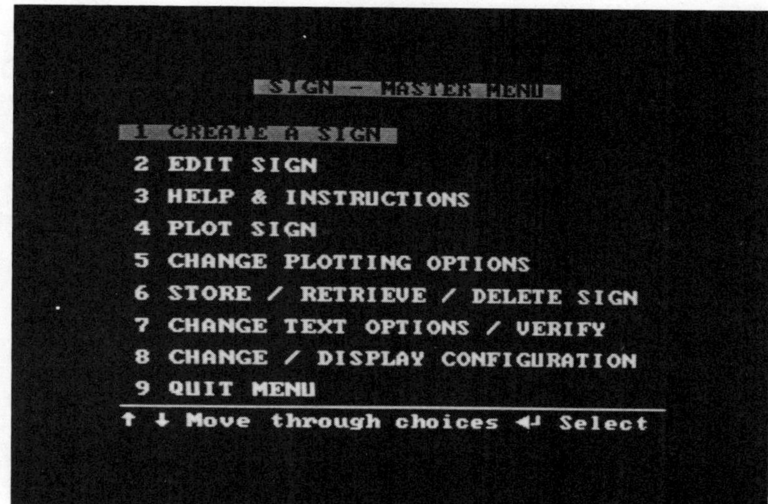

Fig. 11-9. The Sign-Master main menu.

is done with the credits at the end of a movie.

Overhead express does an excellent job both on the screen and on the printer. It offers everything a text/slide package could possibly offer. Its symbol library is sparse, but there are no better packages that have better symbol libraries. Its outstanding ability to handle column and row lines, animation, and scrolling, as well as text, makes this package a must for any business executive today.

SIGN-MASTER

Sign-Master is the text-slide entry by Decision Resources. The package exists solely to produce text charts for paper and 35 mm slides. Sign-Master features many different types of text fonts in various sizes, styles, and colors. Its unique ability is that of adding lines to text. It can produce tables, word charts, signs, and comparisons with just a few keystrokes. Figure 11-9 shows the main Sign-Master screen.

Sign-Master lets you create, change, store, retrieve, and display signs. Signs can be text or text with vertical and horizontal lines. With this easy to use package you can create some excellent text

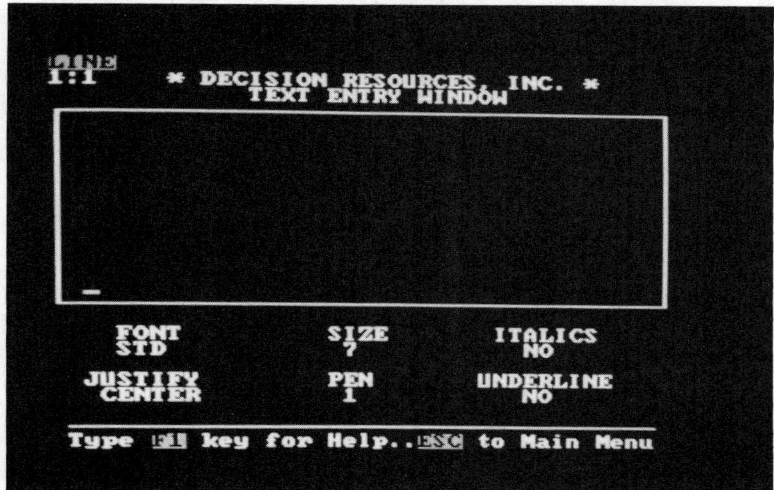

Fig. 11-10. The Sign-Master text entry window.

THE BOTTOM LINE

PROJECTED EARNINGS

(Millions of $)

	78	79	80	81	82
Sales	86.4	121	144	163.8	182
Net Income	5.96	8.8	11.4	13.4	15.7
ROS(%)	6.9	7.3	7.9	8.2	8.6
Mkt. Share	48%	61%	65%	71%	76%

Capital expenditure required: $5 Million

Net present value = $24.25 Million

(opportunity cost of capital = 24%)

Fig. 11-11. The Sign-Master bottom line output.

slides. Figure 11-10 shows the text entry window. This is the area where the contents of each slide is entered. Text is entered as desired. Any line, word, or letter can be styled individually. Styling is done using the area at the bottom of the screen. The font, size, pen number, justification, italics and underlining can all be controlled. There are several different types of fonts. When you want to select a different font, you can scroll through the list of fonts and then choose the one you like.

Figure 11-11 shows a finished display called "The Bottom Line". This was made using a few sim-

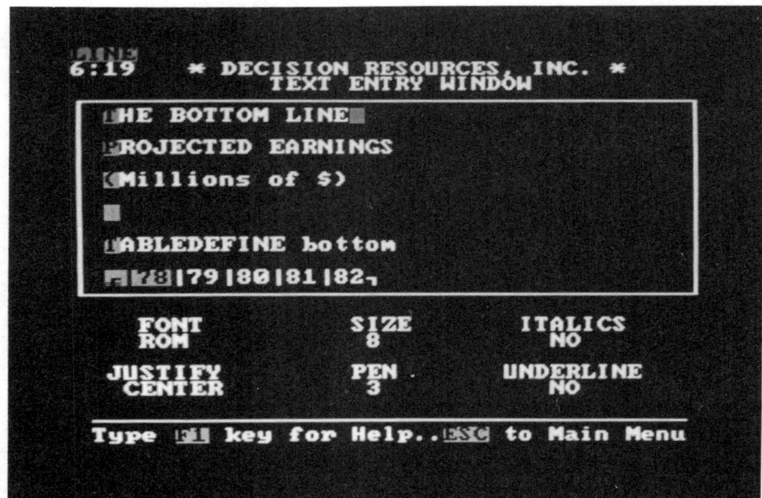

Fig. 11-12. The Sign-Master bottom line text window-part 1.

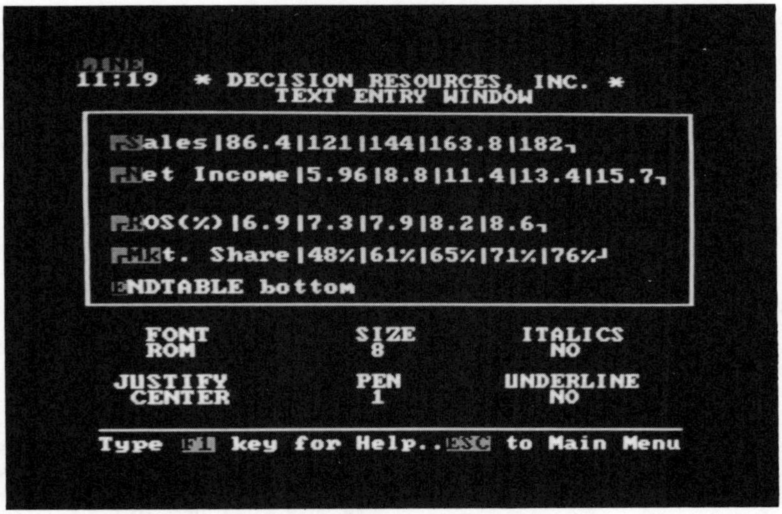

```
11:19   * DECISION RESOURCES, INC. *
              TEXT ENTRY WINDOW

 Sales|86.4|121|144|163.8|182┐
 Net Income|5.96|8.8|11.4|13.4|15.7┐

 ROS(%)|6.9|7.3|7.9|8.2|8.6┐
 Mkt. Share|48%|61%|65%|71%|76%┘
 ENDTABLE bottom

   FONT          SIZE        ITALICS
   ROM            8            NO
 JUSTIFY          PEN        UNDERLINE
  CENTER           1           NO

Type F1 key for Help..ESC to Main Menu
```

Fig. 11-13. The Sign-Master bottom line text window-part 2.

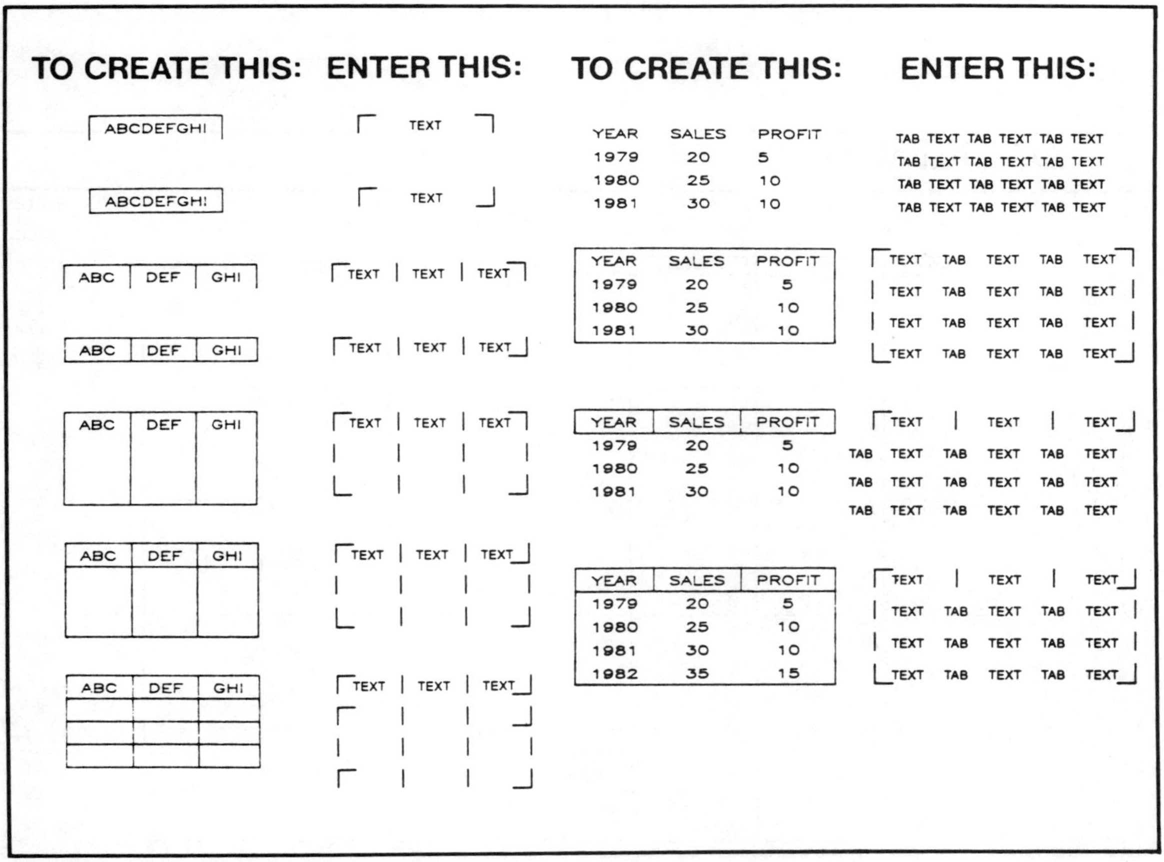

TO CREATE THIS:	ENTER THIS:	TO CREATE THIS:	ENTER THIS:
ABCDEFGHI	┌ TEXT ┐	YEAR SALES PROFIT 1979 20 5 1980 25 10 1981 30 10	TAB TEXT TAB TEXT TAB TEXT TAB TEXT TAB TEXT TAB TEXT TAB TEXT TAB TEXT TAB TEXT TAB TEXT TAB TEXT TAB TEXT
ABCDEFGHI	┌ TEXT ┘		
ABC | DEF | GHI	┌TEXT | TEXT | TEXT┐	YEAR SALES PROFIT 1979 20 5 1980 25 10 1981 30 10	┌TEXT TAB TEXT TAB TEXT┐ | TEXT TAB TEXT TAB TEXT | | TEXT TAB TEXT TAB TEXT | └TEXT TAB TEXT TAB TEXT┘
ABC | DEF | GHI	┌TEXT | TEXT | TEXT┘		
ABC | DEF | GHI	┌TEXT | TEXT | TEXT┐ | | | | └ | | ┘	YEAR | SALES | PROFIT 1979 20 5 1980 25 10 1981 30 10	┌TEXT | TEXT | TEXT┘ TAB TEXT TAB TEXT TAB TEXT TAB TEXT TAB TEXT TAB TEXT TAB TEXT TAB TEXT TAB TEXT
ABC | DEF | GHI	┌TEXT | TEXT | TEXT┘ | | | | └ | | ┘	YEAR | SALES | PROFIT 1979 20 5 1980 25 10 1981 30 10 1982 35 15	┌TEXT | TEXT | TEXT┘ | TEXT TAB TEXT TAB TEXT | | TEXT TAB TEXT TAB TEXT | └TEXT TAB TEXT TAB TEXT┘
ABC | DEF | GHI	┌TEXT | TEXT | TEXT┘ ┌ | | ┘ | | | | ┌ | | ┘		

Fig. 11-14. The Sign-Master tabular create instructions.

BUSINESS ARTS UNIVERSITY

THE COLLEGE OF BUSINESS GRAPHICS OF
BUSINESS ARTS UNIVERSITY
PROUDLY CONFERS THE TITLE OF
DOCTOR OF SIGNS

UPON ______________________________

It shall be declared that from this date forth
the above cited shall be referred to as a DOCTOR OF SIGNS
and heretofore accorded the respect
and praise of all.

DATE_____

Fig. 11-15. A Sign-Master degree.

1984 JANUARY 1984

SUNDAY	MONDAY	TUESDAY	WEDNESDAY	THURSDAY	FRIDAY	SATURDAY
1	2	3	4	5	6	7
8	9	10	11	12	13	14
15	16	17	18	19	20	21
22	23	24	25	26	27	28
29	30	31				

Fig. 11-16. A Sign-Master calendar.

ple keystrokes as shown in Figs. 11-12 and 11-13.

Figure 11-12 shows the title lines and the top of the table; Fig. 11-13 shows how the actual table is built. Graphics characters such as corners and vertical lines are shown intermixed with the text. Though this looks complicated, its really not. Sign-Master provides you with excellent documentation. Figure 11-14 shows a guide for creating tabular data. The corners and vertical lines are controlled with PF keys and the TAB key. Once you have tried one of these, they all become easy; there is no more lining up text or having to make last minute changes because a number has changed.

With Sign-Master you can create an unlimited number of text slides. Some other ideas are shown in Figs. 11-15 and 11-16.

As you can see, Sign-Master is a unique package that can make the creation of text reports easy. If this is the type of presentations you do and you can use high-quality slides and plots, this package is a necessary item in your toolbox.

Chapter 12

Picture Processors Plus

VCN EXECUVISION
PC PAINT
PC ILLUSTRATOR
4-POINT GRAPHICS

It has been said that a picture is worth a thousand words. It could also be said that a graph is worth a thousand numbers. If this is true, a display produced using a picture processor can be worth a million words and numbers. A picture processor is a package that allows the user to create text, graphs, charts, and *pictures*. A picture is just that, a colorful representation or image of a scene. A picture can be a picture of a sailboat or of a company's headquarters. Graphs and text can be added to a picture to produce a very professional and exciting display. Many of the displays created with these picture processors are so attractive that they are shown in the color section that follows page 184.

The measure of the value of a picture processor is not how easy it is to use. Unless you are an artist, you will probably not be able to create a picture worth showing to anyone but your immediate family. There is a direct correlation between the quality of the picture you can produce using any package and your ability to create pictures with a simple set of colored pencils. A professional artist can work wonders with these packages; the average person cannot. You can learn to use a graphics package or a word processor assuming you understand numbers or can write a sentence. The same is not true of a picture processor. Some of the packages in this section come with libraries of predrawn images to make even the least artistic of us professional picture processors.

There are two types of picture processors. The first type is designed for creating pictures from scratch. These packages use commands that allow lines, circles, boxes, and freehand drawings to be placed on the electronic canvas. Usually these allow any geometric figures to be drawn in any color and filled in in many patterns. A good package will allow the editing of the drawing at many levels including the pixel level.

The second type of picture processor is a *graphic enhancer.* This type of software can also create pictures from scratch, but it is better at enhancing graphs, charts, text, and pictures created using other packages. These are very popular today, and most picture processors are now being sold with "capture" programs that allow any image that has been saved using any other program to be loaded and enhanced by the graphic enhancer program.

The most common form of graphic enhancement is the addition of text to an existing graph or chart. Since many packages do not allow you to place text anywhere on the screen, the graphic enhancer fills this void. Graphic enhancers also allow you to change the colors or patterns of bars or lines, draw boxes around the text, and add arrows.

A good picture processor or graphic enhancer should give you the ability to draw virtually anything on a screen, given your skill level. You should be able to "draw" text in a multitude of fonts, colors, sizes, and styles, at different angles and rotations. You should also be able to handle geometric shapes, including squares, rectangles, circles, arcs, ellipses, and any closed polygon. You should be able to paint the closed figures with color or a pattern.

Once the text or shapes are created, you should be able to move or edit them at will. Some packages only allow you to select a contiguous rectangular area to move. Others keep track of each figure or piece of text and allow you to select and move figures even if they are placed on top of other figures. Editing should include several features. You should be able to work at the individual pixel level to "clean-up" pictures. You should be able to add or erase one pixel or several pixels at a time. An undo command is always a great feature; if you make a mistake, you can use undo to reset the screen to the previous version instantly.

Some software developers assume that most people want digitized, professionally drawn pictures and sell add-on libraries of pictures. These pictures can be placed anywhere on the screen and then modified as the user sees fit. These libraries can produce dazzling results when used by even the most inept artist.

The following information is presented for each software package discussed in this chapter.

1. An introduction to the basic philosophies of the package and a discussion of what it is intended to do and who its intended audience is.
2. A presentation of the best or most unusual features that set this product apart from all others.
3. Discussions of the *boot* or first screen, the documentation, the expected learning time, and the tutorials that may be available.
4. A discussion of how the program handles the creation of pictures; what types of text, geometric symbols, special symbols are available; and what types of sizing, colors, patterns, and rotation are allowed.
5. An examination of the package's ability to enhance other packages' data. Does the package come with a screen capture utility? Can it be used to enhance captured screens and allow you to make editing changes? Does the capture program run in the background with any program or just with a select few?
6. A presentation of the types of pictures produced. Can the package also produce its own business graphics that can be modified? Are libraries available with the program?
7. A discussion of the editing commands. Is there an undo command? Are images saved together or overlaid?
8. A discussion of the output quality on the screen, dot matrix printer, Polaroid Palette, and plotter.
9. An evaluation of the overall performance, speed, and error handling, and general comments about the ease of use of the package compared to the results achieved.

You can buy picture processors and graphic enhancers that turn the simplest graph into a completely customized masterpiece. Whether you want simple text slides or complicated pictures, a picture processor may be just what you are looking for.

VCN EXECUVISION

It has been said the Apple started the microcomputer revolution and that IBM has finished it. The same can be said about VCN Execuvision. There have been many picture processors in the first few years of microcomputers. Each one was a little bit better than its predecessor and did a few things differently and a few things better. Then VCN

Execuvision came along and changed the rules. Big business has been using VCN Execuvision ever since. The secret behind this product is not its ease of use, although it is one of the easiest packages to use. Its ability to create and manipulate objects on the screen is good, but again it is not the best of all the packages out on the market. It does well at handling geometric shapes, including points, lines, boxes, circles, and arrows, and allows you to paint areas and change colors. VCN Execuvision features an excellent erase and sketch command that can produce a line or delete an area from just one pixel at a time to nine pixels at a time. It has no zoom feature (It really doesn't need one). Why then, is VCN Execuvision so good?

Anyone who spends their time creating presentations should be using VCN Execuvision. Though it does text slides with great ease, it does so much more. Pictures can be placed anywhere on the screen, moved, rearranged, and cut and pasted to any location on the screen. Any section of the screen can also be animated, giving the effect of a rolling conveyor belt or a flying bird. By attaching several scenes together, you can trace the movement of a part through your company from raw materials to finished goods.

VCN Execuvision is so good because it doesn't exist on the premise that you are an artist. It features the most comprehensive colored image collection that you will probably see for a long while. These libraries are not haphazardly put together; they are divided into well defined categories and include:

The Border Collection
Initials and Decorative Designs
Industry and Business
Professions: Faces and Figures
International Symbols and Landmarks
Maps and Regions
Health and Fitness
Financial Services
Transportation
Computers and Computer Applications

These pictures include digitized and artistic drawings of hundreds of images that fill the screen with great detail. There are also simple figures and figures that contain many smaller figures. Anything can be cut and pasted anywhere else. A tree can be cut out of a forest, a window out of a house, and even a person from a group of people. This lets VCN Execuvision create some of the most amazing pictures ever thought possible.

This package comes in an IBM type binder. It features a multicolor manual with color pictures of hundreds of screen images. The main system comes with several disks of pictures, while the other

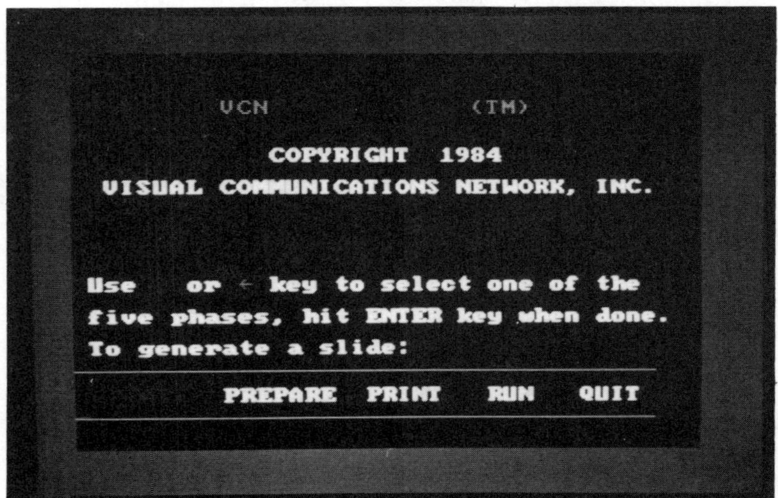

Fig. 12-1. The VCN Execuvision main menu.

The VCN Execuvision main menu.

The VCN Execuvision text menu.

A VCN Execuvision pix slide. Six separate pictures can be cut and pasted from this slide.

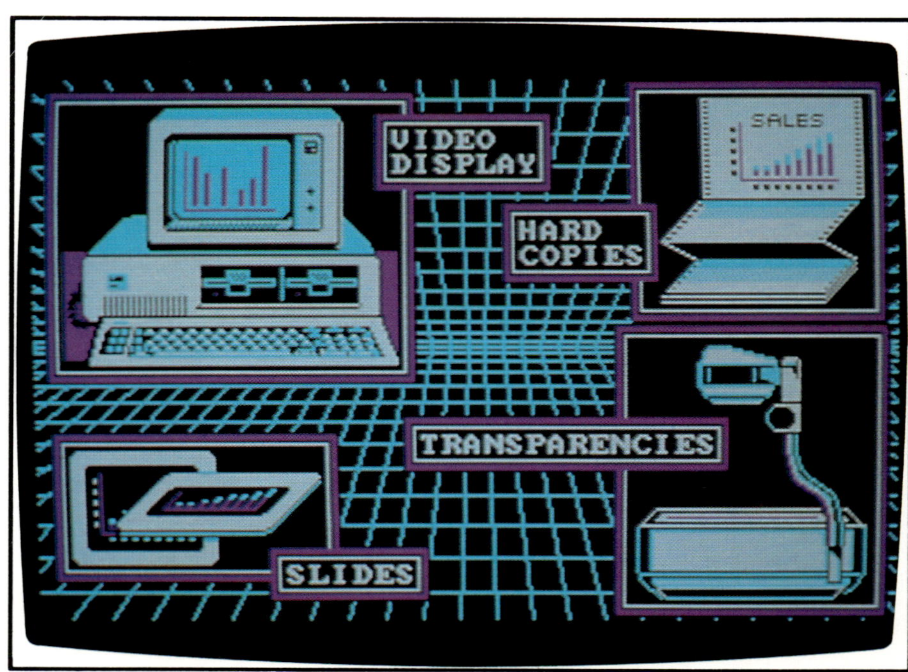

A VCN Execuvision display slide created by combining four pictures from other slides.

A VCN Execuvision display slide created by combining text, a line graph, several pictures, and an appropriate background.

The PC Paint tools screen.

The PC Paint text screen.

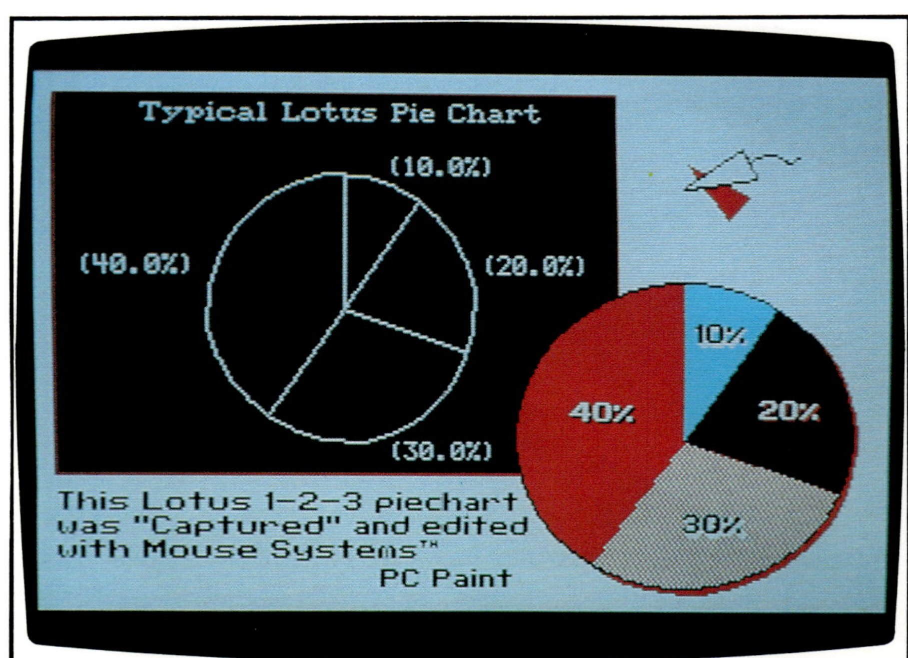

The PC Paint-enhanced Lotus 1-2-3 screen.

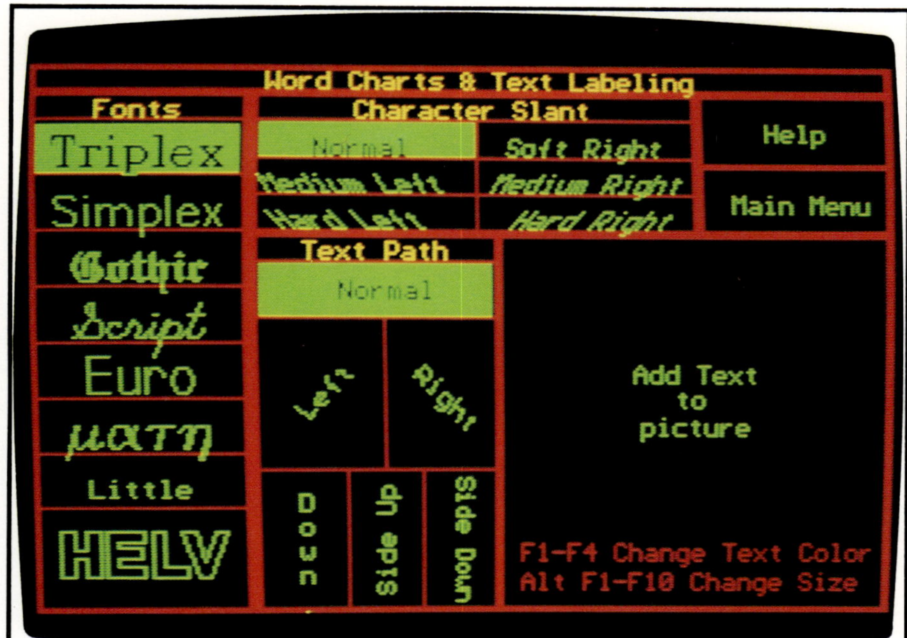

The PC Illustrator text selection menu.

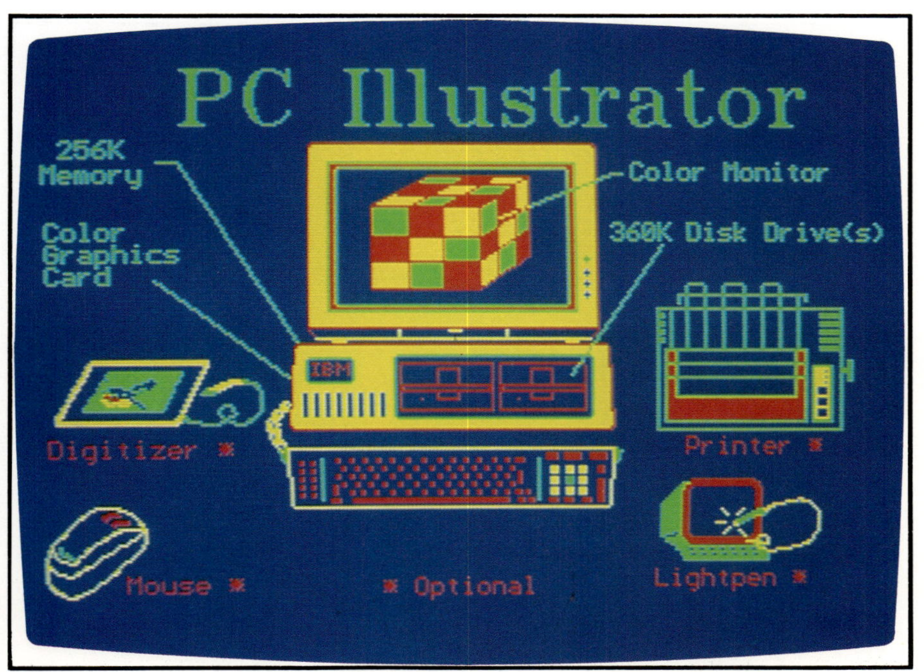

A picture produced using the PC Illustrator.

The space shuttle as produced using the PC Illustrator.

The Golden Gate bridge as produced using 4-Point Graphics.

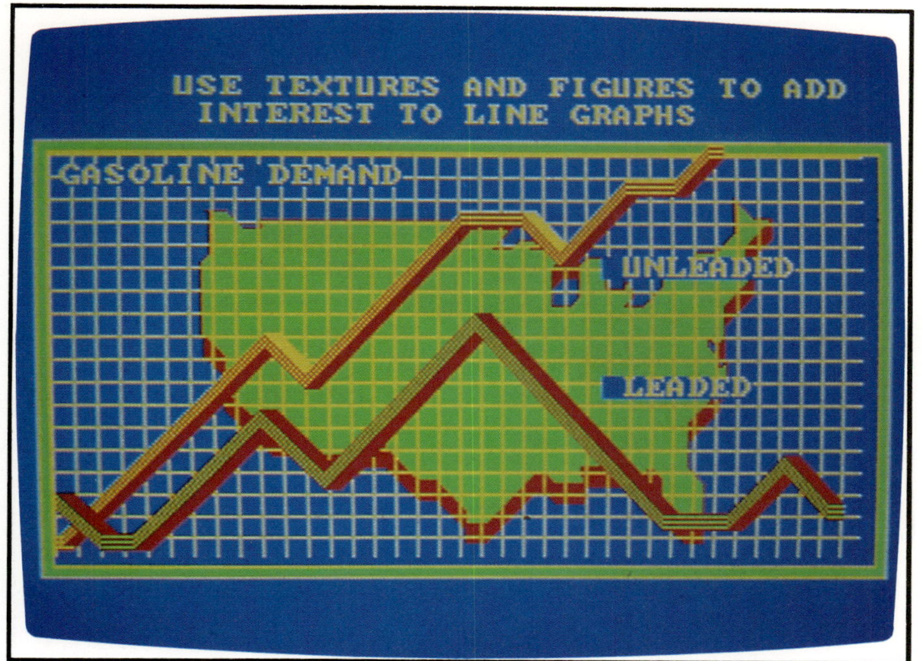

A 4-Point Graphics map and 3-D line graph.

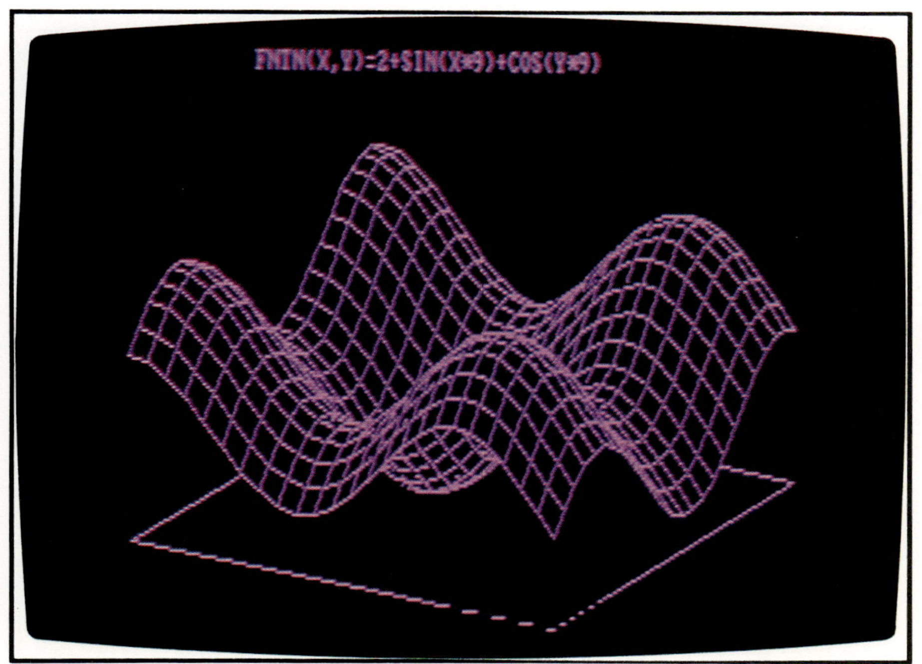

An Energraphics net chart.

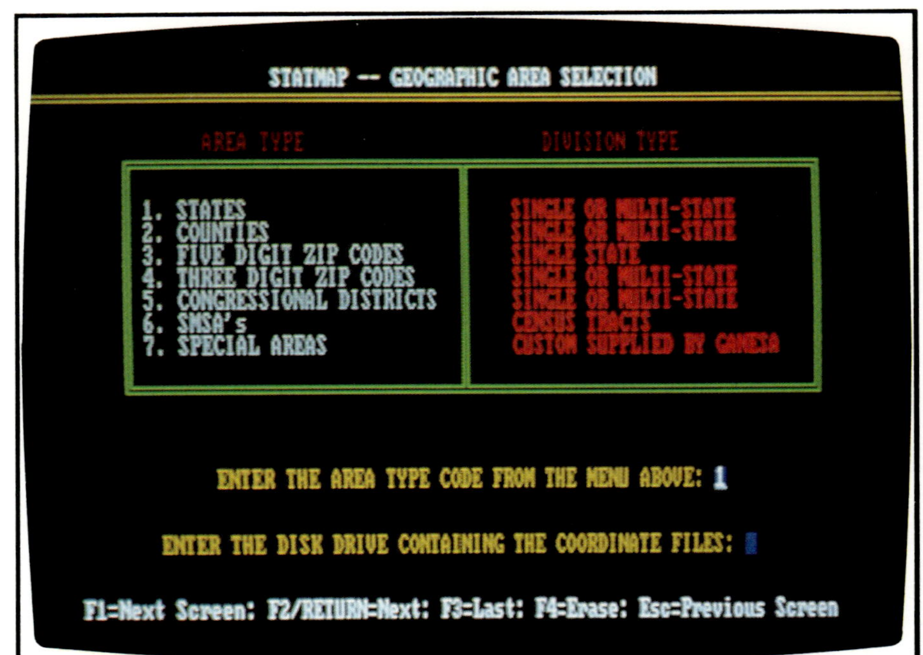

The Statmap create map menu.

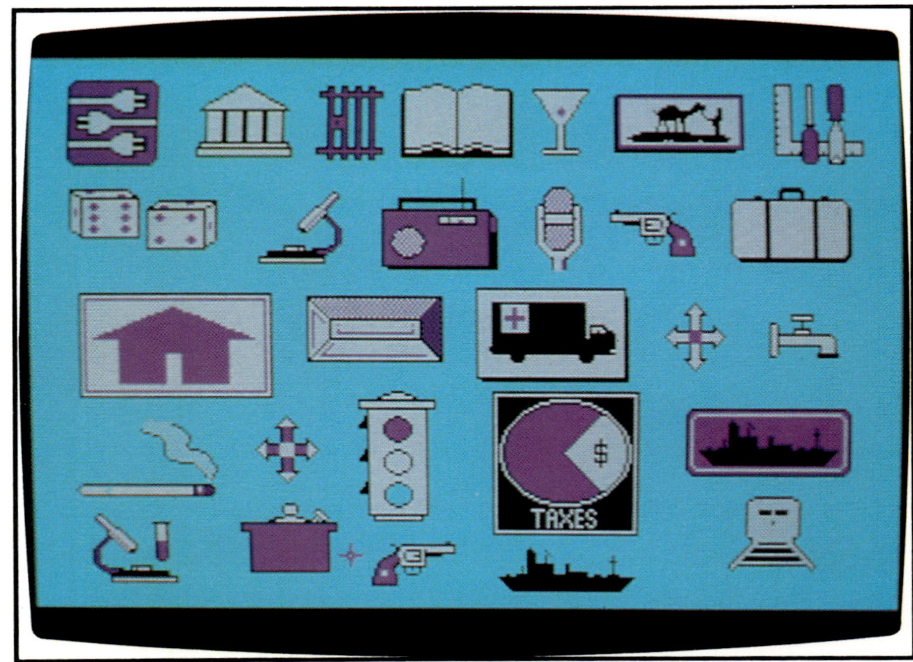

The Graphix Partner library of images.

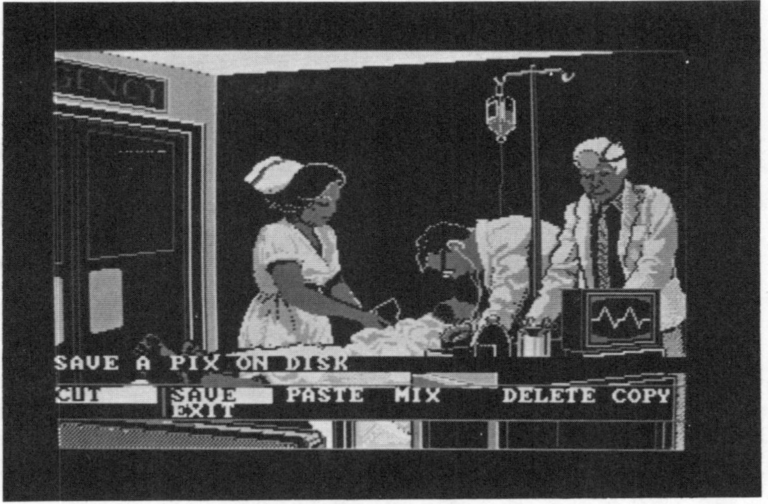

Fig. 12-2. The VCN Execuvision cut menu.

libraries are available separately. In the book there is an excellent tutorial that takes you through all of VCN Execuvision's features. Learning time is only a single afternoon.

VCN Execuvision starts with a main screen as shown in Fig. 12-1. From this screen you can create pictures, sort and delete figures, prepare slide presentations, or even print your images. Once you decide to create an image a separate subsystem places you into the "Create" mode.

The top of page 185 shows a picture after it has been loaded into VCN Execuvision. This is a picture of today's office workers. These pictures are extremely detailed. You may notice a picture on the wall or a graph on one of the terminals. There is a menu bar across the bottom of the page. This lists the create menu items available in VCN Execuvision. This is typical of how this product works. "Object" contains the commands to use geometry to create or enhance pictures. Boxes, diamonds, circles, or arrows can be sized or moved to create the building blocks for images. "Tools" contains the eraser command to erase portions of the screen. You are given a square that can be sized from as small as a 1×1 pixel to as large as 9×9 pixels. As you move across the screen with it while holding down another key everything in the squares path disappears. "Tools" also lets you initialize disks to the special Execuvision format and lets you plot data in bar, line, and pie charts for inclusion in other pictures. "Sketch" is the exact opposite of "Erase". A solid line in the chosen color is left wherever the square cursor has been.

Other menu options include "Color" to recolor the screen in a variety of background and foreground colors, "Motion" to animate a portion of a screen, "Dump" to produce a screen dump, and several items to control the storage and retrieval of pictures.

Figure 12-2 shows a picture of some doctors and nurses at work. The "Cut" menu is also shown. With this function you can take a rectangle that is superimposed on the image, size it to any size, and cut or copy the image anywhere on the same screen or to another screen. You can also cut an image and save it permanently on a disk. Later, you can retrieve it and paste it into another picture. Images are not stored separately. If you put a door on top of a house and later want to remove it, the part of the house that was under the door will also be removed. The house would have to be touched up.

The ability to manipulate text is another important feature of this package. A picture from the Computer Collection is shown at the bottom of page 185. The "Text" menu is about to be used to add some text to the diagram. Several different fonts are shown in the menu. There is another menu that displays several more fonts. There are several dif-

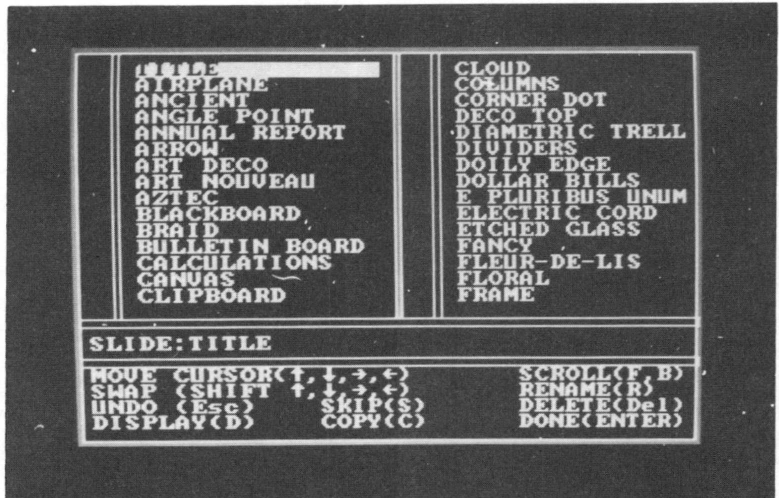

Fig. 12-3. The VCN Execuvision prepare subsystems.

ferent sizes of fonts. The smallest is a Single Dot font that is only 6×8 pixels. There are also large fonts that are 16×24 pixels. Once the font is selected, it can be placed anywhere on the screen in any color from the foreground palette.

Once you have created your slides, you may wish to rearrange them. Figure 12-3 displays the prepare subsystem. With this system, you can rearrange, delete, display, copy, and rename your pictures. Later, if you play them back in a slide show, you will see them in the proper order.

It has been said that a picture is worth a thousand words. The rest of this section will be mostly pictures, as with VCN Execuvision they are usually worth more than a thousand words. They all were taken from a standard IBM Personal Computer screen with no special equipment.

Figure 12-4 demonstrates the use of text to overlay and enhance a picture of the Wall Street Daily.

Graphs and plots can be created and integrated with a picture to make a point. In Fig. 12-5 a graph has been used to show ticket sales at a ski resort.

Slides that contain several images are the focus

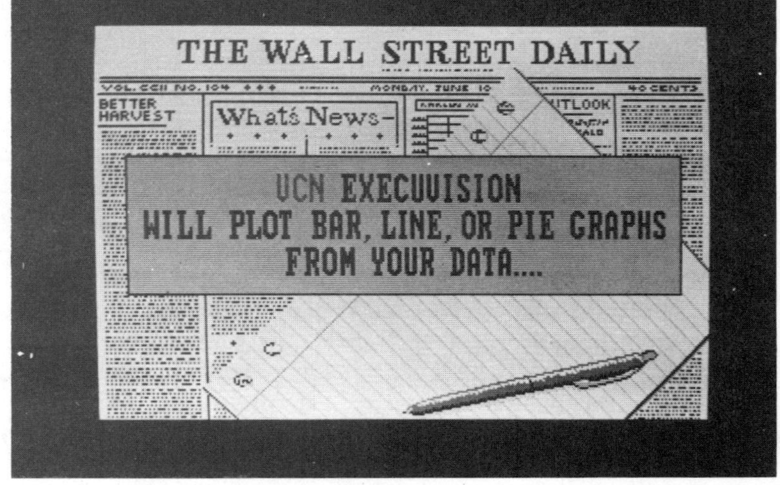

Fig. 12-4. VCN Execuvision text and pictures.

Fig. 12-5. A VCN Execuvision slide with line plot.

of the display at the top of page 186. Six separate pictures known as *pix*, can be cut and pasted from this one slide.

Combining several pixs from different slides can yield an informative slide, such as the one at the bottom of page 186. In this display, an overhead projector, a computer with a video display, a printout and some slides are combined on a grid to make a point about displays.

The display at the top of page 187 shows the combination of text, a line graph, several pictures and an appropriate background.

The VCN Execuvision picture shown in Fig. 12-6 uses both a bar and line graph to show the rising percent of businesses using computers. The detail, from the graph on the businessman's screen to the text on his printer, is amazing for a personal computer screen. Even the lamp and telephone can be cut and pasted somewhere else. The globe placed in front of the graph lends character to the picture and show the qualities of VCN execuvision.

VCN Execuvision has a screen capture utility to grab and enhance other packages' images.

VCN Execuvision allows several types of screen

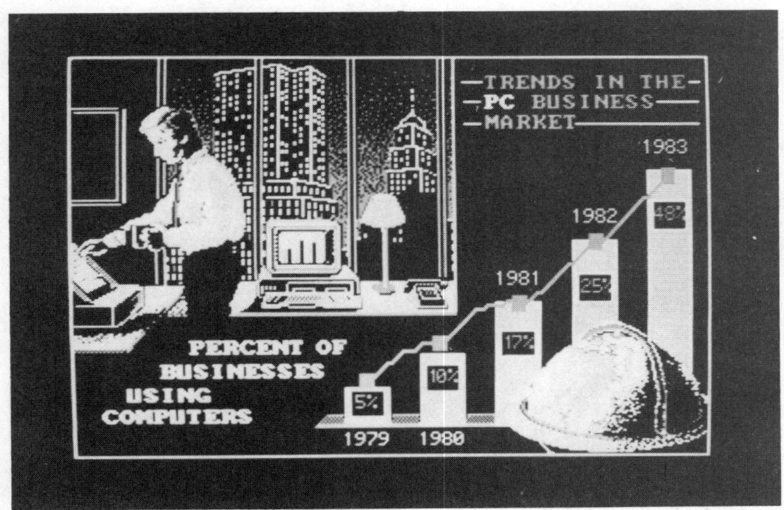

Fig. 12-6. VCN Execuvision businesses using computers chart.

Fig. 12-7. The PC Paint logo and boot screen.

dumps to black and white printers. At the present time you cannot use a color printer or plotter directly from this product. There are color screen dump utilities available from third party vendors.

This package is the premiere package for picture processing. It features a good editor and an amazing picture library. If you want to move beyond text presentations, VCN Execuvision is for you.

PC PAINT

PC Paint is one of the MacPaint look alikes for the IBM PC and its compatibles. PC Paint is among the best of its kind and allows you to create pictures quickly and easily. It requires a mouse, and as shown in Fig. 12-7, it is by Mouse Systems, the producers of a very popular mouse.

As shown in Fig. 12-8, PC Paint uses the left, top, and bottom portions of the screens to display the different commands available. The left side contains a list of the modes available. The four arrows let you move the image around to draw a picture that is larger than the screen. Pencils (like the one that appears in the center of the screen) are used for drawing freehand by moving the mouse and to

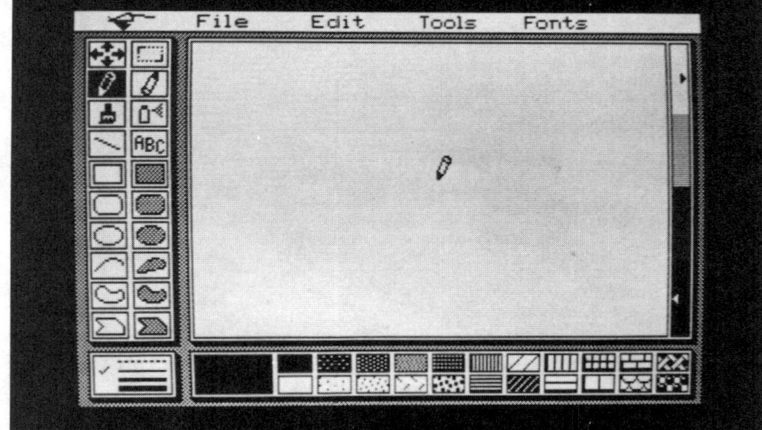

Fig. 12-8. The PC Paint main screen.

erase text. The paint brush, which features a variety of brush types, paints a solid covering. The spray paint can sprays a darker and darker covering. The rest of the left side lets you select closed figures either empty or filled with the pattern selection of your choice.

The patterns appear at the bottom of the screen. You can use the many colors to change patterns into dazzling displays. Some of the more common patterns include bricks, circles, hatching, sparse dots, balls, and even solid shades.

At the top of the screen is a menu line. As you can see in Fig. 12-14 the menus can be pulled down from the top of the screen. Once the menu is pulled down, you can move the menu bar up or down until it rests on the desired selection. The mouse button is then clicked to perform that function. The file menu is used to retrieve and store pictures. The edit menu features an undo command. This allows the last change to the screen to be deleted. This is very useful when you are working on a complicated picture and are likely to make mistakes. You press a couple of keys and the mistake is gone. Edit also contains the cut, copy, and paste functions.

The box at the top of the column immediately to the left of the picture is used to select a portion of the screen. This box can be moved around the screen and resized as large or as small as you want. After a portion of the screen is selected, you can use cut, copy, or paste to manipulate that image. The image in the box can also be rotated and flipped or can have its colors changed from the edit menu.

The tools menu, which is pulled down in the display at the bottom of page 187 has many uses. It can be used to magnify a portion of the screen. When you select a portion of the screen and use the magnify function, the portion of the screen you selected fills the screen. You can then work at the pixel level to turn pixels on or off as you desire. As you do this the image is shown in the corner so you can see the results. In this example magnify could be used to work on an individual shingle.

Using selections from the tools menu you can display the entire screen not just what appears between the borders; you can change brush styles from a square brush to a round brush, for example; you can change the foreground and background colors, and set up grids for measuring figures. The constrain command will help you to force lines to be straight and circles not to be ovals.

The fonts pull-down menu is used to change the font or size of text. Fonts include normal, bold, old english, roman, and another special font. There are three sizes of text. After the text has been placed on the screen, it can be sized and the font changed. Once you stop editing the text, it can no longer be changed. The fonts menu is shown in the display at the top of page 188. The picture in this display is called "Planets" and gives a further indication of PC Paint's ability.

The bottom picture on page 188 is that of a Lotus 1-2-3 graph that has been enhanced. After a screen image was grabbed, using a capture utility, PC Paint was used to enhance the screen. Text was added, pie segments colored, and a background added.

PC Paint can make even the least artistic of us more productive with drawing tools. With this package an artist can work wonders. If you are looking for a painting package that happens to work like MacPaint, this package is for you.

PC ILLUSTRATOR

PC Illustrator probably should be in the chapter entitled "Little Known Packages that do Wonderful Things." You have probably never heard of it, and we almost missed it in preparing this book. Put together by a small company called Computer Graphics Group, this package has the potential to be the best selling picture processor. When it came to us as an undocumented beta test copy, we almost didn't boot it up. After we did however, we were astonished at what we saw. We learned that Computer Graphics Group is small, but they must work hard. When we called late one Friday evening the President answered the phone.

PC Illustrator is a new package that is just now appearing on the market. It uses a very innovative approach to picture processing that allows the user to create text and picture presentations. The main screen sets the tone for the entire package. The icons that you see on the main screen make it amazingly easy to create your pictures and graphs. Figure 12-9 shows these icons.

The icons are unique by themselves. A sinking ship for help, a road sign for an exit, an artist's palette to change color, and a truck to indicate move are just some of the ingenious icons used.

PC Illustrator doesn't leave off here though. You can use lines, curves, arcs, free hand drawing, circles, closed figures, and even symbols. Figures can be cut, copied, moved, and pasted with ease. Patterns can be changed, brush shapes changed, even lines resized. The most amazing thing is that this is just the beginning.

PC Illustrator also has one of the best business graphics systems in any picture processor we have seen. Its graphics are better than a number of standalone graphics packages we reviewed. It includes three dimensional graphics and many mixed charts. It also features a slide show capability that includes instant appearance, slow fade in and dissolve, and an actual curtain being raised to display the image.

Not only is it easy and fun to use, but it is ergonomically sound. It can be run from a variety of devices including the keyboard. When you run it from the keyboard, you use the cursor keys to move around the screen. Instead of using the Enter key to enter selections, you use the 5 key in the center of the cursor keys. This saves a tremendous amount of hand movement. Although you can use a mouse, a light pen, or a digitizer, you may find that it is easier to use the keyboard.

The device selection menu shown in Fig. 12-10 shows some of the more interesting features of PC Illustrator. As mentioned above it can use a keyboard for an input device. That is rare by itself for a picture processor. For example arcs and curves are drawn by specifying a group of points. Line smoothing techniques are used to draw the arc. The more points you place on the page the smoother the line. PC Illustrator also lets you select a mouse, a joystick, a light pen, a digitizer, and even a touch screen simply by selecting the appropriate icon. Device drivers let you switch from one to the other.

PC Illustrator's text handling capabilities are also second to none. The display at the top of page 189 shows some of the text possibilities. There are eight different fonts. These include an excellent script, legible gothic, several roman fonts both serif and sans serif, a little font similar to Lotus 1-2-3, and even a helvetica font for large bold letters (my favorite font).

Any font can be used at any of six slants so a font isn't "wasted" in order to provide just one type of italic font. The text path can be across, down, sideways, and diagonal. These options are invaluable when you are creating graphs and then annotating them. Once you add the text to your picture, you can move it around and change it to any

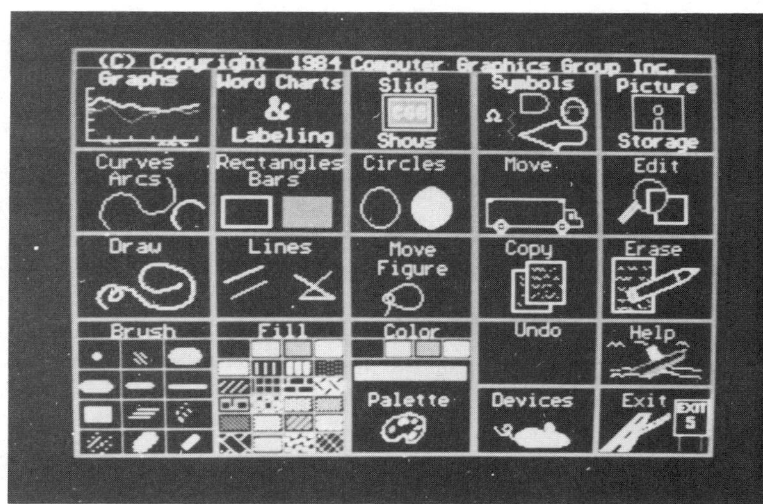

Fig. 12-9. The PC Illustrator logo and boot screen.

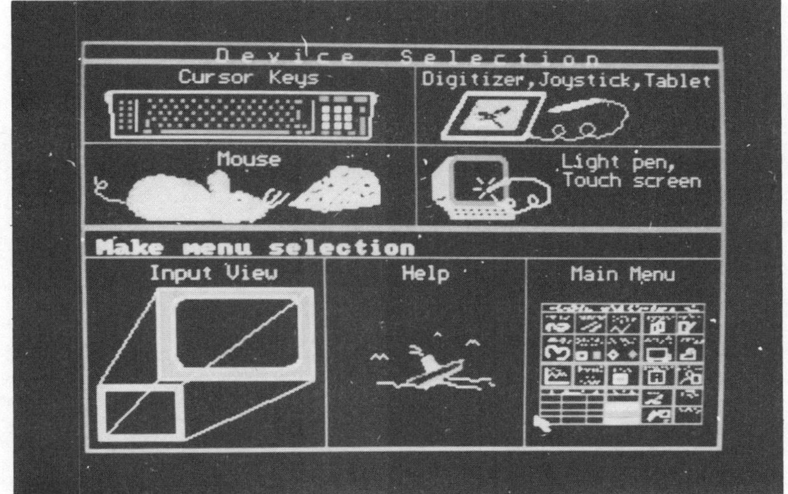

Fig. 12-10. The PC Illustrator device selection menu.

of *ten* sizes and four colors. Text handling capabilities like these have yet to be seen in any other package. The sizing is the best part; with over ten sizes of type available, PC Illustrator is an editor's dream.

The graphics subsystem is also spectacular. You can create, display, edit, delete, and even zoom in on a graph (or any other picture) and work at the pixel level. Figure 12-11 shows the graphic subsystem icons.

As shown in Fig. 12-12, you can create more than 14 chart types, including line, clustered bar, stacked bar, area, pie, mixed, and even three dimensional variations. You can specify hatching patterns, type of grids, and even colors. Once you have filled in this menu, a spreadsheet-like menu is displayed. Labels are entered along the top row, legends along the first column and the data in the middle. Graph types can be readily changed and redisplayed.

Another interesting menu is the picture storage menu as shown in Fig. 12-13. File cabinets are used to store and retrieve files (the draw is open for retrieve). A printer icon is used to print, a glue pot to cut and paste, and a set of disk drives to change

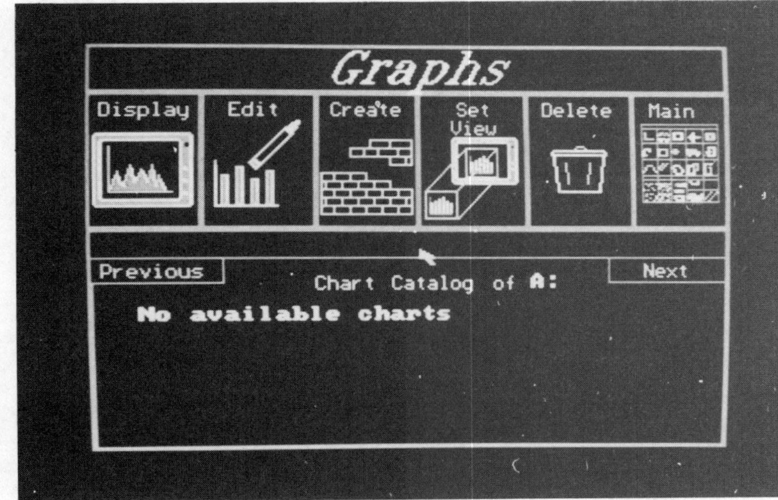

Fig. 12-11. The PC Illustrator graphs subsystem menu.

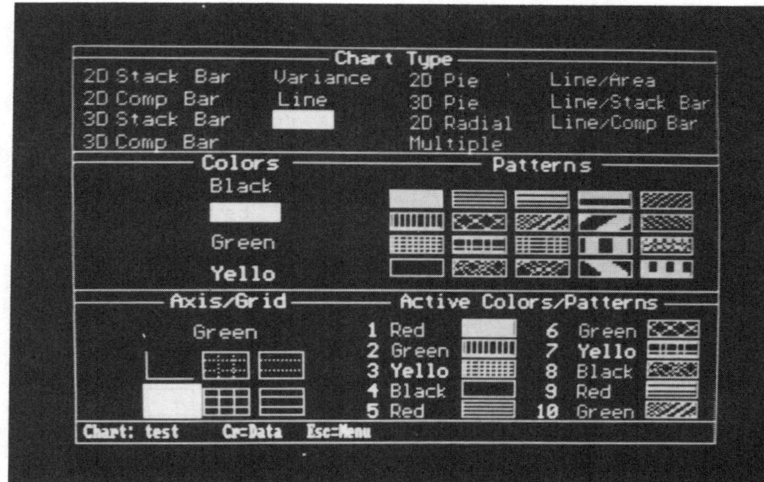

Fig. 12-12. The PC Illustrator graphs selection menu.

the active drive. A wastebasket helps you delete things, and the ever present Titanic is there for your help.

After seeing the icon screens, you are probably wondering what type of pictures PC Illustrator can produce. The displays on pages 189 and 190 suggest its capabilities. Its business graphics are even better, and can be customized through the drawing tools. Objects can be cut and pasted, and a thoroughly delightful slide show can be created. If you are in the market for a picture processor, PC Illustrator deserves a very close look.

4-POINT GRAPHICS

4-Point Graphics is another picture processor known for its use of animation and interesting colorations. It uses a concept called *point mode.* One point mode is used for sketching lines, using dots, text, squares, and other geometric figures. One cursor appears on the screen and can be moved around. In two point mode, there are two cursors. One remains stationary, while the other moves. This mode is used for making rays and vectors. Three point mode is used for parabolas, ellipses, curves, and circles. Four point mode is used to select a portion

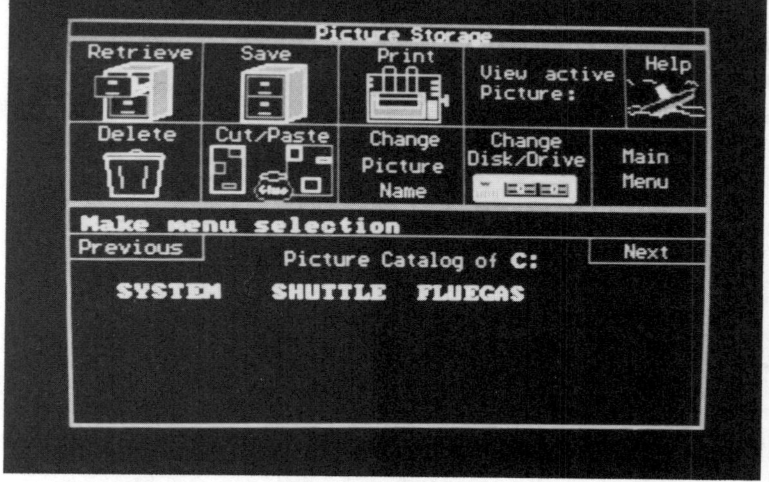

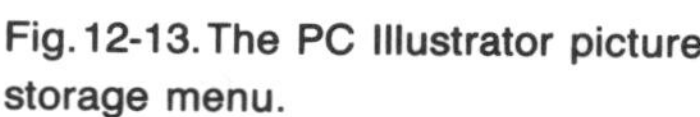
Fig. 12-13. The PC Illustrator picture storage menu.

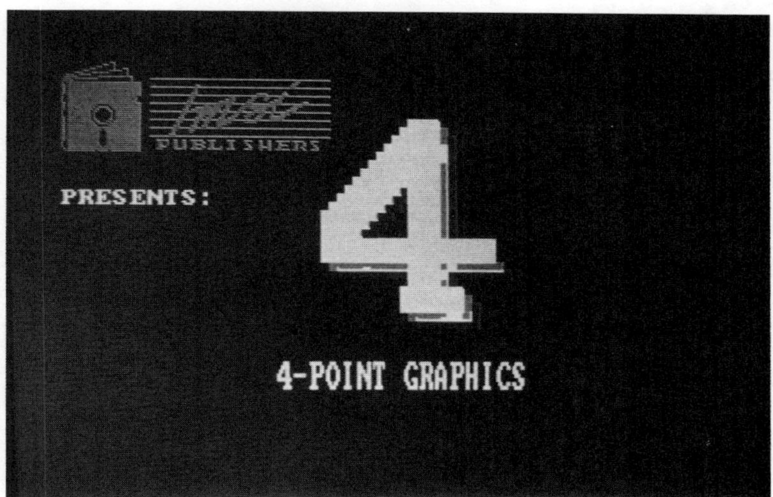

Fig. 12-14. The 4-point graphics boot screen.

of the screen to rotate, invert, enlarge, or copy on the screen.

The boot screen of 4-Point graphics, shown in Fig. 12-14, shows the type of drawing you can do. 4-Point Graphics has some special characteristics that set it apart from some of the other picture processors in this section. It has some of the best slide show and animation capabilities of any package.

Figure 12-15 demonstrates the use of 4-Point to produce a pictograph. The center bars have been replaced by cars, houses, and boats. This is one example of 4-Point's power.

4-Point also allows complex pictures to be produced in several colors. The picture of the golden gate bridge on page 190 shows the detail possible with 4-Point Graphics. The different colors in the picture can be displayed separately if you desire.

The display shown at the top of page 191 shows a map drawn onto a grid. Labels and two three-dimensional lines have been added to produce a professional looking graph that instantly grabs your attention.

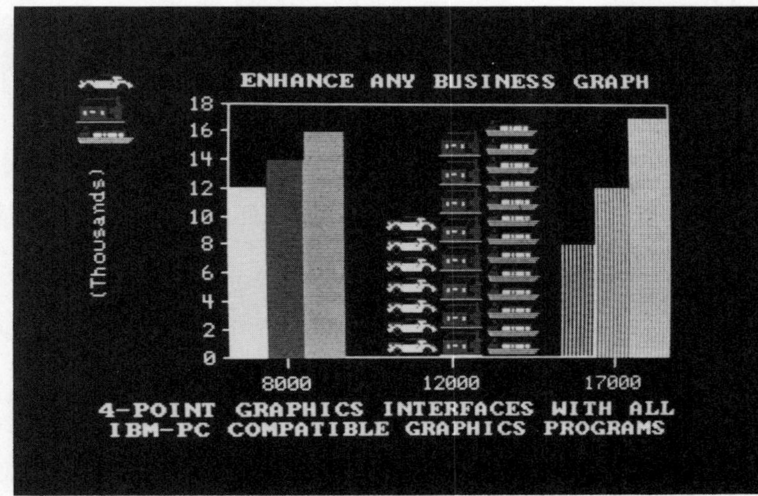

Fig. 12-15. The 4-point graphics pictograph.

These pictures represent a small part of 4-Points power. It features a complete set of routines that can be used to perform standard picture processing tasks and also lets you capture images from other programs. If you are looking for a good picture processor, 4-Point may be for you.

Chapter 13

Highly Specialized Graphics Packages

ENERGRAPHICS
STATMAP

A highly specialized graphics package is one that would not be used by the general population. These would include such things as CAD (Computer Aided Design) packages for electronics diagrams, blueprints, and engineering sketches; modeling packages that feature graphics for output; or any other package that is hard to classify or does something very specific and extra special.

The software described in this chapter include an engineering drawing package and a statistical mapping package.

The following information is presented for each software package discussed in this chapter.

1. An introduction to the basic philosophies of the package and a discussion of what it is intended to do and who its intended audience is.
2. A presentation of the best or most unusual features that set this product apart from all others.
3. Discussions of the *boot* or first screen, the documentation, the expected learning time, and the tutorials that may be available.
4. A discussion of how the program does the special things it does, and what special things make this package a worthwhile package.
5. A discussion of the output quality on the screen, dot matrix printer, Polaroid Palette, and plotter.
6. An evaluation of the overall performance, speed, and error handling, and general comments about the ease of use of the package compared to the results achieved.

When your specialized needs require a specialized package, choose it as you would any other graphics package. Make sure that the package can produce the result you want without excessive effort on your part.

ENERGRAPHICS

Energraphics can be best described as an all around business graphics tool with an added specialty. It is composed of several packages. It can handle some of the best three dimensional business graphics you'll ever see. It also does "normal" busi-

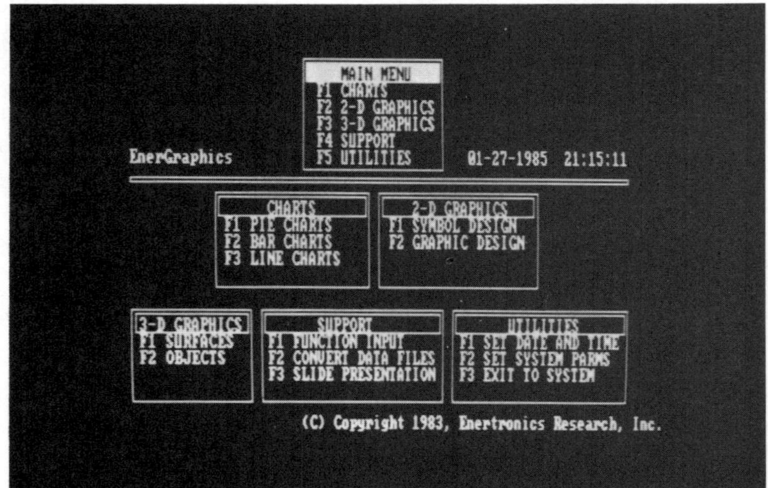

Fig. 13-1. The Energraphics main menu.

ness graphics very well. Its best feature, however, is its ability to produce two and three dimensional engineering drawings. CAD/CAM applications are easily handled with Energraphics. Engineering drawings can be rotated and viewed from different perspectives. There is a symbol generator, and you can work at the pixel level. You can create architectural drawings, house plans, blueprints, mechanical designs, electrical circuit designs, statistical surface drawings, and even slides.

Energraphics is classified as a specialized package because the engineer would find this package most useful. It also does business graphics, but its features are probably more valuable to an engineer or architect.

Energraphics comes in a full size three ring binder. Excellent diagrams instruct the new user in the particulars of the package.

Figure 13-1 shows the Energraphics main menu. There are several options on the main menu found in the top box. The submenus are located below this box. Selections are controlled through the function keys. Energraphics can do simple bar, line, and pie charts. The 2-Graphics menu is used

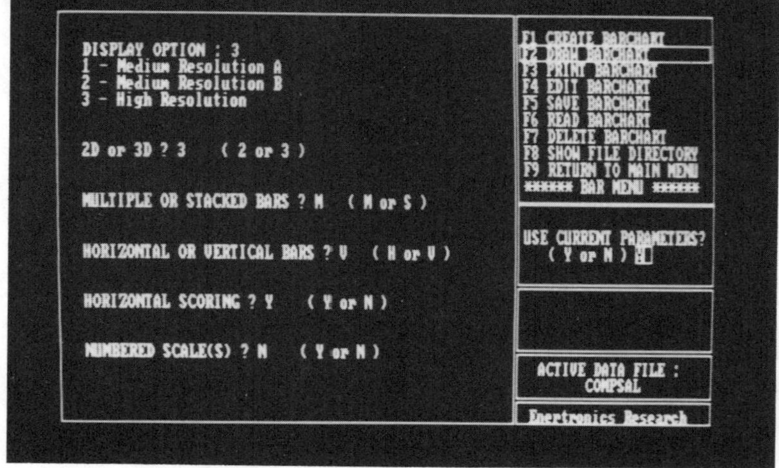

Fig. 13-2. The Energraphics bar chart menu.

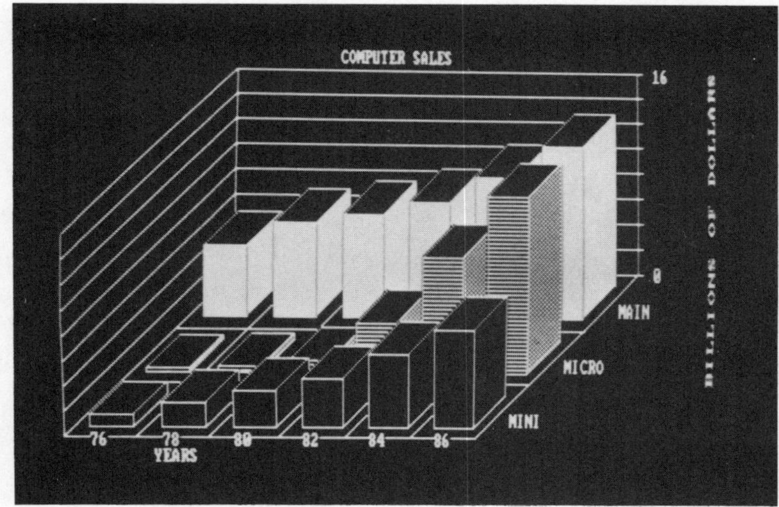

Fig. 13-3. An Energraphics 3-D bar graph.

to select and build two dimensional drawings. The best part of this package is its three-dimensional capabilities.

Figure 13-2 shows a typical edit menu. This menu is for a three dimensional bar chart. After you enter the data, you can enter the display characteristics.

The resulting bar chart appears in Fig. 13-3. Energraphics produces a high quality output on the screen as well as on a printer or plotter. The three dimensional bar chart includes grid lines to make the perspective more pronounced. Energraphics allows you to customize graphics and drawings.

Energraphics can also plot the results of calculations. Three dimensional line charts are also possible. The graph shown at the bottom of page 191, is derived from data taken from a sine and cosine formula. The formula shown results in a "net" chart and can be displayed on the screen or be printed.

Energraphics does its engineering drawings with ease. Figure 13-4 is an engineering drawing of a bolt. It is shown from two different angles. It can be rotated, sized, colored, or manipulated in any other way that might be needed. You can even zoom

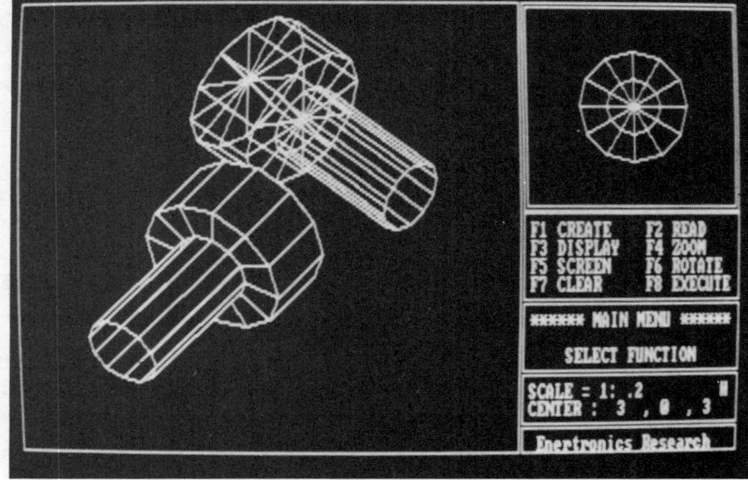

Fig. 13-4. An Energraphics engineering drawing.

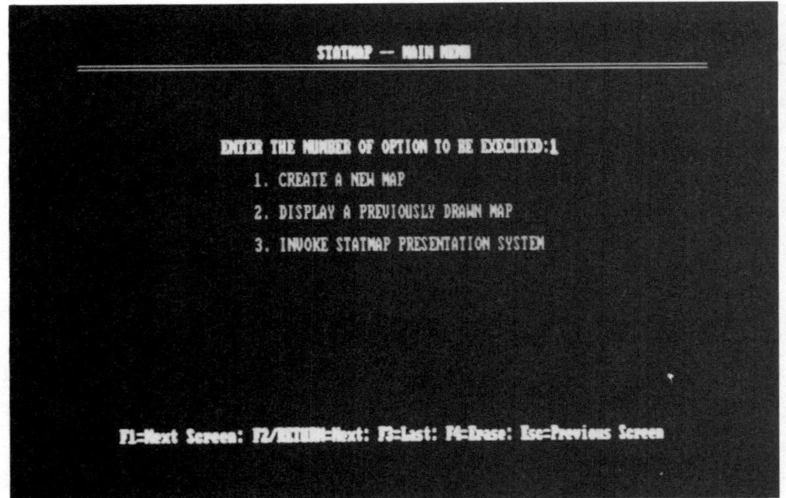

Fig. 13-5. The Statmap main menu.

in on a small part of it and work at the pixel level. The function keys control all the actions.

The pictures shown here were all completed with Energraphics. This highly specialized package can help you perform these types of tasks with great ease. If you are looking for engineering drawing capability at a reasonable price, Energraphics is for you.

STATMAP

Statmap by the Ganesa Group is one of the best mapping packages for microcomputers that you will find. It is used primarily for statistical, marketing, and demographic mapping. It features libraries of the United States by many demographic regions including state, county, zip-code, congresssional district, SMSA census tracts, and even Arbitron ADI's. Map coordinate files are stored by latitudinal and longitudinal coordinates. Foreign countries are also available.

It takes two files to produce a statistical map; one must contain the information for plotting the map itself, and the other must contain the data that is to be plotted. The data that makes up the map of Connecticut might have a state code and several hundred points that would plot the outline of the

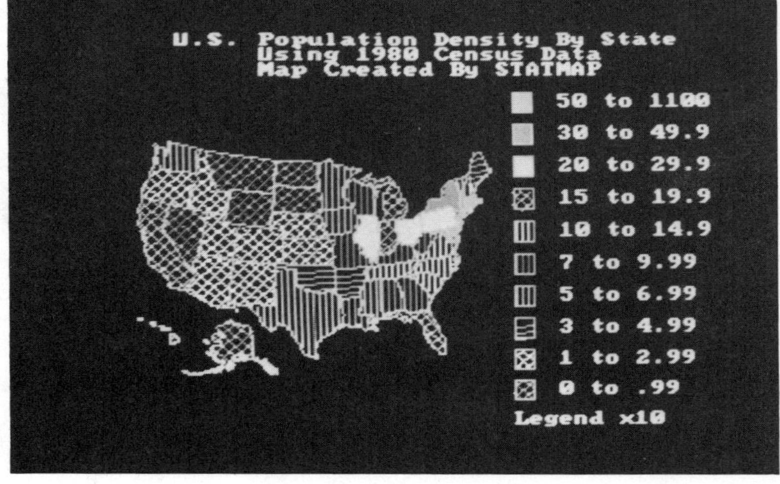

Fig. 13-6. The Statmap United States map.

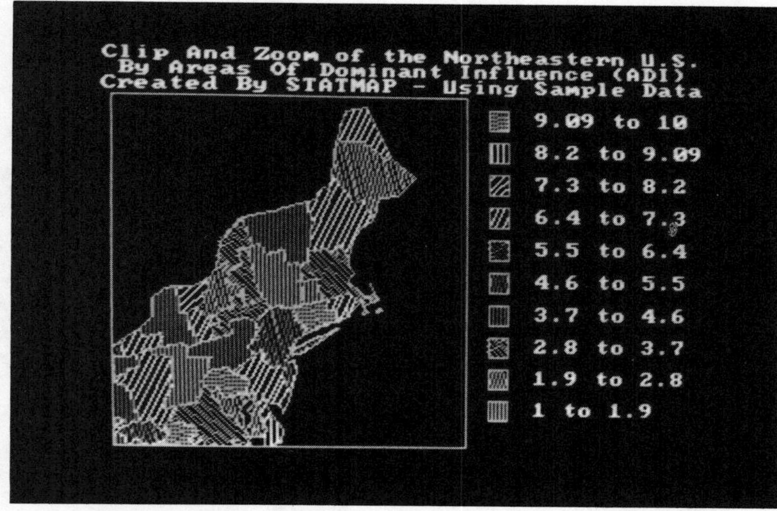

Fig. 13-7. The Statmap clip and zoom feature.

state. This would be the coordinate data. The data to be plotted might simply consist of the state code and a value such as the number of speeding tickets handed out in 1984.

Statmap comes in an IBM style slipcover. Its manual is well documented and contains many figures. Providing you have an understanding of mapping, you can learn to use this package in a few hours.

Figure 13-5 shows the Statmap main menu. The options include creating a new map, displaying an old map, or running the slide show.

Creating a map requires several steps. Fullscreen menus help you choose the data type and the coordinates. The display at the top of page 192, shows the beginning of the map creation process.

The first things to do are to choose the geographic location and select the coordinate system. You would then see another menu that would let you put in the codes and the values.

Once the data has been entered, the map can be drawn. Both on screen and on a plotter the resolution is excellent and the results satisfying. Figure 13-6 shows a sample map of the United States. Shading patterns and legends can be controlled in Statmap.

Another feature of Statmap is the ability to zoom in on a part of a map. Figure 13-7 shows the map of the Northeastern United States only. This feature can be especially useful in showing problem areas or in displaying more detail about an area.

Mapping is important for companies who have nationwide or even statewide interests. If you need a mapping package, Statmap is for you. Its easy-to-use interfaces and crisp output quality make this an excellent specialized package.

Chapter 14

Little Known Packages That Do Wonderful Things

PC GRAPHICS The Grafix Partner
GraphMaker Diagraph

The packages in the previous chapters are well known and best sellers, but they are not the only packages that exist today. The packages in this section have been overlooked, have had little or no venture capital and therefore no multi-million dollar advertising campaign, or are very new and have yet to receive well-deserved publicity.

Almost all of these packages are picture processors in some way. Most are very inexpensive and all have something to offer. These will be looked at in a more overall sense. The best parts of the package will be presented, along with a survey of the capabilities and workings of each program.

These packages include several picture processors, each of which has some interesting qualities; a package that can be used to make graphics easier when you are using Lotus 1-2-3; and a graphic enhancer that captures that captures Lotus 1-2-3 images and then enhances them.

PC GRAPHICS (PCPG)

PCPG also known as Personal Computer Picture Graphics is the brainchild of Eugene Ying. This gentlemen is credited with helping IBM see fit to develop gads of little known packages that do wonderful things. For years employees of IBM were not allowed to sell any products they created, even if they did it on their own time with their own resources. Mr. Ying's package had been distributed under the "freeware" concept, when PC World happened to review it, and the fun began.

Deluged by thousands of requests for his package Mr. Ying soon found himself in the software business (and he was giving it away). This has prompted IBM to rethink their policy, and now IBM sells employee developed software for very tiny sums of money. PCPG is just one of the offerings reviewed in this section. This amazing package is sold at the incredible price of just $29.95. The complete guide to IBM Employee developed software can be obtained by calling 1-800-IBM-PCSW.

PCPG is an unpretentious package that does several amazing things. First it is a picture processor that allows you to create images and text on a screen

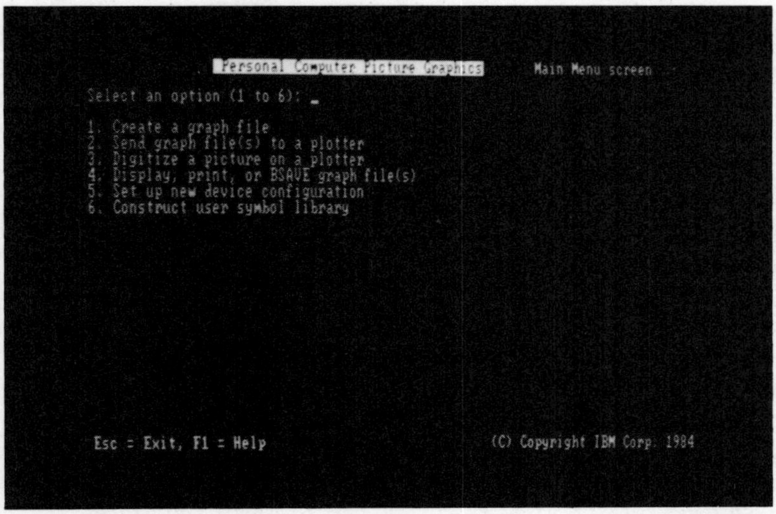

Fig. 14-1. The PCPG main screen.

sized background. Second, it comes with a library of images that rival those in picture processors selling for hundreds of dollars. Now for the really amazing feat: the images are stored separately. This means that you can later move one image around or delete it, even if it lies completely across another image or group of images. Apple's Lisa Draw is the only other package that can do that, to my knowledge. Any image, (and there are hundreds) can also be rotated, colored, and resized in just one keystroke. This is the all-time little-known package that does wonderful things.

PCPG offers several different options from its main menu. These include creating, printing, and saving graphics files. PCPG also allows you to digitize a picture by using a plotter as an *input* device. This option lets you place a picture on the plotter and trace it with the pens; as you trace the picture, it is automatically drawn on your screen. With this you can do simple engineering drawings or CAD/CAM applications.

PCPG also lets you maintain the symbols you create in its own library. Figure 14-1 shows the PCPG main menu.

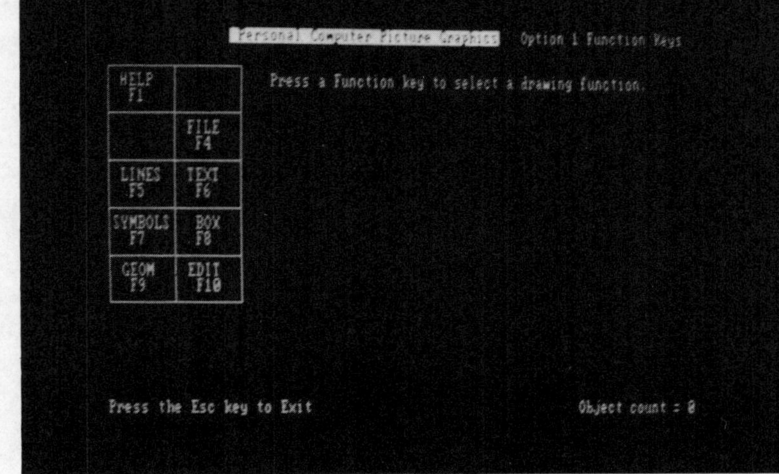

Fig. 14-2. The PCPG create screen.

What then is so wonderful about PCPG? The ability to digitize is nice for those of you who have plotters, but the power of this package lies in the creation of pictures. Figure 14-2 shows the create menu. Everything is function key driven in this menu. Extensive help facilities are available. What you see here however is the tip of the iceberg. PCPG has the most extensive geometric figure library of any package reviewed. Boxes, circles, arc, ellipses, lines, and other closed figures are just some of the preprogrammed geometric figures available.

PCPG also features many different text fonts, each of which can be moved around and scaled to many different sizes. Each object is separate and can be moved at any time without disturbing adjacent or intersecting figures. Each figure can be painted or colored in a variety of palettes.

The true worth of PCPG has yet to be discovered. Its value lies in a truly unique set of symbol libraries, as shown in Fig. 14-3. These include animals, business pictures including computers, flowcharting symbols, zodiac, music and mathematical figures, icons, signs, equipment, vehicles, and miscellaneous pictures. You can also define and store your own pictures in another library.

Figure 14-4 shows a sample symbol library. All together there are several hundred symbols that can be placed on your screen, shrunk or enlarged, moved, rotated, and colored. The final effect is to present a screen that is unique in appearance and can be used by anyone with relative ease.

Figure 14-5 gives an example of the output of this package. PCPG at $29.95 is an outstanding value. Its ability to place objects on top of another as well as its excellent symbol library make this little known package do some wonderful things.

GRAPHMAKER

Here is one of the more unusual packages on the market today. Actually, it isn't a software package at all. Rather, it is a template that works with Lotus 1-2-3 to make producing graphs easier. Graphs can be produced in just one or two keystrokes instead of with the multitude of keystrokes that Lotus 1-2-3 forces you to use.

GraphMaker is produced by a company known as OptionWare (formerly called DDS Development) in Bloomfield, CT. This little known company will soon be well known, as they are quickly capturing the bulk of the template market. A template is a guide or model produced by using a spreadsheet program. It is actually a working model that only needs to have its data filled in. this company takes a new approach to creativity in developing and presenting its wares.

Using nonstandard features of Lotus macros, it fools Lotus into producing some dazzling effects on

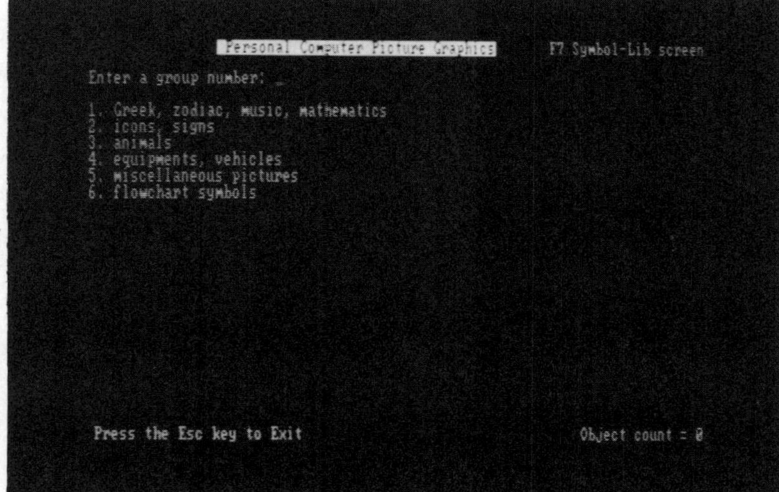

Fig. 14-3. The PCPG symbol libraries.

```
Personal Computer Picture Graphics        F7 Symbols screen

Enter a symbol number: _

 1. hammer        2. screw driv   3. wrench       4. saw          5. clamp
 6. scissors      7. caliper      8. brush        9. hinges      10. lock
11. safe         12. comb        13. racquet     14. palette     15. umbrella
16. plunger      17. scale       18. pencil      19. pen         20. book
21. clip         22. candle      23. shaker      24. nursing bo  25. glass
26. jar          27. fork        28. knife       29. spoon       30. stove
31. refrigerat   32. lens        33. film        34. loudspeakr  35. TV
36. thermomete   37. T square    38. key         39. module      40. lady shoe
41. man shoe     42. boot        43. eyeglass    44. bell        45. mailbox
46. piano        47. bulb        48. pistol      49. rifle       50. bullet
51. bomb         52. parachute   53. car         54. van         55. yacht
56. row boat     57. chopper     58. Boeing 747  59. earth stn   60. satellite
61. rocket       62. submarine   63. calculator  64. CRT         65. modem
66. diskette     67. IBM 370     68. IBM Sys 38  69. IBM 6670    70. IBM PC
71. IBM 3290     72. Displaywrt

Press the Esc key to Exit                        Object count = 12
```

Fig. 14-4. A sample symbol library.

the screen. It uses a common interface to move between its own self-created menus. Through the use of tokens (graphic characters used in writing a Lotus macro to speed up processing), it produces a very fast menu-driven system to create templates.

As you will see, GraphMaker does some wonderful things. OptionWare is not about to stop here though. Over 60 templates are already available in a wide variety of categories including financial statistics, sales and marketing, organization and budget, personnel, sales tools, asset management, cash management, personal organization, private and financial organization, and tax planning.

Some of the more interesting titles include Employee Time Analysis, Customer Mailing List, Credit Card Report, Monthly Calendar, Phone Messages, and Personal Income Tax. Each package uses the same interface making the learning time of the first package (about 30 minutes) the only learning time you will ever spend.

GraphMaker comes in an attractive bubble pack that opens to reveal two pockets. One pocket contains the disk while the other contains the operating

Fig. 14-5. A sample PCPG picture.

instructions. The instructions are produced so they can easily be inserted into an IBM type binder. A colored tab page will let you separate future OptionWare applications that you purchase. On-line help is available as well as an on-line tutorial and demonstration.

Each OptionWare template contains two files. An "AUTO123" file for loading the controlling module, and the application itself. The GraphMaker file is called "GRAPHAK". The "AUTO123" file loads itself automatically when you start LOTUS and the familiar (after you've bought several of these templates) boot screen appears.

This screen lets you choose a short computer-based introduction to OptionWare. Learn about GraphMaker, begin the application, or view a demonstration. After you make a choice, you are taken to a selection menu. Hard disk users will like the option of placing up to fourteen different OptionWare applications on this menu. It features a simple interface to add and delete OptionWare applications. Once the application to be run is selected (floppy disk users will see Graphmaker only), the main program screen is displayed, as shown in Fig. 14-6.

This screen is displayed for only a few seconds before the actual application menu screen is displayed. Figure 14-7 shows the GraphMaker main menu. Each menu in the entire OptionWare line is essentially the same. There are four sections: data entry, review, print and save, and special. The data entry section is used for entering your data and receiving help about Lotus graphs. Review lets you preview your entered data and produce the desired graphs in black and white or color. Print and save lets you save your data to the original file or to create a new file to save multiple versions. After the data has been saved,it can be printed using the Lotus 1-2-3 PrintGraph function. The special section is for clearing the worksheet of data, setting new parameters, and accessing the help screens.

Before you begin to enter data you can choose the number of data series and points on the desired graph. Figure 14-8 shows the graph data selection menu. You can select the number of periods in which to enter data for as many as three data series. These options include from three to twelve periods. These periods are preset to represent months, quarters, or years, but they can be easily changed.

Once you make your selection, OptionWare automatically takes you to a data entry screen, as shown in Fig. 14-9. Even though this system is written in the Lotus 1-2-3 macro language, it maintains control and guides you through the data entry. First it lets you enter the main title and the x- and y-axis titles for the graph. Next, it lets you enter your data series labels for the legend. Finally, OptionWare

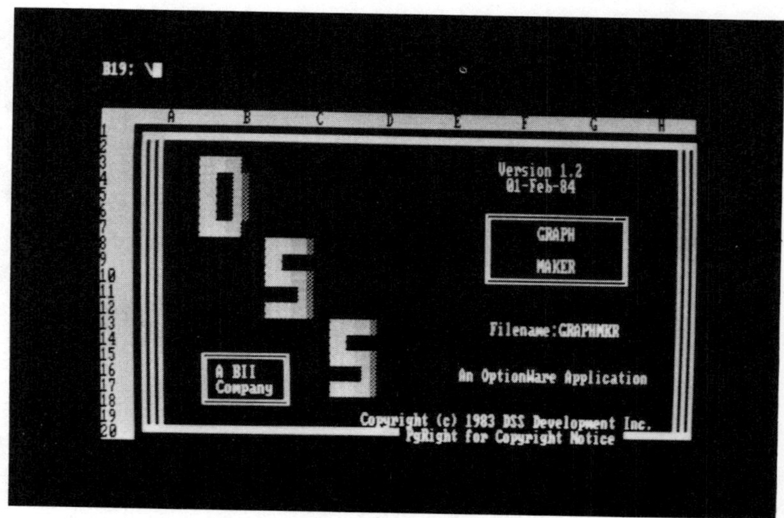

Fig. 14-6. The OptionWare Graphmaker title screen.

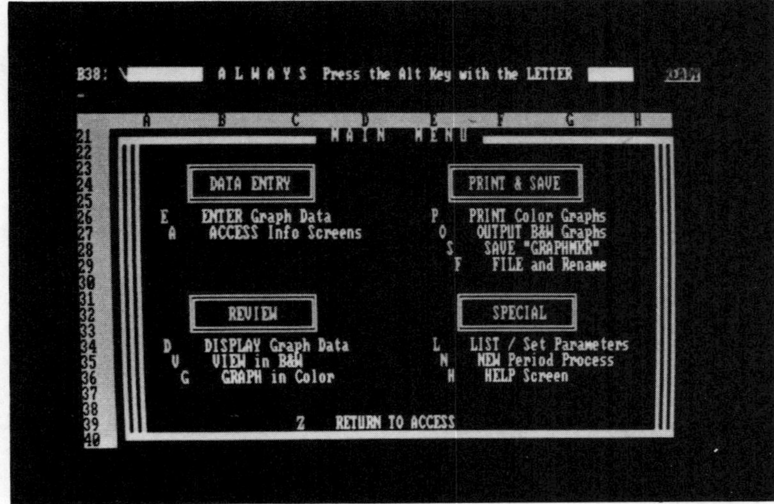

Fig. 14-7. The OptionWare Graphmaker main menu.

places you into the bottom portion of the screen where you can enter data for any of the three series, which in this example have been named Sales, Expenses, and Gross Profits. The period labels, January, February, and March, can be changed to anything you desire. When you are through entering data, you can return to the main GraphMaker menu in just two keystrokes. Whether you choose three periods or twelve, the menus are the same. Three periods at a time are shown in the box and you can scroll to see the rest. OptionWare controls the environment to keep you from getting lost among the cells.

After entering your data you might want to see your data displayed graphically. If you were using Lotus alone, it would involve over 30 keystrokes to set your titles, labels, x- and y-axis variables, graph type and other options. With GraphMaker, you can accomplish the same feat in just 2 keystrokes. Pressing <Alt> <V> starts the black and white graphing process. You see a menu that lets you choose which data you want to see. It looks very similar to the data entry menu, except that it also controls the graph type. The normal default is a bar chart, but you can see any of the Lotus graph types. Figure 14-10 shows this menu. After viewing a

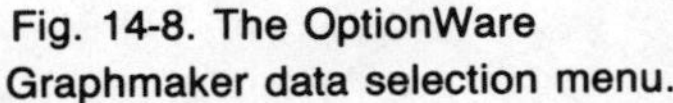
Fig. 14-8. The OptionWare Graphmaker data selection menu.

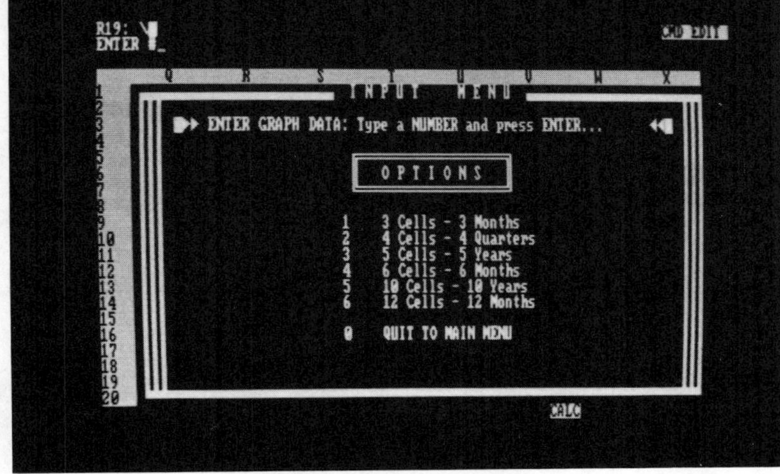

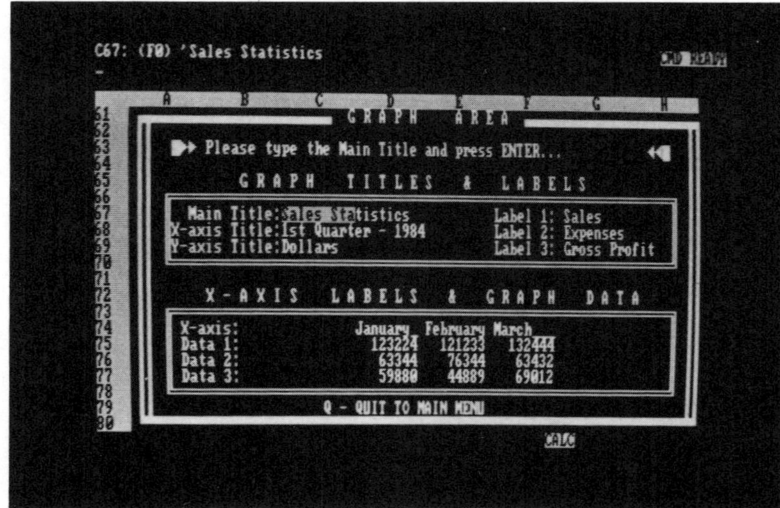

Fig. 14-9. The OptionWare Graphmaker data entry screen.

graph, you are returned to this menu where one keystroke will let you change either the graph type or the data you want to view. Only two keystrokes will change both the data and the graph type and redisplay the graph.

One more keystroke starts the graphing process and viola! You see a perfect Lotus 1-2-3 graph. The graph is shown in Fig. 14-11.

When this package was first presented to us our first reaction was "Oh boy, another macro!" But after viewing the ease of use and consistency throughout this product, we were truly impressed. If this wasn't enough, we decided to try the printing routine. Figure 14-12 shows the printing screen. OptionWare does almost all the work of printing graphics for you. This can be one of the most time consuming chores when using Lotus. OptionWare lets you do it with only a few keystrokes by automatically saving the graph and instructing even the most novice of us how to use the Lotus graphics print program.

OptionWare's performance lives up to its name. It provides you with the opportunity to choose from a variety of well thought out options. If you are a

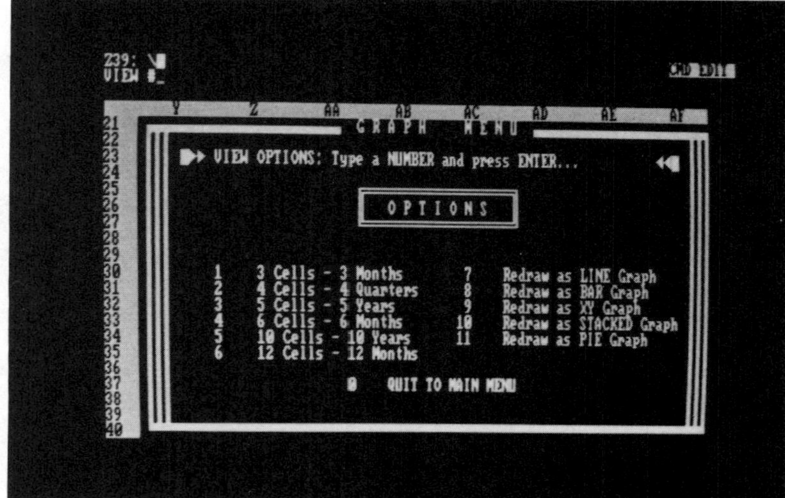

Fig. 14-10. The OptionWare Graphmaker view graph menu.

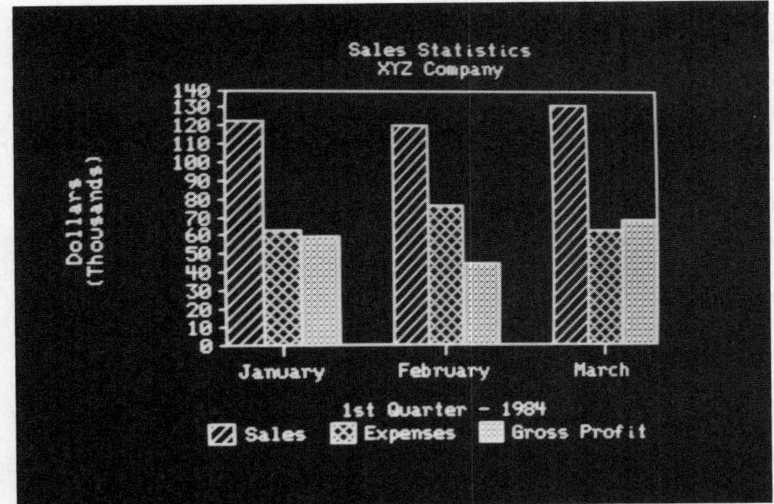

Fig. 14-11. A Lotus 1-2-3 Graph created by OptionWare's GraphMaker.

Lotus expert, you can even customize these templates. We tried to modify GraphMaker and had no problems doing it. The menu screens are stored as perfect screen sizes and not placed haphazardly around the disk. Each is contiguous to the other and can easily be viewed outside of OptionWare. If you are a novice looking for some preprogrammed applications or a Lotus expert looking to dig into the macros, OptionWare is a little known package that can do wonderful things for you.

GRAFIX PARTNER

The Grafix Partner is another little known package that does some wonderful things. Essentially it is a picture processor or a graphic enhancer. It features the standard picture processing functions of multiple text fonts and placements, and geometric figures including boxes, circles, curves, lines, and points. The width of the lines can also be controlled. It also features painting commands and color commands. Moving, copying, cutting and pasting of any part of the screen is easy to accomplish. An erase command lets you erase unwanted portions of the screen.

A Help menu, as it is called, controls all the options. Actually it is a selection menu that is easy

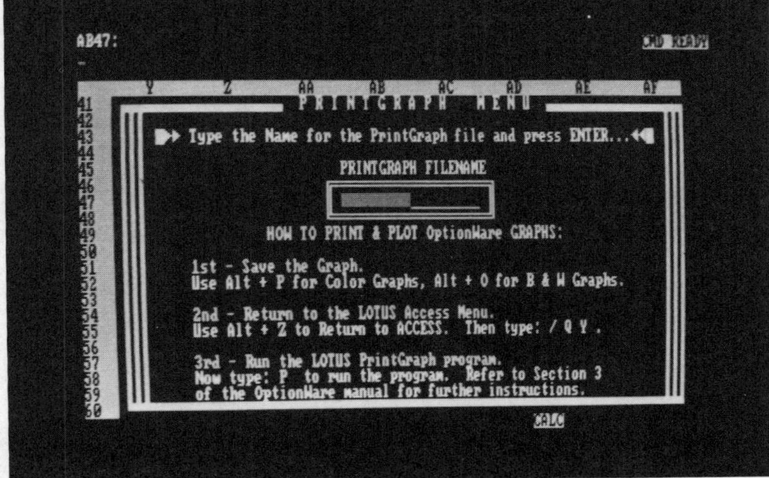

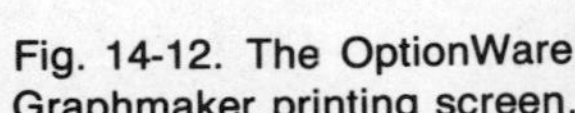

Fig. 14-12. The OptionWare Graphmaker printing screen.

to use. You alternate between this menu and the picture being created.

What then is so wonderful about this package? First, it runs in the background. This package can be placed in the background of your machine and brought up at any time. This by itself is not wonderful, but when you look at why it can do this, you begin to understand the wonder of this little known package.

Lotus 1-2-3 is the most widely used spreadsheet package. Unfortunately it also has some of the worst screen graphics and some of the most difficult to use graphics printing routines. The Grafix Partner can change all of that. By running the Grafix Partner in the background with Lotus 1-2-3 or any other package, you can make instant changes to any graphic.

Imagine the possibilities. You create a Lotus graph. You want to add some pictures to it, put the legend in a box and add some text. You certainly can't do this with Lotus. But, you can with the Grafix Partner. With other packages you could capture the graph, and after leaving Lotus 1-2-3, you could bring up the other program and make changes to your Lotus graph. By then however, you might forget what you wanted to do. With Grafix Partner, you can edit the Lotus graph instantly without ever leaving Lotus.

This allows you to edit the graph while the purpose of the graph is fresh in your mind. When you are creating graphs, the last thing you want to do is to wait many minutes or hours before annotating your graph. By making the most necessary changes right there, you can enhance your thinking process and your graphs.

Grafix Partner contains several fonts including a three dimensional font for very sharp lettering and more importantly a "thin" font that is exactly the same as the font Lotus 1-2-3 uses for text.

After changing the graph to your satisfaction, you can instantly print out the graph without changing disks. When you are in a hurry, this is a great convenience. You can also save the annotated graph for later changes by the Grafix Partner.

Figure 14-14 shows an original graph. After less than two minutes of changes, the graph in Fig. 14-15 appears. It can now be printed out or saved for later changes.

Some of the other features of Grafix Partner include an excellent zoom function that lets you zero in on individual pixels for very fine tuning. An Undo function is provided for correcting errors.

The Grafix Partner comes with a small picture library that can be cut and pasted into other screens as necessary. It allows the capturing of other screens that can also be used to cut and paste as images into other programs. This library is shown at the bottom of page 192.

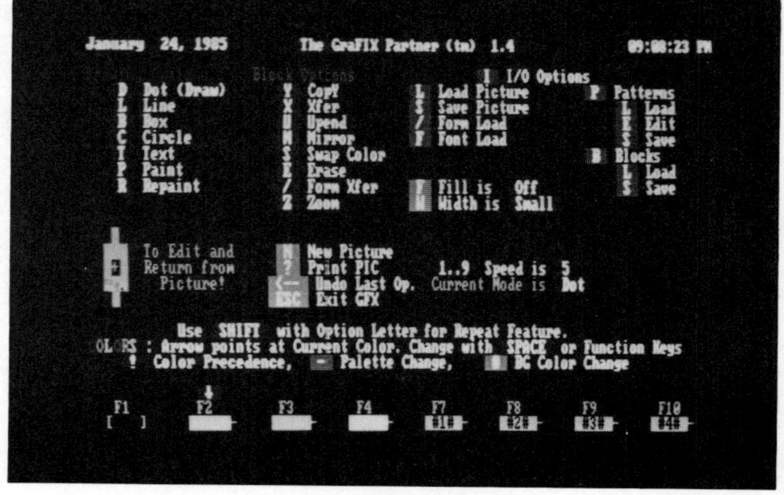

Fig. 14-13. The Grafix Partner help menu screen.

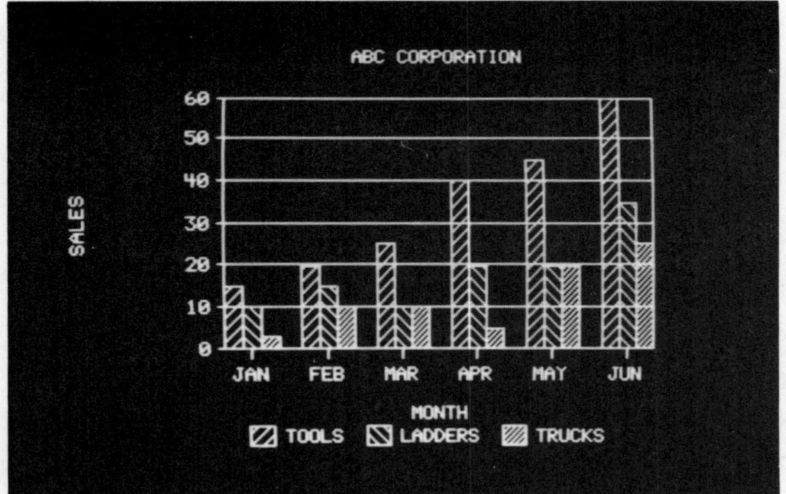

Fig. 14-14. A Lotus 1-2-3 screen.

The Grafix Partner comes with several auxiliary programs. You can edit fonts to change any letter of the font or even create new font libraries. Fonts can be made larger or smaller, narrow or wider, and taller or shorter.

There is also a slide show program included as part of the Grafix Partner. The program called Cycle lets you set the length of time that a picture will be displayed on the screen.

The Grafix Partner is doing wonderful things with Lotus 1-2-3 and a host of other graphics programs. It is an excellent addition to anyone's graphic library.

DIAGRAPH

Diagraph is another little known package that comes to us with some wonderful characteristics. It is a picture processor that presently runs on the Hewlett-Packard 150 Touch Screen and the IBM Personal Computer. It features a symbol library much like PCPG.

Diagraph's unique set of symbol libraries make complex drawings and graphs possible. There are presently over 1500 symbols in the libraries as well as full screen pictures. A symbol is usually something small like a tractor. Picture libraries in-

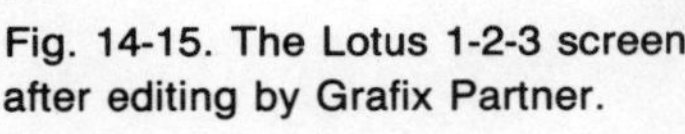

Fig. 14-15. The Lotus 1-2-3 screen after editing by Grafix Partner.

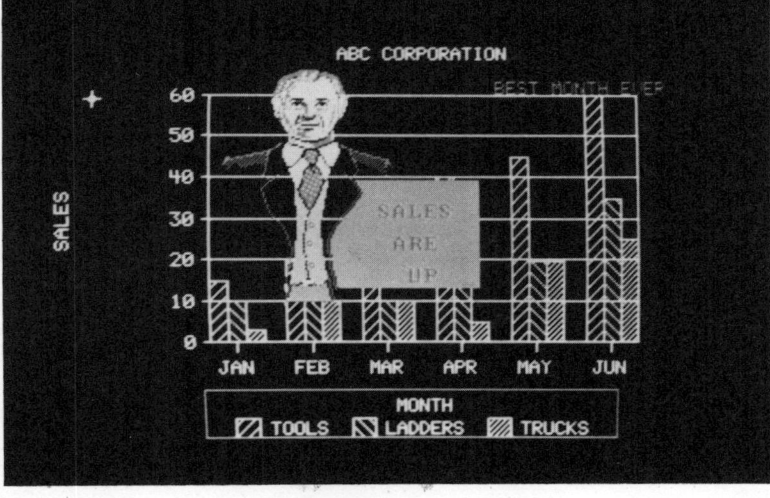

Fig. 14-16. Diagraph sample symbols.

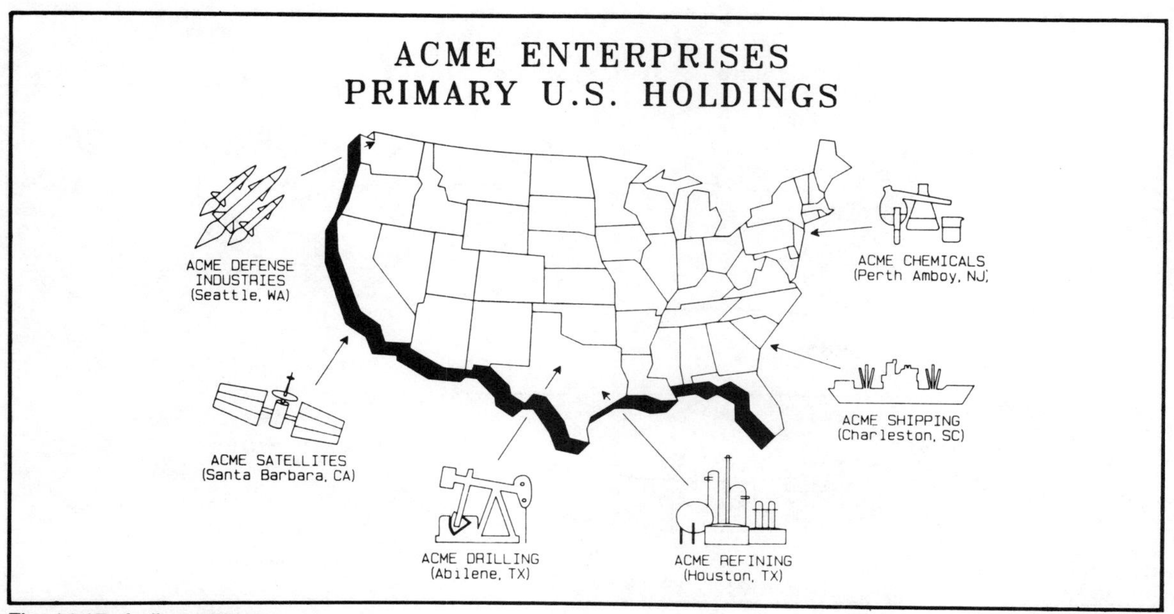

Fig. 14-17. A diagraph map.

clude people, places, things, maps, transportation, office equipment, landscapes, and composition aids. Some of the symbol libraries include banners, boxes, borders, text blocks, word balloons, icons, charting symbols, holiday and seasons, electronic and flowcharting, and data processing equipment. A sample of some symbols appears in Fig. 14-16.

Once you have these symbols you can do some wonderful things with them. Figure 14-17 shows a 3 dimensional map drawn with diagraph. Text and

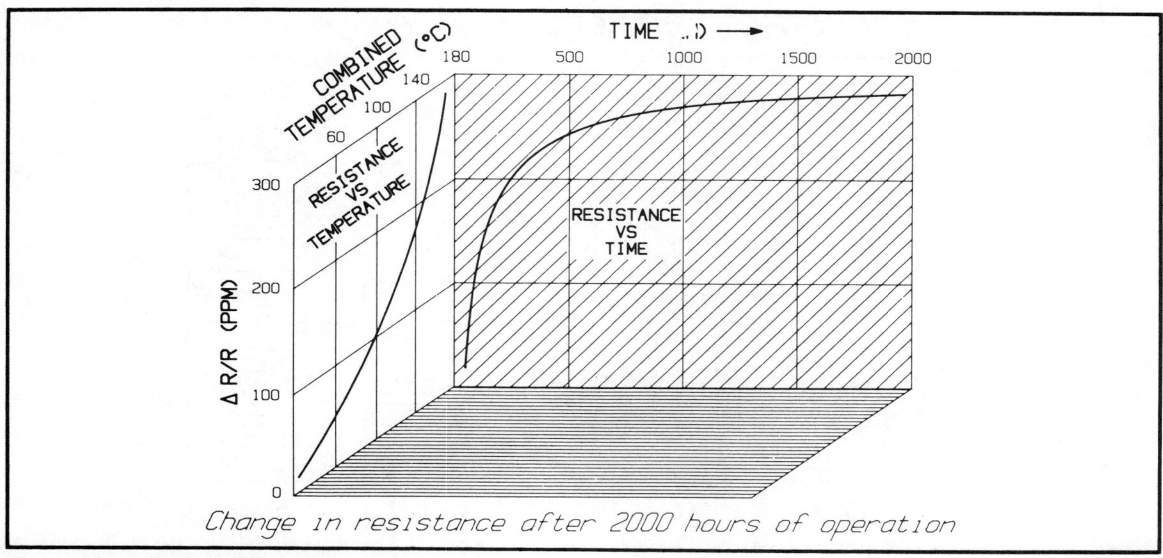

Fig. 14-18. A diagraph 3-dimensional line chart.

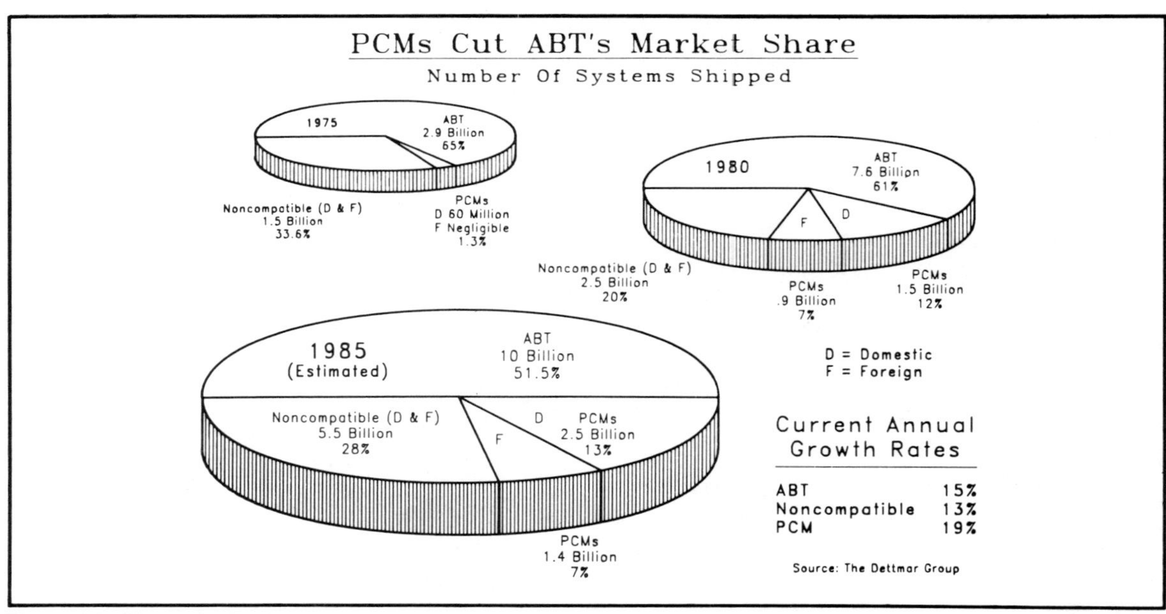

Fig. 14-19. Diagraph pie charts.

symbols have been added to show the location of plants owned by the fictitious Acme aerospace company.

Regular charts can also be constructed. Figure 14-18 shows a three dimensional line chart that displays the results of an engineering study. No other package can produce symbols with the type and clarity of diagraph.

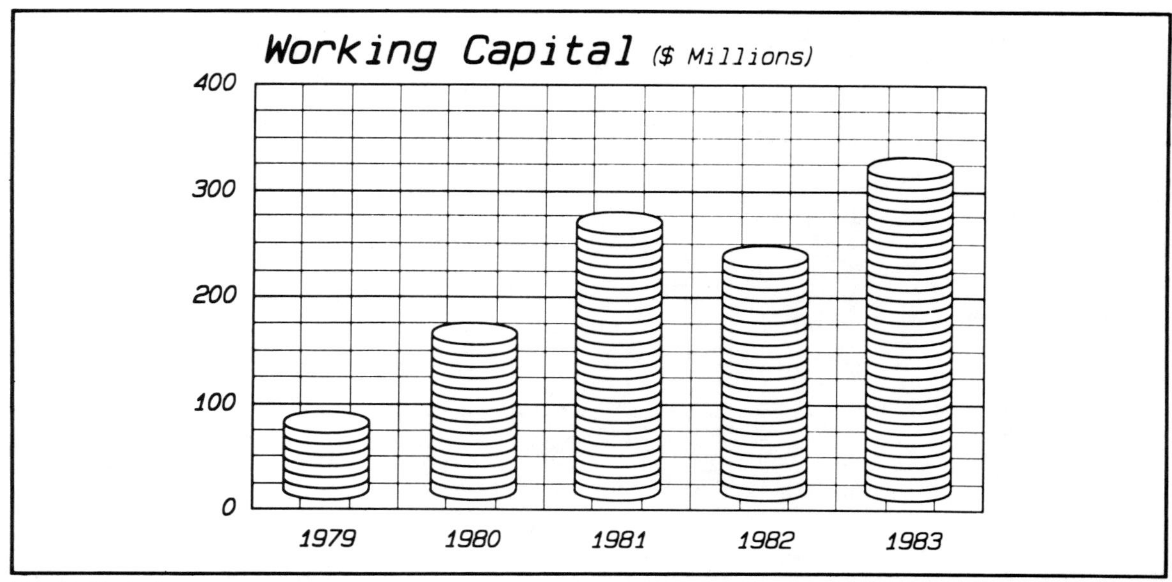

Fig. 14-20. A diagraph pictograph.

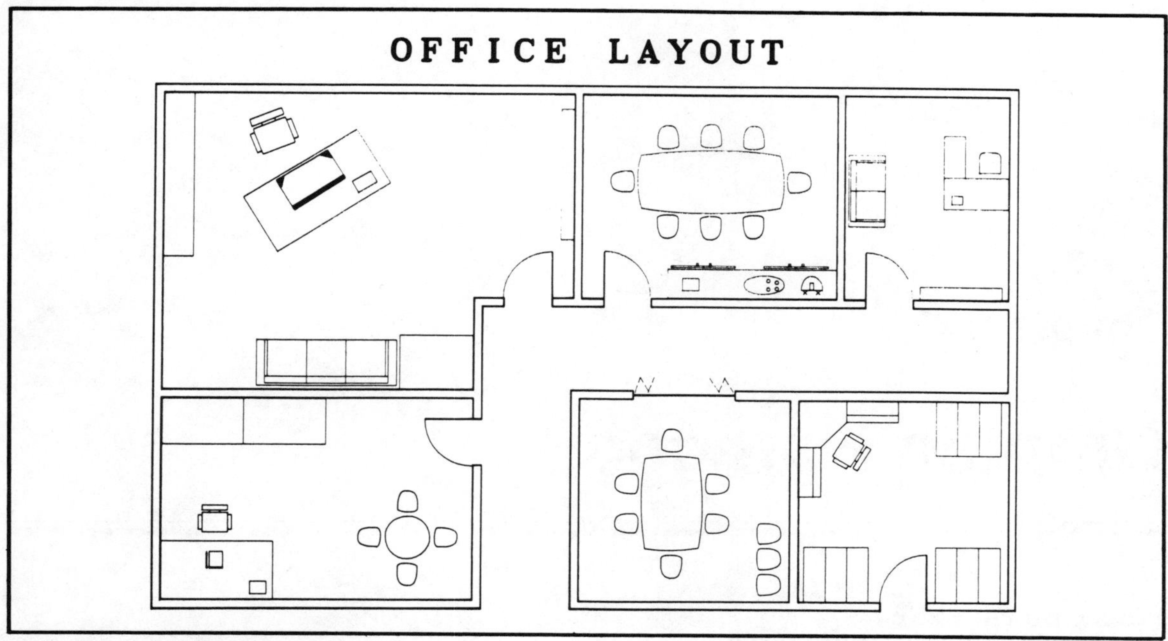

Fig. 14-21. A diagraph office layout.

Diagraph also handles pie charts. Proportional pies have never looked as good as the ones diagraph can make, as shown in Fig. 14-19. A pattern has been added to the edge to simulate a coin.

Diagraph can do what most packages cannot. It allows you to create pictographs easily. Figure 14-20 shows a coin pictograph.

Office layouts and engineering drawings can also be done through the use of lines and symbols. Figure 14-21 shows an office layout created with diagraph.

Diagraph is simple and easy to use. Pictures can be manipulated freely and symbols placed as desired. If you need pictures that aren't too showy, diagraph is another little known package that could do wonderful things for you.

Chapter 15

Graphic Hardcopy

Taking Pictures of Video Screens
POLAROID PALETTE
HEWLETT-PACKARD PLOTTERS
EPSON PRINTERS

No matter how good the software package, if you can't show your creations to your intended audience, you might as well do "hand silhouettes" on a blank screen. There are many ways to show-off your graphics. These include screens, slides, overhead transparencies, and paper. In order to put your creations on slides, overhead transparencies, or paper, however, you will need a slide maker or camera, printer, or plotter.

Figure 15-1 shows this author's workstation for producing graphics. An IBM PC with two half-height floppy disk drives form the basis of the machine. These drives occupy the left disk port. A 10mb Maynard Hard Disk occupies the right slot. Inside the PC is an AST Six-Pack plus with 384k memory. Some of the more voracious packages require 640k today. Due to power problems, there is only an IBM standard color card. An Amdek Color II monitor provides the display. This set up provides all the pictures you have seen in this book. An extra cooling fan sits out of sight in the front air bezel to cool the multitude of boards and ribbon cables.

A mouse systems mouse and TG joystick are used for picture processing. To the right of the computer is a Hewlett-Packard 7470A 2-pen plotter. Next to that is a Polaroid Palette image recorder for making instant prints and slides. On top of that is a Qubie' 1200 baud modem for communicating with the rest of the world. Finally on the far right sits an Epson LQ-1500, which provides near letter quality print and some wonderful (or almost wonderful, as they tend to be light) graphics.

On the market today are several proven leaders in the price/performance race. The hardware shown in this chapter comes from large corporations that you probably have heard of. Though there are many other products available from other companies, these are the ones being used by most corporations and individuals and have such overwhelming shares of the market that they cannot be ignored.

The Palette by Polaroid produces slides and instant prints; plotters by Hewlett-Packard produce multicolor high resolution plots; and graphic printers by Epson and others make crisp black and white or even color copy.

This chapter, however, starts by giving some

Fig. 15-1. A graphics work station.

helpful tips on how to take pictures from your monitor without any special equipment and still produce dazzling results.

TAKING PICTURES OF VIDEO SCREENS

There are many ways to take bad pictures of video screens. There are fortunately only a few good ways to take good pictures. The easiest and least expensive is to use a camera and to shoot the screen. When most people do this, their pictures are extremely bowed at the corners and are usually out of focus, too dim, or too bright.

You cannot easily use a standard instamatic to shoot pictures, nor can you use a flash unit. Taking good pictures is simply a matter of good planning. Follow these simple rules:

1. Use tripod. There is no way to hold a camera in your hands without shaking the camera and causing distortion.
2. Use a 35mm camera with ASA 100 Ektachrome slide film. This is the easiest slide film to find, and it produces brilliant colors.
3. Use a long lens. The standard 50mm lens that comes with most cameras cannot filter out the screen curvature that you get when you shoot at close distances. A 135mm lens is recommended. You can get back about five to six feet and shoot the screen without curvature problems. A longer lens is okay, if you have room to back up and focus sharply.
4. You can shoot at a variety of exposures. It is recommended to shoot in total darkness (except for the image on the screen). Don't worry about the status lights of your computer, monitor, or disk drives. They are faint and won't make a difference.
5. A recommended exposure is f11 at 1/4 sec. If the image is very bright or contains a lot of white text, use f11 at 1/8 second. f11 at 1/2 second is better if the image is darker. Very dark colors, such as deep reds or greens, would force you to shoot at 1 second or greater. For the most part, IBM PC screens should be shot at f11 at 1/4 sec. f8 at 1/2 sec will also produce decent results.
6. Use a shutter release cable to avoid shaking the camera. If you don't have a cable release, use the timer on your camera. If the timer takes ten seconds before the picture is shot, the camera will have time to steady itself from when you pushed the button.
7. Last and not least, make sure you are in focus. Your focusing distance is critical to about one

quarter of an inch. If you move the tripod at all, you must refocus the camera. Try to focus on a vertical line somewhere on the screen.

If you follow these suggestions, you will produce beautiful screen images at a cost of about forty cents per slide. They may not be as good as slides costing fifty dollars apiece, but with the packages demonstrated here they will be very good.

An alternative to taking pictures with a camera and a tripod is to use a Kodak Ektagraphic imager. This is a device that fits over your monitor and comes with its own camera. It is made to take pictures of your screens with no worrying about exposures or f stops, as it is preset. You can buy film for it in single shot print or in slide packs so you don't have to waste an entire roll of film for one shot. The hardware comes with your choice of *cone* (the part that actually sits on the screen), to fit your monitor. The cost of this hardware is under $400.

POLAROID PALETTE

The Polaroid Palette is also a device that allows you to take images from your computer monitor. This is a very high quality device that retails for $1799 and can take pictures with even better quality than the original monitor image. Figure 15-2 shows the Polaroid Palette in use on an IBM Personal Computer.

This system is the ultimate in picture taking. You get everything you need to hook it up and begin working. The system is driven by the Palette box. This box has a very high resolution color monitor built right in. Software provided lets you save screens that appear on your monitor and later put them on the built-in Palette monitor to automatically take the pictures. The pictures can even be recolored by the software in any color you like.

Some packages such as Chart-Master, Sign-Master, DR Draw, DR Graph, and Graphwriter have built-in interfaces to the Polaroid Palette to automatically produce pictures from the graphics packages themselves. When this is done, the resolution of the Palette monitor is used and the effect is that the pictures are as good as those from any graphics house that charges $50 per slide. With the Polaroid Palette, your cost can be as low as seventy cents per slide.

Besides the interfaces from Decision Resources (Chart-Master and Sign-Master), Graphic Communications (Graphwriter), and Digital Resources (DR Draw, DR Graph), the Palette features a routine known as PSAVER. This can be used with every graphics package we could find to produce sharp screen images at your monitor's resolution.

Besides the high resolution monitor and all its associated electronics, the system also comes with a Minolta XG-A 35 mm and a Polaroid instant camera. The Minolta comes with an electronic winder and cable release. The system also comes with an instant slide developer and enough film to get you started. The system comes with software and a complete manual.

The Palette software contains look-up tables allowing the Palette to produce slides or prints in full color, even from computers having only monochrome displays. The computer and software match their exposure to the film being used while allowing the user to control color selection throughout the image. ColorKeys of 72 colors permit up to sixteen colors on a single slide. A "fill" technique minimizes the raster lines that normally show up on slides and prints. Multiple copies and a batch processing routine are also provided.

The Polaroid Palette is compatible with IBM Personal Computers and compatibles such as COMPAQ. It also works with the Digital Equipment Corporation's Rainbow personal computer and the Apple *II*e and II+ computers. Figure 15-3 shows the Polaroid Palette connected to a DEC Rainbow.

If you are interested in easily produced high quality slides and instant prints for a fraction of the cost of a graphics vendor, the Polaroid Palette is for you.

GRAPHIC PRINTERS

There are a multitude of printers that produce graphics available today. The best ones are known as dot-matrix printers. They print each letter or character with little dots. When printing in the graphics mode, their quality becomes quite good.

Epson is probably the best known company in

Fig. 15-2. The Polaroid Palette with an IBM PC.

Fig. 15-3. A Polaroid Palette with a DEC Rainbow.

dot-matrix printers today. Every package that exists today specifically supports Epson printers. The IBM Graphics Printer is actually a reworked Epson printer. Epson has four basic printer. The RX-80 and RX-100 are the low end printers. They are slower than the better quality FX-80 and FX-100. The 80 designates that the carriage is 80 columns wide and will only handle 8 1/2 inch computer paper. The 100 has the wider carriage and handles larger paper. The FX series prints at speeds up to 160 characters per second. This line of printers feature a 2k buffer and allow user-defined fonts to be loaded and printed automatically.

These printers replace the original MX series, which are now obsolete. The RX series can be purchased for as low as $300, while the FX-100 retails for almost $800. These printers handle graphics beautifully. Superior quality dark images allow the tiniest detail to be displayed. There are few better graphics printers than these.

The top of the line dot-matrix printer by Epson is the LQ-1500. Known for its letter quality fonts, this printer produces high quality print speeds of over 200 characters per second in draft mode and 67 characters per second in letter quality mode. The graphics on this machine are weak due to its pin placement. Many packages have yet to write device drivers for it.

The last entry by Epson is the JX-80. This is a color dot-matrix printer that produces acceptable color prints. It features a four color ribbon that produces your graphics in seven colors. The same good graphics available on the RX and FX series are available on the JX-80 but in brilliant colors.

HEWLETT-PACKARD PLOTTERS

The king of the plotters is undisputably Hewlett-Packard or HP as it is widely known. Not only does the company produce a complete line of color plotters, but companies such as DEC and IBM use Hewlett-Packard plotters with their own logos. The next time you see an IBM or DEC plotter, look carefully, it was probably made by Hewlett-Packard.

A plotter is a device that provides very high quality drawings on paper or overhead transparencies. Instead of using a print head as a printer does, a plotter uses a single pen mounted on a device that is capable of placing it anywhere on a page. Usually the paper is moved up and down while the pen moves left and right. By coordinating the movements of the paper and pens, even perfect circles can be drawn precisely and quickly. Nothing matches the resolution or output quality of a plotter. To see the quality of a plotter, you must compare a printed output and a plotted output.

The most popular plotter today is the Hewlett-

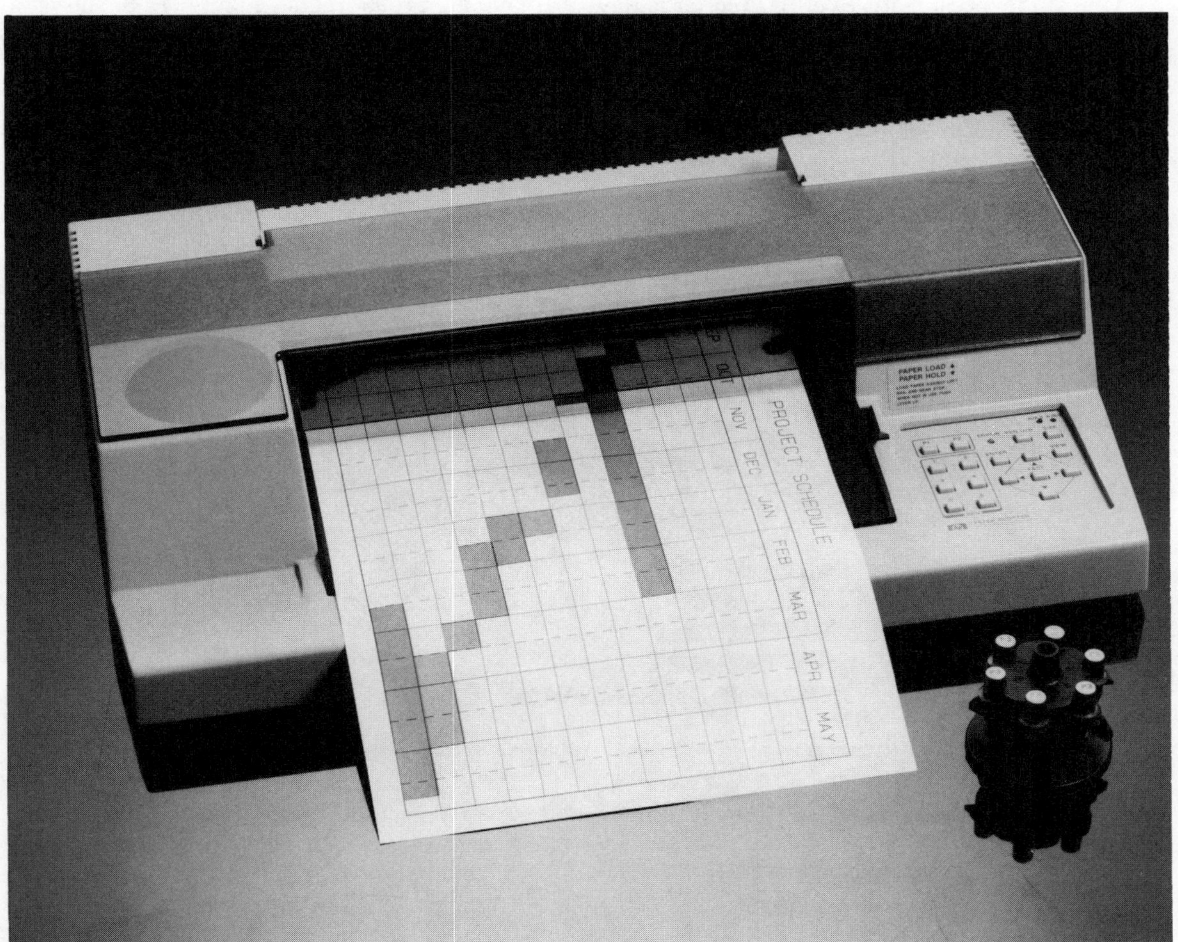

Fig. 15-4. The Hewlett-Packard 7475A six-pen Plotter.

Packard 7475A 6 Pen Plotter. This plotter lets you access six pens without manually changing pens. You can choose from a variety of 10 colors. The plotter can plot on transparencies or on paper as large as 11 × 17 inches. This plotter offers resolution of up to 1/1000th of an inch. Text can be written in any possible size. Colors are solid and bright. Curved lines are smooth and not jagged. Edges can be perfectly aligned in bar and pie charts. There is never a gap or a dark spot where a pen changes direction. You will be amazed at the quality of any Hewlett-Packard plotter. The HP7475 is also very fast. Its pen can moves in speeds up to 15 inches/second. Figure 15-4 shows the HP7475A.

One of the nicest features of this plotter is the fact that virtually every product available specifically supports the Hewlett-Packard plotter. The six-pen carousel is easy to load and protects the unused pens from drying out. When you press the view button, the plotter instantly stops and sends the paper to the front of the plotter to be viewed. When you hit the button again the plotter begins where it left off without any sign that it was interrupted. You can even tell the plotter to rotate the output as it comes from the computer. This machine retails for only $1895.

Hewlett-Packard also makes a low end plotter and a high end plotter. The low end plotter is called the HP7470A. This is a two pen plotter. It can perform almost all of the same functions as the HP7475A, but it requires constant pen changes. For the professional who doesn't need many colors or doesn't mind changing pens, the HP7475A is a real bargain at $1095 retail. Figure 15-5 shows a HP7470A plotter.

The newest addition to the Hewlett-Packard family is the top of the line HP7550 8-Pen Plotter with Automatic Sheet Feed. This plotter has been

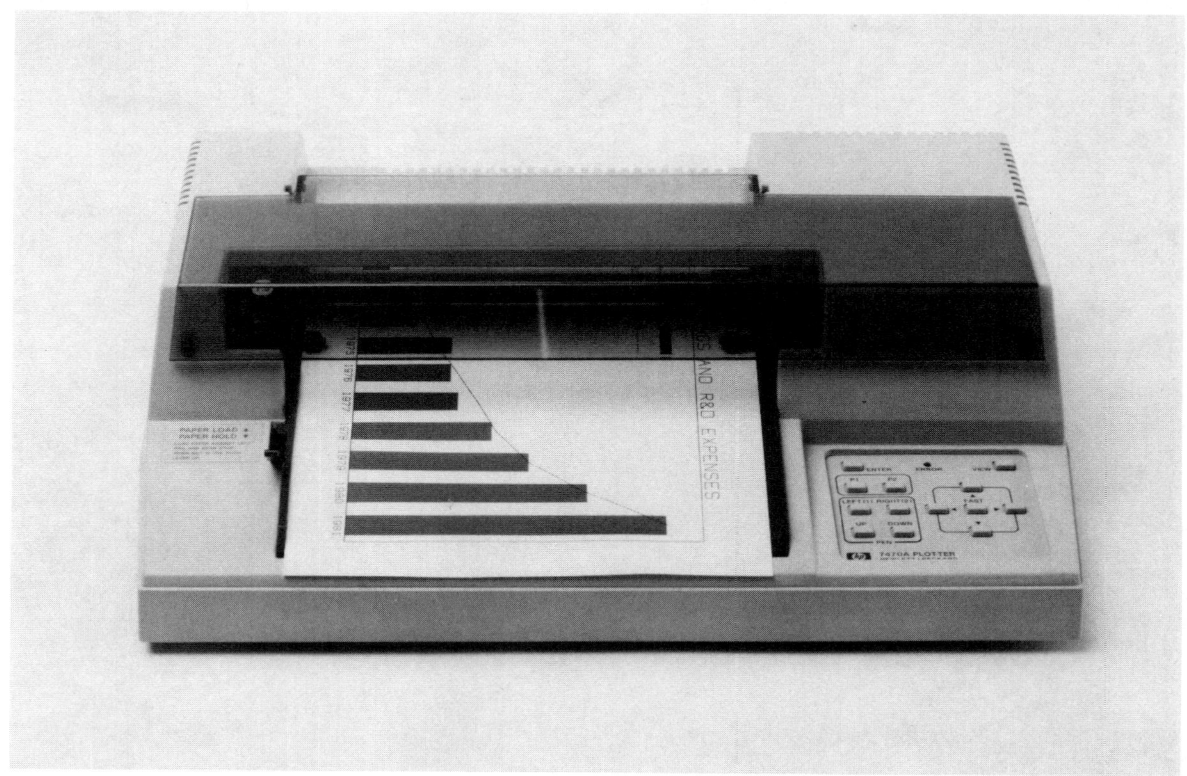

Fig. 15-5. The Hewlett-Packard 7470A two-pen Plotter.

Fig. 15-6. The Hewlett-Packard 7550 eight-pen Plotter.

dreamed about in the business community for years. It has all the features of the HP7470A and the HP7475A and a whole lot more.

Eight pens in the carousel reduce pen change time by 33% when you are using eight colors for complicated graphs. Its features are almost double those of the other plotters. Its maximum speed is over 31 inches/second while producing a resolution of over 25/10,000 of an inch. This is twice the speed and four times the resolution of the HP7470 and HP7475 series. This means that this plotter gives you an eightfold quality and productivity increase. Its cost of $3900 is only twice that of the HP7475, yet it gives you an eightfold increase performance at only twice the price. It also has 33% more pens and the most important feature—an automatic sheet feeder.

The HP7550 can make up to 99 copies of the same graph with a built-in repeat feature; the paper tray can hold up to 150 pages for the plotting of many different graphs. The HP7550 is shown in Fig. 15-6.

No matter what your hardcopy output needs are—paper, overhead transparencies, or slides, todays modern output devices make it quick and easy.

Appendix

The List of Graphics Manufacturers

STANDALONE GRAPHICS SOFTWARE

BPS Business Graphics
Business & Professional Software Inc.
143 Binney St.
Cambridge, MA 02142
(617) 491-3377
Retail Price: $350.00

Chart-Master
Decision Resources
25 Sylvan Road S.
Westport, CT 06880
(203) 222-1974
Retail Price: $375.00

DR Graph and DR Draw
Digital Research Inc.
60 Garden Court
P.O. Box DRI
Monterey, CA 93942
(408) 649-3896
Retail Price:
DR Graph $195.00
DR Draw $295.00

Graphwriter
Graphic Communications Inc.
200 Fifth Ave.
Waltham, MA 02254
(617) 890-8778
Retail Price: $595.00

Microsoft Chart
Microsoft Corp.
10700 Northrup Way
P.O. Box 97200
Bellevue, WA 98009
(206) 828-7400
Retail Price: $250.00

pfs: graph
Software Publishing Company
1901 Landings Drive
Mountain View, CA 94043
(415) 962-8910
Retail Price: $140.00

INTEGRATED SOFTWARE PACKAGES

Framework
Ashton-Tate
10150 West Jefferson Blvd.
Culver City, CA 90230
(213) 204-5570
Retail Price: $695.00

Lotus 1-2-3
Lotus Development Corporation
161 First St.
Cambridge, MA 02142
(617) 492-7870
Retail Price: $395.00

SUPERCALC3 Release2
SORCIM/IUS
2195 Fortune Drive
San Jose, CA 95131
(408) 942-1727
Retail Price: $295.00

Symphony
Lotus Development Corporation
161 First St.
Cambridge, MA 02142
(617) 492-7870
Retail Price: $695.00

The SMART System
Innovative Software
9300 W. 110th St., Suite 380
Overland Park, KS 66210
(913) 383-1089
Retail price: $895.00

TEXT/SLIDE SOFTWARE

Overhead Express
143 Binney St.
Cambridge, MA 02142
(617) 491-3377
Retail Price: $195.00

Sign-Master
Decision Resources
25 Sylvan Road S.
Westport, CT 06880
(203) 222-1974
Retail Price: $245.00

PICTURE PROCESSORS

4-Point Graphics
IMSI Software Publishers
633 Fifth Ave.
San Rafael, CA 94901
(415) 454-7101
Retail Price: $139.00

PC Illustrator
Computer Graphics Group
568 14th Street NW
Atlanta, GA 30318
(404) 876-9469
Retail Price: $149.00

PC Paint
Mouse Systems
2336H Walsh Ave.
Santa Clara, CA 95051
(408) 988-0211
Retail Price: $129.00

VCN Execuvision
Prentice Hall
200 Old Tappan Road
Old Tappan, NJ 07675
(800) 624-0023
Retail Price: $395.00

HIGHLY SPECIALIZED GRAPHICS SOFTWARE

Energraphics
Enertronics Research
150 N. Meramac, Suite 207
St. Louis, MO 63105
(800) 325-0174
Retail Price: $450.00

Statmap
Ganesa Group International
1495 Chain Bridge Road
Suite 300
McLean, VA 22101
(800) 638-2225
Retail Price: $895.00

LITTLE KNOWN PACKAGES

diagraph
Computer Support Corporation
4215 Beltwood Parkway
Dallas, TX 75234
(214) 661-8960
Retail Price: $395.00

Grafix Partner
Brightbill-Roberts and Company Ltd.
120 E. Washington St., Suite 421
Syracuse, NY 13202
(315) 474-3400
Retail Price: $149.00

GraphMaker
OptionWare Inc.
4 Barnard Lane
Bloomfield, CT 06001
(800) 334-2355
Retail Price: $99.00

PC Graphics
IBM Personally Developed Software
P.O. Box 3280
Wallingford, CT 06494
(800) 426-7279
Retail Price: $29.95

GRAPHICS HARDWARE

Hewlett-Packard Plotters
Hewlett-Packard
16399 West Bernardo Dr.
San Diego, CA 92127
(800) 538-8787
Retail Price:
HP7470A $1095.00
HP7475A $1895.00

Polaroid Palette
Polaroid Corporation
575 Technology Square
Cambridge, MA 02139
(617) 577-2000
Retail Price: $1799.00

Index

Edited by Marilyn L. Johnson